ERADICATE
Blotting Out God in America

ERADICATE
Blotting Out God in America

David Fiorazo

ERADICATE: Blotting Out God in America – David Fiorazo
Copyright © 2012

Unless otherwise indicated: Scripture quotations taken from the New American Standard Bible®, Copyright © 1960, 1962, 1963, 1968, 1971, 1972, 1973, 1975, 1977, 1995 by The Lockman Foundation Used by permission." (www.Lockman.org)

Scripture quotations marked (NLT) are taken from the Holy Bible, New Living Translation, copyright © 1996, 2004, 2007 by Tyndale House Foundation. Used by permission of Tyndale House Publishers, Inc., Carol Stream, Illinois 60188. All rights reserved.

Scripture quotations marked (ESV) are from The Holy Bible, English Standard Version® (ESV®), copyright © 2001 by Crossway, a publishing ministry of Good News Publishers. Used by permission. All rights reserved

Scripture quotations marked (NIV) are taken from the Holy Bible, New International Version®, NIV®. Copyright © 1973, 1978, 1984, 2011 by Biblica, Inc.™ Used by permission of Zondervan. All rights reserved worldwide. www.zondervan.com The "NIV" and "New International Version" are trademarks registered in the United States Patent and Trademark Office by Biblica, Inc.™

PRINTED IN THE UNITED STATES OF AMERICA
First edition published 2012

Ankeo Press, Life Sentence Publishing and its logo are trademarks of

Life Sentence Publishing, Inc.
P.O. BOX 652
Abbotsford, WI 54405
www.anekopress.com
Like us on Facebook

ISBN: 978-1-62245-026-8

Library of Congress Control Number: 2012947201

This book is available from www.anekopress.com, amazon.com, Barnes & Noble, and your local Christian Bookstore

Cover Design by Robbie Destocki at Creative Image Design Group

CONTENTS

ACKNOWLEDGEMENTS

This book is dedicated to my Lord Jesus Christ, my Father in Heaven who saved me and the Holy Spirit who guides me. To my wife, Rosanna: thank you, love of my life, for supporting me and encouraging me to persevere. Thank you for enduring the many lonely mornings and evenings as I was researching, writing, and editing this book. I love you! Thank you, Mom, for your compassion and generosity. Thank you for being an example of Jesus. I am so grateful for the love you and Dad gave me growing up. My gratitude also goes to Ma and Pa Di Loreto for your love and support.

A very special thanks to: Mike LeMay, Tony Palacio, Rosanna and her prayer warrior friends - Le Tran, Jenny Newhouse, and Michelle Little; Bill Lauten, Steve Orchard, Bill Ott, and Craig Zolkowski. I also want to thank the staff at Q90 FM for their patience and love. Thank you to the many friends who have helped me through this process by reading and providing early feedback on various chapters, and to friends who have encouraged me.

More thanks! Contributors and pre-editing: Michael Nelson, Rosanna Fiorazo, Mike Marit. Cover Design: Robbie Destocki. Radio commercial and video trailer: Frank Montenegro, Tony Palacio. Website: Amy Spreeman. Photography: Scott Johnson, Tony Reale. Caricature: Scott Wilke Art.

INTRODUCTION TO ERADICATE

Do not conform any longer to the pattern of this world,
but be transformed by the renewing of your mind....
Therefore be careful how you walk, not as unwise men but
as wise, making the most of your time, because the days
are evil. So then do not be foolish, but understand what
the will of the Lord is. (**Romans 12:2, Ephesians 5:15-17**)

Christianity is not the thriving, influential power it once was in America. With a majority of people claiming the Christian tradition, why does our godless culture barely reflect the light of Jesus Christ? Someone recently said, "God may not be dead, but I think a bunch of his people might be." There are two things going on at the same time that contribute to America's decline: Christians are conforming to the world and the agenda to blot out God in America continues to advance at full speed. In this book, we will examine how this is happening and investigate the people and organizations that are the driving forces of immorality. We will scrutinize the major reasons America has fallen away from God.

We're living in sad times when professing Christians know less about the Bible than ever before. Why is this? Many believers are receiving little more than their Gerber's on Sunday mornings and pastors must shoulder some of the responsibility, but individual believers will be held accountable for how we use our time. It's up to us to study God's Word on our own. Decade after decade, the church has been less and less active and vocal in American society and today we're suffering the consequences. We've backed out of culture and have made it easier for those who are hostile toward Jesus Christ to gain control of our country.

There are many whose ultimate goal is to destroy our Judeo-Christian way of life and wipe out evidence of the foundational principles that made us a great nation. The enemy has pawns in his control; some of them are knowingly being used for evil and others naively. In this book, we will examine Hollywood, media, government, public education, and the church. With a background in radio and television, one of my biggest disappointments is in the lies, omissions, and propaganda of media today. The enemy is working from within to ruin America and instead of contending for the faith and resisting, Christians have compromised. Charles Spurgeon once said, "I believe that one reason the church of God at this present moment has had so little influence over the world is because the world has so much influence over the church."[1]

In spite of all its failures, America is still the greatest, most exceptional demonstration of faith, family, and freedom in the world. The war has intensified and there are Christians who don't even know how bad it is. Some don't *want* to know. For instance, according to *Relevant Magazine*, 64% of unmarried Christians in the 18-29 age range have had sex within the last year. A baby is aborted in America every 26 seconds and according to the Alan Guttmacher Institute, seven out of ten women claimed to be Christian at the time they had an abortion! We're going to look at a few conflicting definitions of Christianity.

Recently, pro-life organization Live Action reported on the practice of sex-selective abortions in the United States (Gendercide). Planned Parenthood was exposed again in an undercover video in May 2012.[2] We will thoroughly investigate some of the hidden history of the eugenics movement, Planned Parenthood, and the abortion industry. You will also learn about the biggest influences on the spread of sexual promiscuity in America. Forty percent of all babies born in America are born out of wedlock partly because marriage has been devalued.

Christianity no longer propels this country and by looking at our younger generation, we should be alarmed! Pew Research reports that among Americans between ages 18-29, one-in-four say they are not currently affiliated with any particular religion. Moreover, after just one year of college, 85% of youth turn away from God. Tragically, many young people today coming out of the public school system were not taught properly about America's Christian heritage and were fed a steady diet of liberal opinion. Parents, if you are not helping to educate your kids and build their faith, the world will gladly "program" them for you.

We have lost our moral compass and I'm not just talking about rampant profanity, marketing sex to children in public schools or garbage-infested primetime television programming. I'm not just referring to Hollywood, the lewd lyrics in much of today's music, or the fact our culture has practically accepted baby killing and homosexuality. I'm talking about hostility toward Jesus Christ and open rebellion against God. Americans today justify sins that never, ever would have been allowed fifty years ago. Apathy is killing us, but God's people are also destroyed because of a lack of knowledge (Hosea 4:6). These are desperate times. We must have a sense of urgency, and we cannot remain neutral any longer!

Dietrich Bonhoeffer was a German Lutheran pastor, theologian, and anti-fascist. He was involved in a plan to assassinate Adolf Hitler which led to Bonhoeffer's arrest in 1943 and hanging in 1945. This was just 23 days before the Nazis' surrendered. Bonhoeffer's view of the role of Christianity in the secular world has been very influential. One of his famous quotes is:

"Silence in the face of evil is itself evil. God will not hold us guiltless. Not to speak is to speak; not to act is to act."[3]

The time is short and somehow the church in America must awaken from its slumber. Truth is being suppressed and people are dying without salvation. Some of the content in these pages will be appalling, eye-opening and infuriating. This is not a bad thing unless we do nothing with the information provided. Someone once said decisive moments are fleeting, and when presented must be acted upon or the window of opportunity could close. What is left at that point is regret or pondering what might have been. Too many believers are rolling over and hitting the snooze button.

God is calling us to redeem the time. Peter exhorts believers to prepare their minds for action (1 Peter 1:13), and the apostle Paul reminds us that regardless of what comes against us, God is for us (Romans 8:31). These men died defending the gospel and glorified the Lord in the process. Are we ready to commit to truly living what we believe? Would you do it for your Savior?

Jesus Christ lived a radical, counter-cultural life. He obeyed God the Father and transformed the world. He overcame the power of the enemy. Jesus relentlessly resisted sin, opposed legalism, and confronted hypocrisy. He loved unconditionally, he forgave freely, and he sacrificed himself completely. He spoke the truth boldly, exhibited humility, and lived with integrity. He is the Light of the world. He is our standard and our goal; the only way to the Father. Following his example may cause people to ridicule and hate us. What an honor!

Though we share a common Constitution, country and culture, Americans are greatly divided over many issues, but none more important than the person of Jesus Christ. Either people accept and advance biblical truth, or they refuse and resist it. There is no neutral ground, but some Christians are trying to live with one foot in church and one in the world.

The choice is ours: we can face the reality of what is happening in America and take action, or we can look the other way. It's time to know your spiritual allies. This republic under God continues to be a threat to atheism, communism, socialism, and tyranny in the world. We get to decide what direction we want this country to take in the coming years.

I never thought I'd live to see the day America would be threatened from within. The Obama White House has proven to be the most biblically hostile administration in the history of the United States. In a recent speech to the Human Rights Campaign (HRC), the largest lesbian, gay, bisexual transgender (LGBT) advocacy group and political lobbying organization in the United States, President Obama told the audience they will "see a time in which we as a nation finally recognize relationships between two men or two women as just as real and admirable as relationships between a man and a woman."[4]

We saw the vitriol of those who oppose Christian values when Chick-fil-A president Dan Cathy took a stand for traditional marriage and was attacked for his beliefs. There's one thing we need to know: Though liberals and activists have the megaphone of the media, they are a malignant minority. According to the 2010 census, same-sex couples comprise *less* than one-half of 1 percent of the American population![5] Faith, family, and marriage are bedrocks of our great nation, and we have taken these blessings for granted. Let's contrast the 44th president's values with the 16th president. One hundred and fifty years ago, President Abraham Lincoln recognized what he believed was God's hand of judgment on America. People were taking freedom for granted. Here is part of his 1863 proclamation:

"We have been the recipients of the choicest bounties of Heaven. We have been preserved, these many years, in peace and prosperity. We have grown in numbers, wealth and power, as no other nation has ever grown. But we have forgotten God.

"We have forgotten the gracious hand which preserved us in peace, and multiplied and enriched and strengthened us; …we have become too self-sufficient to feel the necessity of redeeming and preserving grace, too proud to pray to the God that made us! It behooves us then, to humble ourselves before the offended Power, to confess our national sins, and to pray for clemency and forgiveness."[6]

We aren't that different today and the church is running out of time to seek God's face and turn from our wickedness. Christians are suffering from complacency and many have grown lukewarm. In this book, we will examine why approximately 50 million Americans claiming to be born again appear to have such a marginal impact on society. If it is often difficult to tell the difference between a Christian and an unbeliever outside of Sunday morning, the enemy is winning. He is waging an effective campaign, but the final battles have yet to be staged.

"There is no neutral ground in the universe; every square inch, every split second is claimed by God and counterclaimed by Satan." – **C.S. Lewis**

The church must reengage in the culture war. America is in disarray, and people are losing hope. There are two paths America can take: one leads to further moral erosion and socialism, ultimately ending in destruction, while the other path leads back to God and a revival of Christianity. There will always be opposition, but you and I believe in an unshakable God and with Him, we can make a difference.

A remnant of faithful, Bible-believing soldiers have been pretty lonely for decades as they have prayed and worked. They have purposely gone outside the walls of their churches to impact society for Jesus Christ even though secular progressives have told them to keep their faith to themselves. This book may upset you, but it will also encourage you to join the cause, fight the good fight, and choose Christ over culture.

One person has potential to impact countless lives for Jesus Christ and eternity. Author and historian Edward Everett Hale once said:

> "I am only one, but I am one. I cannot do everything, but I can do something. What I can do I should do, and with the help of God, I will do."

God is being blotted out of America. Christians are being silenced by accusations of hate and intolerance; and our very freedoms are being threatened. The government, media, Hollywood, the abortion industry, and academia are not going to defend Christian values—it's up to you and me. If we love God with all our hearts, we will take a stand for truth. We can trust him to be our rock, refuge and strength (Psalm 46:1). I pray we will be faithful servants of Christ and stop the downward spiral of Christian silence. America and the church really need us to understand the times and heed God's call right now…while there's still time.

> *Wake up! Strengthen what remains and is about to die, for I have not found your deeds complete in the sight of My God. Remember, therefore, what you have received and heard; obey it, and repent. But if you do not wake up, I will come like a thief, and you will not know at what time I will come to you* (**Revelation 3:2-3**).

ENDNOTES

1 http://www.spurgeon.org/sermons/1906.htm
2 http://liveaction.org/blog/
   sex-selective-abortion-thrives-in-america-courtesy-planned-parenthood/
3 http://www.qotd.org/search/search.html?aid=1575&page=2
4 President Obama speech transcript, HRC, 10/10/2009 http://blogs.suntimes.com/
   sweet/2009/10/obama_human_rights_campaign_sp.html
5 http://www.washingtontimes.com/news/2011/sep/27/
   census-households-led-by-gay-couples-rose-80-perce/?page=all
6 http://holydays.tripod.com/linc.htm

CHAPTER 1

WHY TRUTH MATTERS

YOUR WORLDVIEW AFFECTS EVERYTHING

In the beginning was the Word, and the Word was with God, and the Word was God. He was in the beginning with God. All things came into being through Him, and apart from Him nothing came into being that has come into being. ...And the Word became flesh, and dwelt among us, and we saw His glory, glory as of the only begotten from the Father, full of grace and truth – (**John 1:1-3, 14**).

What we believe about truth affects everything we do in this life. How we view God, people, and how we understand the world – past, present, and future – depends on what we believe about absolute truth. If there are no absolutes, then anything goes! As Christians, what we believe about absolute truth depends on what we believe about Jesus Christ and the Bible. The Old Testament refers to God as the God of truth (Isaiah 65:16). The Word of God is perfect. From indisputable historical facts to archeological evidence, the Bible has yet to be proven inaccurate or wrong.

Enemies of truth can make up stuff about the Bible, write their books attempting to debunk Scripture, and create their own documentaries with lies and fabrications, but it won't change the fact that God's Word is eternal. Does truth depend on where we were raised, what church we attended, what a teacher taught us, or what the media says is true? Does truth change with the times, technology or circumstances? What is truth?

Jesus prayed to the Father in the presence of His disciples and said: Sanctify them in the truth; Your word is truth (**John 17:17**).

According to the Bible, truth is the self-expression of God. Truth is that which is consistent with the mind, will, character, and being of God. There is complete unity between the written Word of God and the perfect expression of God in Jesus Christ. The Bible tells us Jesus existed in the beginning. In the New Testament, Scripture is called the Word of Christ (Colossians 3:16). The person of Jesus Christ and the Holy Word of the living God then are in full agreement. This is the basis from which we must discern, perceive, and reason. There is no ambiguity whatsoever!

Try defining truth apart from God or without universal absolutes and see where that gets you. Apparently, there is plenty of confusion not only in the world, but also in the church regarding how truth is defined and understood. There are professing Christians who say they believe in "most" of the Bible. Really? We don't have the option to pick and choose only those Scriptures that suit us or the verses we agree with. The entire Bible is true or our faith is a lie.

The sum of Your word is truth, And every one of Your righteous ordinances is everlasting (**Psalm 119:160**).

Furthermore, in the book of Revelation, Jesus is called Faithful and True (Rev. 19:11) when He returns to conquer and reign. Here's where our worldview starts, and it takes faith: Either God *is* or God *is not*. This is something many grapple with. God created all things, but how did He come into existence?

Before the mountains were born, Or You gave birth to the earth and the world, Even from everlasting to everlasting, You are God (**Psalm 90:2**).

God existed in the beginning, before anything and everything. All we need to know is that when Moses asked, God said to him, *I AM WHO I AM* in Exodus 3:14. We get *Lord* from the original name of God, *YHWH*, which is derived from the verb *HAYAH*, meaning "to be." Our faith also holds that Jesus is God.

For no man can lay a foundation other than the one which is laid, which is Jesus Christ (**1 Corinthians 3:11**).

Truth has been under attack from the very beginning of time, and in America, opposition to Jesus Christ has intensified. People are avoiding, denying, and suppressing the truth more than ever. They can ignore it, they can mock it, and they can pretend it does not exist, but that changes nothing. The sad thing is there is some debate about what is true even among Christians!

In 1995, approximately fifty percent of *Christians* said there are moral truths which are unchanging, and that truth is absolute, not relative to the circumstances. Not surprisingly, ten years later in 2005, The Barna Group conducted a poll revealing only 35% of Americans believe in absolute standards of morality, that right and wrong do *not* change with time or circumstances.[1] (33% didn't even know how to respond!)

ESTABLISHING A CHRISTIAN WORLDVIEW

A person's worldview is a significant step toward self-awareness, self-knowledge and self-understanding. Your worldview as a Christian needs to be based on a foundation of God's Word. Our sovereign God is not surprised, but it must grieve His heart to see the condition of our country, the world, and the church today. Holiness and righteousness are practically meaningless to some religious folks. The Word of God is being watered down, truth is being diluted, and this has led to moral and cultural confusion.

Here's a quick example: I'm pro-life and sure hope you are as well. I have learned that even in the church, believers have different views on abortion and when life begins. This proves either we don't read our Bibles as much anymore, or we believe the talking heads. Especially in the church, building on a foundational worldview of biblical truth is paramount.

In a Crosswalk.com article, Michael Foust wrote:

"Barna defines a biblical worldview as believing that: moral absolutes exist; the source of truth is the Bible; the Bible is "accurate in all of the principles it teaches," salvation is by grace alone; Jesus lived a sinless life; believers have a duty to witness; Satan is real and not just a symbol; God is the "all-knowing, all-powerful maker of the universe who still rules that creation today."[2]

This worldview is the foundation for *every* decision you make in life. I don't care who you are, how old you are, where you live, or what kind of family you grew up in; if you have not considered *exactly* how your personal beliefs, philosophy, and worldview were formed, it is time to take a serious look at what you believe and why.

We must be undaunted in establishing God's Word as the basis of our thinking, our faith, and our lives. If we don't make this critically important decision, we'll be in danger of seeing the world through our own feelings, personal experiences, opinions, Hollywood, media, and what others have told us, instead of through God's eyes. Some of us have lived much of our lives believing what we have heard or read at one time, instead of believing what God says. May the Lord have mercy on our biblical illiteracy!

All Scripture is inspired by God and profitable for teaching, for reproof, for correction, for training in righteousness – (**2 Timothy 3:16**).

Is it possible to live authentically and effectively as a Christian and not believe the entire Bible word for word? If you do not believe in parts of the Bible, then how can you trust God's Word in its entirety? Is Jesus a liar? Did he only really mean *most* of the things He said? This is where people living on a spiritual fault line panic at the first sign of a life-shaking trial, revealing their foundation wasn't very solid.

You may be reading this right now and God is nudging you to evaluate what you think about truth. Jesus promised his followers the Holy Spirit would guide them into all truth (John 16:13). If you think the Bible is a history book or a moral guide, then you are missing out on knowing Jesus. Evangelical Christian theologian, author, and pastor, Francis Schaeffer stated:

"Truth always carries with it confrontation. Truth demands confrontation; loving confrontation nevertheless. If our reflex action is always accommodation regardless of the centrality of the truth involved, there is something wrong."

The battle over what is true divides people. This is the state of America today because if opponents of truth can convince people to believe that God doesn't exist, then there are no moral restraints and anything goes. In his book, *78 - How Christians Can Save America*, author and radio talk show host, Peter Heck, included a fascinating interaction with a caller to his program. Here's a portion:

James: "...There are different ways of looking at the world, and there are different perspectives people have, and ...saying that this is a concrete right, and this is a concrete wrong may be true given your perspective, but it's not maybe true given mine...."

Peter: "...do you realize that Hitler was doing what he thought was right? He was merely speeding up the evolutionary process. He was attempting to bring about a master race and exterminate all the riff-raff. It's the same thing Planned Parenthood was founded to do. Get rid of all the lesser folks. Now, maybe you don't agree with his strategy, but he just had a different perspective on how to improve the lives of humanity than Mother Theresa, but ultimately they both wanted the same thing, right?

"What if I said that it would have been better for Mother Theresa to kill all those impoverished people she lived with? Take them out of their misery! Why is this perspective wrong? ... There has to be a truth that is fixed, that is right for all men, or we're in a lot of trouble."[3]

The truth established from the beginning is God. He is eternal. Though humanists have made progress in their goal to blot out God, ultimately it will be impossible. Even if they could eradicate Christianity from America one day, we know He is everlasting; He is the beginning and the end, and He holds the universe in his hands.

The grass withers, the flower fades, but the word of our God stands forever (**Isaiah 40:8**).

IF AT FIRST YOU DON'T BELIEVE, START WITH THE TRUTH

In my personal conversations with people who do not believe the Bible is the Word of God, my intention is never to try to force them to believe or to convince them about Jesus; that's the job of the Holy Spirit. My job is to speak honestly to whoever will listen and allow God to work through me. Some people simply don't *want* to believe, and that is the beauty of free will. We serve a loving God who refuses to force His creation to worship Him.

The road to life is a narrow one, but whoever believes in Jesus can have everlasting life because God is no respecter of persons. Take the necessary time to thoroughly examine the Scriptures. Even though God knows some will refuse to believe no matter what, He desires all people to know the truth and be saved through Jesus Christ because there is only one God (1 Timothy 2:3-5), and Christ is the only Mediator between God and man.

If someone gave you this book, and you are not a follower of Jesus Christ, it's not too late to be saved unless you are simply unwilling to ask. Please search your heart right now and see if you honestly *want* to know the one true God personally. He loves you and He is waiting for you with open arms. He is the only God who is alive! It's not wrong to have doubts, but those doubts need to be dealt with – and He's knocking right now.

If you are sincerely ready to accept God's will for your life, here's a prayer God always answers: "Father in heaven, please show me *the truth* about who Jesus Christ is." He *wants* to reveal His love and truth to you and show you His plan for your life. God never promises an easy life, but He does promise us a better life. Our part is the faith, His part is the fulfillment.

> *Call to Me and I will answer you, and I will tell you great and mighty things, which you do not know* (**Jeremiah 33:3**).

It is easy for people to criticize what they do not understand. The Bible tells us the message of the cross is foolishness (1 Cor. 1:18) to unbelievers because God frustrates those who think they are intelligent or wise. Proverbs 3:7 warns us to not be wise in our own eyes. After all, who can fully comprehend a perfect God?

Without question, this is the great mystery of our faith: Christ was revealed in a human body and vindicated by the Spirit. He was seen by angels and announced to the nations. He was believed in throughout the world and taken to heaven in glory (**1 Timothy 3:16** NLT).

Jesus is the cornerstone, which is one reason why there is so much division over him. Everything written in the Bible concerning Him is true. On the other hand, some think Jesus was simply a persuasive teacher, the leader of a rebellion, or even a lunatic because of the claims He made. According to Jesus, He is the bread of life, the door, the gate, the light, the truth, and the way. Jesus said He was not of this world and that He overcame the world.

Before His crucifixion, Jesus told His disciples He was going *back* to heaven to prepare a place for them and then return for them because He wanted His followers to be with Him in God's glory. He also told them they should know where He was going and how to get there. Thomas said to Him, *Lord, we don't know where you are going, so how can we know the way?* Jesus answered:

I am the way and the truth and the life. No one comes to the Father except through me. If you really knew me, you would know my Father as well. From now on, you do know him and have seen him (**John 14:6-7**).

This statement by Jesus Christ must be dealt with, because it does not allow for wiggle room. The Bible is the God-breathed, Holy Spirit-inspired Word of life. If you doubt the Bible can be infallible, since it was written by men, then you are putting God in a box.

Above all, you must understand that no prophecy of Scripture came about by the prophet's own interpretation. For prophecy never had its origin in the will of man, but men spoke from God as they were carried along by the Holy Spirit (**2 Peter 1:20-21**).

Is anything too hard for the Lord? God's ways are higher than ours, and if we believe in the Creator then we must believe He gives us our intellect. Without a creator, without a design, and without a plan, you and I are just cosmic accidents living a purposeless, random existence.

After all, *without* God, our lives are based on ourselves (we're number one!) and on living for today. But if God's Word is true, and we really are sinners in need of rescue, then there must be right and wrong, true and false, good and bad, light and darkness, and moral absolutes.

Our godless society has been heading full speed away from Christ, and many people seem to hate the very truth that could save them! As a whole, our secular progressive culture has denied the truth of God and the authority of the Bible, in order to defend and justify their unholy living. The result is chaos, confusion, moral relativism, self-exaltation, and countless forms of spirituality *apart* from Christianity. It is difficult for the natural man to grasp the sovereignty, omniscience, and omnipotence of a perfect God. Even in the church, doctrine divides denominations and the best of Christians. Riding the fence with a foot in two different worldviews is not an option.

CHRIST BEFORE ALL THINGS

> *John [the Baptist] testified about Him and cried out, saying, "This was He of whom I said, 'He who comes after me has a higher rank than I, for He existed **before** me* (**John 1:15**).

> *Then God said, "Let Us make man in **Our image**, according to Our likeness; and let them rule...* (**Genesis 1:26**).

> *God, after He spoke long ago to the fathers in the prophets in many portions and in many ways, in these last days has spoken to us in His Son, whom He appointed heir of all things, **through whom also He made the world.** And He is the radiance of His glory and the exact representation of His nature, and upholds all things by the word of His power...* (**Hebrews 1:1-3**) (Emphasis mine).

These verses confirm and bear witness to the fact Christ existed before He came to live on earth for 33 years. This can be hard to grasp with our human minds, but it is essential to understanding the truth. It also reinforces the Trinity; God the Father, God the Son, and God the Holy Spirit. Believers don't consider the creation account often enough. All things were created by Him and for Him. **Colossians 1:17** tells us *He [Jesus] is before all things, and in him all things hold together.* In addition, Jesus said the following in **John 5:39, 40, and 46:**

> *You search the Scriptures because you think that in them you have eternal life; it is these that testify about Me; and you are unwilling to come to Me so that you may have life.... For if you believed Moses, you would believe Me, for he wrote about Me.*

The religious leaders flipped out when they heard Jesus say this, and then they blew a gasket when Jesus told them He existed before Abraham (John 8:56). This challenges us to dig deeper into our faith. John R.W. Stott was an English Christian leader and was very influential in the worldwide evangelical movement. He said it is the uniqueness of Christ that we defend:

> "So, because in no other person but Jesus of Nazareth did God first become human (in his birth), then bear our sins (in his death), then conquer death (in his resurrection) and then enter his people (by his Spirit), he is uniquely able to save sinners. Nobody else has his qualifications."[4]

Most Christians don't have a problem with the above assertions or Scriptures, but some have a hard time with being saved by grace alone. A few religions overemphasize good works – doing as much as you can to be accepted by God or to get to heaven – which is not what the Bible teaches. In Ephesians 2, Paul writes that we are saved only through faith because of God's grace. Grace is undeserved favor. Grace has nothing to do with our efforts.

However, it is also important to balance out our faith and good deeds because faith without actions is useless. We are to live what we believe in full expression and demonstration of our faith. The Bible also teaches faith works through love (Gal. 5:6). But please do not miss the point that there is absolutely nothing you or I can do to get God to love us more or accept us more. Nothing in all creation can separate us from the love of Christ (Rom. 8:38-39).

Then there are others who don't think they need to put their trust in Jesus to go to heaven. They might say, "I am a good person. I have never murdered or raped anybody. I try to follow the Golden Rule. I love the planet and recycle, and I even volunteer." I would ask them if they think Jesus was a good person.

> *As He was setting out on a journey, a man ran up to Him and knelt before Him, and asked Him, "Good Teacher, what shall I do to inherit eternal life?" And Jesus said to him, "Why do you call Me good? No one is good except God alone* (**Mark 10:17-18**).

No one is good enough on their own to approach a holy God. He also made the point that we are incapable of keeping the commandments, so how can anyone be saved by trying to be good through their own efforts?

Have you ever lied, stolen anything, coveted something someone else had, hated someone in your heart (murder), or lusted after another person (adultery)? Have you always honored your mother and father? Have you ever idolized a person or a thing over God? (Like a Hollywood actor, rock star, sports team, athlete, celebrity, bike, car, boat, house, etc.) Have you ever taken the Lord's name in vain? Not one of us is good, and it's impossible for us to keep the laws and commandments of God on our own. That's why the gospel truly is *very* good news. Those of us who confess Jesus is our Lord and Savior, believing in our hearts, are forgiven, saved, set free, redeemed, restored, sanctified, and blessed. We have a bright future and an eternal hope!

PRAY FOR THOSE WHO REFUSE TO BELIEVE

I recently had a good conversation with a very liberal guy who is not a Christian. Though he didn't believe the Bible is God's Word or that Christ alone is Lord, he listened to what I shared. Sadly, the conversation left his heart unchanged. He complimented me on being a person of conviction even though he disagreed with me.

> *But a natural man does not accept the things of the Spirit of God, for they are foolishness to him; and he cannot understand them, because they are spiritually appraised* (**1 Corinthians 2:14**).

The natural man may be wise according to the world's wisdom and intellect, but that won't get him very far when it comes to discerning spiritual things. His pride, earthly success, degrees and worldly education prevent him from admitting he needs God. Though this person I talked with hasn't read much of the Bible, he had formed strong beliefs and negative opinions about Christianity and religion in general. Not only that, but he also taught this worldview to his children, and they now take bits and pieces from many religions.

I call it *cafeteria Christianity*. They choose what they want, when they want it, and avoid what they don't like in the Bible. It is being dangerously mired in the mucky middle. But if you have an unwavering faith in Jesus Christ built on the solid foundation of God's Word, your beliefs will not be shaken. Your faith will withstand the debates, opinions, talking points, arguments, and attacks of opponents. We don't have all the answers, so we don't need to pretend we do.

I love the Lord because He changed my heart. I am convinced about the truth of Jesus Christ because of massive evidence – archeological, biblical, and historical – and years of personal research and study. This other person was just as convinced in his views by his upbringing, by liberal friends, and higher education. We both believe our convictions are right and true. So what is the lesson? Don't get discouraged when you talk to someone who simply doesn't *want* to believe. Pray for them. The results are in God's hands.

The more I study the Bible, the more I realize I need to learn. Our responsibility is to *always be ready to make a defense to everyone who asks you to give an account for the hope that is in you, yet with gentleness and reverence* (**1 Peter 3:15**). Are you prepared to explain the reason for your faith in Christ? The Holy Spirit will instruct us and teach us. People may not know exactly what they're looking for, but they are searching. Everyone has a void only Christ can fill. We are ambassadors for Christ commissioned to share the truth, so speak it with boldness.

> *Because, if you confess with your mouth that Jesus is Lord and believe in your heart that God raised him from the dead, you will be saved. For with the heart one believes and is justified, and with the mouth one confesses and is saved... For everyone who calls on the name of the Lord will be saved* (**Romans 10:9-10, 13 ESV**).

Biblical truth has been forced out of the public square, followed by a purposeful shift away from Christianity in America to the point where we are confused about church and state issues. Since truth matters, we need to look at what our founders believed and how this country was established on free speech and religious freedom. While doing this, we must understand the founder's intent and the connection between God and government in the United States.

ENDNOTES

1 http://www.barna.org/barna-update/article/5-barna-update/174-most-adults-feel-accepted-by-god-but-lack-a-biblical-worldview

2 http://www.crosswalk.com/1345335/

3 Peter Heck, 78 How Christians Can Save America; 2011 Attaboy Press, page 45-49

4 http://www.christianitytoday.com/ct/2003/september/2.50.html

CHAPTER 2

GOD, THE GOSPEL AND GOVERNMENT

We Recognize no Sovereign but God, and no King
but Jesus. – **Patriot John Hancock** (1737 – 1793)
First Signer of the Declaration of Independence

Let each citizen remember at the moment he is offering
his vote that he is not making a present or a compliment
to please an individual – or at least that he ought not so
to do; but that he is executing one of the most solemn
trusts in human society for which he is accountable to
God and his country. – **Samuel Adams** (1722 – 1803)

America's future is being threatened by those who have successfully rewritten some of our history. Distortions about America's origins and heritage have poisoned our education system, our government, and the national media. We may not have been paying attention, but children across America probably were. Having learned a much different history than you and I once learned in public schools, many of these young people are now out of college and have moved on to join the work force.

Of all people, Christians should care the most about this country. We've lost the moral influence we once had in public schools, and to be blunt, government education has been hijacked by progressives. They have several agendas which we will expose when we investigate the National Education Association, but right now it's important to look at some of our history. People from all over the world flock to America to escape communism, socialism, oppression, and tyranny, and when they reach our shores exhausted, hopeful and thankful, they know they have come to a good nation, and what they've heard about our freedom is true.

People of deep faith ventured to this land to start a new life, one independent of government and free of its control. Christians once permeated every aspect of American culture, from academia and the arts to politics and the press. They were hard-working farmers, ministers, and small business owners. They had a strong, godly, moral influence in public life. That solid foundation began at home with educating their children with the Scriptures and strengthening their families. They taught about faith, love, honor, respect, and responsibility. Parents studied the Bible and took its application seriously.

> *Hear, O Israel! The* LORD *is our God, the* LORD *is one! You shall love the* LORD *your God with all your heart and with all your soul and with all your might. These words, which I am commanding you today, shall be on your heart. You shall teach them diligently to your sons and shall talk of them when you sit in your house and when you walk by the way and when you lie down and when you rise up* (**Deuteronomy 6:4-7**).

The earliest established American universities held the Bible in high esteem and were saturated with Christian influence and instruction. Harvard University is the oldest institution of higher learning in the United States, established in 1636 by vote of the Great and General Court of the Massachusetts Bay Colony, just 16 years after the pilgrims arrived at Plymouth Rock. Harvard was founded by ministers who realized the need for training clergy for the new commonwealth.

Adopted in 1692, Harvard's early motto was *Veritas Christo et Ecclesiae*, meaning "Truth for Christ and the Church." Ten out of the first twelve Harvard presidents were ministers, and in its earliest classes, half the graduates also became ministers. Further proving the Bible was established in early American education, Harvard's 1646 "Rules and Precepts" included the following:

> "Let every Student be plainly instructed, and earnestly pressed to consider well, the maine end of his life and studies is, to know God and Jesus Christ which is eternal life (John 17:3) and

therefore to lay Christ in the bottome, as the only foundation of all sound knowledge and Learning. And seeing the Lord only giveth wisdom, Let every one seriously set himself by prayer in secret to seeke it of His (Prov. 2:3)."[1]

Extremely high levels of biblical discipline continued with the "Harvard College Laws of 1700" which required students to observe strict rules, and in order to earn their bachelor's degree, "read the Old and New Testament into the Latin tongue, and resolve them logically." Systematic theological instruction was inaugurated in 1721, and by 1827 Harvard became a nucleus of theological teaching in New England.[2] However, during this time, Unitarian liberals were infiltrating Harvard. Soon, the institution that operated with the presupposition that education should be predicated upon the Scriptures as the starting point for wisdom and knowledge would remove Christ and the church from its motto leaving only "Veritas" in 1836.

It has been said churches, individuals, and institutions never slide closer to God; they only slide away. If this fall happened at Harvard, the university where Samuel Adams, John Adams, and John Quincy Adams received their higher education, rest assured it has happened at every other university in America! Liberals secularized Harvard to the point that by 1850, it was referred to as the "Unitarian Vatican." Just like today's church in America, it was the gradual neglect of the study of Scripture, discipline, and prayer that led them away from truth to the moral relativism that occupies Harvard, most universities, and even some churches today.

In his 1988 farewell address to the nation, President Ronald Reagan said:

> "So, we've got to teach history based not on what's in fashion but what's important. ...If we forget what we did, we won't know who we are. I'm warning of an eradication of the American memory that could result, ultimately, in an erosion of the American spirit."

FOUNDERS INTENT

We have lost our founders vision of educating children in the Bible and have handed them over to learn from the government. The U.S. Department of Education and NEA curriculums are not exactly what our founders had in mind. I come from a family of teachers, and most people go into education for the right reasons, but if teachers are not grounded in biblical truths or conservative principles, many eventually get sucked into the liberal indoctrination matrix.

One Christian teacher friend of mine was asked to remove her Bible from view when it was on her desk. This is the very book most of our founders believed in and relied upon! Another Christian friend was asked to take down a photo of his favorite president, Ronald Reagan, in his classroom. You may remember what happened to a New Jersey teacher in 2011 when she made a Facebook post saying homosexuality was a sin. Naturally, that comment sparked media-infused activism. Vikki Knox, a Christian teacher in a public school made comments in response to a large, prominent display the school had put up celebrating gay, lesbian, bisexual, transgender (GLBT) history month. Hundreds turned up at the school to protest, calling her a hateful, intolerant bigot, for starters.[3]

By the time many students get to college, they've most likely exited high school supporting several of the following: abortion, gay marriage, environmentalism, evolution, illegal immigration, man-caused global warming, social justice, and the Democratic Party. The government takes its agenda seriously. Over eighty percent of students leave their Christian faith after just one year of college. College takes impressionable kids to the hyper-liberal level. Most young people figure if their professors say the Bible isn't true or that there is no God, they must be right. After all, they have a PhD! Professors tell them what to think, and you don't dare challenge them. One thing higher education does is produce more progressives.

According to survey averages, approximately 85% of college professors are liberal, Democrat, or progressive compared to 15% conservative, Republican, or Christian. Remove Christian teachers and professors, add some atheists and socialists; remove the Bible and prayer from schools and add the promotion of homosexuality, other religions, and political correctness, and we've got a dangerous combination that has drastically strayed from what our founders intended.

> "Our constitution was made only for a moral and religious people. It is wholly inadequate to the government of any other."
> – **President John Adams** (1735 – 1826)

For over 225 years, the greatest influence in America has been the Gospel of Jesus Christ. Brave pioneering settlers fought the elements and illnesses to arrive on our shores so they could freely worship the Lord our God. The Founding Fathers were determined to live in complete freedom. They fought to establish the Declaration of Independence, the Constitution, and the Bill of Rights for a free people. This Republic under God was ambitious and revolutionary. They enacted a philosophy of government the world had never seen. These courageous leaders pledged their lives, their fortunes, and their sacred honor to lay the foundation for these great United States. To reach their goal of freedom, they had to go through a bloody, costly war against the mightiest military power in the world at the time.

It took tremendous sacrifice to make this society a reality; it takes no less of a sacrifice today by our brave military personnel to preserve our Republic. We must never take this ongoing sacrifice for granted, nor should we think our liberty can be maintained by itself. Early American patriots battled against and overcame tyranny to gain individual freedom to live, work, and worship. They recognized every blessing and every good thing comes from God (James 1:17).

> "We hold these truths to be self-evident, that all men are created equal, that they are endowed by their Creator with certain unalienable Rights that among these are Life, Liberty and the pursuit of Happiness."

This preamble in our Declaration of Independence has been called one of the best-known statements in the English language, containing the most potent and consequential words in American history.[4] This passage came to represent a moral standard to which the United States should strive. Sadly, in the last 50-100 years, its importance in public education, government, and in the mainstream media has been minimized dramatically.

John Quincy Adams was elected as the sixth President of the United States. Some historians suggest there was a time when he became unpopular with his followers because he often put principle *before* party. Imagine that! Grounded in biblical instruction, in a letter to his father, John Adams, John Quincy Adams wrote:

> "The Sermon on the Mount commends me to lay up for myself treasures, not on earth, but in Heaven. My hopes of a future life are all founded upon the Gospel of Christ..."

Signer of the Declaration of Independence, Charles Carroll, further stated: "Without morals a republic cannot subsist any length of time" and went on to say that those who opposed Christianity are undermining a morality that is "the best security for the duration of free governments." The movement to blot out God in America goes against everything these men and this country originally stood for. Our Founding Fathers would be appalled if they could see the blatant moral, fiscal, and societal decline in America today.

Did you know at least six of the original thirteen American colonies had official, state-supported churches? Moreover, at the request of Mr. Robert Aitken in 1782, Congress approved the purchase of 20,000 Bibles from Holland to give to the American people. Many states also required those seeking elected office be of the Christian faith, and past presidents and members of Congress often encouraged prayer and other religious activities. What they did *not* do is tell people what church, denomination, or religion to adhere to, even though they personally and collectively followed the principles and standards of the Bible and Christianity. In the early days of America, Christians were visible and effective in every aspect of society. They were looked up to, respected, and their contributions were valued. Many of our founders were theologically trained and could have been ministers.

Tradition holds that a few hours before his death on October 24, 1852, Daniel Webster said, "The great mystery is Jesus Christ – the Gospel. What would the condition of any of us be if we had not the hope of immortality?" Webster was one of America's most prominent conservatives and statesmen. From his bed, he began to recite the Lord's Prayer and made this request: "Hold me up; I do not wish to pray with a fainting voice..." Daniel Webster's last coherent words were: "I still live."[5] Here is a warning and admonition from this great American Patriot:

> "If we abide by the principles taught in the Bible, our country will go on prospering and to prosper; but if we and our posterity neglect its instruction and authority, no man can tell how sudden a catastrophe may overwhelm us and bury all our glory in profound obscurity...

> "Finally, let us not forget the religious character of our origin. Our fathers were brought hither by their high veneration for the Christian religion. They journeyed by its light, and labored in its hope. They sought to incorporate its principles with the elements of their society, and to diffuse its influence through all their institutions; civil, political, or literary."
> – **Daniel Webster** (1782 – 1852)[6]

Early in American history, men of faith and principle understood the importance of Christians living as salt and light in our culture. Today, however, this great nation is being poisoned from within while America falls further away from the God that blessed us.

TO THE REPUBLIC FOR WHICH IT STANDS...

We are clearly not the same America. It is astounding to me how radically the country most of us love has changed. As Christians, we've stepped back and have allowed an anti-biblical, anti-American, socialist sentiment to gain ground. There has also been disagreement regarding what America is, and what we stand for. A good example of this apparent confusion is over The Pledge of Allegiance, written in 1892:

> "I pledge allegiance to my Flag and the Republic for which it stands, one nation, indivisible, with liberty and justice for all."

The word "my" was soon replaced with "the" and then the words "of the United States" were added. The final change in the Pledge of Allegiance occurred on Flag Day in 1954 when President Dwight D. Eisenhower approved the addition of the words "under God." He was rightly concerned about a communist movement in America and as he authorized this change, President Eisenhower said:

> "In this way we are reaffirming the transcendence of religious faith in America's heritage and future; in this way we shall constantly strengthen those spiritual weapons which forever will be our country's most powerful resource in peace and war."

It is important to emphasize that America is more than a republic. We are a constitutional republic! This is an important distinction. As John Adams so aptly put it, "We are a nation of laws, not of men." We are not a democracy, and not a democratic republic. We are united as one nation. In other words, we are not a loose confederation of states. Our rights come from God, not legislators. The U.S. Constitution defines us as one people, indivisible. Each of us is recognized as possessing certain liberties, and we are all treated equally under the justice system.

Let's look a bit closer at the difference between a democracy and a republic. The traditional definition of a democracy is in stark contrast to the modern revision of the term. To briefly summarize, a democracy is government operated and ruled by direct majority vote of the people. The majority calls the shots on policy matters through public meetings or by voting on referendums. If the mob decided rape was to go unpunished, they would set a new law. A democracy is the system that chose Barabbas over Jesus. The Framers of our Constitution were rightfully fearful of pure democracy. (See the Occupy Wall Street movement.)

A republic, however, is where the general population elects leaders to represent them who, in turn, make policy decisions on their behalf and then pass laws to govern. America is a republic where power is separated between three branches of government: the executive, judicial, and legislative. The Constitution declares that The United States "shall guarantee every State in this Union a Republican form of government" (Article IV, Section 4). Electing the best, most godly people to govern is our best hope to stop the downward spiral and turn the country around.

While researching the differences between a democracy and a republic, I came across some fascinating information. About the time our original thirteen states adopted their new constitution in 1787, Alexander Tyler, a Scottish history professor at the University of Edinburgh, had this to say about the fall of the Athenian Republic some 2,000 years earlier:

"A democracy is always temporary in nature; it simply cannot exist as a permanent form of government… A democracy will continue to exist up until the time that voters discover they can vote themselves generous gifts from the public treasury.

"From that moment on, the majority always votes for the candidates who promise the most benefits from the public treasury, with the result that every democracy will finally collapse due to loose fiscal policy, which is always followed by a dictatorship.

"The average age of the world's greatest civilizations from the beginning of history has been about 200 years

"During those 200 years, those nations always progressed through the following sequence:

1. From bondage to spiritual faith
2. From spiritual faith to great courage
3. From courage to liberty
4. From liberty to abundance
5. From abundance to complacency
6. From complacency to apathy
7. From apathy to dependence
8. From dependence back into bondage[7]

I am concerned America may be somewhere between numbers six and seven.

ANTI-GOD GOVERNMENT GAMES

One of the biggest lies of our generation trumpeted by progressives and the national media is that there is a *constitutional separation of church and state*. The debate came to the forefront of American news a few years back when a controversy erupted over a 5,300 pound granite monument in Alabama. Evidently, some atheists were in an upheaval over what was written on the granite: **the Ten Commandments!** With the help of the ACLU, they filed a lawsuit. By the way, those same words out of the Holy Bible are inscribed on the U.S. Supreme Court building in Washington D.C. Believing in the Constitution, Alabama Supreme Court Justice Roy Moore had the audacity to install the monument with the "offending religious references" in the state courthouse rotunda, and it became a controversy.

How far will Americans allow this judicial assault to go when enemies of God keep tearing at the fabric of our country? Truth alert: **There is no mention of any "separation of church and state"** in the U.S. Constitution. This idea that anti-Christian activists claim in their agenda to blot out God comes from an 1802 letter to the Danbury Baptists that Thomas Jefferson wrote about a healthy "wall of separation." Family Research Council's Robert Morrison explains:

> "It is that phrase – honestly misunderstood or deliberately misconstrued – that has fueled so much of the anti-religious fervor of secular elites, activist judges, and atheizers. But one thing ought to be clear from Thomas Jefferson's actions in those days: Preaching the Word of God and speaking of Jesus Christ on federal property cannot be banned."[8]

The letter was written during the time Thomas Jefferson's former Virginia neighbor, cheese maker, and Baptist preacher delivered a biblical sermon during a worship service in the U.S. House of Representatives! President Jefferson, Secretary of State James Madison, and most government representatives were in attendance. Does this sound like someone wanting to prevent Christianity from influencing government?

Author and historian David Barton writes about Thomas Jefferson's exchange with the Baptist Association in Connecticut affirming Jefferson believed God, not government, was the author and source of our rights. The idea was to prevent government from interfering with those rights. Barton explained:

> "Very simply, the "fence" of the Webster letter and the "wall" of the Danbury letter were **not** to limit religious activities in public; rather they were to limit the power of the government to prohibit or interfere with those expressions."[9]

The sooner we spread the truth, the sooner a few more uninformed citizens will wake up. Humanism and secularism are on the rise and offer a very present threat. Much of our rich Christian heritage has been rewritten or removed entirely from text books and public education. Evil is at work. Knowing how corrupt and deceptive man can be and how wicked the human heart, Thomas Jefferson once said:

> "I tremble for my country when I reflect that God is just, that His justice cannot sleep forever."[10]

Some believe God is already judging America, and others say His final judgment is right around the corner. With the massive increase in corruption and deception in government, we often forget it all results from sin and our sin nature. Perhaps God is allowing Christians to suffer the consequences of the politicians we have elected to represent us. America must turn back to God!

Laws continue to be passed, bills signed, and policies implemented that either go against our biblical values or threaten another one of our freedoms. This is not what our Founding Fathers intended. According to several polls in early 2012, over 72% of Americans said the country is headed in the wrong direction. Even some people who voted for "hope and change" in 2008 are now hoping to change it back.

Our founders understood the ways of man, the dangers of too much power, and the potential for tyranny so they established a Constitution to protect the people. They created checks and balances in an attempt to hold government accountable, while providing for individual freedoms at the same time. They placed the highest of values on religious freedom.

We've strayed dramatically away from their vision to the point of electing a president who does not seem to respect America. Why does he insist on radically transforming the United States? President Obama downplays America's greatness, disrespects the Constitution, seems embarrassed of our history, and enacts policies against the Word of God. It is our job to put faith, character, and integrity back on the priority list of who we elect, not how well someone speaks in public or reads a teleprompter. In 2008, Barack Obama singled out Christianity and voiced his concerns about religions that encourage evangelism:

> "The difficult thing about any religion, including Christianity, is that at some level there is a call to proselytize. There's the belief

that if people haven't embraced Jesus Christ as their personal savior, they're going to hell."[11]

Barack Obama has become one of the biggest presidential advocates in our history for abortion, gay marriage, GLBT education, and class warfare – a major tenet of Marxism. He also stated "our schools are there to teach *worldly* knowledge and science. I believe in evolution, and I believe there's a difference between science and faith."[12]

Christians should strongly oppose legislation that favors the destruction of human life. We should also be against laws that penalize marriage and families, taxing married couples at a higher rate than those who are gay, single, or living together. That said, regardless of who is in office, we are called to submit to the authorities and pray for those in high positions because God allowed them to be placed there. The candidates we elect should represent our interests and carefully decide how to spend *our* tax dollars. They advance social policies and implement economic and foreign policies that affect us.

Opponents of Christianity have even used the First Amendment against churches and individuals. They are often quick to point out that not one church or religion may be respected or promoted by government, but they stop there. They conveniently fail to read after the comma in the First Amendment. Congress may not prohibit (forbid, hinder, prevent) Americans from freely worshipping. Part of this very important Amendment is the freedom of all speech. **Government may NOT abridge** (shorten, reduce, deprive, cut-off) **our speech, including when we talk about Jesus Christ in public.** But that doesn't mean they won't try to silence us.

> "Congress shall make no law respecting an establishment of religion, or prohibiting the free exercise thereof; or abridging the freedom of speech, or of the press; or the right of the people peaceably to assemble, and to petition the Government for a redress of grievances."

God has blessed America, but I can't help but think of America's current president and how far to the opposite end of the spectrum he is compared to most of our founders. The Washington Times' Jeffrey Kuhner said the president's goal is to purge Christianity from civil society and to marginalize religion from the public square. I'm not sure about all religions but it does appear the president makes no apology for promoting the antithesis of Christianity.

President Obama publicly recognized several Muslim holy days in 2011, but he ignored Easter and the resurrection of Jesus Christ, the foundational bedrock of Christianity. He also refused to acknowledge our National Day of Prayer, approved more funding for Planned Parenthood, and has declared June national Gay Lesbian Bisexual Transgender month for two years in a row. Mr. Obama is against any kind of restriction on abortion and one of his first acts as president was to sign a bill (Mexico City Policy) allowing federal money to be spent on overseas abortions. He has quoted the Islamic holy book, the Quran, in speeches such as in Cairo in 2009. People of faith may be starting to take notice. According to the Barna Group, toward the end of 2011, President Obama had an unfavorability rating of 94% with Evangelical Christians.

> "America will never be destroyed from the outside. If we falter and lose our freedoms, it will be because we destroyed ourselves." – **President Abraham Lincoln** (1809 – 1865)

One problem within our country is with judicial activism in America. In February 2012, the Ninth Circuit Court (the Ninth Circus) out of San Francisco trounced on millions of Californians who voted on Proposition 8 which defined and favored marriage as being between a man and a woman. This is the way progressives think. The liberal court justices overturned the voter-approved ban on same-sex marriage, saying it is unconstitutional.[13]

The 2012 Presidential election will decide America's future and could have a domino effect on judicial decisions as there are three Supreme Court Justices who may be retiring soon. This could leave three open appointments for either conservative or liberal nominees! The country really needs you: your witness, your faith, your time and your voice. If you have any hope whatsoever for America to reverse its decline, please be informed and vote **biblical values** on Election Day.

In early February 2012, in an interview in Cairo, American Supreme Court Justice Ruth Bader Ginsburg, though her job is to uphold our

Constitution, gave the impression it is dated and irrelevant. When asked to give her opinion regarding the type of government Egypt should adopt as they try to rebuild their country following the Arab Spring, she said, "I would not look to the U.S. Constitution, if I were drafting a constitution in the year 2012."

Instead, Ruth Bader Ginsburg – a U.S. Supreme Court Justice who supposedly uses the U.S. Constitution as the basis for her judicial decisions – suggested they look at South Africa's Constitution as a guide for their new government! For the record, Ginsburg, one of the most liberal Justices in U.S. history was appointed by – drum roll... (Wait for it), Bill Clinton.

Some believe America has come close to destroying our constitutional system of government and do not think we will recover. Author and educator Samuel Blumenfeld wrote that a "socialist cancer" has infected our culture. He implied that even with the Tea Party movement and the rise of Christian conservatism, it may not be enough to stop the decline.

> "The disease, long and slow in developing, has spread throughout our public education system, our universities, and many of our cultural institutions.... The coming election in November may very well determine whether or not this Constitutional Republic can be saved or is gone forever."[14]

If you are a believer in Jesus Christ, you must understand how ideas liberals in government promote are focused on moving America away from any influence of God and biblical truth. Tragically, the church has been apathetic toward politics throughout much of this unholy transformation. Will enough Christians wake up and help sound the alarm for the sake of America?

> "The people are responsible for the character of their Congress. If that body be ignorant, reckless, and corrupt, it is because the people tolerate ignorance, recklessness, and corruption..."
> – **President James A. Garfield** (1831-1881)

American government and culture has been hijacked by many promoters of evil. How should we respond? We can start by exposing the darkness and by raising awareness. Jesus told us not to hide under a table but to let our light shine. Why? It only takes a sliver of light to overcome thick darkness. It only takes a small dedicated movement of conservative Christ-followers who are committed to stand for truth and against sin and corruption.

Evidence shows cultural Marxism has saturated our country. (To those over 30 this may sound shocking; to those under 30, you may be asking, "what's Marxism?") We'll cover this in a later chapter on the "isms." It has taken generations, but it has happened: our traditional American culture that was once established on Judeo-Christian principles has succumbed to political correctness (PC). Marxism's goal is for a one world government and power leading to communist rule. Christianity is in the way of this quest for power.

Multiculturalism is the criticism of and opposition to Western culture and its founding worldview of Christianity. It is a dressed up and politicized version of cultural relativism – the doctrine that *every* group has its own distinct but equally sound patterns of perception, thought, and values. As I write this, the Obama administration is promoting more spending, tax increases, and they have enabled more than 100 million Americans to rely on government for some form of welfare. They speak out of both sides of their mouths, and behind the mask of a benign celebration of diversity (PC) lies a deeply corrosive rejection of all general norms, rules or truths. It is an ideology by which the elites rule and gain more power by advancing their agenda, and it's happening right under our noses.

LIGHT IN THE POLITICAL DARKNESS

> *For this is what the Lord has commanded us: "I have made you a light for the Gentiles, that you may bring salvation to the ends of the earth* (**Acts 13:47**).

God can save souls through faith in the Lord Jesus Christ, but you and I are the vessels He has chosen to work through and to have influence where He places us; this includes the political arena. To get the country back on track will take work and prayer. It will take a movement of committed people of faith and the application of sound doctrine and Scriptural truth in our personal lives to be reflected in society. Writing for Townhall, author Frank Turek reminds us that Jesus said "go" into every part of the world.

> "Christians are to be salt and light in everything they do, be it in their church, in their business, in their school, or in their government…. If you think "preaching the Gospel" is important like I do, then you ought to think politics is important too. Why? Because politics and law affects your ability to preach the Gospel!"[15]

As Christians, politics is not the number one priority, and God will allow what He allows regardless of how we vote. The political process is, however, one important way we can ensure a safer, more traditional, family-oriented society while we're here, if enough Christians vote their convictions instead of their wallets. One election will not fix a country as off track and morally impoverished as we have become, but our history has proven it takes just a few brave citizens whose faith and worldview is one of biblical Christianity to positively impact countless Americans.

Founding Father and President John Adams once said every American citizen should "examine politics with a Christian spirit and neglect all party loyalty…." It's far too rare to hear this kind of sentiment today. Too many believers blindly vote along party lines even though the candidates they vote for often support policies that go directly against their religious beliefs! This must be acknowledged as irresponsible or lazy, and then remedied.

In **Exodus 18:21**, God gives Moses some guidelines for choosing leaders:

> *You shall select out of all the people able men who fear God, men of truth, those who hate dishonest gain.*

John Jay, Founding Father and First Chief Justice of the United States (1745 – 1829) stated:

> "Providence has given to our people the choice of their rulers, and it is the duty as well as the privilege and interest of our Christian nation, to select and prefer Christians for their rulers."

We must pray for a spiritual awakening and be informed about the candidates and issues. America is a better nation when the people take more responsibility and when the government is held accountable. Since the media refuses to do this, it is up to you and me. As good as a revival would be for America, it is still not the end goal. In his book *Fire Breathing Christians*, author Scott Alan Buss said:

> "The good things realized by a return to conservative governing principles are only of lasting, genuine benefit insofar as they are shaped and linked to our understanding of Christ and His perfect Word.... We of all people should know that true and lasting success cannot be realized any other way. As Christ and the Gospel have been marginalized in our society, liberalism has metastasized.... Only when Christ and the Word of God are exalted in all areas of life (and yes folks, that includes the political) by those who claim Him as Lord can there be any real hope of reversing the cultural plunge that has come to America."[16]

A CALL TO ACTION

According to alarming statistics, only about 50% of Christians in America are registered to vote! Even more disappointing, only about half of those actually show up at the polls. If we do the math that means about 75% of Christians are *not* helping decide who is elected to run the country. If just another 25% of Bible-believing Christians got involved, elections wouldn't even be close because that amounts to millions of Americans.

I came across an inspiring prayer for elections in America that was sent out to many Catholic parishes and placed in church bulletins. I credit leaders in any church for speaking up and taking a stand for life and for America. Honestly, I'd love to hear more Christian Pastors and Ministers send prayers like this to their congregations. This is from one of the country's most vocal opponents of abortion, Father Frank Pavone:

> "O God, we acknowledge you today as Lord, not only of individuals, but of nations and governments. We thank you for the privilege of being able to organize ourselves politically and of knowing that political loyalty does not have to mean disloyalty to you. We thank you for your law which our Founding

Fathers acknowledged. We thank you for the opportunity that this election year puts before us, to exercise our solemn duty not only to vote, but to influence countless others to vote, and to vote accordingly.

"Lord, we pray that your people may be awakened. Let them realize that while politics is not their salvation, their response to you requires that they be politically active.... Awaken them that the same hands lifted up to you in prayer are the hands that pull the lever in the voting booth; the same eyes that read your Word, are the eyes that read the names on the ballot, and that they do not cease to be Christians when they enter the voting booth.

"Awaken your people to a commitment to justice, to the sanctity of marriage and family, to the dignity of each individual human life, and to the truth that human rights begin when human lives begin, and not one moment later! Lord, we rejoice today that we are citizens of your kingdom. May that make us all the more committed to being faithful citizens on earth. We ask this through Jesus Christ our Lord, AMEN."

As a friend of mine from the south used to say, "If that don't light your fire, your wood is wet." Regardless of your denomination, I wish the beliefs of each church and the words of church leaders would make their way all the way down into the hearts of those sitting in the pews and seats. The lip service of some believers in America has become tedious.

Irish author and philosopher Edmund Burke once said:

"All that's necessary for the forces of evil to win in the world is for enough good men to do nothing."

It takes a remnant of undaunted, Bible-believing, God-fearing Christians to make a difference, and it begins with you and me. We can start by impacting those in our immediate circle of influence. The church may have lost some of its light, but I believe it is not too late to, with a sense of extreme urgency, encourage as many Christians as possible to get back to the basics and influence our country for the God who has blessed us. We must honor Jesus Christ by discerning and voting accordingly.

The good news is God is not finished with this country yet, and more Christians are waking up and speaking up today than we've seen in many years. More and more conservatives are participating in the political process, and this is a very good thing. If we want to make a difference and prevent the complete takeover of our Republic, then we had better understand how critical every single election is from this point forward. May God's will be done for our country. The last time I checked, He is still sovereign, Jesus Christ is still Lord, and the Holy Spirit is still moving.

You and I are responsible for how we use our time, talents, and treasure. One day, every person alive and dead will bow before the King of Kings – whether they loved Him and believed in Him or whether they hated and rebelled against Him – and *every knee will bow and every tongue will confess that Jesus Christ is Lord* (**Phil. 2:10**). We have His Word on it. In the meantime, there are many battles to be fought, and our faith needs to be strong for the days ahead. We've touched briefly on government and next, we need to scrutinize public education in America.

> "The time has come that Christians must vote for honest men, and take consistent ground in politics or the Lord will curse them... Christians have been exceedingly guilty in this matter. But the time has come when they must act differently... God will bless or curse this nation, according to the course Christians take." – **Reverend Charles G. Finney** (1792-1875)

ENDNOTES

1 http://www.christianity.com/ChurchHistory/11630203/
2 http://en.wikipedia.org/wiki/History_of_Harvard_University
3 http://www.christianpost.com/news/
   nj-teachers-facebook-comments-spark-gay-rights-protest-58358/
4 http://en.wikipedia.org/wiki/United_States_Declaration_of_Independence
5 America's God and Country: Encyclopedia of Quotations, William J. Federer, June/2000
6 http://www.goodreads.com/author/quotes/31180.Daniel_Webster

7 http://deathby1000papercuts.com/2011/02/
democracy-countdown-usa-how-long-do-we-have/
8 http://www.frc.org/issuebrief/
deeds-not-words-what-the-founders-really-did-on-religious-freedom
9 http://www.wallbuilders.com/libissuesarticles.asp?id=65
10http://www.monticello.org/site/jefferson/quotations-jefferson-memorial
11 http://blogs.cbn.com/thebrodyfile/archive/2008/06/03/2004-interview-obama-
talks-about-jesus-heaven-and-sin.aspx
12http://www.worldviewweekend.com/worldview-times/print.
php?&ArticleID=4073
13http://www.reuters.com/article/2012/02/07/
us-usa-gaymarriage-california-idUSTRE8160HO20120207
14Samuel Blumenfeld; 3/14/2012, http://www.thenewamerican.com/opinion/
sam-blumenfeld/11191-can-america-be-cured-of-its-marxist-cancer
15Frank Turek, 10/31/2010 http://townhall.com/columnists/frankturek/2010/10/31/
jesus,_christians_and_politics/page/full/
16 Scott Alan Buss, Fire Breathing Christians, (2010 Revolution Press) page 53

CHAPTER 3

THE NEA AGENDA: MORE MAN, MORE MONEY, LESS GOD

"In my view, the Christian religion is the most important and one of the first things in which all children under a free government ought to be instructed.... No truth is more evident to my mind than that the Christian religion must be the basis of any government intended to secure the rights and privileges of a free people." – **Noah Webster,** original "Father of American Scholarship and Education"

"There is no God and no soul. Hence, there are no needs for the props of traditional religion. With dogma and creed excluded, then immutable (unchangeable) truth is also dead and buried. There is no room for fixed, natural law, or permanent moral absolutes."[1] – **John Dewey,** modern "Father of American Education"

According to a 2011 poll, confidence in U.S. public schools dropped to 34% and in 2012 it is a mere 29%.[2] Back in 1979, approximately 53% of Americans were happy with the public school system according to a Gallup poll. Education had already been declining, and that same year, President Jimmy Carter created the United States Department of Education (USDE), one of the richest government gravy trains in American history with a current annual budget of over $71 billion.

Upgrading education to cabinet level status was opposed by many outside the Democratic Party. They saw the department as unconstitutional, arguing the Constitution doesn't mention education and deemed it an unnecessary and illegal federal bureaucratic intrusion into local affairs, funded by taxpayers. Some say the creation of the Department of Education was payback for the support Carter had received from the teachers' unions.

It is no coincidence that in every presidential election since Carter created the USDE, the National Education Association (NEA) has endorsed or supported Democratic candidates. Today, the Department of Education has over 17,000 employees and an enormous annual budget of over $68.1 billion. When Carter was voted out of office, President Ronald Reagan promised to eliminate the Department as a cabinet post, but due to the Democrat-controlled House of Representatives at the time, he was not able to follow through.

There continues to be opposition to the Department today from conservatives who see it as an undermining of states' rights, libertarians who believe it gives government way too much power, and from concerned American citizens who see massive spending without adequate results to justify it. We can't blame the economic behemoth fully on Carter. It was Lyndon Johnson who passed the Elementary and Secondary Education Act of 1965 as part of Johnson's so-called "War on Poverty." That act was the most far-reaching federal legislation affecting education ever passed by Congress.

The Federal Security Agency was upgraded to Cabinet-level status in 1953 as the Department of Health, Education, *and* Welfare. At that time, there was strong opposition and resistance to federal aid to education. It was not until Lyndon Johnson was elected in 1964 that liberals and progressives were given the political power to hand the NEA whatever it asked for – and they got it on a silver platter! The Johnson Democrats gifted the NEA with access to the U.S. Treasury. It was quite the nifty scheme using the Elementary and Secondary Education Act. Today, children of the poor are educated free, K-12, and are eligible for preschool Head Start, Perkins Grants, Pell Grants and student loans for college.

Lyndon Johnson told Americans this was the way to build a Great Society. Those "Great Society" social reforms included new major spending programs that addressed education, medical care, urban problems, and transportation. What has happened since? We have seen a full-throttle decline into social decomposition. Federal and state spending on social welfare is approaching $1 trillion a year, $17 trillion since the Great Society was launched. Those massive programs were one of the catalysts that have put America on the path to economic chaos, and eventually, toward socialism.

Colin Gunn, producer and director of the documentary *IndoctriNation,* pointed out that people are starting to wake up to the damaging effects of a "government controlled education monopoly."

> "We now are facing all these problems in America – high taxation, welfare dependency, government debt – and as Christians and conservatives we have to see we can't solve those problems until we solve the public schooling problem."

STUPID IN AMERICA

Leave it to Stossel. John Stossel, author, journalist, Fox News contributor, and host of "Stossel" did a 2012 special on ABC's *20/20.* It was an attempt to investigate public schools in America, but schools refused to give him and his camera crew access to classrooms. Stossel wanted to show Americans what goes on behind the scenes in public school classrooms. They first tried New York City schools, but were denied access. All they wanted to do was to "tape typical classrooms, but were turned down in state after state."

Finally, school officials in the Washington, D.C. district handpicked a few of their best students and allowed *20/20* to give cameras to them to tape classroom activity. One of the selected schools was labeled by *Newsweek* as one of the best in America. The NEA wanted their best to be reflected. However, what they saw from the *best* school was alarming: classroom chaos, misbehavior, and a lack of discipline along with the disrespect of teachers. Stossel reported:

> "'Stupid in America' is a nasty title for a program about public education, but some nasty things are going on in America's public schools, and it's about time we face up to it."

Another poll asking parents about their kid's public school showed 76% are satisfied with the school. This seems to contradict the findings of the poll noted earlier. Let me get this straight: one poll says the majority of Americans are not confident in public schools, but this poll says the majority of parents are satisfied with the schools *their* kids attend. How do we explain this apparent discrepancy? The fact is they really don't have much information to go on. Since there is little school competition, how do parents know if the public schools are good, if there is nothing to compare them to?

Jay Greene, author of *Education Myths*, points out that if money was the solution, the problem would have been solved. More money has not helped American kids.

> "We've doubled per pupil spending, adjusting for inflation over the last 30 years, and yet schools aren't better.... National graduation rates and achievement scores are flat, while spending on education has increased more than 100 percent since 1971."[3]

When you compare international education, the results are even more revealing. At age ten, American students take an international test and score well above the international average. But by age fifteen, when students from 40 countries are tested, the Americans place 25th. They do worse than kids from poorer countries that spend much less money on education, ranking behind not only Belgium, but also Poland, the Czech Republic and South Korea. What happens in that five-year period that contributes to lower test scores?

One of the problems John Stossel pointed out in his investigation was that even if a school was horrible, our taxes still fund it. There is little incentive for a school district to bust its collective hump to outscore another district, and in many school districts across the country, it is almost impossible to fire a bad teacher. Because of union contracts, most teachers get paid about the same regardless of performance – a recipe for mediocrity.

In New York, it took six years (of litigation) to fire a teacher because of sexual misconduct, and thanks to the teachers union, though the teacher was prohibited from teaching, he continued to receive full pay. He received over $300,000 pay and benefits without stepping into the classroom. New York City Schools' Chancellor Joel Klein said he employs dozens of teachers he's afraid to let near the kids, so he has them sit in what are called rubber rooms. This year he will spend $20 million to "warehouse teachers in five rubber rooms" as an alternative to firing them! Klein said:

> "In the last four years, only two teachers out of 80,000 were fired for incompetence."

How can anyone argue this is the most effective use of taxpayer money? Even former Apple CEO, Steve Jobs criticized the NEA and other teacher unions for their lack of support for voucher programs, merit pay, and the removal of bad teachers. On February 17, 2007 at an education reform conference in Texas, Steve Jobs said:

> "What kind of person could you get to run a small business if you told them that when they came in they couldn't get rid of people that they thought weren't any good?"[4]

Accountability seems to be lacking, but that doesn't stop the money from pouring in to fund education.

FUNDING DEMOCRATIC CONTROL

The National Education Association is the largest labor union in the United States, representing public school teachers, faculty and staff at colleges and universities, plus retired educators. The NEA has 3.2 million members and is headquartered in Washington, D.C. With thousands of affiliates across the country, the NEA employs over 550 staff and has a budget of more than $307 million per fiscal year. It is part of Education International, the global federation of teachers' unions. The NEA is a major supporter of liberal organizations and contributes heavily to the Democratic Party.

The NEA asserts itself as "non-partisan," but critics point out the NEA has endorsed and provided support for *every* Democratic Party presidential nominee from Jimmy Carter to Barack Obama. Conversely, the NEA has *never* endorsed any Republican or third party candidate. All the way back in 1983, U.S. Senator Steve Symms tried to warn that the NEA had become "the most powerful special interest group in the U.S.," and that political lobbying had increased federal education spending massively in the last 20 years.

"In 1982, their contributions of $1,183,215 and their army of
"volunteer" campaign workers helped elect 222 congressmen
– a majority of the House of Representatives. But instead of
using its influence to improve the quality of American education, the NEA has presided over the virtual crumbling of our
nation's schools."[5]

That was thirty years ago. How does a public employee union continue to receive federal funding while it openly supports one political
party? Based on required filings with the federal government, it is estimated that between 1990 and 2010, nearly 91% of the NEA's substantial
political contributions went to Democratic Party candidates and liberal
causes. In addition, union dues that are confiscated, I mean, collected
from teachers, add up to around $40 million each year and are disbursed
to state affiliates and political issue campaigns.

The school district's payroll office deducts union dues from each
teacher's paycheck as a lump sum. The money is transmitted at regular
intervals to the local union affiliate, which keeps its share and transmits
the remainder to the state affiliate, which keeps its share and transmits
the remainder to the national affiliate. NEA has an affiliate in every
state and claims 14,000 locals. Whoever came up with this scheme was
a genius. President Thomas Jefferson clearly understood the problem
with involuntary dues, fees or taxation when he said:

"To compel a man to furnish contributions of money for the
propagation of opinions which he disbelieves and abhors is
sinful and tyrannical."[6]

I have talked with teachers who have money taken from each paycheck and do not agree with the political causes their dues end up
funding. In many schools across the nation there are Christian teachers
who are afraid to speak up because they will be either discriminated
against or ridiculed. If this doesn't raise concern, let's take a look at the
money flow from progressive (and many anti-Christian) groups to the
NEA and then back out to those organizations.

In 2008, the combined total of contributors to state and federal
campaigns, political parties, and ballot measure committee was over

$56 million.[7] The following is partial list of recipients that benefit from NEA funding:

Americans United for Separation of Church and State, Gay and Lesbian Alliance Against Defamation (GLADD), Democratic Leadership Council, Sierra Club, Jesse Jackson's Rainbow/PUSH Coalition, Media Matters for America, Center for American Progress, National Council of La Raza, Amnesty International, the now-defunct ACORN, Women's Voices, Women Vote, NAACP, Congressional Black Caucus Foundation, American Rights at Work, Ballot Initiative Strategy Center, Gay, Lesbian and Straight Education Network (GLSEN), and many others.

This country is blessed with many good public school teachers whose character, morals or beliefs do not line up with the NEA, but it's a shame they are being represented by such a self-serving, hyper-partisan group of activists. Their quest for power should be concerning. In 1978, the top lawyer for the NEA, Bob Chanin, warned about protecting collective bargaining at all costs, saying, "It is well-recognized that if you take away the mechanism of payroll deduction, you won't collect a penny from these people…I think it has to do with the nature of the beast…."

Chanin retired in 2009 and gave a fiery speech in which his primary focus was money, power, and control. In July 2009 in San Diego, California, the annual NEA Convention took place and on the final day, outgoing general counsel, Bob Chanin, gave his good-bye pep talk. He mentioned the fact that in 1963, Wisconsin was the only state with a public sector labor law. In the next few years, there was a legislative explosion when more than twenty-five states enacted statutes giving teachers the right to engage in collective bargaining.

A revolution was in the making. Well into his lengthy speech, Bob Chanin mentioned the resistance some have shown toward the direction of public education saying:

> "Why are these conservative and right-wing bastards picking on NEA and its affiliates? I'll tell you why: It is the price we pay for success. NEA and its affiliates…are the nation's leading advocates for public education and the type of **liberal, social and economic agenda** that these groups find unacceptable….

"And that brings me to my final and most important point, which is why, at least in my opinion, NEA and its affiliates are such effective advocates. Despite what some among us would like to believe, it is not because of our creative ideas. It is not because of the merit of our positions. **It is not because we care about children. And it is not because we have a vision of a great public school for every child.**

"NEA and its affiliates are effective advocates because we have power. And we have power because there are more than 3.2 million people who are willing to pay us hundreds of millions of dollars in dues each year."[8]

Chanin credited the liberal changes in the NEA to collective bargaining, which he noted helped support teacher strikes and establish a political action committee. This also enabled NEA to speak out for affirmative action and defend homosexual rights, about which Chanin boasted "the more we said and did, the more we pissed people off."

Part of their power grab was to control changes in curriculums. The NEA has been gradually implementing an anti-Christian agenda starting with the youngest children they can access. Secular Humanist, John Dunphy, wrote an essay in 1983 *A Religion for a New Age* for *The Humanist* magazine, stating:

> "The battle for mankind's future must be waged and won in the public school classroom by teachers who correctly perceive their role as proselytizers of a new faith.... The classroom must and will become an arena of conflict between **the old** and the new – **the rotting corpse of Christianity, together with all its adjacent evils and misery,** and the new faith of humanism."[9] (Emphasis mine)

The 'out with old Christianity' sentiment has been obvious, but with massive amounts of money continually pouring into the NEA, shouldn't there be better results when it comes to what kids are learning and retaining? Was money misappropriated? How was their massive funding allocated? Let's take a closer look.

THIRTY YEARS OF MEDIOCRITY

Growing up, I loved having summers off, and it was an added blessing that the whole family had the same time off and could go on vacations together. We also spent quality time at our summer cottage on a small lake. My parents both worked in education for decades, and they loved their jobs. I remember them bringing work home with them quite often. My mother would sit in the recliner in our living room, correct papers and work on lesson plans for the next week. Talking to my mother today, she says that the NEA changed through the years. They implemented new policies, supported causes she did not agree with, but her biggest concern was the change in curriculum. Suddenly, there was more focus on social studies than on the basics; reading, writing, and math. She also noticed a gradual decline in student behavior and learning.

The National Commission on Excellence in Education came out with a report exclaiming America's educational foundations were eroding, and the level of mediocrity in public schools threatened the future of our nation. This 1983 report went on to say we allowed this to happen, but if a foreign power had tried to force a mediocre educational standard on America, "we might have viewed it as an act of war."

Ten years later in 1993, the U.S. Department of Education did a survey of adult literacy in America costing $14 million. You guessed it – people were shocked by the results. The report found half of the adult population (over 90 million at the time) had such poor literacy skills, people were barely able to deal with computers and other high-tech additions to our society. These adult Americans had spent more time in school than previous generations, and more money was spent to educate them!

Skipping ahead to 2007, the National Endowment for the Arts did a comprehensive survey on American literacy that revealed horrendous results once again. The report was named *Reading at Risk* and Chairman, Dana Gioia, openly stated they were not happy to issue the results to the public and admitted the report revealed a "bleak assessment of the decline of reading's role" in America. Gioia went on to warn we were losing the new generation, and due to poor reading, they'd not come close to reaching their potential, further stating:

"For the first time in modern history, less than half of the adult population now reads literature, and these trends reflect a larger decline in other sorts of reading. Anyone who loves literature or values the cultural, intellectual, and political importance of active and engaged literacy in American society will respond to this report with grave concern."[10]

It would be redundant to list more reports, studies and surveys done on public education revealing disappointing results. One thing the NEA seems to excel at is ignoring negative reports about problems in education. These stories fade away, and Americans barely catch the headlines. If reading in America is rapidly declining, especially among youth, what is being done to correct the problem? Something is definitely not gelling. America spends more money on education than any nation in world history.

Because the NEA wanted to make sure taxpayers were getting something for their investment, they did a follow-up study two years later. Get this: with no mention of the cause or a solution to this major problem, they released a 99-page study called "To Read or Not to Read: A Question of National Consequence," finding an increasing number of adult Americans were not even reading one book a year! In this report, 72% of high school graduates were also deemed by employers as "deficient" in writing in English.

We already knew math was a weak area, and now it was confirmed reading and writing skills were declining. Compared to thirty-one industrialized nations, American fifteen-year-olds ranked fifteenth in reading scores, behind Poland, Korea, France, Canada and others. This time, NEA Chairman Dana Gioia again showed grave "concern" over the results and said:

"I've done a lot of work in statistics in my career and I've never seen a situation where so much data was pulled from so many places and absolutely everything is so consistent."

At least we're consistently awful. Gioia went on to note the "catastrophic falloff" once kids get into their teens. In this technology age and electronic culture, something must be done, or kids may stop reading altogether. She and the NEA called for *immediate* changes in the way we're educating kids, especially in high school and college. I wouldn't hold my breath. Gioia somberly concluded that because of these failures "the majority of young Americans will not realize their individual, economic or social potential."[11]

During the public employee union protests in Wisconsin, a 2011 report was done by the U.S. Department of Education clearly showing **despite the massive increase in spending, student test results have stayed about the same or even got worse**. Nationwide, only 30% of public school eighth graders earned a rating of "proficient" or better in reading, and the average reading score on the National Assessment of Educational Progress (NAEP) test was 262 out of 500.[12]

Since the State Capital in Madison was hijacked by union protesters for months on end, let's highlight Wisconsin. In a ten-year comparison of school testing from 1998 to 2008, student scores stayed the same on reading tests. During this same ten year period, Wisconsin public schools increased their per pupil expenditures from $4,956 to $10,791. Let's do the math here. Ten-year spending increased approximately $5,835 per student, yet that massive increase did not add a single point to test scores. The sad and unfortunate fact made headlines as: "Two-Thirds of Wisconsin Public School 8th Graders Can't Read Proficiently – Despite Highest Per Pupil Spending in Midwest."[13]

The evidence is overwhelming that NEA curriculum and policies are not helping the kids. In fiscal year 2008 alone, the federal government provided over $669 million in subsidies to the public schools in Wisconsin. The SAT verbal scores for the class of 2011 are the lowest on record! Combined **reading and math scores have fallen to their lowest level since 1995.**[14]

Author and educator, Dr. Samuel Blumenfeld, confirmed what many knew, government schools are not truly educating, but they are indoctrinating. He warns atheistic influences are gaining momentum in America and only concerned conservative citizens can stop the power grabs. Blumenfeld pulled no punches when he answered this question, **'what are the American people getting for their tax money?'**

"The drugging of over four million children by their educators to cure Attention Deficit Disorder, a steep decline in literacy, and an anti-Christian philosophy of education. If it were not for the growth of the home-school movement and the restoration of educational freedom by this dedicated remnant, the country would in time become a totalitarian society controlled by behavioral psychologists and corrupt politicians."

Reports have been done. Whistles have been blown. Information has been available over the last three decades that has been rightly critical of the NEA containing the same list of problems: decreasing test scores, poor academic performance, high dropout rates, ineffective curriculums, student violence, and even low teacher morale. The NEA's solution is more money for education, better health plans, smaller class size, higher teacher pay, new buildings, new curricula, more computers, more....

Could it be government-level leaders and NEA decision makers do not have the same worldview as most Americans and don't want the same kind of education we do? Enter socialist John Dewey. Dewey once plotted a long-range, comprehensive strategy that would reorganize primary education to serve the needs of socialization. "Change must come gradually," he wrote. "To force it unduly would compromise its final success by favoring a violent reaction." In other words, Dewey was saying that implementing socialistic ideas had to be done slowly; otherwise those who truly cared about educating children would become angry and resist.

JOHN DEWEY – THE "FATHER OF MODERN EDUCATION"

Longtime member of the American Federation of Teachers, atheist and "progressive" philosopher, John Dewey, has had tremendous influence on education. He taught at Columbia University, The University of Michigan, and Chicago University. Through the years, Dewey was a member of many Marxist organizations and a totalitarian socialist who wanted government to take over all education via government schools. Dewey rejected traditional religion and moral absolutes and is considered the epitome of liberalism by many historians, sometimes even portrayed as "dangerously radical."

John Dewey and his colleagues are responsible for deciding that since high literacy was an obstacle to their progressive agenda, the NEA needed to reduce emphasis on reading. Dewey's agenda has produced absolutely tragic results in American education. He and a few other progressives brought in the system of "social studies." Naturally, this direction soon edged God out of public school curriculums as Dewey disparaged schooling that focused on traditional character development. It's no wonder today's youth have a distorted view of our founders.

> "The general principles on which the fathers achieved independence were the general principles of Christianity. I will avow that I then believed, and now believe, that those general principles of Christianity are as eternal and immutable as the existence and attributes of God." – **John Adams**

Dewey wanted to transform America into a secular and socialist country and had major support from the Rockefellers. In order to move toward that end, he, along with other progressives, concluded the young must be less educated and less informed than their parents. John Dewey was also a trainer of teachers and a creator of curriculums. He spent a good portion of his adult life attempting to reconstruct the American system.

In 2005, HUMAN EVENTS asked a panel of 15 conservative scholars and public policy leaders to compile a list of the **Ten Most Harmful Books** of the 19th and 20th Centuries.[15] **John Dewey's 1916 book *Democracy and Education*** made the list as the fifth most harmful book over two centuries! The Communist Manifesto by Karl Marx was first on the list, and Hitler's *Mein Kampf* was number two. (Marx's *Das Kapital* was number six, immediately after Dewey)

Karl Marx once said that "The first battlefield is the rewriting of history."

While teaching at Columbia University in 1935, John Dewey came up with his own list of the twenty-five most influential books since 1885. Number one on the list was *Das Kapital* by Karl Marx. So the father of modern education, Dewey, considered Marxism pretty important, even going so far as to say it was "one of the greatest modern syntheses of humane values." Number two was a famous 1887 novel by Edward Bellamy. In *Looking Backward*, Edward Bellamy depicted a happy, socialist America where greed and material want ceased to exist; harmony prevailed, the arts and sciences flourished, and an all-powerful government and bureaucracy were efficient and fair. Bellamy saw America becoming socialist by way of consensus rather than revolution.

This is exactly what Dewey wanted in America. In his 1934 essay, "The Great American Prophet," Dewey claimed capitalism imposed a restriction on freedom and "socialized industry and finance" would be the vehicle by which people would reach their full potential. How could he believe that, and why write so much about Dewey? He changed NEA curriculums!

Six years earlier John Dewey traveled to the former Soviet Union with others from the NEA and studied the communist education system. It was 1928, and the Soviet system of Socialist education was very similar to China's system. Dewey was apparently manipulated and was not given the full picture as the Soviets only showed him what they planned for him to see. The Bolsheviks had invited Dewey and enjoyed his work so much they translated his books into Russian.

In Dr. Paul Kengor's 2010 book, *Dupes and the Religious Left,* Dr. Paul Kengor talks about how the Bolsheviks rolled out the red carpet for Dewey in Russia and even implemented the same books by Dewey that teachers' colleges and education departments in the United States have used to "train a century of public school educators." When he came back praising their development of progressive education ideas, Kengor writes, "He did exactly what Stalin hoped, promoting the 'new world' he discovered in the USSR." In one account, Dewey hailed the "restoration" of Russia's churches when everyone knew the Bolsheviks were demolishing churches.[16]

THE HUMANIST MANIFESTO

As part of his agenda, John Dewey co-authored and signed the *Humanist Manifesto* in 1933. Humanism is a worldview that focuses on human values and concerns, attaching prime importance to people rather than on a divine or supernatural being. The *Humanist Manifesto* is a philosophy and value system which does not necessarily include belief in any personal deity or "higher power." It referred to Humanism as a religious movement to transcend and replace previous religions.

This philosophy promoted by John Dewey refutes the salvation of God. In fact, Dewey promoted the teaching of the Theory of Evolution in order to popularize humanism.

Evolution denounces any existence of God; if there is no God, there is no need for salvation. John Dewey was adamantly opposed to anything that supported the Christian faith. He believed the children needed to be re-educated away from the traditional values of the parent. He felt this would make them better citizens for the new world order. He also believed in the redistribution of wealth and called for universal socialism. Dewey had an alarming philosophy:

> *"You can't make socialists out of individualists. Children who know how to think for themselves spoil the harmony of the collective society, which is coming, where everyone is interdependent."*

Dewey was the first honorary president of the NEA and a major influence on school curriculums. What a drastic contrast between John Dewey and early American settlers whose primary goal and desire, where education was concerned, was for their children to be able to read the Bible proficiently and live its principles freely. In 1936, the NEA stated one of its reformed goals: "We stand for socializing the individual." Apparently, Dewey and his ilk were effective enough to transform the system so that 88% of Christian children deny their faith by the time they graduate from college.

"I don't want a nation of thinkers. I want a nation of workers."
– **John D. Rockefeller**

DUMBING DOWN AMERICA – DELIBERATELY?

Charlotte Iserbyt worked in the Department of Education during the Reagan administration in the 1980's as a Senior Policy Advisor in the Office of Educational Research and Improvement. What she learned about controversial methods and programs being federally funded was so disturbing she felt she had no choice but to blow the whistle on the public school system. She gathered evidence that showed how "good teachers across America have been forced to use controversial, non-academic" curriculums, and how the "international, national, regional, state and local agendas for education reform are all interconnected and have been for decades."

Naturally, Charlotte was fired from her department when they found out she was collecting information, but by that time she already had thousands of pages of copied documents from the Education Department's files! She would eventually reveal insider information by writing a gargantuan book called *The Deliberate Dumbing Down of America: A Chronological Paper Trail,* which was first published in 1999.

In the Preface to her book, Iserbyt said that the United States is fighting a secret war in the public schools in which children are the captive targets. It is a war most Americans – especially parents – are ignorant about. This war has been waged, not by a foreign enemy but by our own government, and it produces "the death of intellect and freedom." Iserbyt said traveling and spending a decade in Europe's socialist countries changed her life.

Upon returning to the U.S., she realized "America's transition from a sovereign constitutional republic to a socialist democracy" would come about through government implementation of the system at every level: federal, state and local. The use of behavior modification would be used in schools to promote acceptance of the "system's" control.

Iserbyt mentioned her concerns with outcome-based education and the methods of B.F. Skinner, as well as values clarification, which was renamed "critical thinking." She wrote that regardless of the changing labels, critical thinking is nothing but "pure, unadulterated destruction of absolute values of right and wrong upon which stable and free societies depend, and upon which our nation was founded."

If you're wondering how Iserbyt began her journey as a "resister," she placed the first document in her education files back in 1973. It was an invasive questionnaire her fourth grade son brought home from school called "All About Me" containing highly personal questions about his family. She said its purpose was to find out the student's values and state of mind, how he felt and what he liked. Iserbyt concluded:

> "With this knowledge it would be easier for the government school to modify his values and behavior at will – without, of course, the student's knowledge or parents' consent."[17]

The same year Iserbyt published her outstanding work, three-time New York City Teacher of the Year and 1991 New York State Teacher of the Year, John Taylor Gatto, wrote a letter to the op-ed pages of the Wall Street Journal announcing his retirement. Part of the letter said he no longer wished to hurt kids to make a living. Hearing something like this from a respected teacher makes you wonder what they were doing in New York public schools.

In the 2011 documentary *IndoctriNation*, John Taylor Gatto exclaimed:

> "Is there an idea more radical in the history of the human race than turning your children over to complete strangers and having those strangers work on your child's mind – out of your site – for a period of twelve years? Could there be a more radical idea than that? Back in colonial days in America if you proposed that as an idea they'd burn you at the stake... It's a mad idea."[18]

Public schools are now a place where kids can get many kinds of drugs, free condoms from Planned Parenthood, and plenty of sex. They're taught about sex practices, and students are encouraged to experiment, not only with a boyfriend or girlfriend, but with same sex partners. It's no wonder kids are leaving schools with their faith and virginity shattered.

John Taylor Gatto is also the author of many books including *Weapons of Mass Instruction: A Schoolteacher's Journey through the Dark World of Compulsory Schooling*. In this book, he suggests public schools deliberately – through the agenda of the NEA – harm children by "crippling imagination" and discouraging critical thinking. Gatto goes so far as to say the function of compliant teachers ends up being to "render the common population manageable." The NEA, through the government, has embraced humanism full throttle.

> "The education of all children, from the moment that they can get along without a mother's care, shall be in state institutions at state expense." – **Karl Marx**

The consequences of public schools accepting and promoting this socialistic worldview have been disastrous. If human beings are not unique, individual creations of God; if we have no meaning, purpose, or value aside from this temporary life, then any life can be disposed of because it can be declared that it's no longer useful and can no longer serve its purpose on this earth. We see this dangerous philosophy in justifying abortion and end of life "counseling," as well as in those who judge the handicapped or mentally retarded as less capable or productive.

Imagine if the opposite was taught in public schools. What a difference it would make in the very lives of precious kids, if they were taught the truth, that God created each one of them in His image and that He has a beautiful plan and purpose for each life. Founder and signer of the Declaration of Independence, Benjamin Rush (1746-1813) once said:

> "We profess to be republicans, and yet we neglect the only means of establishing and perpetuating our republican forms of government, that is, the universal education of our youth in the principles of Christianity by the means of the Bible.

> "For this Divine Book, above all others, favors that equality among mankind, that respect for just laws, and those sober and frugal virtues, which constitute the soul of republicanism."

From our earliest history, the founders knew how important it was for children to know and study the Bible and how dangerous it would be without the Christian worldview.

IF GOD IS NOT WELCOME, ANYTHING GOES

Remove the Bible, prayer, and the Pledge, confuse kids about moral absolutes and just about anything can be taught under the guise of education. The presence of the Ten Commandments once established an environment of standards and morals. Today, schools are filled with propaganda such as man-caused global warming and earth worship, political correctness, sex education and birth control, anti-bullying campaigns, selling the need for vaccinations, and the minimizing of our history and the founders influence.

Some believe there was a purposeful 'blocking of parents' from their children's education process. Writing for *Worldview Times*, Tom DeWeese talked about the federal influence in school curriculums with the addition of behavior modification as well as an overall global (rather than local) outlook. DeWeese stated:

"In short, the modern environmental movement was chosen as the shock and awe tactic to force America into the global village. Over the next three decades these forces combined to rapidly and drastically change America in a very significant way.... Change the attitudes, values and beliefs of just one generation and America will forget its founding principles and fall in line with the globalist world view."[19]

Hillary Clinton published a 1996 book called *It Takes a Village: And Other Lessons Children Teach Us*. She minimized the traditional family and declared organizations outside the family could meet children's needs. Clinton asserted *society* (she means "government") is obligated to do its part to meet those needs. The church must defend the sanctity of life and marriage. Marriage is the foundation of the family, and a healthy family is the foundation to a strong society. At least that's how it used to be.

It was the Clinton administration that opened the door to teaching about the history and practices of Muslims, which was a key change in school textbooks. If Darwinism, environmentalism, and homosexuality weren't enough, now kids are taught to be open to Islam. In 1995, President Bill Clinton directed his Secretary of Education, Richard W. Riley, to prepare guidelines for religious expression and activities in America's schools. They declared government schools may not provide religious instruction, but can "teach about religion."

Dr. Karen L. Gushta is a Research Coordinator for Coral Ridge Ministries in Florida and a former multi-level teacher. She is the author of the book *The War on Children: How Pop Culture and Public Schools Put Our Kids at Risk*. Writing about the teaching of Islam in public schools in America, she noted that results of a study were released in 2008 by the American Textbook Counsel. Dr. Gushta said the 48-page report was:

"Islam in the Classroom: What the Textbooks Tell Us." Of particular significance is the portion of the Council's report regarding seventh-grade world history textbooks, since many seventh-grade curricula, following the lead of California schools, now require students to receive instruction and engage in activities to learn about Islamic history, culture, the Qur'an, and the religious practices of Muslims.[20]

Welcoming tolerance whitewashes terrorism. In 2002, the NEA was criticized for a series of lesson plans called "Remember September 11" which appeared on its website. The NEA was evidently urging teachers to **remove all references to Muslim terrorists** in lesson plans about the September 11 attacks. These plans appeared on NEA's Health Information Network Website and suggested teachers discuss "historical instances of American intolerance." The site also mentioned how Japanese Americans were treated during WWII. (Americans are the bad guys.) Ellen Sorokin wrote about this in *The Washington Times* on August 20, 2002. She titled it "NEA Plan for 9/11 Not Backed By Teachers."

Evidently, the American Federation of Teachers (AFT) released a statement: "The AFT disagrees with the lesson plans found on the NEA Website. The AFT does not support a blame-America approach in particular and wishes to distance itself from the entire document." Critics cited the controversy as another example of political correctness gone awry. This foundational problem is the removal of our Judeo-Christian educational principles from public education.

"Education without values, as useful as it is, seems rather to make man a more clever devil." – **C.S. Lewis**

GAY IS OK – GOD IS NOT

According to a former chairman of the NEA Ex-Gay Educators Caucus, one of the NEA goals is "changing public opinion on homosexuality, starting with the youngest generation." Under the guise of safe schools, meaning schools should "raise awareness of homophobia" and intervene when GLBT students are harassed, a 2005 ruling in California basically told parents to stay out of school business. The Palmdale School District had conducted a survey about "psychological barriers to learning" in which elementary school children were asked questions of a sexual nature, and when parents learned their children had received this questionnaire, they sued the district for the right "to control the upbringing of their children by introducing them to matters of and relating to sex." Both the district court and the Ninth Circuit Court of Appeals rejected that the parents had any such right.[21]

It was a shocking ruling in the case known as *Fields v. Palmdale School District,* essentially saying traditional fundamental parental rights "[do] not exist beyond the threshold of the school door." Most of us can see the government and school are overstepping their boundaries in public education as a whole. Another part of this ruling stated:

> "Once parents make the choice as to which school their children
> will attend, their fundamental right to control the education of
> their children is, at the least, substantially diminished."

How do these surveys and curriculums get into the schools in the first place? Recently retired public school teacher, Meredith Berg, found out at the 2008 NEA annual convention. What she learned was so appalling it made her ask if these were "the kind of people we want teaching our children." Berg was most disappointed by the number of radical delegates – thousands of which wore buttons saying "The 'Christian Right' is neither" as well as "Gay rights are civil rights" – wanting to pass resolutions and implement NEA policies authorizing members to lobby government for homosexual education. Not surprisingly, some of the NEA goals include:

- The "right to reproductive freedom" (Abortion on demand)
- Government-run health care
- The implementation of diversity, tolerance, and anti-bullying programs
- Gun control
- The opposition to English as the official language in America (even though more than 80% of Americans favor it)

Berg, a former high school teacher, called the resolutions "far outside the realm of education." The NEA fiercely opposes any competition for public schools such as vouchers, tuition tax credits, or parental option plans. Berg noted the NEA oppose homeschooling unless kids are taught by state-licensed teachers and use a "state approved curriculum." The unions want control. Berg continued:

> "They also want to bar homeschooled students from partici-
> pating in any extracurricular activities in public schools (even
> though their parents pay school taxes too!). Their Diversity
> Resolution makes it clear that schools are to teach about 'sexual
> orientation,' and 'gender identification,' even for preschoolers!" [22]

Meredith Berg is another of the many concerned teachers or former teachers to actually see first hand what is going on and have the courage to disagree. She emphasized there are many, very good teachers with Christian values who are not involved in the radical efforts, but are afraid to speak up. They understand the NEA is ruining America's schools and in turn, taking our nation down the road to destruction.

> "Give me four years to teach the children and the seed I have
> sown will never be uprooted." Marx disciple – **Vladimir Lenin**

Meanwhile, back at headquarters in Washington, D.C., the resignation of Kevin Jennings was a major news story ignored by the media on May 23, 2011. Jennings was the "Safe Schools Czar" for the Obama administration, and after I read what he promoted in public schools, it almost made me sick to my stomach.

Jennings was the founder of the Gay, Lesbian and Straight Education Network (GLSEN), and one look at GLSEN's recommended reading list should cause alarm. There are books encouraging the sexualization of children regardless of "orientation" and a reading list for teachers on down to grade schoolers. Kevin Jennings had been known to encourage sex between adults and minors. CNS News reported:

> "In April, he spoke at an assembly at a public school in Mary-
> land where he compared those who oppose homosexuality to
> supporters of slavery and racial segregation." [23]

During his fourteen-year tenure at GLSEN, Jennings touted his homosexual activism and included the fact that since 1995, he increased the number of public school-based and student-led pro-homosexual clubs, such as Gay-Straight Alliances, from 50 to 4,300 today. Did you get that number? With the NEA's cooperation, Jennings was responsible for adding **more than 4,200 new clubs in public schools that promote homosexuality**. They have representatives saying one of the problems with education today is kids aren't taught enough about sex. This brings us to Diane Schneider, who said:

> "Oral sex, masturbation, and orgasms need to be taught in education."

Diane Schneider is a high school health educator in Spring Valley, New York. She is very active with GLSEN in the Rockland County area, where she is its co-chair. She advises the Gay-Straight Alliance group in her high school and is an online professor for New York State. Schneider is a trainer for the NEA, teaching LGBT Trainers. When speaking to the United Nations Population Fund, she told the audience that comprehensive sex education is "the only way to combat heterosexism and gender conformity!"

Diane Schneider spoke to a panel against homophobia and, representing the NEA, opposed abstinence-based sex education. Schneider proclaimed, "...and we must make these issues a part of every middle and high school student's agenda."[24]

This is what the NEA promotes at a UN conference? She also implied family and religion are two things that hold back the advancement of homosexuality.

CLINTON EXPANDS WHAT CARTER STARTED

Jimmy Carter gets credit for starting the U.S. Dept. of Education, and Bill Clinton gets credit for expanding the bureaucracy. The homosexual lobby helped get Clinton elected as president in 1992 in return for his promises to further their agenda in public schools. So naturally, at the 1993 NEA convention, President Bill and First Lady Hillary Clinton were in the front row. According to Concerned Women for America, when President Clinton spoke, he confirmed their partnership and actually told the audience his "goals for America closely parallel those of the NEA," further stating:

> "And I believe that the president of this organization would say we have had the partnership I promised in the campaign

in 1992, and we will continue to have it. ... You and I are joined in a common cause, and I believe we will succeed."[25]

That same year at the Minneapolis convention, delegates adopted new resolutions, including B-9. The resolution, introduced by the Gay, Lesbian, and Straight Teachers Network, states the NEA supported "the celebration of a Lesbian and Gay History Month as a means of acknowledging the contributions of lesbians, gays, and bisexuals throughout history."

With the help and support of the Clinton administration, a "Day of Silence" (DOS) was introduced in 1996. DOS is a full school day the NEA dedicates to raising awareness about bullying and hate – primarily to stifle any student who might believe homosexuality is wrong – or God forbid, a sin. On the Day of Silence in public schools across America, a pro-gay message is often sent to the students, with teachers and administrators frequently promoting homosexuality, bisexuality, and transgenderism over the course of the day, with the explicit backing of GLSEN.

Linda Harvey, founder of the Christian pro-family Mission America, has followed the GLSEN movement closely. Harvey writes that the goal for DOS is to "exploit the tender sympathies of kids to promote approval of homosexuality and gender confusion." Obviously, the enemy is Judeo-Christian morality. Harvey stated:

> "GLSEN teaches students that homosexuals and gender-confused people are 'silenced' and under persecution by those who object to this behavior, and that traditional moral beliefs cause bullying. No hard, objective data exists to support this contention, and the event itself causes hostility, confusion, and division."[26]

Bullying is wrong no matter who is doing it and no matter who is being bullied. The problem many Christians have with things like DOS going on in public schools is that there is no tolerance of religious speech for those who believe in the Bible and who do not agree with their agenda. Apparently, those who do not support a special school day devoted to gay indoctrination are expected to be silent.

It's not hard to understand why an average of six thousand students every year are leaving public schools for private education or home-schooling. Homeschooling parents pay about $550 – $1,600 per year to educate their child; by comparison, taxpayers fork over more than $10,000 per student in the public education system with far less successful results.

SHOW ME THE MONEY

While the Wisconsin State Capital was overtaken by powerful labor unions in 2011, Governor Scott Walker was working to fix the $3.6 billion deficit left by the Jim Doyle administration. Something had to change, spending cuts had to be made, and Walker decided to limit collective bargaining for public employee unions. The protests went on for months, and the unions even forced a recall of Governor Walker. Paid for by all state taxpayers, the $16 million recall election produced the same result it did in November 2010 as Walker was again overwhelmingly voted in by the majority of Wisconsin citizens, this time by an even greater margin.

The teachers' unions claim their political action is best for the children, but sources show the average public employee makes several times more than the average citizen. This is not counting health insurance and retirement packages. Due to collective bargaining, there are even bus drivers in Milwaukee who make $117,000 a year, and in Madison, seven garbage men made more than $100,000 in 2010.

In the Milwaukee area, high school teacher salaries ranged as high as $122,000 all the way up to $170,000 for supervisory staff. Just like in Wisconsin, nationally, collective bargaining weakens the ability of America to compete with other parts of the world not only in education, but in manufacturing and other areas.

The protests in Wisconsin were heated and at times intimidating. There was plenty of foul language, and both communist and socialist groups had a presence there. Something else had to be behind this behavior. While navigating around the NEA website, I was shocked to find on their recommended reading list, right there in plain sight, *Rules for Radicals* by Saul Alinsky, "The American Organizer." The 1971 book articulated a socialist strategy for gaining political power to redistribute wealth. Talk about bullying, Chicago politics, and thuggery.

Why would the NEA want teachers to learn about fascist, radical, socialist-inspired methods of protesting? America found out why in 2011 when public employee unions and socialist groups took the Wisconsin state capital hostage. On the NEA website, it called Alinsky "an inspiration to anyone contemplating action in their community." It also recommended his 1946 book *Reveille for Radicals*, about the principles and tactics of "community organizing."

The Alinsky method is to: agitate, aggravate, educate, organize, ridicule, pressure, and polarize. What does this have to do with teaching children and improving education? For now, let's state some specific examples of his tactics and techniques – otherwise known as "rules" for activists and protesters. According to its own website, the NEA talked about making people more effective activists and encouraging them "not to worry too much about getting his or her hands dirty. It's all a part of the job, he [Alinsky] seems to say."[27]

Since the NEA recommended his books and wants teachers to be effective protestors, let's take a gander at the content. This is very eye-opening to most of us in Wisconsin who witnessed the vociferous union demonstrations that caused chaos, state division, and property damage, all over the collective bargaining issue. As an activist trainer, Saul Alinsky counseled organizers and activists to cause confusion, fear, and retreat. The Wisconsin teachers who participated were just following instructions. Alinsky wrote about always keeping the pressure on the enemy, saying, "Marching mobs of chanting demonstrators accomplishes this objective."

Some Alinsky techniques include the staging of loud, defiant protest rallies expressing rage over some particular "injustice." He talks about giving the impression there are more people behind the protests than there actually are. It's a scare tactic they use to make onlookers think their movement is going to increase. Alinsky taught about intimidation, saying, "Power is not only what you have, but what the enemy thinks you have."[28]

Remember the following "rules" the next time you see big union or Occupy protests, and it will make sense. According to the profile for Saul Alinsky on the Discover the Networks website:

> "...whenever possible the organizer must deride his enemy and dismiss him as someone unworthy of being taken seriously because he is either intellectually deficient or morally bankrupt."

He advised organizers to "laugh at the enemy" in an effort to provoke "an irrational anger."

> "Ridicule," said Alinsky, "is man's most potent weapon. It is almost impossible to counterattack ridicule. Also it infuriates the opposition, who then react to your advantage...."

Among the most vital tenets of Alinsky's method were the following:

> "Make the enemy live up to their own book of rules. You can kill them with this, for they can no more live up to their own rules than the Christian Church can live up to Christianity."

> "No organization, including organized religion, can live up to the letter of its own book. You can club them to death with their 'book' of rules and regulations."

> "Practically all people live in a world of contradictions. They espouse a morality which they do not practice.... This dilemma can and should be fully utilized by the organizer in getting individuals and groups involved in a People's Organization...."

Why discuss this? The NEA encourages its employees to emulate Saul Alinsky. They aim to achieve their goals at any cost. ***Author's note:*** *The recommended reading page on Saul Alinsky and his books has recently been scrubbed from the National Education Association's website. (The original link was: http://www.nea.org/tools/17231.html)*

CELEBRATING COMMUNISM?

On July 29, 2010, the NEA promoted Mao's launch of "People's Republic" of China on the anniversary of the repressive communist regime's violent founding. The NEA website has a page called Diversity

Events[29] and listed October 1, 2010 as the day to celebrate Chairman Mao's successful revolution. Should this surprise us?

The NEA has been advocating multiculturalism for decades and has minimized the foundational Western worldview. Author, columnist, and National Radio and TV host, Brannon Howse, suggested the true term is Cultural Marxism. Howse believes this move was consistent with the NEA philosophy of rejecting the traditional family. In a World Net Daily interview on this story, Brannon Howse said he was "appalled but not shocked because of the National Education Association's long love affair with communism…." They know if the family unit is broken down in America that the government will grow bigger, due, in part, to the reliance on welfare. Discussing the NEA, Howse stated:

> "They support feminism, which is antifamily, anti-father. They openly write about the need to destroy the father, the male, the leader of the home, the defender and the provider…. They are for a progressive, liberal, anti-American worldview and **most of the teachers who pay dues to the NEA do not agree with the liberal stances….**

> "Their friends are at work, to try to show that social justice, or communism, or progressive ideology is good. The antithesis, Christianity, is evil…Communists hate traditional America."[30]

When this story came to the public's attention and WND contacted the National Education Association, an official told World Net Daily no one from the organization was available for comment. *Editor's note: After this report appeared, the reference to the founding of Chairman Mao's "People's Republic" was removed from the NEA website.*

THE BIBLE IS "QUESTIONABLE MATERIAL"

The Sheboygan, Wisconsin School District backed up a February 2012 decision by James Madison Elementary School Principal, Matthew Driscoll, deciding that a Bible verse is "questionable material." The result was the confiscation of a second grader's valentines.

It all started when a second grader added the wrong message to the candy he wanted to give out for Valentine's Day: John 3:16, a Bible verse.

Dexter Thielhelm wanted to put the verse with the candy and give them to his James Madison Elementary school friends. Another offending message, "Jesus loves you," was written on the rolled up Bible verse. His siblings helped Dexter put all the valentines together. Apparently, the problem in public schools is you can use the word "love" but you can't use any reference to religion.

According to the Wausau Herald, Dexter's mother, Melissa Wolf, said she didn't know the Christian message, *For God so loved the world that he gave his one and only Son, that whoever believes in him shall not perish but have eternal life,* would be objectionable by the school and was unhappy with the way principal Matthew Driscoll handled the situation.[31]

Even though the School District's assistant superintendent of student and instructional services said there is not a "specific district policy dealing with the distribution of religious verses on Valentine's Day," the reason they gave for confiscating the boy's valentines was that other second graders expected to receive a valentine, not a "religious verse." It must be noted that Wolf has a son who attends a private school in the same school district, Lake Country Academy. He had no problems sharing the identical Christian valentines at his charter school.

FREE SPEECH FOR ALMOST EVERYONE

Again in Wisconsin, in January 2012 at Shawano High School, Brandon Wegner, a fifteen-year-old student wrote an editorial column in the school paper in support of children being raised in a home by a mother and a father. He cited Scriptures and other sources to back up his point, including verses opposing homosexuality because it is considered a sin.[32]

Both sides of the debate were printed in the school paper as Wegner's article was "released in conjunction with an opposing viewpoint provided by another student, Maddie Marquardt," the copy editor for the paper. In her article, Marquardt countered by arguing that "gay couples should be able to adopt because the foster system is broken, and children need a two-parent home."

A homosexual parent wrote a formal complaint to the school that Wegner's opinion was "constituted as hate speech," and some kids might commit suicide because he voiced his Christian beliefs. The School District issued an immediate written statement calling the article "offensive" and saying it "cultivated a negative environment." Superintendent Todd Carlson went so far as to call Wegner's opinion piece "bullying."[33]

Maddie Marquardt was never questioned about promoting homosexual adoption in the same paper. Brandon Wegner's article was wrong because he used the Bible as a reference, and he supported a traditional family view. This is today's NEA. In a meeting following the incident, Superintendent Todd Carlson asked Wegner if he regretted writing the column, and Wegner said no. Carlson then allegedly told Wegner he had to be "one of the most ignorant kids to try to argue with him on this topic," and threatened to suspend him.

Liberty Counsel, a nonprofit public interest law firm and ministry, took Wegner's case and called the situation "shocking" and "outrageous." Liberty Counsel's Matthew Staver sent a letter to the school stating: "The [District] humiliated Brandon in front of everyone, prevented him from his exams, and jeopardized his academic progress." According to the lawyer, Wegner's parents were never notified about his meetings with the school district.

WHAT CAN BE DONE?

When God is blotted out of education and government, immorality increases. Sin creates an atmosphere and an environment for more evil. If sin is not dealt with according to the Bible, it will infect everything in its path and will fertilize a culture of corruption.

The Bible tells us everyone who does evil hates the light, and the reason they don't come to the light is they are afraid their deeds will be exposed (**John 3:20**). So if we look at these problems in spiritual terms, it is clearly not just an issue of educators, money or curriculums. It goes much deeper and much higher, to top levels of the NEA and the U.S. Department of Education. Change won't take place without changed hearts. It is vital we raise awareness about these concerns, and parents must be as active as possible in their children's education process.

Author and former teacher, Dr. Dennis Laurence Cuddy, compiled an exhaustive study, "The Grab For Power: A Chronology of the NEA." I suggest anyone in the field of education or interested in the history of the change in direction of public schools take the time to read this research. In his conclusion about the union power grab, Dr. Cuddy stated:

"But the battle for America's schools is not over. Concerned Women for America and other pro-family organizations will not surrender the American education system to the NEA. We will continue to monitor America's schools, educate the public, and encourage legislators to support only family-friendly legislation that truly promotes educational excellence."[34]

I have heard it said one of the single most important things concerned citizens can do to combat the misuse of public schools is get involved in their community. Attend meetings, speak up, volunteer, and let the NEA know you are paying attention.

Parents have many alternatives. Classical On-Line Schools such as Freedom Project Education (www.fpeusa.org) teaches in the tradition of America's Founders. There is also the possibility of advocating the installment of a Biblical curriculum in local public school districts. This is happening right now in many schools across America. Learning about the Bible helps students understand its influence on world history as well as what motivated our founders to risk their lives and sacrifice in order to form a Republic under God in America.

The National Council on Bible Curriculum in Public Schools' (NCBCPS) curriculum has been voted into over 2,235 high schools in thirty-eight states so far, and there is now an on-line curriculum available. "Over 550,000 students have already taken this course nationwide, on the high school campus, during school hours, for credit." From Bible-inschools.net, the NCBCPS is:

"...introducing the electronic version of their course "The Bible in History and Literature." This version will be for students to use on their school computers and will include not only the text from the original textbook, but it also includes movies, DVDs, and slides."[35]

Public schools are failing. If the NEA refuses to relent on its anti-Christian, anti-American agenda, if they do not make an effort to respect the values and beliefs in the majority of American homes, then parents should seek private alternatives, remove their children from public schools and find chartered schools, Christian schools, or try home schooling. The choices are: let the NEA shape your child's worldview or take responsibility to raise him or her in a way in which you would approve.

Conservative Christian teachers currently in the public school system find themselves in a quagmire of sorts. They have invested time and treasure in their college education and ongoing training. Some of their families could not make it without their salary. Others have been teaching for years and had no idea about the deeper agendas of their mother ship, the NEA, and the U.S. Dept. of Education. We need to pray for them to stand strong in the faith and be the salt and light Jesus Christ commanded us all to be wherever we work. They may not be able to change the union, but they sure can impact the formation of a young child's worldview. There is no easy answer and no quick fix, but getting back to America's founding ethics, principles, and values would be a good start.

In 1788, **Noah Webster** said:

> "Every child in America should be acquainted with his own country. He should read books that furnish him with ideas that will be useful to him in life and practice. As soon as he opens his lips, he should rehearse the history of his own country."

Yes, my friend – let's rehearse America's true history, not what has been rewritten.

> *Train up a child in the way he should go, Even when he is old he will not depart from it* (**Proverbs 22:6**).

Around the same time that John Dewey was pushing Humanism in American education, studying Karl Marx, and preparing to influence the NEA; Planned Parenthood's founder, Margaret Sanger was pushing birth control, eugenics, and preparing to influence Americans to accept abortion and population control. We're headed there next.

ENDNOTES

1 http://www.worldviewtraining.com/book/chapters/dmrsh.html
2 http://www.gallup.com/poll/148724/Near-Record-Low-Confidence-Public-Schools.aspx
3 http://abcnews.go.com/2020/Stossel/story?id=1500338#.T2TOiPWCeZR
4 http://en.wikipedia.org/wiki/National_Education_Association
5 http://www.cwfa.org/brochures/nea.pdf
6 http://en.wikipedia.org/wiki/Virginia_Statute_for_Religious_Freedom
7 http://www.followthemoney.org/database/top10000.phtml?PHPSESSID=6a8f67e0d24618da7d8b1a960ecbc670
8 http://www.youtube.com/watch?v=bqn1rvv7Fis&feature=PlayList&p=4B61C3ABDB9A16FB&playnext=1&playnext_from=PL&index=16
9 http://americanvision.org/3383/the-demise-of-secular-humanism-by-the-hands-of-secular-humanists/
10 http://www.thenewamerican.com/opinion/sam-blumenfeld/6877-national-endowment-for-the-arts-sounds-alarm-on-literacy
11 http://www.cbsnews.com/2100-201_162-3520163.html
12 http://cnsnews.com/news/article/two-thirds-wisconsin-public-school-8th-graders-can-t-read-proficiently-despite-highest
13 http://cnsnews.com/news/article/two-thirds-wisconsin-public-school-8th-graders-can-t-read-proficiently-despite-highest
14 http://www.thenewamerican.com/opinion/sam-blumenfeld/10848-public-education-the-sick-dinosaur-on-fed-life-support
15 http://www.humanevents.com/article.php?id=7591
16 http://www.crosswalk.com/news/dr-paul-kengor-on-dupes-and-the-religious-left-part-ii-11639924.html
17 Charlotte Iserbyt, The Deliberate Dumbing Down of America: A Chronological Paper Trail, 1999; Conscience Press, Preface
18 http://defendingcontending.com/2011/10/29/indoctrination-2/
19 http://worldviewweekend.com/worldview-times/article.php?articleid=6597
20 www.onenewsnow.com/Perspectives/Default.aspx?id=1314254
21 http://www.parentalrights.org/index.asp?Type=B_BASIC&SEC={F36BF540-C568-46FD-B0CA-AC76E4754112}
22 Meredith Berg, The Radical Agenda of the NEA; http://www.wisconsinchristiannews.com/view.php?sid=3278
23 http://cnsnews.com/news/article/homosexual-activist-kevin-jennings-leaving-obama-administration
24 http://theothermccain.com/2011/03/04/the-global-orgasmatron-for-kids/
25 http://www.cwfa.org/brochures/nea.pdf
26 http://americansfortruth.com/2012/04/13/ten-reasons-to-walk-out-on-the-april-20-day-of-silence/
27 http://www.nea.org/tools/17231.htm
28 http://www.discoverthenetworks.org/individualProfile.asp?indid=2314#_edn70
29 http://www.nea.org/grants/38831.htm

30 World Net Daily, NEA: Let's celebrate communism, http://www.wnd.com/2010/07/184721/

31 http://www.wausaudailyherald.com/apps/pbcs.dll/article?AID=/201202160429/WDH0101/302170017

32 http://www.lc.org/index.cfm?PID=14102&AlertID=1360

33 http://www.christianpost.com/news/wis-student-censored-punished-by-school-for-gay-adoption-beliefs-68061/

34 http://www.cwfa.org/brochures/nea.pdf

35 http://www.bibleinschools.net/

PLANNED PARENTHOOD'S BURIED HISTORY

MARGARET SANGER AND AMERICA'S CULTURE OF DEATH

For you created my inmost being; you knit me together in my mother's womb. I praise you because I am fearfully and wonderfully made; your works are wonderful.... My frame was not hidden from you when I was made in the secret place, when I was woven together in the depths of the earth. Your eyes saw my unformed body; all the days ordained for me were written in your book before one of them came to be (**Psalm 139:13-16**).

"It is a vicious cycle; ignorance breeds poverty and poverty breeds ignorance. There is only one cure for both, and that is to stop breeding these things. Stop bringing to birth children whose inheritance cannot be one of health or intelligence. Stop bringing into the world children whose parents cannot provide for them. Herein lies the key of civilization."[1]
– **Margaret Sanger**

Ninety-six. Remember this number. A baby is aborted at a Planned Parenthood facility somewhere in America every 96 seconds. In that same amount of time, Planned Parenthood receives $1,056 taxpayer dollars. That equals eleven dollars a second and allows them to abort 910 lives every day. How did it get to the point in America where we kill our own and call it a choice? It sure did not happen overnight, but it does occur – *Every 96 seconds....*

Abortion is the number one killer in the United States, above cancer, heart disease, accidents, and everything else that causes death. According to the Alan Guttmacher Institute, one-third of all women in the United States will have an abortion before the age of forty-five. Nationwide, less than 1% of abortions are cases of rape or incest, contrary to liberal talking points. The number of abortions from all clinics and providers in America is estimated to be 3,600 a day,[2] equaling one abortion every twenty-four seconds.

Planned Parenthood was busted in 2010 in a series of undercover videos that brought national attention to their corrupt use of our tax dollars. Some of their employees were caught on tape giving advice to a couple on how to obtain abortion services for underage sex workers.[3] Reporting on abortion is not on the media's agenda, so I'm thankful for Live Action President Lila Rose and others who have exposed the truth. It is beyond atrocious that Planned Parenthood receives federal funding.

As I watched one of the sting videos, I noticed a portrait of Margaret Sanger proudly displayed in the lobby of a Planned Parenthood office. In order to better understand the influence of Planned Parenthood on America, it is critically important to investigate and expose Margaret Sanger for who she was and for what she believed. It is impossible to divorce Sanger from today's Planned Parenthood.

In fact, Alexander Sanger is continuing his grandmother's work as Goodwill Ambassador for the UN Population Fund and by serving as chairman of The International Planned Parenthood Council. New estimates indicate there have been between 55 and 60 million abortions since the monumental Supreme Court decision, Roe v. Wade, to legalize abortion in 1973. Americans, slaughtered by abortion, total *ten times* the number of Jews who died under the Nazis.

EUGENICS: SHOCKING HISTORY OF A WARPED WORLDVIEW

Most everyone would consider Adolf Hitler pure evil, and yet few people know he was as inspired by the eugenics movement in America as Margaret Sanger was about Germany's progress. Eugenics is the study of or belief in the possibility of improving the qualities of the human species or a population, especially by such means as discouraging reproduction by persons having genetic defects or presumed to have inheritable undesirable traits (negative eugenics) OR, encouraging reproduction by persons presumed to have inheritable desirable traits (positive eugenics). Hold on to your coffee while we connect some dots. In her 1922 book *The Pivot of Civilization*, Margaret Sanger wrote:

> "Constructive Eugenics aims to arouse the enthusiasm or the interest of the people in the welfare of the world fifteen or twenty generations in the future. On its negative side it shows us that we are paying for and even submitting to the dictates of an ever increasing, unceasingly spawning class of **human beings who never should have been born at all** – that the wealth of individuals and of states is being diverted from the development and the progress of human expression and civilization."[4]

What Adolf Hitler did to millions of Jews through eugenics and sterilization, Margaret Sanger has dwarfed by pioneering a movement causing the abortion of over one hundred million babies in the United States alone. Planned Parenthood founder Margaret Sanger promoted a eugenic ideology that eventually led to the gas chambers in Germany. A truth seeking, fair-minded person cannot read Sanger's writings without seeing her influence in America and the world. Sanger's publication, *The Birth Control Review,* was founded in 1917 and through the years, she often published articles from eugenicists such as Ernst Rudin.

Ernst Rudin (1874-1952) was a psychiatrist who worked as Adolf Hitler's director of genetic sterilization and founded the Nazi Society for Racial Hygiene, which was Germany's racial purity program. But what most people fail to realize is it was the United States that led the forced sterilization movement which began on the mentally ill and on prisoners. Between 1907 and 1939, more than 30,000 people in twenty-nine states were sterilized, many of them unknowingly or against their will, while they were incarcerated in American prisons or mental institutions. Nearly half the operations were carried out in California.[5]

Lothrop Stoddard (1883-1950) was a sophisticated racist and colleague of Margaret Sanger. Stoddard was a graduate of Harvard and author of *The Rising Tide of Color against White Supremacy* in 1921. He was a co-founder of the Birth Control League with Sanger. Lothrop

Stoddard described the eugenic practices of the Third Reich as "scientific" and "humanitarian" and even went so far as to say that the "Jew problem [is] already settled in principle and soon to be settled in fact by the physical elimination of the Jews themselves from the Third Reich."

In 1932, Margaret Sanger published "A Plan for Peace" in the April issue of her *Birth Control Review*, which included the following as part of her agenda:

> "To give certain dysgenic groups in our population their choice of segregation or sterilization. To apportion farm lands and homesteads for these segregated persons where they would be taught to work under competent instructors for their entire lives.

> "The first step would thus be to control the intake and output of morons, mental defectives, epileptics.

> "The second step would be to take an inventory of the secondary group such as illiterates, paupers, unemployables, criminals, prostitutes, dope fiends; classify them in special departments under government medical protection, and segregate them on farms and open spaces as long as necessary for the... development of moral conduct.

> "Having corralled this enormous part of our population and placed it *on a basis of health instead of punishment*, it is safe to say that fifteen or twenty millions of our population would then be organized into soldiers of defense – defending the unborn against their own disabilities."[6]

Ernst Rudin's article, "Eugenic Sterilization: An Urgent Need," was also published in 1932 in Sanger's *Birth Control Review* journal. The following year, Rudin drafted the Nazi Sterilization Law in Germany which originally called for the sterilization of "schizophrenics," "alcoholics," and "manic-depressives" – the subjects of Rudin's research. As these legal sterilizations began, programs were already underway to sterilize "black" Germans and expanded to include Jews, Gypsies and, in the words of Rudin, other "inferior race types." This led to the establishment of a killing program that began at several of Germany's psychiatric hospitals. The first to die were between 375,000 and 400,000 mental patients and others deemed to be racially, physically, or mentally unfit.

Rudin publicly praised Adolf Hitler for making his "more than thirty-year-old dream a reality" by imposing "racial hygiene" upon the German people. To help you understand the timeline, it was only one year after Sanger delivered her Peace Plan that Hitler signed the infamous Law for the Prevention of Hereditarily Diseased Offspring.[7] Margaret Sanger and Ernst Rudin were both influenced by the population control theories of Thomas Robert Malthus.

Thomas Malthus (1766-1834) was an English scholar and mathematician who believed that, "The power of population is indefinitely greater than the power in the earth to produce subsistence for man."[8] Malthus was both influential and controversial in his raising economic fears of overpopulation and concerns about a shortage of food and resources, which later proved to be unfounded. He literally believed in the survival of the fittest, and that the poor were not worth feeding. According to author George Grant in his revealing book on Margaret Sanger called *Killer Angel*, in one of the six editions of "An Essay on the Principle of Population," Malthus wrote:

> "All children born, beyond what would be required to keep up the population to a desired level, must necessarily perish, unless room is made for them by the deaths of grown persons. We should facilitate, instead of foolishly and vainly endeavoring to impede, the operations of nature in producing this mortality."[9]

He believed mankind was to blame for human suffering and Malthus was also a key influence in the lives of Charles Darwin and Karl Marx. The plot thickens.

H.G. Wells (1866-1946), the famous British author, was another elitist who believed in eugenics. Speaking at a dinner honoring Margaret Sanger, Wells said "The movement she started will grow to be, a hundred years from now, the most influential of all time in controlling man's destiny on earth." While traveling abroad to promote her birth control cause, Sanger met H.G. Wells, a devout Darwinian atheist. During his marriage to Amy Robbins, H.G. Wells had affairs with a number of women, including Margaret Sanger.

Wells was a believer in eugenics and even wrote the introduction for Sanger's book *Pivot of Civilization*. Wells implies in his writing that there was a shift at that time in regard to how people looked at birth control due to the "inferior citizens," and that the new civilization was saying to the old, "We want fewer and better children who can be reared up to their full possibilities." At the end of Sanger's book introduction, H.G. Wells writes:

> "Mrs. Sanger with her extraordinary breadth of outlook and the real scientific quality of her mind has now redressed the balance. She has lifted this question from out of the warm atmosphere of troubled domesticity, in which it has hitherto been discussed, to its proper level of a predominantly important human affair."[10]

Leon Whitney (1894-1973), a dog-breeding specialist, had an article published by Sanger in June 1933 entitled "Selective Sterilization" that praised and defended the Third Reich's pre-holocaust "race purification program." Whitney was secretary of the American Eugenics Society, and he called for the sterilization of ten million "defective" Americans when the U.S. population was approximately 126 million.

It is well documented that the Birth Control League (BCL) pushed to get political influence and used the wealth of its leaders to "sell" abortion and birth control well beyond the United States. Leon Whitney once said, "While we were pussyfooting around...the Germans were calling a spade a spade."[11] In 1938, Margaret Sanger's sex education and family limitation programs were accepted in Sweden, the first free nation to permit abortion.

After World War II had concluded, the horrors of eugenics and Nazi atrocities – including the use of concentration camps, human experimentation, and the gas chamber – were exposed. Sanger acted deceptively and quickly to attempt to distance herself and the BCL from the Third Reich's "Final Solution." Her idea to change the name of her organization was a shrewd one, desiring no trace of her close Nazi associations. Until that time, the birth control and the eugenics movements were nearly impossible to separate.

BIRTHING PLANNED PARENTHOOD

*The Birth Control Federation of America (BCFA) members voted unanimously at a special January 29, 1942 meeting to change Sanger's organization's name to the Planned Parenthood Federation of America.

By then, BCFA had thirty-four state league affiliates. The state leagues followed suit in changing their name and bylaws. Particularly, the New York State Federation for Planned Parenthood's old bylaws stipulated the object was:

> "To develop and organize on sound *eugenic*, social and medical principles, interest in and knowledge of *birth control* throughout the State of New York as permitted by law."[12]

The new bylaws replaced "birth control" with "planned parenthood." "Eugenics" was dropped in 1943 because of its unpopular association with the German government's race-improving eugenics theories.[13]

At the Nuremberg Trials in 1945, Allied prosecutors recited the appalling account of Nazi crimes, including the practice of forced sterilization. One of the excuses given by the German Socialists who defended their drastic population control measures was that they were inspired by the progress of the birth control movement in the United States, which was not a lie. By 1956, abortion became legal in eleven more European nations, and within another few years, UN Agencies would begin to subsidize Planned Parenthood programs in many other countries.

MARGARET SANGER'S BIOGRAPHICAL TIMELINE

Early 1900's: How did Margaret Sanger develop an obsession with abortion, birth control, and eugenics? Sanger was born to poverty-stricken Irish immigrant parents in Corning, N.Y. in 1879 and grew up in a family of eleven children. Her father was an atheist, and her mother was Catholic. Both of her parents were socialists. Her mother, Anne, died of tuberculosis and cervical cancer, and it is said Margaret blamed her father for having too many children.

Margaret Sanger became an atheist, a feminist, Marxist, and an avowed socialist who was angry at what she considered an unsatisfactory system of capitalism in America that included poor working conditions for young white women. In her autobiographical book, *My Fight for Birth Control,* Sanger wrote that she "associated poverty, toil, unemployment, drunkenness, cruelty, quarreling, fighting, debts, and jails with large families."

Sanger rose to affluence when she dropped out of nursing school after three months to marry a wealthy architect. They eventually settled in Greenwich Village. She wanted to do something to help prevent "unnecessary suffering," and she would later describe the birth of her first son as agonizing and "mental torture." She once noted the experience of giving birth as a factor "to be reckoned with." Her first marriage fell apart, and one of her children – whom she admitted to neglecting – died of pneumonia at age four.

She convinced herself that she wasn't right for family life, stating she was not a "fit person for love or home or children or anything which needs attention." In a rare 1957 interview, Sanger admitted to journalist Mike Wallace that she was a staunch feminist and added, "I naturally didn't want to see all the women take all the suffering from child bearing and of pregnancy."[14]

1914: Margaret Sanger coined the term "birth control" in 1914, the year after she separated from her first husband. She then launched "The Woman Rebel,"[15] an eight-page monthly newsletter with the slogan "No Gods, No Masters," insisting a woman be "the absolute mistress of her own body." Sound familiar? Sanger strongly felt women needed to be at the same level as men in society. In 1916, she launched the monthly periodical *The Birth Control Review* and wrote articles for the Socialist Party publication *The Call.* Believing so much in limiting the populations of those she deemed unworthy of bearing children, she went so far as to advocate married couples must submit applications in order to have children.

1918: In "Morality and Birth Control," Sanger wrote:

"Birth control is the first important step a woman must take toward the goal of her freedom. It is the first step she must take to be man's equal. It is the first step they must both take toward human emancipation."[16]

1920: In her book *Woman and the New Race* Sanger explicitly called her work in birth control "nothing more or less than the facilitation of the process of weeding out the unfit, of preventing the birth of defectives or those who will become defectives."[17]

Two years later, in *The Pivot of Civilization*, she wrote, "Our failure to segregate morons who are increasing and multiplying ... demonstrates our foolhardy and extravagant sentimentalism."[18] She had already shown her racist views toward blacks and seemed to take an alarming step here that furthered her quest for power. Who on earth is qualified to make these determinations about who is a moron, and how would these morons be segregated?

1923: Under the auspices of the American Birth Control League (ABCL), she established the Clinical Research Bureau (CRB). It was the first legal birth control clinic in the U.S. (renamed Margaret Sanger Research Bureau in 1940). It received crucial grants from **John D. Rockefeller, Jr.'s** Bureau of Social Hygiene from 1924 onward. The grants were made anonymously to avoid public exposure of the Rockefeller name with her agenda.

Rockefeller and his wealthy colleagues would work behind the scenes to encourage federal intervention, thus imposing their will on the U.S. Congress. They needed the United States government to be an ally in order for Sanger to further the eugenics agenda. His family also consistently supported her ongoing efforts in regard to population control.[19] Rockefeller followed in the footsteps of his great grandfather, a strong believer in the population control ideals of Robert Malthus.

1926: Sanger gave a lecture on birth control to the women's auxiliary of the **Ku Klux Klan** in New Jersey.[20] In 1927 she helped organize the first World Population Conference in Geneva, and in 1931, Sanger founded the Population Association of America with Henry Pratt Fairchild, formerly the secretary-treasurer of the American Eugenics Society, at its head. Fairchild, a leading racist and anti-Semite, wrote *The Melting Pot Mistake*, a book that severely denigrated Jews. And from researching various Sanger biographies, it appears she admired Karl Marx and Mao Zedong. After all, Margaret Sanger once said,

"The most merciful thing that a large family does to one of its infant members is to kill it."[21]

Approximately 78% of Planned Parenthood *clinics* are in minority communities. Abortion rates in other inner cities across America are quite high as well, and it makes you wonder if the original vision of Margaret Sanger to reduce minorities is becoming a reality right before our eyes. To give you some perspective, the nationwide rate for pregnancies ending in abortion is about twenty percent. Margaret Sanger believed "we have divinity within us," so who needs God? Planned Parenthood's early goals asserted that its "core clients" are "young women, low-income women, and women of color."

They shed innocent blood, the blood of their sons & their daughters ... and the land was polluted with blood... (**Psalms 106:38**).

According to Concerned Women for America and other sources, in 1929, the American Birth Control League laid the groundwork for a clinic in Harlem, a largely black section of New York City. This was ten years before Margaret Sanger created The Negro Project. It was the dawn of the Great Depression, and at the time, blacks faced harsher conditions of desperation because of widespread racial prejudice and discrimination. From Sanger's perspective, Harlem was the ideal place for this experimental clinic, which officially opened on November 21, 1930. Many blacks looked to escape their adverse circumstances and along came a clinic to offer "help." This brings us to one of the darkest skeletons in Planned Parenthood's closet.

THE NEGRO PROJECT

William Edward Burghardt Du Bois, a sociologist and author, helped found the National Association for the Advancement of Colored People (NAACP) in 1909 to improve the living conditions of black Americans. Before World War II, Margaret Sanger was fairly outspoken about her views on other races. Sanger shrewdly used the influence of prominent blacks to reach the masses with her message. Du Bois was an open admirer of Joseph Stalin and according to his biography was influenced by Karl Marx. He was investigated by the FBI due to his socialist writings and later would join the Communist Party.

Sanger invited Du Bois and a host of Harlem's leading blacks including physicians, ministers and journalists, to form an advisory council to help direct the Harlem clinic and control births in the community. The prejudice and discrimination that blacks endured made their struggle even more difficult, which seemed to further justify reducing their population and restricting their reproduction. In his 1932 essay on birth control in Sanger's *Birth Control Review,* Du Bois accepted the conventional wisdom that "the more intelligent class" uses birth control. He wrote:

> "The mass of ignorant Negroes still breed carelessly and disastrously, so that the increase among Negroes, even more than the increase among whites, is from that part of the population least intelligent and fit, and least able to rear their children properly."[22]

{Where in the heck are black Christian conservatives on this issue? While blacks and Hispanics comprise only 28% of the population in the country today, they account for nearly 60% of all abortions! In New York, the statistics are even worse. According to CBS News and LifeNews.com, a 2011 study by the New York City health department shocked pro-life advocates across the country when it was discovered 41% of pregnancies end in abortion.}[23]

1939: Next, Margaret Sanger selected **Dr. Clarence J. Gamble** of Procter and Gamble, to be the BCFA regional director of the South. Gamble wrote a memorandum in November of 1939 entitled "Suggestions for the Negro Project" in which he recognized "black leaders might regard birth control as an extermination plot." He suggested black leaders to be placed in positions where it would *appear* they were in charge. Sanger responded to Gamble in a letter on December 10, 1939, where she stated:

> "The most successful educational approach to the Negro is through a religious appeal. We do not want word to go out that we want to exterminate the Negro population and the Minister

is the man who can straighten out that idea if it ever occurs to any of their more rebellious members."[24]

It is clear she had strategic plans to set up birth control clinics in poor New York City neighborhoods to target "Blacks, Hispanics, Fundamentalists, Jews, and Catholics."

1942: Sanger secretary Florence Rose helped sell abortion to black religious leaders because there was opposition to Sanger's birth control ideas. Rose noted a meeting with a Planned Parenthood Negro Division board member, Bishop David H. Sims (African Methodist Episcopal Church), who offered whatever assistance he could give.

Bishop Sims agreed to begin the "softening process" among the representatives of different Negro denominations at meetings with the Federal Council of Churches and its Division of Race Relations. With Margaret Sanger's efforts to find wealthy donors combined with her pestering of politicians, their efforts really paid off after the horrors of World War II threatened her work.

1950: By this time, virtually the entire black leadership network of religious, social, professional, and academic organizations had endorsed Planned Parenthood's program. In less than fifteen years, Donald B. Strauss, chairman of Planned Parenthood World Population, urged the 1964 Democratic National Convention to liberalize the party's stated policies on birth control and to adopt domestic and foreign policy platform resolutions.

Irony alert: The very party that helped Sanger reach her goal to control parts of our population, and years later to far surpass that goal, claims to be the party that supports minorities and women! Approximately 80 percent of African American, Hispanic, and inner-city women typically, albeit ignorantly, vote for pro-abortion Democrats. *That's* good marketing.

HOW DID THIS HAPPEN IN AMERICA?

The evil of abortion has been successfully sold to the American people as health care, women's rights, freedom of choice, and an issue of privacy. According to Day Gardner, current President of The National Black Pro Life Union and Associate Director of National Pro Life Center on Capitol Hill, more than 15 million black children have been aborted in America. Gardner said abortion is the number one killer of black people in this country and is responsible for "killing more African Americans than accidents, heart disease, stroke, crimes, HIV-AIDS and all other deaths ... COMBINED!" In 2007, Day Gardner explains:

> "What bothers me is we are very quick as a people to recognize racism everywhere else except the one place that truly affects all of us. Most blacks will say nothing when abortion facilities are placed purposefully in minority and poor communities. This is no accident! ...More than 37% of all abortions are performed on black women. Last year alone, more than 400,000 black babies were killed by abortion."[25]

The proof is indisputable. Mark Crutcher, President of Life Dynamics, also offered several statistics to support similar claims in his documentary about black genocide called *Maafa 21*. He said a black child in the United States is five times as likely to be aborted as a white child. He maintains more African-American children die in abortion mills in less than four days than the number of African Americans killed by Ku Klux Klan in 150 years.

"The most dangerous place for a black child in the U.S. is his mother's womb," Crutcher asserts. The filmmakers calculate abortion has reduced the black population in the United States by about 25 percent![26] Ironically, African-American women tend to be more pro-life than white women today, yet they have three times the abortions. Margaret Sanger would be thrilled that the Left has successfully implemented her elitist eugenics strategy of reducing the black and minority populations in America. Why is there not a greater public outcry over this genocide in our country? With more than 79% of clinics in minority neighborhoods, there are more than 1,400 black abortions a day in America.

Alan Guttmacher, who immediately succeeded Sanger as President of the Planned Parenthood Federation of America, exclaimed, **"We are merely walking down the path that Mrs. Sanger carved out for us."** Guttmacher was also vice-president of the American Eugenics Society and founder of the American Association of Planned Parenthood Physicians. He founded abortion studies and supported tax-subsidized birth control programs. Guttmacher was also a proponent of controlling the world birthrate.

Alexander C. Sanger (current chairman of the International Planned Parenthood Council) is Margaret Sanger's grandson. While in charge of Planned Parenthood of New York City in 1991 he proclaimed, "Right now, we have three clinics in this city and I want ten more. We currently have a small storefront office in central Harlem, and it is my first priority to see if we can transform that into a clinic.... **With all her success, my grandmother left some unfinished business, and I intend to finish it.**" [27]

Decade after decade, Planned Parenthood achieves devastating results in part by using tactics made famous by number one radical Saul Alinsky and his 'power at any cost' agenda. To move this culture of death forward, Margaret Sanger and her political minions issued legal challenges, organized protests, used tactics of civil disobedience and sophisticated propaganda campaigns.

TAXPAYERS FUNDING BIG BUSINESS

Planned Parenthood is the largest abortion provider in the country. In their own 2010 report, they received $487.4 million in taxpayer money. The organization also had a nice $18.5 million profit! Do they really need our help? They average 332,000 abortions a year, and 46% of Planned Parenthood's income comes directly from the very accommodating American taxpayers.

Because of legalized abortion, close to 53 million *Baby Boomers* (someone born during the demographic birth boom from 1946 and 1964) never had the chance to be born. That's quite a bit of missing tax revenue for our struggling economy, but thanks to abortion mills like Planned Parenthood those people were not given a chance to live and to help sustain us in our retirement by paying into the system.

Tragically, abortion is a *huge* money-making scheme. Depending on gestation of the fetus, the average cost of an early abortion per customer can range from $400 to $2,200. Approximately forty percent of their annual income is from abortions totaling over $156 million. Some may argue Planned Parenthood offers other services. This is true – and counseling is one of those services. If they make money with *every* single abortion, but lose money if a young woman changes her mind and walks out their door, which way do *you* think Planned Parenthood "counsels" girls?

Of all pregnant girls and women seen by Planned Parenthood, 91% end up having abortions. First of all, thank God for the nine percent! Recent statistics show **the ratio of aborted babies to adoption refer-rals is 340 to 1.**[28]

For every one potential adoption, 340 lives are destroyed. The Democratic Party believes abortion is health care. Do you buy that? Total Planned Parenthood health center income from all of their "services" is nearly $405 Million. When we add the federal funding to this figure, it is over $1 billion dollars! Planned Parenthood has now grown to nearly 900 clinics across America.

THE MEDIA CELEBRATES MARGARET SANGER'S LEGACY

In the mainstream media, abortion is supported and even celebrated. For example, **Katie Couric** did a documentary on Margaret Sanger on PBS in 1998. Later, during Couric's time at CBS, Deacon Greg Kandra was the editor of Katie's blog and a contributor to the CBS Evening News. Greg once wrote about the photos of famous women on the walls in Couric's office such as Amelia Earhart, Eleanor Roosevelt, Audrey Hepburn...and Margaret Sanger. In 2000 when she was on NBC, Katie Couric honored Margaret Sanger as a heroine for the millennium on *The Today Show.* Sanger was described by Couric as vivacious, healing, and "powerfully driven."[29]

By the way, it is worth mentioning that each year Planned Parenthood presents its Margaret Sanger Award to recognize "outstanding contributions to the reproductive health and rights movement." Past recipients include liberals like Jane Fonda, Phil Donahue, Ted Turner, and in 2009, Secretary of State **Hillary Clinton** who once exclaimed on video how much she admires and is "in awe" of Margaret Sanger. People like Couric, Clinton, Jane Fonda, Oprah, the ladies on TV's *The* (Liberal) *View* and other Hollywood elites, and the mainstream media like to depict Christians, conservatives, and others who oppose abortion as extreme, anti-choice, or old fashioned.

Ending the life of a baby is not a right, but it does happen to be an unfortunate choice many people support. I personally refuse to accept the changing terminology people use to sugar coat a brutal procedure. I've heard it said many ways to water down abortion, but Ashley Judd floored me in 2008 when she called ripping a baby apart in the birth canal a "Women's right to privacy and reproductive freedom." I almost gagged when she said that.

We shouldn't look down our noses at Judd because this mentality is so prevalent in Hollywood it's the norm. They are products of their anti-Christian, Humanist worldview. They need the salvation of Jesus Christ. If the truth about abortion was reported honestly by the national media, I believe fewer Christians would vote for pro-abortion Democrats. You and I must take the time to help inform those who still care. Father Frank Pavone is known for promoting the whole truth and says, "America will not reject abortion until America sees abortion."

Nothing surprises God, and if you've had an abortion, you do not have to walk around feeling defeated or isolated anymore. You are loved, so reach out to Him, knowing He is waiting for you to take that first bold step to being completely restored. God may be able to use your painful experience to help others. Don't keep living with the pain by putting it off. Here is one heartbreaking testimony about how abortion can affect a family:

> "My daughter had an abortion 9 years ago.... Now I understand why she almost drank herself to death. I HATE PLANNED PARENTHOOD. Had they not been available she would have come to me. She admits this. She is so sorry and it feels like a 'death of her very soul.' I just found out, and have started the grieving process for my grandchild. God, it hurts so bad. Evil has visited our family and left us in ruins. I curse Planned Parenthood and their supporters." [From the Center for Bio-Ethical Reform][30]

GOD VS. SANGER: CONTRASTING VIEWS ON LIFE

The Bible teaches us God had plans for you and me and for every baby in the womb. Every human life is created in the image of God. Look at Scriptures from the Bible compared to quotes from the writings of Margaret Sanger. If you believe as I do that only God has the authority to determine the end of one's life and that the deliberate destruction of any human life is sin, these comparisons will be eye-opening for you.

But when God, who had set me apart even from my mother's womb and called me through His grace, was pleased to reveal His Son in me so that I might preach Him among the Gentiles... (**Galatians 1:15**).

"As an advocate of birth control I wish ... to point out that the unbalance between the birth rate of the 'unfit' and the 'fit,' admittedly the greatest present menace to civilization, can never be rectified by the inauguration of a cradle competition between these two classes. In this matter, the example of the inferior classes, the fertility of the feeble-minded, the mentally defective, the poverty-stricken classes, should not be held up for emulation.... On the contrary, the most urgent problem today is how to limit and discourage the over-fertility of the mentally and physically defective."[31] – **Sanger**

My times are in Your hand; Deliver me from the hand of my enemies... (**Psalm 31:15**).

"In conclusion, I cannot refrain from saying that women must come to recognize there is some function of womanhood other than being a child-bearing machine...Until capitalism is swept away, there is no hope for young girls to live a beautiful life during their girlhood... There is no hope that a woman can live in the family relation and have children without sacrificing every vestige of individual development."[32] –**Sanger**

Before I formed you in the womb I knew you, and before you were born I consecrated you; I have appointed you a prophet to the nations (**Jeremiah 1:5**).

"A functioning Communistic society will assure the happiness of every child, and will assume the full responsibility for its welfare and education ... where there are no legal restrictions, no religious condemnation, and where birth control instruction is part of the regular welfare service of the government." – **Sanger**

Make no mistake; Margaret Sanger knew what she was doing. It just seems hard for most of us to comprehend. The spiritual battle is going on all around us. Satan is the father of lies and the author of evil. I am sure he celebrates Planned Parenthood and its successful agenda of death today. There are too many to list, but Sanger also published such articles as "Some Moral Aspects of Eugenics" (June 1920), "Birth Control and Positive Eugenics" (July 1925), and many others including "A Code to Stop Overproduction of Children."

Margaret Sanger biographer and historian, David M. Kennedy, said her primary goal was not to encourage marriage but to "increase the quantity and quality of sexual relationships." The birth control movement, she said, freed the mind from "sexual prejudice and taboo." Sanger was a proponent of free love and abortion. Prior to Alfred Kinsey, she was largely responsible for the so-called 'sexual revolution' which has destroyed millions of families, debased countless women, and influenced America's downward moral slide.

In *The Woman Rebel* back in 1922, Sanger wrote:

"Our objective is unlimited sexual gratification without the burden of unwanted children.... Women must have the right to live ... to love ... to be an unmarried mother ... to create ... to destroy.... The marriage bed is the most degenerative influence in the social order."[33]

I could not complete this chapter without giving "credit" to Faye Wattleton, the President of Planned Parenthood Federation of America from 1978 to 1992 who said..."We are not going to be an organization promoting celibacy or chastity." On May 2, 1979, Wattleton proclaimed:

"I believe Margaret Sanger would have been proud of us today if she had seen the directions that we have most recently in this organization taken."[34]

She also said **Planned Parenthood is proud to be "walking in the footsteps of Margaret Sanger."** Speaking up for minorities, Wattleton was paid in the six-figure range and was the youngest and first African American President of Planned Parenthood. Ironically, this influential pro-abortion woman is the founder and president of the Center for the Advancement of Women.

FINAL WORDS ON SANGER

This is all part of a horrible legacy of darkness and death, and people like Margaret Sanger will have to stand before a holy God one day to be judged. You may wonder how Sanger felt in terms of health, success, and quality of life. Was she happy and proud of her accomplishments? The answer is no – and yes. In his biography on Margaret Sanger, Dr. George Grant thoroughly covers her unhappy upbringing that we touched on earlier. Sanger said she was agitated and disturbed in her early years which led to much bitterness in her life. This unhappiness caused her eventual fixation with drugs, alcohol and the occult.

Sanger died September 6, 1966, a week before her eighty-seventh birthday. Grant writes:

> "[She] had nearly fulfilled her early boast that she would spend every last penny of James Slee's [her second husband] fortune. In the process, though, she had lost everything else: love, happiness, satisfaction, fulfillment, family, and friends."[35]

For most of us, it is incomprehensible that Margaret Sanger continues to be defended and honored by many liberals, progressives, and Democrats in Washington, D.C. and across America. By voting Democrat, even some Christians who know better still put party before policy which is a shame. Writing for National Review, Chuck Donovan penned an article, "Margaret Sanger and the War on Compassion," in which he wrote that Sanger's dream had been realized in many ways:

> "For generations the sterilization of the poor and the vulnerable has been a reality pushed by government agencies and population-control groups...Currently, roughly 90 percent of unborn children diagnosed with Down Syndrome are aborted.

Obsessed with plucking the 'weeds' from the human garden, Sanger and her fellow eugenicists lost sight of what it means to be human."[36]

The elite media not only approves of Planned Parenthood, but they also help promote the sexual revolution in America, abortion on demand, and legislation that funds abortion providers.

The following line from *Pivot of Civilization* allows a particularly telling glimpse of Sanger's "compassion" and her motives:

"Remember our motto: if we must have welfare, give it to the rich, not to the poor."

Sanger's views naturally led her to strike out against the institution of marriage and the family. "The marriage bed," she wrote, "is the most degenerating influence in the social order." Sanger advocated instead a "voluntary association" between sexual partners. She thus sought to supplant the family as the most fundamental unit of society with relationships directed toward the sexual gratification of cooperating individuals.[37]

PLANNED PARENTHOOD TARGETS CHILDREN

Planned Parenthood makes the most money from women under thirty and especially from return customers who had their first abortion as a teenager. Their website tells teens how to legally get an abortion without informing their parents, even in states with laws generally mandating a parent give consent to, or at least be informed of the abortion.[38]

One of their ads targeting young people states, "If your parents are stupid enough to deny you access to birth control and you are under 18, you can get it on your own. Call Planned Parenthood." They also provide sex talks in public schools. One employee lectured students at Ramona High School, Riverside, CA, saying:

"At Planned Parenthood you can also get birth control without the consent or knowledge of your parents. So, if you are 14, 15 or 16 and you come to Planned Parenthood, we won't tell your parents you've been there. We swear we won't tell your parents."

As for the potential fathers of a preborn baby, abortion providers, feminists and liberals oppose any rights for them even if those fathers-to-be are concerned, loving husbands. They seem to have no problem with leaving a man out of the abortion decision. As much as Planned Parenthood might want us to think they are pro-family planning, their existence drastically weakens the family and "Preventing Parenthood" may be a more appropriate name.

Abortion would not be as big of a business if not for the sexualization of children in America through the successful efforts of Hollywood, the media, government and especially public schools. Planned Parenthood and their affiliates promote promiscuity and sexual experimentation to young, impressionable children. If you've been out of school for a while, you'd be shocked at the propaganda being pushed on kids today. They are even targeting children too young to be thinking about the opposite sex in adult situations.

Planned Parenthood gets into classrooms by lobbying state legislatures in order to mandate their Sex Education curriculum. They have done a good job of selling the "safe sex" lie and promoting a worry-free message of sex without consequences. One result ends up being millions of teen pregnancies which lead either to abortions or to sexually transmitted diseases. Either way, Planned Parenthood makes money from these young clients. Kids often go to these clinics to get help for treatment of their STD, and certain medications can be quite expensive. To make things worse, some STD's are incurable, so they can end up as a life-long customer of the very agency that promoted a sexually active lifestyle – a regretful reminder of their foolish teen choices.

From a business standpoint, it makes sense that Planned Parenthood would aim for young kids with developing hormones. Give 'em condoms and a PP business card along with the message of experimentation and safe sex in order to increase the rate of teen sexual activity. Typically, Planned Parenthood's agenda looks like this:

- Dupe the public into believing their main goal is women's health services

- Lobby for increased federal funding through American taxpayers

- Re-elect pro-abortion Democratic representatives

- Influence public school curriculums with the help of the NEA

- Get young kids and teens addicted to sex and encourage experimentation

- Sell them birth control – and when kids catch a sexually transmitted disease,

- Sell them testing services

- When a young girl gets pregnant, sell her an abortion

- *[wash – rinse – repeat]*

A natural expression of our anti-Christian culture, the concepts of abstinence, purity, and self-restraint are nowhere to be found. Their message is blatant indoctrination intended to increase Planned Parenthood's business income. School films routinely portray Sanger as a pioneer for women's rights. If you happen to visit New York City you can visit 'Margaret Sanger Square.' Heck, even the United States Postal Service issued a stamp in honor of what would have been her 100th birthday in 1979! Has America's conscience been seared? Unfortunately, yes – and the only answers are truth, love, and the Gospel of Jesus Christ.

In his book *78: How Christians Can Save America*, Peter Heck addresses our confusion:

> "Is it anything but society's moral confusion that says if you hold an infant's head inside the birth canal while inserting scissors and suction tips to extract its brain, you are completing a 'legitimate medical procedure'; but doing the same thing with the infant's head outside the canal is first degree murder?"[39]

Too many people seem indifferent toward the cruel evil of abortion. We need to pray for a miracle in our country that we will somehow value life once again so innocent babies in the future will have a chance to live. Maybe one of the aborted babies would have discovered a cure for cancer. Imagine who might have been born all these years. We also must allow our voices to be heard in the efforts to defund Planned Parenthood. Support the pro-life movement.

In **Jeremiah 6:10** the Bible states:

> *To whom can I speak and give warning? Who will listen to me? Their ears are closed so they cannot hear. The word of the LORD is offensive to them; they find no pleasure in it.*

It is not surprising the world chooses not to listen, but this attitude of apathy has crept into Christianity. Imagine if at least one committed church in each district in your state actively fought for the unborn in public, it could influence and radically change the culture. Although some have become desensitized to abortion, I'm not saying the church as a whole doesn't care. I'm saying abortion is not being talked about very much. If your Pastor is not leading on the life issue, then maybe God wants you to lovingly remind him.

We must pray America miraculously develops a conscience again, and that Christian hearts are softened. We must also elect more conservative, pro-life, pro-family representatives to local and state legislatures. This truly is one of the most important battles in our culture. Practicing Christians must lead by example if we are to have a greater impact in America for Christ and defend precious lives.

Planned Parenthood continues to receive over $360 million in taxpayer subsidies each year. Did you remember the number from the beginning of this chapter? Ninety-six. In the United States of America, a baby with a beating heart, cells, and nerve endings is aborted at a Planned Parenthood facility every 96 seconds.

In the twenty minutes it took the average reader to finish this chapter, Planned Parenthood received about $13,250 in taxpayer dollars ($11 every second). During this same time, approximately **thirteen babies were just given a death sentence** instead of being given a right to life, liberty and the pursuit of happiness. Another human life is denied at a Planned Parenthood clinic...**somewhere in America...every 96 seconds**.

> *I have set before you life and death, blessing and cursing; therefore choose life, that both you and your descendants may live* (**Deuteronomy 30:19**).

Next, let's investigate the beliefs and background of the most pro-abortion president in the history of America and compare his values to what most Bible-believing Christians value.

ENDNOTES

1 What Every Girl Should Know-Margaret Sanger 1915
2 http://www.movementforabetteramerica.org/abortionindex.html
3 Undercover 'Sex Work' Videos Fuel Congressional Campaign Against Planned Parenthood; February 03, 2011 FoxNews.com
4 The Pivot of Civilization Sanger, Margaret 1922 Dangers of Cradle Competition (Project Gutenberg) Page 72
5 http://www.jewishvirtuallibrary.org/jsource/Holocaust/disabled.html
6 A Plan for Peace, Margaret Sanger; Birth Control Review (April 1932, pp. 107-108)
7 http://en.wikipedia.org/wiki/
   Law_for_the_Prevention_of_Hereditarily_Diseased_Offspring
8 Malthus T.R. 1798. An essay on the principle of population. Chapter 1, p13 in Oxford World's Classics.
9 George Grant, Killer Angel (Franklin, Tennessee: Ars Vitae Press, 1995), 50.
10 H.G. Wells Easton Glebe, Dunmow, Essex., England. http://www.infoplease.com/t/hist/pivot-civilization/2.html
11 Leon Whitney; George Mason Univ. History News Network, http://hnn.us/articles/1796.html
12 Tanya L. Green, 5-10-2001, The Negro Project; Margaret Sanger's Eugenic Plan for Black Americans, CWFA and http://citizenreviewonline.org/special_issues/population/the_negro_project.htm
13 Robert G. Marshall and Charles A. Donovan, Blessed are the Barren: The Social Policy of Planned Parenthood (San Francisco: Ignatius Press, 1991), 24-25.
14 M.Wallace interview 1957; http://www.hrc.utexas.edu/multimedia/video/2008/wallace/sanger_margaret.html
15 "Margaret Sanger Clinic, Statement of Significance". National Historic Landmarks Program. 1993-09-14. Retrieved 2010-03-09.
16 "Morality and Birth Control," February-March, 1918, pp. 11,14.
17 http://www.bartleby.com/1013/18.html Women and the New Race, page 18
18 http://blackgenocide.org/archived_articles/sanger04.html
19 Harr, John Ensor; Johnson, Peter J. (1988). The Rockefeller Century: Three Generations of America's Greatest Family. New York: Charles Scribner's Sons. pp. 191, 461-62. — crucial, anonymous Rockefeller grants to the Clinical Research Bureau and support for population control
20 Sanger, Margaret (2004). The Autobiography of Margaret Sanger. Courier Dover Publications. p. 366
21 Margaret Sanger, Women and the New Race (Eugenics Publ. Co., 1920, 1923)

22 W. E. B. Du Bois, "Black Folk and Birth Control," Birth Control Review 16 (June 1932): 166-167.

23 http://www.cbsnews.com/2100-201_162-7222625.html

24 http://www.citizenreviewonline.org/special_issues/population/the_negro_project.htm

25 http://www.catholicnewsagency.com/news/black_prolife_leader_says_abortion_ratios_point_to_racism/

26 The documentary Maafa 21: Black Genocide in 21st Century America, Maafa21.com

27 "Another Sanger Leads Planned Parenthood." The New York Times, January 23, 1991, page B2

28 http://www.lifesitenews.com/news/planned-parenthood-2010-report-4874-million-in-taxpayer-money-329445-unbor/

29 http://www.jesus-is-savior.com/Evils%20in%20America/Abortion%20is%20Murder/murderhood.htm

30 http://www.abortionno.org/index.php/are_you_pregnant_and_considering_an_abortion/

31 "The Eugenic Value of Birth Control Propaganda," October 1921, page 5.

32 Margaret Sanger, What Every Girl Should Know, 1915

33 Margaret Sanger (editor). The Woman Rebel, Volume I, Number 1. Reprinted in Woman and the New Race. New York: Brentanos Publishers, 1922.

34 http://www.ewtn.com/library/PROLENC/ENCYC067.HTM

35 George Grant, Killer Angel: A Biography of Margaret Sanger, 1995, 2000, 2010

36 Chuck Donovan and Nora Sullivan, Margaret Sanger's War on Compassion 12/21/2011 http://www.nationalreview.com/articles/286203/margaret-sanger-and-war-compassion-chuck-donovan

37 http://www.catholiceducation.org/articles/population/pc0027.html

38 plannedparenthood.org, 3/7/11

39 Peter Heck, 78 : How Christians Can Save America, page 44

CHAPTER 5

PRESIDENT OBAMA'S FAITH & FRUIT: ACTIONS SPEAK LOUDER THAN WORDS

*For you were formerly darkness, but now you are Light in the
Lord; walk as children of Light; ...Do not participate in the
unfruitful deeds of darkness, but instead even expose them.*
(Ephesians 5:8, 11)

"In selecting men for office, let principle be your guide.
Regard not the particular sect or denomination of the candidate – look to his character." – **Noah Webster, 1789**

When asked about President Obama's faith during an interview in
February 2012, Franklin Graham gave an opinion and was ganged up
on. He answered honestly, but evidently it was not the correct answer.
All Graham said was that when the president proclaims faith in Jesus
and his actions don't match his words, it is not authentic Christian
faith. Most of us know the powers that be at MSNBC wanted to set Mr.
Graham up so they could attack what he stands for – biblical Christianity. I get it, that's part of the game in the elite media. We need to be
prepared when those who are hostile to Christianity frame the debate.

The question should *not* be "is someone a Christian or not" because
we can't know a person's heart. The question in this case should be "What
kind of Christian is President Obama?" We'll analyze this interview
with Franklin Graham in the lions' den on MSNBC in a few moments.
It is so fascinating I highly recommend you look it up on YouTube. We

can only measure a person's faith by what the Bible teaches. Compare and contrast.

Every one of us is under the same scrutiny because we worship a holy God. If we say we are a Christian, do our lives reflect the teachings of Jesus Christ and the Word of God? In the chapter about truth, we established the fact that a person's faith and worldview affects *every* decision he or she makes. It is ludicrous to ignore the religious background of the President of the United States, the most powerful public office in our country. The problem is most Americans ignored Barack Obama's history before he was elected president.

When Solomon took over the throne of his father, King David, he knew what a great responsibility it was to lead all the people. God told Solomon to ask Him for whatever he wanted (2 Chron. 1:10). Solomon could have had anything, but he asked for wisdom and knowledge so he could rule over the people wisely. He didn't ask for power, social justice or wealth redistribution, and not universal healthcare, not more funding for abortion, not environmental investments, not amnesty for illegal immigrants, and not gay rights – he wanted wisdom to govern diligently.

In this chapter, we will simply look closely at what the president has said and what he has done. We will also look at what shaped his worldview and what policies he has promoted and enacted as elected leader of *all* American people. If we listen to what President Obama says regarding Christianity and then observe what he does, it can be confusing; things don't add up. The Bible is not ambiguous. However, I agree with what a blogger on a Christian site wrote: "It's not my place to judge Obama's faith. I can see the fruit he bears, and I don't like what I see. I need to pray for him more."

IN HIS OWN WORDS

When running for U.S. Senate in Illinois in 2004, Barack Obama was interviewed by *Chicago Sun-Times* columnist Cathleen Falsani. It was on Saturday, March 27 at 3:30 p.m. inside of Café Baci on Michigan Avenue. To save time, we'll primarily include his responses to her questions:

OBAMA: "I lived in Indonesia, the largest Muslim country in the world, between the ages of six and ten. My father was from Kenya, and although he was probably most accurately labeled an agnostic, his father was Muslim...I'm rooted in the Christian tradition. I believe that *there are many paths to the same place*, and that is a belief that there is a higher power, a belief that we are connected as a people....

"So, my mother, who I think had as much influence on my values as anybody, was not someone who wore her religion on her sleeve. We'd go to church for Easter. She wasn't a church lady... The way I came to Chicago in 1985 was that I was interested in community organizing, and I was inspired by the Civil Rights movement... One of the churches that I became involved in was Trinity United Church of Christ. And the pastor there, Jeremiah Wright, became a good friend. So I joined that church and committed myself to Christ in that church.

"I'm a big believer in tolerance. I think that religion at its best comes with a big dose of doubt...They [people] get confused sometimes, they watch Fox News or listen to talk radio. That's dangerous sometimes. But generally, Americans are tolerant, and I think recognize that faith is a personal thing...."

FALSANI: "Who's Jesus to you?"

OBAMA: "Jesus is an historical figure *for me*, and He's also a bridge between God and man, in the Christian faith....

"I think it's perfectly consistent to say that I want my government to be operating for all faiths and all peoples, including atheists and agnostics.... I find it hard to believe that my God would consign four-fifths of the world to hell."

FALSANI: "Do you believe in heaven?"

OBAMA: "What I believe in is that if I live my life as well as I can, that I will be rewarded. I don't presume to have knowledge of what happens after I die...."

FALSANI: "What is sin?"

OBAMA: "Being out of alignment with *my* values." [1]

Let me first point out that neither of Barack Obama's parents believed in Jesus Christ, but somehow Obama ended up following the Christian "tradition." What does that mean? He also said "there are many paths to the same place," and that there is a "higher power." The Bible clearly establishes there is one narrow path to eternal life through faith in Christ, and there is no power or name is higher than Jesus Christ. Contrary also to popular tepid teachings, there are not many pathways (plural) to heaven.

Jesus was not vague when in **John 14:6,** He said He alone is *the way, the truth, and the life.* The Apostle Paul wrote *there is no other name under heaven given to men by which we must be saved* (**Acts 4:12**). Barack Obama also suggested people who watch Fox News are confused, intolerant, and that it was even "dangerous."

Barack Obama said Jesus was an "historical figure." (Not Savior, Messiah or the Son of God.) As far as heaven and hell, the Bible is very clear, and sadly, some Christians today believe the same thing as Barack Obama. "How can we really know?" they seem to ask. Obama emphasized living his life the best he can (works) to maybe get rewarded, and he seemed to think our government was inefficient for atheists and agnostics. This tells me he does not respect our Christian roots. Finally, to Obama, sin means being out of alignment with his own values – not the values of Jesus Christ or the Word of God.

FRANKLIN GRAHAM & FOUR CONFUSED LIBERALS

Let's go back to the interview mentioned earlier. This was one of the most fascinating exchanges I've seen in a long time. The Franklin Graham interview mentioned earlier had the elite media grinning and spinning. They asked Graham on MSNBC's *Morning Joe*, "Do you believe President Obama is a Christian?" The *first* thing Franklin Graham said was "I think you have to ask President Obama." The host fired back "So you don't take him at his word when he says he's a Christian?" Graham calmly responded that since Obama has said he's a Christian "I just have to assume that he is. But the question is 'what is a Christian?'" This is typically the best part of any Franklin Graham interview as he shares the gospel message.[2]

After hearing the entire gospel presentation which followed Graham's responses, one of the co-hosts still came back with, "So by *your* definition, he's not a Christian?" And it went back and forth for another round when another host said, "I just don't get it, Reverend, I mean I don't want to harp on this but...." The interview was almost as entertaining as it was infuriating. The next subject was Obama's upbringing, and Graham was asked if he thought Obama was a Muslim. Here is his patient, well-informed response:

> "Under Islamic law, under Shariah law, Islam sees him as a son of Islam, because his father was a Muslim, his grandfather was a Muslim, his great-grandfather was a Muslim. So under Islamic law, the Muslim world sees President Obama as a Muslim, as a son of Islam. That's just the way it works.

> "Now those Christian minorities throughout the entire Arab world are under attack. A *Newsweek* magazine cover story last week was about the massacre of Christians in the Islamic world. From Europe all the way through the Middle East to Africa into East Asia, Muslims are killing Christians. The president can come out and make a statement demanding that if these countries do not protect their minorities, no more foreign aid from the United States.... The society in these Islamic countries is *not* protecting the Christians anymore.

> "These Christians are having their churches burned....Women are being raped. They're being murdered. Because under Shariah law Muslims can take a Christian's property, take a Christian's life, can take his daughter. And this is what is happening. The governments are not able to protect the minorities in the society. And they're unwilling to protect them.

> "If a government is not going to protect the minorities, we should not give them one dollar of U.S. aid ... And he's got the power of the White House," Graham complained. "He could be speaking

to these countries right now, demanding that they protect the Christians in those countries. He's been quiet about it.

"We [Samaritan's Purse] have an aid station in Southern Sudan. The Sudanese dropped bombs on it right before Christmas. We have a Bible school. Just two weeks ago the Sudanese air force dropped eight bombs on that Bible school. Why doesn't the president come out and try to bring peace to the Sudan?"

Amazingly, none of the panelists interrupted or disagreed! However, they did go right back to their agenda. One of the panelists accused Graham of a double standard for saying earlier that he considered Rick Santorum a Christian because he and Santorum share many of the same values. Franklin Graham responded, "You have to look at what a person does with his life. Anybody can *say* they're a Christian." The woman on the panel kept giving Graham condescending glances and another co-host smugly implied Graham was being judgmental by assessing other people's faith. The funny thing is – that's why they had him on the show! Graham responded to the criticism with:

> "You guys go through the newspapers every day. You're checking off articles that are written. I look at a person's political interests, but more importantly I look at their spiritual interests. I'm not judging them. But you have to go by what a person says and how they live their life."[3]

So then, you will know them by their fruits (**Matthew 7:20**).

In 2008, American citizens, Christians included, refused to judge Barack Obama by his own words, his stance on abortion, gay marriage, and by his questionable Chicago history and radical activism. I don't dislike the man, but I'd much rather have someone else in the White House. I do pray for his heart to be softened and for him to be humbled, but I also pray for him to be saved if he isn't already. Let's talk policy.

On January 22, 2012, President Obama put in place a new mandate forcing religious employers to pay for birth control and drugs that may cause abortions. Then after the backlash, his administration revised the birth control mandate to require insurance companies to make this provision. Obama has also mandated and then provided for additional embryonic stem cell research with taxpayer funds. During his term as president, he has continued to nominate pro-abortion activists to federal appeals court positions and has made pro-abortion judicial picks.

His administration is full of leftist, pro-abortion advocates whose past records should be alarming to Christians. President Obama has also cut funding for abstinence education. Conversely, he announced $50 million in funding for the UNFPA, the UN population agency that has been criticized for promoting abortion and working closely with Chinese population control officials who use forced abortions and involuntary sterilizations! The Obama administration also shut out pro-life groups from attending a White House-sponsored health care summit, but Planned Parenthood and other pro-abortion groups were invited.[4]

In October 2009, President Obama gave the keynote address at the annual Human Rights Campaign dinner in Washington, D.C. Among those joining the president were Lady Gaga, Tipper Gore, and the cast of Fox comedy *Glee*. The Human Rights Campaign is dedicated to promoting homosexual issues education and changing legislation to favor gay rights. President Obama began by praising the gay community for making strides in equal rights and he pledged to deliver on major campaign promises.

He said heterosexuals still "hold fast to outworn arguments and old attitudes" and that we "deny you [gays] the rights most Americans take for granted." In his speech, the president boldly proclaimed what no other president in American history had articulated regarding the institution of traditional marriage. Here are some direct quotes from the transcript of President Obama's 25-minute speech:[5]

> "I want to thank the Human Rights Campaign for inviting me to speak and for the work you do every day in pursuit of equality on behalf of the millions of people in this country who work hard in their jobs and care deeply about their families – and who are gay, lesbian, bisexual, or transgender." (Applause) …

> "Now, I've said this before, I'll repeat it again – it's not for me to tell you to be patient, any more than it was for others to counsel patience to African Americans petitioning for equal rights half a century ago." (Applause)

* [*dropping a Civil Rights comparison, slavery...REALLY?!* df]

"My expectation is that when you look back on these years, you will see a time in which we put a stop to discrimination against gays and lesbians – whether in the office or on the battlefield. (Applause) ...I am committed to these goals. And my administration will continue fighting to achieve them....

"I support ensuring that committed gay couples have the same rights and responsibilities afforded to any married couple in this country. (Applause) ...I've required all agencies in the federal government to extend as many federal benefits as possible to LGBT families as the current law allows.

"And I've called on Congress to repeal the so-called Defense of Marriage Act and to pass the Domestic Partners Benefits and Obligations Act. (Applause) And we must all stand together against divisive and deceptive efforts to feed people's lingering fears for political and ideological gain.

"...Day by day, law by law, changing mind by mind, that is the promise we are fulfilling."

It appears there are times when President Obama interprets Scripture as he sees fit, and he ignores the Bible when it doesn't conform to his view. This president has been a master at double speak. When he criticizes the free markets and complains that capitalism is unfair, yet at the same time grants waivers and bailouts to favored organizations that support his Party, he's not fooling us anymore. Ultimately, what he does and says is between him and God, but the evidence compiled in this chapter is a fraction of what is available concerning President Obama's faith.

ALL THE PRESIDENT'S FRUIT

Here are some examples of President Obama's policies that reflect his and his administration's views of Christianity – or lack thereof:

1. Speaking to a friendly audience of campaign donors in April 2008 in San Francisco, Barrack Obama talked about

average Americans saying, "And it's not surprising then that they get bitter, they cling to guns or religion or antipathy to people who aren't like them or anti-immigrant sentiment or anti-trade sentiment as a way to explain their frustrations."[6]

2. Obama ends National Prayer Day services at White House: President Truman signed the first National Prayer Day proclamation; President Reagan made it permanent. For years, it was a staple on the WH calendar – but not in May 2009, President Obama's first year in office.[7]

3. President Obama is the *first* president in America's history to mention non-believers in an inaugural address when he said, "We are a nation of Christians and Muslims, Jews and Hindus and non-believers."[8]

4. Obama nominated three pro-abortion US ambassadors to the Vatican; The Vatican vetoed all three amid a growing dispute between the White House and the Roman Catholic Church over the new administration's support for abortion rights.[9]

5. President Obama *continues* to omit 'Creator' From Declaration of Independence: During a speech in Rockville, Maryland on October 18, 2010, he once again *omitted* the mention of man's Creator as the source of his unalienable rights. This isn't the first time.[10]

6. President Obama misquotes the National Motto, saying it is "E pluribus Unum" rather than "In God We Trust" as established by federal law. [November 10, 2010]

7. Although he filled posts in the State Department, *for more than two years* Obama did not fill the post of religious freedom ambassador, an official who works against religious persecution across the world; he filled it only after heavy pressure from the public and from Congress.[11]

8. The Department of Veterans Affairs was consistently censoring Veteran's prayers by banning them from saying the words "God" and "Jesus" during funeral services at Houston National Cemetery.[12]

9. The Obama administration released its new health care rules in 2011 that override religious conscience protections for medical workers in the areas of abortion and contraception. Forcing private insurance plans to pay for morally controversial offerings such as contraception, sterilization, and abortifacients raises obvious questions regarding freedom of conscience.[13]

10. Unlike previous presidents, Obama avoided any religious references in his Thanksgiving speech. "The president said his family was 'reflecting on how truly lucky we are.'"[14]

11. Obama lifts restrictions on U.S. government funding for groups that provide abortion services or counseling abroad, forcing taxpayers to fund pro-abortion groups that either promote or perform abortions in other nations. He signed the order just three days into his presidency. [Jan. 20, 2009][15]

12. The Obama administration requires rewriting of government documents and a change in administration vocabulary to remove terms deemed offensive to Muslims including jihad, jihadists, terrorists, radical Islamic, etc. [April 7, 2010][16]

13. President Obama directs the Justice Department to stop defending the federal Defense of Marriage Act. 2/23/11[17]

14. The Obama administration refuses to investigate videos showing Planned Parenthood helping alleged sex traffickers get abortions for victimized underage girls.[18]

15. Obama allows homosexuals to serve openly in the military, reversing a policy originally instituted by George Washington in 1778.[19]

16. While every White House traditionally issues hundreds of official proclamations and statements on numerous occasions, this White House avoids traditional biblical holidays and events, but regularly recognizes major Muslim holidays, as evidenced by its 2010 statements on Ramadan, Eid-ul-Fitr, Hajj, and Eid-ul-Adha.[20]

17. Obama's Muslim advisers block Middle Eastern Christians' access to the White House.

18. The Obama administration makes apologies for Korans being burned by the U. S. military, but when Bibles were burned by the military, numerous reasons were offered why it was the right thing to do.[21]

*For an exhaustive list, see David Barton's WallBuilders "The Most Biblically-Hostile U.S. President."[22]

One of the interviews I remember from 2008 – next to elitist Charlie Gibson's condescending "peering over his glasses" interrogation of Sarah Palin – was George Stephanopoulos's interview with Barack Obama. Rarely do you see a friendly correction and interruption by a media personality. Talking about the verbal attacks going back and forth between campaigns:

Obama: "The McCain campaign said 'look, these liberal blogs that support Obama are out there attacking Governor Palin. Let's not play games...you're absolutely right that John McCain has not talked about my Muslim faith, and you're absolutely right that—"

[Stephanopoulos interrupts]

Stephanopoulos: "Christian faith."

Obama: "...my Christian faith and, uh, what I'm saying is that he hasn't suggested—"

[Stephanopoulos interrupts again]

Stephanopoulos: "...that there are connections."

Obama: "...that I'm a Muslim."[23]

There's nothing like a little coaching from the cheering section to get the proper message out.

NO DIFFERENCE BETWEEN WRIGHT AND WRONG

I like the word "connections." It's too bad Stephanopoulos and the liberal media completely avoid it where Obama is concerned. If you make a decision to attend a church and become a member, can we assume you believe in their doctrines and agree with the theology of that church? If you were going to the same church for over twenty years, if the pastor performed your wedding and you considered him a good friend, would his teachings become part of your worldview? In 2008, the media did their best to avoid mentioning Jeremiah Wright, Barack Obama's mentor. The few times their relationship was brought up the media completely downplayed it. Why?

His church in Chicago, Trinity United Church, believes and teaches Black Liberation Theology – a theology rooted in Marxism. Obama was given a pass in 2008 when he said the anti-American, racist, socialist views of his pastor were not his views. Yet in his book, Obama refers to his Caucasian grandmother as "a typical white person." During his first presidential campaign, he was unwilling to wear an American flag lapel pin. Michelle Obama said she was never proud of her country until her hubby won the Democratic nomination for president.

Here is one of Jeremiah Wright's more infamous sermon quotes from 2003:

> "The government gives them the drugs, builds bigger prisons, passes a three-strike law and then wants us to sing *God Bless America*. No, no, no, God damn America! That's in the Bible – for killing innocent people ... God damn America for treating our citizens as less than human. God damn America for as long as she acts like she is God and she is supreme."[24]

What did candidate Obama say when he was asked about the sermon? He wasn't there, of course. Was this a one-time outburst by Wright? An ABC News review of dozens of Rev. Wright's sermons, offered for sale by the church, found repeated denunciations of the United States and the treatment of black Americans. One member of the congregation told ABC, "I wouldn't call it radical. I call it being black in America."

Day Gardner, president of the National Black Pro-Life Union commented on Wright:

> "There are many black people who were offended by his anti-American slurs, because we, as black people have a vested interest in this great country... I'm tired of being made to feel – by our own people sometimes, such as Rev. Wright – that we are disconnected from what we are. I am an American."

The 2008 Obama campaign tried to downplay the friendship between Wright and Obama. Rev. Wright baptized their daughters and is credited by Obama for the title of his book, *The Audacity of Hope*. In the interview cited earlier, Obama was asked where he went for guidance.

> "Well, my pastor [Jeremiah Wright] is certainly someone who I have an enormous amount of respect for...Father Michael Pfleger [radical liberal priest] is a dear friend, and somebody I interact with closely."

During the period of Obama's attendance at Wright's Trinity United Church, the Chicago church was *openly* allied with Louis Farrakhan (Nation of Islam leader, renowned for his hatred of Whites and Jews). Wright gave Farrakhan his 2007 Empowerment Award! Farrakhan delivered multiple guest lectures at the church and sources confirm Wright and Farrakhan have known each other for over twenty-four years. Farrakhan has called the real evil in America "the idea that undergirds the setup of the Western world, and that idea is called white supremacy." Al Sharpton, Jeremiah Wright, and Barrack Obama each helped Farrakhan organize his Million Man March event. Do these "connections" matter?

> "God will destroy America by the hands of the Muslims. ... God will not give Japan or Europe the honor of bringing down

the United States; this is an honor God will bestow upon Muslims." – **Louis Farrakhan, 1996**

"Nothing is more powerful than the black church experience."
– **Barrack Obama, 2004**

"Fact number one: We've got more black men in prison than there are in college. ... Fact number two: Racism is how this country was founded and how this country is still run...Barack knows what it means living in a country and a culture that is controlled by rich, white people. Hillary would never know that." – **Jeremiah Wright, 2007**

BLACK LIBERATION THEOLOGY

Twenty years in the same church means nothing according to the progressive Democratic media. Let's start with defining *Liberation* Theology: it is a political movement and Christian theology which interprets the teachings of Jesus Christ in terms of liberation from unjust economic, political, or social conditions. Liberation theology teaches the New Testament gospels can be understood only as calls for social activism, class struggle, and revolution aimed at overturning the existing capitalist order and installing, in its place, a socialist utopia where today's poor will unseat their "oppressors."

The movement began in Latin America in the 1950's – 60's and teaches that God is the liberator of those oppressed by ruling classes. It came to America through theology professor James Cone, who was influenced by Malcolm X and the Black Power movement. So, where President Obama and Wright are concerned, Black Liberation Theology teaches all Scripture must be interpreted through the black experience.

The chief architect of black liberation theology, James Cone was Professor of Systematic Theology at the Union Theological Seminary in New York City and author of several books including *Black Theology and Black Power*. Cone views America as a racist nation with no hope of redemption. One of the tasks of this movement, according to Cone, is to analyze the nature of the gospel in light of the experience of blacks victimized by white oppressors. In *A Black Theology of Liberation,* Cone stated:

> "What we need is the divine love as expressed in Black Power, which is the power of Black people to destroy their oppressors here and now by any means at their disposal. Unless God is participating in this holy activity, we must reject His love."

Implying that America was founded for white people, Cone calls for "the destruction of whiteness, which is the source of human misery in the world." He advocates the use of Marxism as a tool of social analysis to help Christians to see "how things really are."[25]

> "Cone believed that Jesus was black and that everyone must 'become black' to be saved ... When you join the side of the oppressed, you become black," said Bishop Van B. Gayton of the International Community of Christian Churches as he pointed out the ideology's shortcomings. "Cone denies the fact that God is for all people."

The Marxist roots of this theology are evident, and obviously, not all black churches support this theology. Black religious leaders in Wright's generation are burdened by Cone's teachings which helped lay a foundation that enables many to embrace Marxism. There is also an emphasis on collective salvation when the black "community" overcomes oppression. Sadly, this theology encourages a victim mentality and government dependency.

Trinity Church's promotion of its 12-point Black Value System asks members to measure the worth of all activity in terms of "positive contributions to the general welfare of the Black Community and the Advancement of Black People toward freedom," while pledging adherence to the Black Worth Ethic and "Allegiance to All Black Leadership Who Espouse and Embrace the Black Value System."[26] Those who adhere to biblical Christianity honor, revere, and give allegiance to the Lord Jesus Christ alone. The notion of "blackness" is not merely a reference to skin color, but rather is a symbol of oppression. When Jeremiah Wright says, "Jesus was a poor black man," it is because he lived in oppression at the hands of "rich white people."

"The history of all hitherto existing society is the history of class struggles." – **Karl Marx**

American Thinker's Kyle-Anne Shiver visited Obama's church in early 2008. She described Jeremiah Wright's sermon as fiery, but not overly controversial, and seemed basically to be a "call for all good congregants to support Barack Obama for President." Shiver explained she had spent months trying to fathom how "Marxist philosophy wound up emblazoned with a cross and a pulpit" while pretending to rely on the authority of the Bible. She came away with far more questions than answers.

What was revealing to Shiver was her visit to the church bookstore following the service. The books were much more political than religious in nature including numerous books prominently displayed by Wright's mentor, James H. Cone. Shiver's warnings are clearly pointed:

"Now that I have read a number of the books that presumably Wright's congregants (including Barack Obama) have also read, I can only conclude that the thing tying these volumes together is not Christianity, nor any real religion, but the political philosophy of Karl Marx."

Books referring to the oppressor and oppressed, freeman and slave, class struggles, and societal revolutions may be fine for a library or history collection, but these and many others were in the Chicago church's store. These aren't ideas from the *Holy Bible*, but the *Communist Manifesto*. The danger of Cone and Wright's teachings is that their claim to a new theology unites the black power of Muslims and Malcolm X with the Christianity of Martin Luther King Jr.

Just the fact Cone is a hero of today's black power preachers should be telling enough. This is the emphasis of the teachings from Obama's church. Kyle-Anne Shiver added:

"Understanding that black liberation theology is Marxism dressed up to look like Christianity helps explain why there is no conflict between Cone's 'Christianity' and Farrakhan's 'Nation of Islam.' They are two prophets in the same philosophical (Marxist) pod, merely using different religions as backdrops for their black-power aims."[27]

On June 8, 2006, Barack Obama was the keynote speaker at Jim Wallis' Call to Renewal conference, "Building a Covenant for a New America." Following his address, in an interview by the United Church News, he cited "the teachings of the UCC (United Church of Christ) as foundation stones for his political work."

> "Religious thinkers and activists like my friend Jim Wallis and Tony Campolo are lifting up the Biblical injunction to help the poor as a means of mobilizing Christians against budget cuts to social programs and growing inequality."

> "Moreover, given the increasing diversity of America's population, the dangers of sectarianism have never been greater. **Whatever we once were, we are no longer just a Christian nation; we are also a Jewish nation, a Muslim nation, a Buddhist nation, a Hindu nation, and a nation of nonbelievers.**"[28]

> "And even if we did have only Christians within our borders, whose Christianity would we teach in the schools, James Dobson's or Al Sharpton's?"[29]

Many of us tried sharing our concerns about Barack Obama before the 2008 election. In his May 2008 article "The Marxist Roots of Black Liberation Theology," author Anthony Bradley warned about then Senator Obama, asking if Black Liberation Theology is helping unite the country. He concluded "preaching to a congregation of middle class blacks about their victim identity" divides people and fosters a distorted view of reality. Bradley wrote that Wright and Obama's theology has stirred up resentment and separatism:

> "'Economic parity' and 'distribution' language implies things like government-coerced wealth redistribution, perpetual minimum wage increases, government subsidized health care for all.…

> "Black Liberation Theology, originally intended to help the black community, may have actually hurt many blacks by promoting racial tension.… As the failed 'War on Poverty' has exposed, the best way to keep the blacks enslaved to government as 'daddy'

is to … seduce blacks into thinking that upward mobility is someone else's responsibility."[30]

Hundreds of conservative authors, bloggers, and columnists wrote about these issues prior to the 2008 elections. We must learn from recent history, even if it hurts. American citizens were warned (just not by the media) time and time again that if elected, Obama would push the most leftist, radical policies in American history. But millions voted for charisma and eloquence rather than character and experience, and many citizens didn't pay attention to the issues.

Aside from his controversial church, it surprised me Americans didn't have reservations about Obama's stance on key biblical issues. In addition to what we've already covered, another goal of his administration has been to expand "gay adoption," which would create intentionally motherless and fatherless homes. When asked whether being "gay" was a choice, he responded, "I don't think it's a choice. I think that people are born with a certain makeup."[31]

We must be more active in electing godly leaders. Christian Coalition's Chuck Colson implied that no matter who runs the country, laws will be passed that promote someone's morals and values. He wrote:

> "The popular notion that 'you can't legislate morality' is a myth. Morality is legislated every day from the vantage point of one value system being chosen over another. The question is not whether we will legislate morality, but whose morality gets legislated. Laws establish, from the view of the state, the rightness or wrongness of human behavior."

THE VERDICT

Let's not be afraid to say it: President Obama may believe in parts of the Bible, but his policies reveal a different view of Jesus and Christianity than many of us understand. By his own admission, he does not believe the Word of God is inerrant and God-breathed. Barack Obama seems to have built his own brand of faith on a foundation of liberalism and post-modernism. He confuses people by declaring he is a Christian, and as Franklin Graham clearly stated, his actions and policies do not line up with biblical principles.

He has continually shown he does not support Christianity's most essential truths and traditional morality. Is this an accurate observation? Some don't agree. These are dark days.

This is the verdict: Light has come into the world, but men loved darkness instead of light because their deeds were evil (**John 3:19** NIV).

President Obama needs the forgiveness of Jesus Christ just as you and I do, and if he is a backslidden Christian, he needs to return to the Lord and humbly repent. If, however, he is sincerely living out a different gospel than what the Bible teaches, then someone must reach him with the truth. He's the President of the United States, but he is just an imperfect man of flesh and blood. Though he is the product of his past, his associations, and his environment, no one is without hope.

It's been said that Americans vote with their wallets, that the economy, jobs, and taxes trump all other issues in an election. Too many people continue pulling the voting booth lever for anti-life, progressive Democrats. Abortion is the measure for judging a society's righteousness. What does it say of a people, regardless of the economy, when we allow more than one million unborn babies to be murdered every year in the name of choice?

Republicans, Independents, Libertarians, and some conservative Democrats got out the vote in 2010 that created an avalanche in Washington, D.C. (a "Shellacking" as President Obama called it) I believe that was a first step in the right direction. Will common sense conservatism score a victory again in 2012? Hopefully, politicians remember that outcome from those midterm elections where Republicans picked up 680 seats around the country. Way to go, Tea Party! According to recent approval ratings for the Obama administration it looks like more Americans are fed up. One election means nothing if everyday believers and concerned citizens like you and me don't wake up and take our own walks with Christ more seriously.

If Mitt Romney gets elected president, though that would be a step in the right direction, there is still plenty of corruption in both parties, and politics is not the 'be all – end all.' It is when people turn back to

God and put their trust in Jesus Christ, when lukewarm believers recommit to Him, when we impact the political process, and when Christians have greater influence in our culture for godliness, we all win. God will have His way in the end. He governs over dictators, kings and presidents. But until Christ returns, we are called to hold candidates up to the highest of standards. They must be scrutinized with the Truth and the light of Scripture. As long as we still have a free country, America deserves nothing less.

> "The hope of a Christian is inseparable from his faith. Whoever believes in the Divine inspiration of the Holy Scriptures must hope that the religion of Jesus shall prevail throughout the earth. Never since the foundation of the world have the prospects of mankind been more encouraging to that hope than they appear to be at the present time. And may the associated distribution of the Bible proceed and prosper till the Lord shall have made *Bare His holy arm in the eyes of all the nations, and all the ends of the earth shall see the salvation of our God.*" (Isaiah 52:10)
> – **President John Quincy Adams** (1767-1848)

How does a president with such an anti-Christian administration continue to get away with promoting sin, expanding the size and power of government, signing executive orders, appointing unaccountable czars, and enacting policies that most Americans disagree with? He is protected by the media.

ENDNOTES

1   Barrack Obama, Chicago Sun Times 3/27/2004 Interview with Cathleen Falsani http://blog.christianitytoday.com/ctpolitics/2008/11/obamas_fascinat.html

2   http://www.youtube.com/watch?v=-7LAlLtZauQ Franklin Graham on MSNBC 2/21/2012

3   http://blogs.wsj.com/washwire/2012/02/21/rev-franklin-graham-questions-obamas-romneys-christian-faith/

4   A Pro Life Compilation; Updated 2012, http://www.lifenews.com/2010/11/07/obamaabortionrecord/

5   President Obama speech transcript, HRC, 10/10/2009 http://blogs.suntimes.com/sweet/2009/10/obama_human_rights_campaign_sp.html

6   http://blog.christianitytoday.com/ctliveblog/archives/2008/04/obama_they_clin.html

7   Los Angeles Times, http://latimesblogs.latimes.com/washington/2009/05/obama-cancels-national-prayer-day-service.html

8 President Barack Obama's Inaugural Address, 1/20/2009, http://www.white-house.gov/blog/inaugural-address/

9 Chris McGreal, "Vatican vetoes Barack Obama's nominees for U.S. Ambassador," The Guardian, April 14, 2009.

10 Meredith Jessup, "Obama Continues to Omit 'Creator' From Declaration of Independence," The Blaze, October 19, 2010

11 Thomas F. Farr, "Undefender of the Faith," Foreign Policy, April 5, 2012

12 "Houston Veterans Claim Censorship of Prayers, Including Ban of 'God' and 'Jesus'," Fox News, June 29, 2011

13 Chuck Donovan, "HHS's New Health Guidelines Trample on Conscience," Heritage Foundation, August 2, 2011

14 Joel Siegel, "Obama Omits God From Thanksgiving Speech, Riles Critics," ABC News, November 25, 2011

15 Jeff Mason and Deborah Charles, "Obama lifts restrictions on abortion funding," Reuters, January 23, 2009.

16 'Islamic Radicalism' Nixed From Obama Document," CBSNews, April 7, 2010

17 Brian Montopoli, "Obama administration will no longer defend DOMA," CBSNews, February 23, 2011.

18 Steven Ertelt, "Obama Admin Ignores Planned Parenthood Sex Trafficking Videos," LifeNews, March 2, 2011

19 George Washington, The Writings of George Washington, John C. Fitzpatrick, editor (Washington: U. S. Government Printing Office, 1934), Vol. XI, pp. 83-84, from General Orders at Valley Forge on March 14, 1778.

20 "WH Fails to Release Easter Proclamation," Fox Nation, April 25, 2011

21 Military burns unsolicited Bibles sent to Afghanistan," CNN, May 22, 2009.

22 David Barton, 2/29/2012, America's Most Biblically-Hostile U. S. President; http://www.wallbuilders.com/LIBissuesArticles.asp?id=106938#FN51

23 George Stephanopoulos, Obama, 2008 interview, http://www.youtube.com/watch?v=SVn59TC2QqM

24 Brian Ross, Obama's Pastor: God Damn America; 3/13/2008; http://abcnews.go.com/Blotter/DemocraticDebate/story?id=4443788&page=1#.T11t2PWCeZR

25 http://www.discoverthenetworks.org/viewSubCategory.asp?id=796

26 http://www.renewamerica.com/article/080505

27 Kylie-Anne Shiver, American Thinker, Obama, Black Liberation Theology, and Karl Marx 5/28/2008; http://www.americanthinker.com/2008/05/obama_black_liberation_theolog.html

28 CBN News http://www.cbn.com/CBNnews/204016.aspx

29 Barrack Obama, Call to Renewal speech, 6/08/2006 http://blogs.suntimes.com/sweet/2006/06/obama_on_faith_and_politics_an.html

30 *Anthony B. Bradley, Action Institute;* http://www.acton.org/pub/commentary/2008/04/02/marxist-roots-black-liberation-theology

31 Time.com, Obama, People Are Born Gay, 2012, http://newsfeed.time.com/2010/10/15/obama-people-are-born-gay-must-fight-back-against-cyberbullying/

CHAPTER 6

TRUTH HAS LEFT THE MEDIA

ETHICS IN JOURNALISM

"I want to do everything I can to make this new
[Obama] presidency work." – **Chris Mathews**,
MSNBC host – November 6, 2008

A few years ago, the Pew Research Center found 92% of Americans now use multiple platforms to get their daily news. With failing newspapers and increased technology, more and more people are using a wider variety of news sources. Distrust of those in the media is at an all-time high, and confidence in media is at all-time lows, but why? Are media elites just out of touch with the average American? Maybe they've been groomed in a liberal bubble of sorts. Maybe they are submitting to secular-progressive bosses. One thing is certain; the media today has an anti-Christian agenda as well.

It obviously wasn't always like this in America. Early in this nation's history, our founders realized the need for government accountability, and they had the help of the print media. Before the Freedom of the Press clause in the First Amendment, it was against the law to print anything considered by the government to be seditious libel even if it was true. It now guarantees people can publish any lawful material without fear of punishment, even if that material is critical of the government.

Our founders ensured the press was free to inform American citizens, protect them from tyranny, and to help keep government in check. There was also a time, before the 1960's, when the media as a whole cared about truth, ethics, integrity, and fairness in their news product. Ironically, there was more accountability two hundred years ago when only a handful of newspapers existed. Today, with thousands of print, radio, and TV outlets plus electronic media, there is far less government accountability and more corruption. How do we explain this?

MY WAKE-UP CALL

People tend to believe half-truths or lies, if they are repeated often enough. What happened in 2008 should be taught in journalism classes and should go down as the final nail in the coffin of media objectivity. The character assassination, personal attacks, and brutal political assault on former Alaska Governor Sarah Palin should never have been allowed to happen. I've never seen so much hatred toward one person trumpeted by the media. It should be something fair-minded Americans won't soon forget.

This was why I began writing and blogging more frequently. I made a vow right then that I would do whatever I could to stand for truth, share the real news, and expose the glaring double standards in the media. What we see today is certainly not journalism. Even as I edit this chapter, the tragic shooting rampage in Aurora, Colorado at the premiere of *The Dark Night Rises* just took place, and ABC News reported the killer was a conservative Tea Party member. They had the wrong guy! It was a mistake; they issued an apology and retraction later in the day, but they put another person's life in danger. How irresponsible! This is the new normal.

The mainstream media has, for decades now, been infiltrated by elites, liberals, progressives, and socialists. They are typically in their thirties and forties, were indoctrinated at liberal universities, support the Democratic Party platform, support the Occupy Wall Street movement and pretty much despise or dismiss the Bible. Be assured today's media are part of the agenda to blot out God in America. They are supportive of Planned Parenthood, big government, the NEA, Islam, Hollywood, homosexuality, and the Christian "social justice" Left.

I discuss truth quite a bit in this book, and though we know the Bible is the ultimate truth, we should be no less concerned about truth in our country, culture, and media. They don't even try hiding their bias anymore. The fact that the Christian worldview is not popular in today's society shouldn't be surprising to us, but we are American citizens, and we deserve to know the facts and the truth about issues affecting America.

LISTEN, READ, WATCH

If you still watch the news on TV, it is now necessary to pay very close attention. Notice not only *what* is being said but *how* the news is being handled and packaged. There is often a subtle, and sometimes not so subtle, framed graphic or headline on the TV screen. This headline can often tell a story without even hearing the news anchor. The headline can also indicate a slant or bias depending on how it is worded. As the news people report a story, we can usually hear a tone in their voices as well. At other times an important story can be omitted altogether if it does not reflect the news editor's worldview. This "sin of omission" happens much too often.

We tend to forget news anchors, editors, and reporters are not unlike us; they have deep beliefs and established politics, opinions, and worldview. Unfortunately, they often report the news from their perspective. It is most obvious when the anchors talk faith or politics. When someone is reporting the news about a particular conservative or Republican in a newscast, they sometimes use unappealing photos while the anchor is reporting. There are many factors involved in putting a story together. It is all part of the delivery of the "product." We must understand some news outlets are definitely biased, and we need to listen, read, and watch!

Here is a quick example of local media bias from 2011 on a story about Governor Scott Walker; a pro-life, pro-family, Christian conservative whose father is a pastor. This particular Wisconsin political newscast caused me to email the General Manager and ask that his station report more fairly. In the story, the first thing the viewer sees is a video image close-up of a "Recall Walker" button on someone's jacket. The segment was then introduced by the news anchor: "The recall battle is on.... Angry voters gathered tonight in Appleton." The next video footage we see is liberal Democrat Steve Kagen, (voted out of office in 2010) teaching activists how to gather recall signatures. The introduction to the story was thirty seconds. (Cut to angry activist saying, "We gotta get him out.") The female reporter goes on to report, "Organizers are training a volunteer army in sessions like this one state-wide!"

The first time you heard from "the other side" was not until one minute and thirty-seven seconds into the segment. It was a Republican who said he was supporting Governor Scott Walker, which was part of a twenty second video clip concluding with a brief response by Scott Walker. (Cut to activist saying, "He's making war on the 99 percent.") The co-anchor then closed the story by saying, "In addition to the training sessions, the recall organizers say they are setting up offices around the state," and then named four cities activists could go to for protestor training. The entire news segment was two minutes and forty-six seconds (2:46). It was a laughable lack of balance. The station GM replied to me and told me he'd forward my concerns to the News Department.

In 2009, the Pew Research Center released a report on how the public evaluates the news media concluding: "Press Accuracy Rating Hits Two Decade Low." It showed "just 29% of Americans say that news organizations generally get the facts straight, while 63% say that news stories are often inaccurate."[1] Accuracy and bias have been concerns to people for years now, and more Americans have caught on.

Let's take a look at basic journalistic standards. Pew studies and analyzes news content and the performance of the press. They are non-partisan, non-ideological, and one of their goals is to help citizens develop a better understanding of what the press is delivering. Pew provides a lengthy description and explanation of each of the following principles, but these are quite straight forward. Contrast this list with today's media.[2]

PRINCIPLES OF JOURNALISM

- Journalism's first obligation is to tell the truth

- Its first loyalty is to citizens

- Its essence is a discipline of verification

- Its practitioners must maintain an independence from those they cover

- It must serve as an independent monitor of power

- It must provide a forum for public criticism and compromise

- It must strive to make the significant interesting and relevant

- It must keep the news comprehensive and proportional

- Its practitioners must be allowed to exercise their personal conscience

We already know most Americans don't believe the media reports fairly. Where does media loyalty lie? Do the elite media monitor the power of the United States government regardless of whether there is a Republican or Democrat in the White House? Do they report on social issues with no bias? Let's investigate.

REPORTING ON ABORTION

Recent polls have shown a majority of Americans – an average of about 70% – believe abortion is morally wrong. According to a 2011 Gallup poll, 61% say abortion should be illegal. Next to preaching the gospel, this is *the* most important Christian battle in the public arena. We rarely hear much about abortion in the news media.

According to Life News, while 72% of Americans feel abortion should have some restrictions placed on it by law,[3] only 3% of media people do. Translation: the media often believe or desire the exact opposite of the majority of citizens to whom they report the news.

In January 2012, pro-life groups from all over the country again held their annual March for Life and Walk for Life rallies on the anniversary of Roe vs. Wade week. At what other time in America do more than half a million people rally and protest for the same cause every single year? Why do you think the media would not want to give this important subject air time? The pro-life cause is not part of their narrative or their party's platform.

Naturally then, when the West Coast Walk for Life drew over 40,000 people *and* the Washington, D.C. March for Life rally grew to over 400,000, neither event received much media coverage. Even though the AP barely mentioned the massive rally, they did display a short story with [ready?]… a photo of three pro-abortion activists who were opposed to the event! *The New York Times* did not have *any* coverage of 400,000 concerned Americans in the nation's capital, but did however mention the fact Rand Paul (Republican) was arrested at the airport on his way to speak at the March for Life event.[4]

Rand Paul's arrest turned out to be bogus, but that didn't stop the *Times* from giving you "all the news that's fit to print." They simply refuse to be objective because the media elites think they know better, and no one holds them accountable. As a general rule of thumb, estimated numbers at pro-choice marches are doubled or multiplied while numbers at pro-life events are either cut in half, minimized or ignored. This is interesting given that the pro-life movement is much larger than the civil rights movement ever was, for example.

Writing about the Culture War in America, author and professor Peter Kreeft identified abortion and the media as two of the major battlefields in America. He points out that we can see anything on TV today except the truth about **abortion, the most frequent medical procedure in America:**

> "…it is extremely difficult to find the biological and medical facts about how an abortion is performed. …There is a total media censorship of the facts. …most women who abort … do not believe their 'fetus' was 'only tissue' or 'only potential life' (as they are told by Planned Parenthood), but believe they killed their baby."[5]

Celebrated as freedom of choice, abortion has been covered up by the mainstream media. What a disservice, especially to women who've gone through the grief, guilt, and the anguish of regret.

HOW MEDIA ELITES THINK

We cannot fully understand why the media reports the way they do unless we analyze their beliefs and standards. When we consider that Walter Cronkite, though he was a staunch Democrat, was possibly one of the last fair news anchors in America, it's quite clear how long this liberal media slide has gone practically unchecked.

The following data was selected from various surveys and polls regarding the ethics, views, beliefs, and habits of leading journalists in today's media, including (but not limited to) those representing the *New York Times, Washington Post, USA Today, Time, Newsweek, U.S. News & World Report, Wall Street Journal*, ABC, CBS, NBC, and PBS.

ABORTION: Nearly all of the media elite **(97%) agreed "it is a woman's right to decide whether or not to have an abortion,"** and five out of six (84%) agreed strongly. More than half of the respondents said *abortion should be legal under any and all circumstances*, including the late-term procedure commonly known as Partial Birth Abortion, where the abortionist punctures a living baby's skull and suctions out its brain before the infant's head passes from the birth canal.[6]

HOMOSEXUALITY: Three out of four journalists (73%) agreed "homosexuality is as acceptable a lifestyle as heterosexuality," and 49% agreed strongly.[7]

CHURCH: 57% said they attend worship services only "a few times a year," **7% attend regularly,** and 10% attend "almost every week."[8]

PRAYER: Only 33% of journalists supported prayer in public schools compared to 74% (almost three-fourths) of the general public who supported prayer.

ADULTERY: Only **15% of journalists regarded adultery as wrong** while more than half of respondents said adultery could be acceptable under certain circumstances.[9]

POLITICS: Just 6% of journalists would admit to being Republicans among the journalists working at *prominent* news organizations. Just 18% of *all* elite media surveyed said they were Republicans.[10]

CAPITALISM/CLASS WARFARE: 75% agreed the "government should work to reduce the income gap between rich and poor." Only 30% agreed "private enterprise is fair to workers."

REAGAN: In evaluating former President Reagan's performance in office, only 17% of elite journalists gave him an "excellent" or "good" mark.[11]

CONSERVATIVES: The percentage of self-identified conservatives in the elite media...**7%.**[12]

PROGRESSIVES: A total of 31% described themselves as "very liberal" or "liberal" with 49% maintaining they are "moderate."[13]

GAY MARRIAGE: Nearly three in five journalists (59%) favored laws allowing "two men or two women to marry each other." Among the general public, only 28% favored same-sex marriage.

[SEE MEDIA RESEARCH CENTER, MRC.ORG, 'MEDIA BIAS BASICS' – JOURNALISTS' VIEWS][14]

Let's jump into a few case studies: major news stories that barely or rarely made the news because they would have reflected negatively on the Obama administration.

SOLAR SCANDALS & GREEN TECHNOLOGIES

"We have to spend more money to keep from going bankrupt."
– **Joe Biden** 7/16/2009

Through the massive economic stimulus, the Obama administration funneled money to their Democratic allies, and even with all the evidence, the media protects their failures and disregards the American people in the process. The Energy Department has provided almost $35 billion in loans, loan guarantees and conditional commitments to renewable energy companies. Here is a condensed rundown of some big government, big green energy, **solar failures:**

Solyndra solar manufacturer, which we'll highlight in a minute, received a $535 million loan guarantee from the Department of Energy (DOE) stimulus paid for with our tax dollars and went BANKRUPT!

Fisker Automotive, the electric vehicle manufacturer, received a $529 million DOE stimulus loan and has gone through layoffs.

Abound Solar received a $400 million DOE stimulus loan guarantee and has declared bankruptcy. A123, the battery maker, received a $249 million stimulus grant from the DOE and has had layoffs.

Enerl, another battery maker, received a $118.5 million stimulus grant and went BANKRUPT. (Enerl was #67 on the White House list of 100 Projects that are Changing America)

Nevada Geothermal Power, Internal audit for the firm that received a $98.5 million stimulus loan guarantee revealed $98 million in net losses and significant debt. **Beacon Power**, another solar company, received a $43 million DOE stimulus loan guarantee and has gone bankrupt.[15]

SILENCE ON SOLYNDRA

I don't know who this embarrasses more, the Obama administration or the mainstream media that punted on this story. Even an AP report showed Solyndra was hemorrhaging hundreds of millions of dollars for years *before* the Obama administration signed off on the original $535 million loan guarantee in September 2009! The Fremont, California-based company was the first renewable-energy company to receive a loan guarantee under a stimulus-law program to encourage green energy. Obama touted the "investment" into Solyndra as a model.

Michigan Republican Fred Upton, chairman of the Energy and Commerce Committee, warned:

> "In this time of record debt, I question whether the government is qualified to act as a venture capitalist, picking winners and losers in speculative ventures and shelling out billions of taxpayer dollars to keep them afloat."

Solyndra announced bankruptcy on August 31[st,] 2011, and in October, the Media Research Center released a study that exposed the three networks (ABC, CBS, and NBC) because they rarely mentioned the scandal, just the opposite of their reporting on Enron, an energy company with Republican ties:

> "In just the first two months of 2002, the ABC, CBS and NBC evening newscasts cranked out 198 stories on the Enron debacle,

compared to just eight (at the time of this study) on Obama's Solyndra, which is **a 24-to-1 disparity.**"[16]

How was this not news? When government takes $535 million and pours that much money into a losing cause, it completely wastes taxpayer money that was supposed to go toward immediate job creation. How about investing in the private economy and giving it a better chance to succeed? There is no substantial proof green jobs are going to be successful in the near future. In fact, according to the *Washington Post*: "Instead of creating 65,000 jobs, *as promised*, the $38 billion loan program which included Solyndra could only claim 3,545 jobs."[17]

The Obama White House and his DOE stuck with Solyndra because its largest financial backer was George Kaiser, a major financial donor to Obama. Accuracy in Media's Roger Aronoff stated, "This goes against the media narrative that Obama operates on a higher ethical plane than previous scandal plagued politicians."[18] An entire month after Solyndra declared bankruptcy, a Pew survey found that 43% of Americans "had never even heard of the scandal." As for MSNBC, their primetime lineup went months without even acknowledging Solyndra.

It gets worse. In April 2012, another California solar company supported by the Obama administration declared bankruptcy. The latest casualty is **Solar Trust for America**, which received $2.1 billion in loan guarantees from the Department of Energy! According to the *Washington Examiner*, Energy Secretary Steven Chu touted the deal as "the largest amount ever offered to a solar project."[19]

The media will not tell the truth and serve American taxpayers. They are dedicated to keeping bad news from the public if it does not fit their narrative.

OPERATION FAST AND FURIOUS

In June 2012, U.S. Attorney General Eric Holder was voted in Contempt of Congress by 259 members of the House of Representatives for stonewalling the investigation into the Operation Fast and Furious scandal. The media calls it "a show" by Republicans. I'll let you decide. In all of American history, no sitting Cabinet member has been held in contempt of Congress until now. President Obama even stepped in and used his "executive privilege" to protect Eric Holder. If Holder did nothing wrong, why not cooperate with the investigation? What's Holder hiding?

The media keeps glossing over corruption, and those of us who are informed have watched in astonishment. The Obama administration defies laws on marriage, immigration, gambling, marijuana, and pornography, and conservatives are fed up. In this case, American guns were used in the deaths of U.S. Border Patrol Agent Brian Terry, Immigration and Customs Enforcement Agent Jaime Zapata, and approximately 300 Mexican citizens. The gun used in Terry's death was purchased in Arizona, and the gun used in Zapata's death was purchased in Texas. Both were "Fast and Furious" guns.

From 2009 to 2011, the Obama administration's Bureau of Alcohol, Tobacco, Firearms and Explosives (ATF) ran Operation Fast and Furious (a.k.a. Project Gunrunner), a program to track U.S.-purchased firearms headed to Mexican drug cartels in order to get to cartel heads. Critics believe the real purpose of the operation was to undermine the Second Amendment by vilifying gun owners and sellers so the government could enforce stricter gun laws in America. Either way, it went terribly wrong.

One problem with the plan was that our DOJ didn't even notify Mexican authorities that thousands of semi-automatic firearms were being sold to people in Arizona thought to have links to Mexican drug cartels. ATF agents "were ordered not to intercept the smugglers, but rather to let the guns 'walk' across the U.S.-Mexican border and into the hands of Mexican drug-trafficking organizations."[20]

Fast and Furious was botched when over 1,400 guns, including AK-47's, were lost. The operation was halted in December 2010 after two weapons the department lost track of were found at the murder scene of U.S. Border Patrol Agent Brian Terry. His family has since filed a lawsuit charging that the top federal prosecutor in Phoenix lied to them about the guns found at the crime scene in an attempt to hide the weapons' connection to the ATF's operation. The media has made this a political issue, and Holder has even accused Republicans of racism.

Rep. Darrell Issa, House Oversight Committee chairman, and Sen. Charles Grassley (R-Iowa) requested the Justice Department release thousands of documents related to the inner workings of Fast and Furious. The Justice Department has delivered fewer than 8% of the 80,000 documents. Issa also released a report suggesting top Department of Justice officials had extensive knowledge of and involvement in Operation Fast and Furious.

Justice headquarters "had much greater knowledge of, and involvement in, Fast and Furious than it has previously acknowledged," the memo reads. Writing for *Forbes*, author Frank Minter asked, "is it even conceivable that Attorney General Eric Holder didn't know about this secret program? And if he didn't, shouldn't he have?"[21]

However, in February 2011, the Justice Department sent a letter to Congress denying the operation even existed! Ten months later, the Department retracted the letter. Then, Eric Holder insisted he did not even know about the program until early 2011. After months of investigation, the Justice Department finally acknowledged the allegations were true. Why did it take nearly nine months for the Department to acknowledge Holder's earlier denials were false?

In other words, he lied. Why did senior Justice Department officials who knew about and received briefings on the operation fail to stop it? By the way, former ATF Director Kenneth Melson began talking to investigators and pointed to a cover up. Melson was moved to a new position with the ATF. Four more ATF officials were reassigned or promoted by the Obama administration to other positions in Washington D.C.

Naturally, Holder not only received support from President Barack Obama after the hearing, but White House spokesman Jay Carney said, "He absolutely stands by the Attorney General, thinks he is doing an excellent job." Can Americans still have confidence in their chief law enforcement agency, the Department of Justice? Even if Holder resigns, it appears the media successfully protected the president, and regardless of the deaths caused by Fast and Furious, the flawed and reckless gun operation will not go down as Obama's Watergate after all.

OCCUPY WALL STREET VS. THE TEA PARTY

Two of the biggest public movements in America in many years have been the Tea Party and Occupy Wall Street. Here is your first comparison to digest: Occupy Wall Street drew more broadcast network stories in the first nine days of coverage (24) than the Tea Party drew in the first nine months (19). With that blatant discrepancy under our belts, let's briefly describe the two movements.

The Tea Party is a conservative grassroots populist movement funded by individuals from states across the country as well as some wealthy donors. The Tea Party endorses cutting government spending, cutting taxes in general, reducing the national debt, and adherence to the United States Constitution. They also aim to call awareness to any issue that challenges the security, sovereignty, or domestic tranquility of America. The massive stimulus spending and the passage of Obamacare were two major catalysts that galvanized the movement. Most participants include those who possess a strong belief in the foundational Judeo-Christian values embedded in our founding documents. They identify with various religious groups and lean Republican or Independent.

Occupy Wall Street (OWS) is a well-organized, nationally *and internationally* funded social movement protesting the disparity of wealth in America, capitalism, greed, corporations, and big business. Vancouver, Canada-based *AdBusters*, an anti-consumerist publication that sounded the initial call for the protests, is funded in part by the leftist Tides Foundation,[22] a major recipient of George Soros's funding. MoveOn.org, another Soros venture, has rallied support. The primary OWS goal is equal distribution of wealth by government through taxes. Other goals include more jobs for college graduates, corporate regulation, and bank reform. Some demand the government pay off their student loans. Most participants include those who are young (average age 31), liberal, and lean Democrat or Independent.

The three main networks, ABC, CBS and NBC flooded their morning and evening newscasts in October 2011 with thirty-three full stories or interview segments on the Occupy Wall Street protests for the month. In contrast, the Tea Party movement was initially ignored before receiving a total of only thirteen stories in all of 2009.[23]

This is blatant bias. The big three networks continued to overlook the OWS arrests, cases of violence, property damage, public health concerns, anti-Semitism, and sexual assaults that occurred in various cities hosting protests. There have been at least nine reported deaths, and the media also failed to report on the OWS money trail leading to big unions such as SEIU.

The very acts of radicalism or violence that the same media accused the Tea Party of, without substantial proof I might add, seemed to escape their notice. The story ratio was nineteen favorable to only one critical on OWS. (For a total of 190 to 10) When confrontations erupted between the police and the protestors, the networks, being sympathetic to the OWS cause, were much more likely to pin the blame on police. The Occupy numbers keep increasing so I have been unable to confirm an exact total of arrests for both movements. It appears less than ten people have been arrested at over 300 Tea Party rallies across the country since 2009.

Contrast this with approximately 7,380 documented Occupy Wall Street protestors arrested in 117 cities as of August 2012.[24]

Arrests have ranged from civil disobedience and disturbing the peace to assaulting police officers, trespassing, public defecation and urination, drunkenness and drug use, vandalism, and at least one rape (Philadelphia). Gideon Oliver, who represents OWS with the National Lawyers Guild in New York, said that about 2,000 had been arrested in New York City alone. Police rap sheets show over seventy-five incidents of sexual assault, violence, anti-Semitism, extortion, perversion, and lawlessness. Nancy Pelosi encourages their freedom to protest, and President Obama said, "We are on their side," showing support for the movement.

Occupy Wall Street has been publicly supported by many other prominent Democrats. Although some activists cannot clearly explain what the Occupy goals actually are, there is an obvious anti-American theme as flags are flown upside down, desecrated, or burned. Some protesters openly admit to being Socialists, Communists and Marxists, but not once has a media report on the three main networks used these labels to describe any of the protestors. These groups support OWS:

Communist Party USA, Louis Farrakhan and Nation of Islam, CAIR, American Nazi Party, Marxist Student Union, and Socialist Party USA.

Conversely, Tea Party participants hold their flags up high at rallies, are proud of the founders and America's Constitution; some are families, some are retired, and the protests are peaceful. The Democratic National Committee called them "rabid right-wing extremists." ABC said they were a "mob." CNN accused them of "rabble rousing." Harry Reid called them "evil mongers." Nancy Pelosi said they were "un-American." Anderson Cooper and other media elites simply insulted these patriotic Americans. I won't mention how bad MSNBC's coverage has been.

POLITICAL CORRECTNESS & FEAR OF ISLAM

You may have heard of the 2011 conviction of Mohammad Shafia and his wife, Tooba Yahya, for the murder of their three teen daughters and Rona Amir Mohammad, Shafia's first wife in a polygamous marriage. Their four bodies were found June 30, 2009, in a car submerged in a canal in Kingston, Ontario. The prosecution said one of the daughter's parents found condoms in her room as well as photos of her wearing short skirts and hugging her *Christian* boyfriend, a relationship she had kept secret. Shafia's first wife wrote in a diary that her husband beat her and "made life a torture."

According to Sharia Law, if a family member deviates from the strict Muslim teachings and the Quran, they can be executed by other family members. These "honor killings" are allowed under the Taliban in Afghanistan and in some other parts of the world. An AP report neglected to mention the fact that the convicted murderers are Muslim. They were described as "Afghan." In fact, the only religion mentioned in the AP dispatch is Christian (used while describing the boyfriend of one of the daughters).

Also describing the family as Afghan, the *USA Today* did not mention Sharia Law, Islam, or Muslim in the article. The *New York Times* headline read, "Afghan Family Members Convicted in Honor Killings." I give them credit for at least mentioning honor killings in the headline. It is sad the media refuses to connect a religion with the crimes.

Brian Williams reported the story on NBC's Nightly News:

"A verdict has been reached in a murder case that's gotten a lot of attention because it involved so-called honor killings of family members. In this case, it was an Afghan family living in Canada. It is a culture clash getting a lot of attention to our North."

Did you notice he or NBC news editors inserted the words "so-called?" You will typically see this tactic when a network or news organization wants to downplay the truth. NBC's Kevin Tibbles was the reporter on the story and describing the motivation for the violence, he stated the victims were killed by "a strict religious family that felt it had been disgraced." He mentions that the religion of the family led them to murder yet fails to name that religion.

We continually see the media candy-coating politically incorrect facts. Author and truth defender, Pamela Geller, notes that Muslims are responsible for 91% of honor killings worldwide and that Islamic law stipulates no penalty for a parent who kills their own child. Geller passionately commented on the verdict and bias:

"Yet the media's malevolent enthusiasm to self-enforce the blasphemy laws under the Shariah ('do not offend Islam') has extinguished whatever humanity they might have had. Islamic gendercide is epidemic in Muslim countries and an increasing problem in the West as Muslim populations grow.

"Instead of expressing repulsion and outrage at the systematic murder of girls yearning to be free and shining a light on this monstrous religious slaughter, the media have gone to irrational (even criminal) lengths to deny the connection of this honor killing, and every honor killing, to Islamic law."[25]

Imagine how a newscast would be presented if a Baptist, Lutheran, Catholic, or Christian father murdered his daughter for having an abortion. Political correctness is dangerous; it obscures the truth and often discriminates against Christians. It allows certain people and groups to avoid scrutiny for destructive actions, and it prevents our government from taking proper steps to investigate or prevent suspicious religious behavior before tragedy strikes.

Major Nidal Malik Hassan is the Muslim gunman who had ties to Al Qaeda and had business cards with SOA (Soldier of Allah) printed on them. He shouted "Allahu Akbar!" while killing fourteen people and injuring thirty-two others at Fort Hood, Texas in 2009. Internal Army reports indicate officers within the Army had discussed what they characterized as Hasan's tendencies toward radical Islam since 2005. An army psychiatrist, Hasan fired a total of 214 rounds at American soldiers, and when the shooting ended, he was still carrying 177 rounds of ammunition.

Naturally, the media kept a lid on this premeditated act of murder. Investigations discovered e-mail communications between Hasan and Yemen-based cleric Anwar al-Awlaki, who quickly declared Hasan a hero proclaiming "fighting against the U.S. army is an Islamic duty." How did the Defense Department classify the Fort Hood massacre? An act of "workplace violence."

MEDIA SILENT ON THE SILENCING OF CHRISTIANS

Another case that barely made headlines was in January 2012 when Lieutenant General William Boykin, a three star Delta Force leader and American hero, was pressured to withdraw from speaking at the United States Military Academy at West Point. It only took a few Muslim and atheist cadets to complain about General Boykin's Christian faith and silence his scheduled talk about the importance of prayer in a leader's life.

Nihad Awad of CAIR (The Council on American-Islamic Relations) proudly released a statement saying that it had successfully prevented retired Lt. Gen. Boykin from speaking because they preferred "a spiritual message that promotes tolerance and mutual understanding." A committed Christian, General Boykin has faced danger for his country on missions in places like Iran, Somalia, and Grenada, yet his faith has made him a target at home. In contrast, the following headline was happily reported in the news the month before: US Navy 'First Kiss' Goes to Lesbians for First Time in American Military History.

In May 2010, the Pentagon withdrew Franklin Graham's invitation to speak at a National Day of Prayer event. Mr. Graham had said he loves Muslim people and wants them to know God loves them, and that they can be saved through Jesus Christ. In an interview, Franklin Graham said Islam "is not the faith of this country, and is not the religion that built this nation. The people of the Christian faith and the Jewish faith are the ones who built America."

What did Franklin Graham do on the National Day of Prayer that year? He showed up anyway and quietly prayed on the sidewalk outside the Pentagon. "I have a son in Afghanistan, and I came today to pray for our men and women that serve this nation," he said. "They risk their lives every day to protect our freedom. So my prayer was that God would watch over them."[26]

GOODNIGHT WALTER, GOOD-BYE JOURNALISM

Back in the 1970's when most network news was reported without bias and opinion, people would watch the evening news and catch up on the most important things happening in the country. Admittedly a staunch Democrat, news anchor Walter Cronkite was known as the most trusted man in America. Times have changed, and today's mainstream media is more like a PR machine for the Democratic Party.

Three decades later, *Time*'s cover story on Obama after just six months in office read, "Obama's start has been the most impressive of any president since FDR." Remember their cover story on Bush in the first 100 days of his presidency? There wasn't one. In 2003, however, *Newsweek did* do a cover story called: "Bush & God – Why His 'God Talk' Worries Friends & Foes." The nine-page article dissected Bush's upbringing and "questionable" Christian influences.

In his campaign for president, Barrack Obama promised to change the political culture in Washington and bring in the most transparent administration in American history. In January 2009, Obama stated: "These [health care] negotiations will be on C-SPAN, and so the public will be part of the conversation and will see the decisions that are being made." Wrong. The intense meetings over the massive legislation took place behind closed doors. Did the media hold the president to his promise? Nope. They acted like they saw nothing, heard nothing, and so they reported nothing.

Who can forget Nancy Pelosi infamously saying "we need to pass the bill so you can find out what's in it."[27] If Romney were president and a Republican made that statement, it would be broadcast non-stop and front page news. The Obamacare behemoth was over 2,000 pages long, and the Democrats rammed it through with no intention of listening to the American people. They resorted to their overused tactic of blaming Republicans for not compromising.

ADMISSION OF BIAS

Author Michael Malone is a true journalist, and his grandmother was one of the first women reporters for the *Los Angeles Times*. One week before the 2008 presidential election, in his column for ABC News (of all places), Malone wrote a four-page article entitled "Media's Presidential Bias and Decline" blasting his profession. He suggested that the volume of bias in election coverage was both bewildering and "appalling."

The media was playing a "very dangerous game" with the Constitution, and he found himself literally shouting at the TV screen during news reports! Malone was disgusted by what he witnessed. Here's a brief part of his honest 2008 analysis:

"But worst of all, for the last couple weeks, I've begun – for the first time in my adult life – to be embarrassed to admit what I do for a living. A few days ago, when asked by a new acquaintance what I did for a living, I replied that I was "a writer," because I couldn't bring myself to admit to a stranger that I'm a journalist. You need to understand how painful this is for me. I am one of those people who truly bleeds ink when I'm cut. I am a fourth-generation newspaperman....

"But nothing, nothing I've seen has matched the media bias on display in the current presidential campaign. No, what I object to (and I think most other Americans do as well) is the lack of equivalent hardball coverage of the other side – or worse, actively serving as attack dogs for the presidential ticket of

Sens. Barack Obama, D-Ill., and Joe Biden, D-Del. If the current polls are correct, **we are about to elect as president of the United States a man who is essentially a cipher, who has left almost no paper trail, seems to have few friends… and has entire years missing out of his biography.**

"Why haven't we seen an interview with Sen. Obama's grad school drug dealer – when we know all about *Mrs. McCain's* addiction? Are Bill Ayers and Tony Rezko that hard to interview? Are all those phony voter registrations that hard to scrutinize? And why are Sen. Biden's endless gaffes almost always covered up, or rationalized, by the media?"[28]

Like Michael, many of us yelled at the TV as well as witnessed some of the worst reporting in our history. You've heard it said that two things that divide America are politics and religion. They both came into play in the 2008 election cycle.

CONCLUSION

Not everyone in the media is evil. Many have been brainwashed at some point in their education or in their careers. We may not be able to turn back the tide of bias, but let's raise more awareness by sharing the truth. We may not be able to hold the media accountable, but we can expose their hypocrisy. Plenty of Americans still do care.

I often question the spiritual discernment of Fox News host, Bill O' Reilly, but he has been right on target regarding the Culture War. He also says that people should help unmask the media's bias because it is hurting America. Writing about the brutal media attacks on Sarah Palin, he stated:

"With Barack Obama in the White House…the left sees a major opportunity to knock out Judeo-Christian traditions, replacing them with a secular philosophy…Americans need to wake up and smell the corruption."[29]

Let's stay informed and network. There appears to be some progress thanks in part to the Internet, the Tea Party, and millions of concerned citizens who have never been involved in political action in the past.

New media is one key to gaining ground in the information war when it comes to defending and promoting traditional values. If you're online, use your time wisely. People listen to people they trust. Remember, if you don't say anything, there are some in your circle of influence that think what they're getting is news.

Truth has left the media, and this leaves us with the responsibility to inform ourselves. The fight for morality and truth is just one of the battles we face as believers in an entertainment-driven culture with growing anti-Christian influence. In the next chapter we are going to look back at the media malpractice in 2008 that made history as the most biased ever. It was embarrassing how openly Hollywood and the media attacked Sarah Palin and yes – we will examine why they love to hate her.

> "I want to create a society that is more equitable, where... there are liberal ideas presented and conservative ideas presented in Hollywood, in academia, and in the mainstream media and let the consumer choose." – Author, journalist, and media mogul **Andrew Breitbart** (1969-2012)

ENDNOTES

1 Pew Research Center; 9/13/09 - Press Accuracy Rating Hits Two Decade Low http://www.people-press.org/2009/09/13/press-accuracy-rating-hits-two-decade-low/

2 http://www.journalism.org/resources/principles

3 http://www.lifenews.com/2012/01/25/pro-lifers-use-new-media-to-protest-march-for-life-blackout/

4 http://www.christianpost.com/news/did-the-media-forget-about-the-march-for-life-68116/

5 Kreeft, Peter, A Defense of Culture Wars: A Call for Counterrevolution, http://peterkreeft.com/topics-more/culture-wars.htm

6 http://archive.frontpagemag.com/readArticle.aspx?ARTID=32928

7 Spring 2001 issue of The Public Interest; Stanley Rothman and Amy Black

8 Princeton Survey Research Associates; May 24, 2005. Journalists' ethics and attitudes.

9 S. Robert Lichter, then with George Washington University, and Stanley Rothman of Smith College, 1981

10 The American Journalist, 1986: Indiana University journalism professors David H. Weaver and G. Cleveland Wilhoit

11 New York-based newsletter, Journalist and Financial Reporting, 1988

12 The Pew Research Center for The People and The Press; May 2004, in association with the Project for Excellence in Journalism

13 Princeton Survey Research Associates; May 24, 2005. Journalists' ethics and attitudes.

14 Media Research Center, Bias Basics – Journalists' Political Views http://www.mrc.org/biasbasics/biasbasics.asp

15 http://townhall.com/tipsheet/townhall.comstaff/2012/07/13/doe_officials_calls_loan_program_that_produced_solyndra_an_enormous_success

16 Media Reality Check, Networks Keeping Viewers In the Dark on Solyndra Scandal - http://www.mrc.org/realitycheck/realitycheck/2011/20111011093017.aspx

17 Washington Post, Solyndra Struggles to Create Jobs, 9/14/2010, http://www.washingtonpost.com/politics/obama-green-tech-program-that-backed-solyndra-struggles-to-create-jobs/2011/09/07/gIQA9Zs3SK_story.html

18 Accuracy In Media; Roger Aronoff, Measuring Liberal Bias— By Numbers and By Examples http://www.aim.org/aim-report/measuring-liberal-bias%E2%80%94by-numbers-and-by-examples/

19 http://campaign2012.washingtonexaminer.com/blogs/beltway-confidential/solar-company-bankrupt-despite-win-win-doe-loan/459621

20 http://www.forbes.com/sites/realspin/2011/09/28/fast-and-furious-just-might-be-president-obamas-watergate/

21 http://www.forbes.com/sites/realspin/2011/09/28/fast-and-furious-just-might-be-president-obamas-watergate/

22 http://www.discoverthenetworks.org/articles/Tides%20Foundation%20and%20Tides%20Center1.htm

23 A Tale of Two Protests: MRC study http://www.mrc.org/realitycheck/realitycheck/2011/20111013100045.aspx

24 http://occupyarrests.moonfruit.com/

25 Atlas Shrugs Pamela Geller, http://atlasshrugs2000.typepad.com/atlas_shrugs/honor_killings_islam_misogyny/

26 Newmax, 5/6/2010 Franklin Graham Prays in Front of Pentagon as Nation Celebrates Prayer Day, http://www.newsmax.com/Headline/graham-national-prayer-day/2010/05/06/id/358072

27 http://blog.heritage.org/2010/03/10/video-of-the-week-we-have-to-pass-the-bill-so-you-can-find-out-what-is-in-it/

28 Michael S. Malone, "Media's Presidential Bias and Decline", ABCnews.com, Oct. 24, 2008, http://abcnews.go.com/Business/story?id=6099188&page=1

29 https://www.billoreilly.com/newslettercolumn?pid=26893

CHAPTER 7

WHY THEY LOVE TO HATE SARAH PALIN

MORE MEDIA MAYHEM

[In this chapter we may encounter some unexpected turbulence. Please stay calm and keep your seat belts fastened. This is a non-denominational book, and we may not agree on every course adjustment. Our final destination is what truly matters. What you are about to read is a true story, and names have not been changed.]

"If John McCain wins, this woman [Sarah Palin] will be one seventy-two-year-old man's heartbeat away from being president of the United States, and if that doesn't scare the hell out of you, it should." – **Jack Cafferty**, CNN host

"They shouldn't have the right to call themselves Christian, for they have no Christ-like attributes. I am a feminist and a Christian – and when I see Sarah Palin – I see neither. And it is official. She is evil." – **Margaret Cho**, Comedienne

If the world hates you, you know that it has hated Me before it hated you. If you were of the world, the world would love its own; but because you are not of the world, but I chose you out of the world, because of this the world hates you (**John 15:17-19**).

Jesus Christ was hated. In other countries, Christians are persecuted and killed. In America, we're carving out new territory where fewer people are ashamed to spew hatred under the guise of free speech. Sarah Palin is hated, not for what she has done, but for who she is – a pro-life Christian conservative. She is also hated because she is a strong, family-oriented, successful career woman. Liberal Feminists can't stand her because she accomplished so much in public office while raising five children. She seems genuinely happy with her life and that bugs them too. The foundational reason they hate her, however, may be that her joy comes from an authentic faith in Jesus Christ. Palin promotes a passion for life. She loves her God, her family, and her country.

Furthermore, she is attractive, she brings ratings to every program she appears on, and has authored two best-selling books. Her eight-part documentary, *Sarah Palin's Alaska* on TLC broke ratings records with nearly 5 million tuning in for the premiere.[1] Though she had to develop a thick skin, she is sensitive, vulnerable and, of course, human. This is a point we often miss about famous public figures. She is like you and me, and many of us are like her.

What do I mean by that? Tens of millions of patriotic Americans identify with her in some way. She gained popularity for being herself and by representing traditional values. When we live to glorify Jesus, some people will feel guilty. Moreover, darkness does not like being exposed and will lash out at any sign of a serious threat. It is important to recognize the spiritual undercurrent to this reaction, and it comes from a dark, evil place. The lesson is this: when we choose to live as a committed Christian, it shines light on sin and on the way others have chosen to live.

In a 2011 *Newsweek* profile of HBO *Real Time* host, Bill Maher, Maher said:

> "When I point out that Sarah Palin is a vainglorious braggart, a liar, a whiner, a bully who sells patriotism like a pimp, and the leader of a family of inbred weirdoes straight out of *The Hills Have Eyes*, that's not sexist. I'm saying it because it's true."

THE TRIG EFFECT

A living, glaring, obvious reminder that Sarah Palin is seeking God's heart is the fact she and her husband Todd gave birth to a child with Down syndrome. The Palins welcomed their son, Trig, as the special gift from God that he is. By choosing life and being in the public eye, they showed a watching world in 2008 that every human life is to be valued instead of a "problem" to be dealt with as the pro-abortion crowd believes. That alone makes this mob furious.

On April 20, 2011, liberal blogger Jack Stuef attacked three-year-old Trig Palin on his birthday. Blogging for Wonkette, Stuef suggested Trig was a product of incest and that he was actually Bristol Palin's son:

> "Is Palin his true mother? Or was Bristol? (And why is it that nobody questions who the father is? Because, either way, Todd definitely did it.) It doesn't matter."

Jack Stuef then made fun of Trig by re-posting a poem published by a member of Team Sarah on the coalition's website that begins:

> "Oh, little boy what are you dreaming about." Stuef retorted, "What's he dreaming about? Nothing. He's retarded!"

Addressing Trig, Stuef sarcastically expressed hope that the boy would eventually die in combat. Stuef wrote:

> "We can hardly wait for fifteen years from now, when you will finally be able to vote and will be sent off by your mother's junta to fight the Union in the Great Alaska War. It'll be quite a loss. You're the smartest one in that family."[2]

Feminists supposedly champion women's rights, but when Sandra Bernhard joked about Sarah Palin being gang-raped, the media didn't utter a word. The Left can spout their hate about Palin, Tim Tebow, Michelle Bachmann or Kirk Cameron, and we hear little about it in the media. The media also attacked Republican Presidential candidate Rick Santorum in 2012 because he opened up about social issues. Apparently, an unspoken rule is you don't dare talk about limiting abortions, birth control, and protecting marriage in America. Santorum also had the audacity to attend evangelical Christian churches while campaigning and allowed pastors to pray for him! Sarah Palin did the same thing back in 2008.

SOME KNOW NOT WHY THEY HATE

We've all been there – and it's flabbergasting. We get into a conversation with a person who firmly believes something without much knowledge or understanding to back up their view. When you ask for factual examples or question them at all, their reply is often irrational. In an article for *Front Page Magazine*, "Why the Left Hates Sarah Palin," writer and producer Evan Sayet wrote about hanging out at his favorite coffee shop in the hopes of doing his writing and converting a few liberals. Because encounters such as this are common, you might relate. Describing an interaction at the coffee shop, Sayet wrote:

> "Today, the conversation turned to Sarah Palin and my latest acquaintance blurted out: 'Oh I *hate* her.' Since she did not yet know my politics, and since we were in Los Angeles, it is clear that she expected to hear back what you usually hear back in this city: 'Yeah, I hate her, too.' Instead, I asked her why.

> "At this point I could have predicted her response because it's the same response you get from liberals no matter who on the Right you're talking about: 'Because she's stupid.'

> "I replied: 'Being stupid is no reason to hate someone, but tell me, which one of her policies do you disagree with?' It wasn't hard to predict her response: 'All of them!'

> "I continued to push. 'Well, then, if it's all of them, it should be easy for you to name one.' Her reply? 'They're too many to list.' 'So don't list them, just give me one,' I said.

> "This went on for a while until my new acquaintance finally admitted that she didn't know any of Ms. Palin's policies. Before she ran off... I looked her in the eyes and said, 'If you don't know any of her policies, perhaps you should look into them.' She promised she would. She won't."[3]

Palin's daughter, Bristol Palin, also received her share of venomous attacks beginning with her decision to keep her baby (the nerve!) after becoming pregnant at seventeen. It came at the most inopportune time early in the 2008 presidential campaign. Since her mother was on the Republican VP ticket, Bristol received much public scrutiny from those who not only hated her for being a Palin, but loathed her "choice" to have a baby instead of aborting. The fun continued in 2010 when Bristol decided to compete on *Dancing with the Stars*. The way Bristol dealt with the nonstop criticism proved the Palin family has very thick skin and that they really try not to care about what hateful, ignorant or jealous people think.

The very next year in 2011, hatred erupted from the Left when Sarah Palin announced she would *not* run for the presidency in 2012. Also, Palin's political action website had targets on congressional districts across the country where Republicans needed to win. Democrats have done the exact same thing on their strategy maps. In "Sarah Palin and the War for America's Soul," author and managing editor of *World Net Daily*, David Kupelian, mentioned the fact some in the media and many on the Left actually blamed Palin for the January shooting in Arizona that injured more than a dozen people, killed six, and severely injured Democratic Congresswoman Gabrielle Giffords. Kupelian wrote:

> "The irrational hatred toward Sarah Palin cannot be explained in the usual terms of politics and ideology. The traditional divide of 'liberal versus conservative' or "Democrat versus Republican" cannot explain such dark, almost other-worldly expressions as 'I hope she dies gnashing her teeth' or death threats against the Palins' *children*."[4]

TWEETING HATE

Proclaimers of civility and tolerance want to take away our guns, but they want Sarah Palin shot. I share the following, especially for those who say there is hatred on *both* sides. Shortly after that Arizona shooting, the haters filled Twitter and encouraged violence against the former Alaska Governor. One person called Palin supporters "radical right wing retards." Here are a fraction of the "Tweets" that blasted across the Internet:

"My hatred for Palin continues to grow. I think this woman should be assassinated."

"Can somebody please shoot Sarah Palin?"

"I hope Sarah Palin dies an ugly death and takes her moronic hate with her."

"I am very nonviolent, but somebody needs to shoot Palin's toes off."

"Save a wolf – shoot Sarah Palin: just saw that on a bumper sticker, ha ha"

"I may hate Sarah Palin, but I wish no real violence upon her. Just an inoperable tumor is all."

"Sarah Palin is the single most dangerous threat to the future of the human race. Somebody should shoot her."

"Join us in praying to God that Sarah Palin contracts cancer and dies."

"I hope Sarah Palin dies a slow and painful death."[5]

The Left can be quite hypocritical, and media will not hold them accountable for their actions. They demand respect for every religion except Christianity. Leftists can either no longer hold back their hatred toward Palin, or they don't care anymore who knows about it. If a Democrat is even mildly insulted, the media is sure to report it. The Bible warns about calling evil good, and calling good evil (Isaiah 5:20); those who *substitute darkness for light and light for darkness.'* If people simply disagree with Sarah Palin or anyone else on policies or politics, that's fine. Let's discuss the issues. The problem is that their disagreement with her worldview evolves into an irrational hatred of her as a person.

In a 2011 *Townhall* article called "The Cowardly Character Assassination of Sarah Palin," author, commentator, and journalist Michelle Malkin wrote:

"Hollywood savaged Palin. Journalists mocked her. Liberal blogs slimed her. Opponents cursed her, Photoshopped her, hacked her e-mail, hanged her in effigy, called her bigot, Bible-thumper and bimbo, and attacked her husband and children. But nothing Palin endured compares to the treatment she's receiving from these backstabbing blabbermouths who worked on the same campaign she poured herself into...."[6]

Put yourself in her shoes, and tell me if you'd keep going strong. Sarah Palin has been labeled "The Most Powerful Female Politician in the World" as recently as 2012. She attracts large audiences and sells out speaking engagements. She continues to carry great influence in political opinion. Palin also has a massive, energized base of conservative Americans that love her, buy her books, respond to what she says in the media, and when necessary will defend her reputation. She has galvanized conservatives like no other political figure since Ronald Reagan, and God has used the whole fiasco to bring about good.

But as for you, you meant evil against me; but God meant it for good, in order to bring it about as it is this day, to save many people alive (**Genesis 50:20** NKJ).

MEDIA MALPRACTICE AND THE 2008 PRESIDENTIAL RACE

What the mainstream media did during the presidential campaigns and election of 2008 was not only embarrassing, it was glaring evidence of their overt allegiance to the Democratic Party. There were journalists who left the profession because of their association with blatant bias and corruption, and Americans lost complete trust in the media's ability to deliver an unfiltered story. The good news is millions of truth seekers now get news from alternative sources, and this is creating a new wave of citizen journalism: concerned individuals sharing important factual information.

The debate in 2008 began with John McCain's age (which I agree was an issue) and with Sarah Palin's experience (which shouldn't have been an issue). First, a quote from a young, green, liberal Senator:

"You know, I am a believer in knowing what you're doing when you apply for a job. And I think that if I were to seriously consider running on a national ticket, I would essentially have to start now, before having served a day in the Senate. Now, there are some people who might be comfortable doing that, but I'm not one of those people." – **Senator Barack Obama**, 11/08/2004

Hollywood and media elites believe experience only matters if a candidate is a Republican. Though I was not sure John McCain could win in 2008, (an old white-haired moderate Republican and Veteran running against a young, black, charismatic, liberal Democrat and smooth orator) McCain's four years as a member of Congress and twenty-five years in the United States Senate did not seem to be important to the media. Tragically, it was not important to many Americans either. The media did, however, point out McCain's age, his past bout with skin cancer, and the fact he couldn't raise his arms over his head (due to the torture he endured as a POW). It was a brilliant strategy: 'he's old, look at his white hair!'

Since John McCain was not a conservative, he was easily cast aside as not being a threat to Barack Obama. There was, however, a very real and present danger to Democrats in Sarah Palin: a popular, attractive, and charismatic, walk-the-talk conservative. She represented practically everything liberal elites and socialists oppose. So they hated her.

"There's a one out of three chance, if not more, that McCain doesn't survive his first term, and it'll be President Palin! It's like a really bad Disney movie, 'The Hockey Mom.' Oh, I'm just a hockey mom from Alaska, and she's president. She's facing down Vladimir Putin and using the folksy stuff she learned at the hockey rink. It's absurd." –Actor **Matt Damon**, 9/9/2008

THE CONTRAST

Sarah Palin began her career in public service back in 1992, and by the time she was Alaska's Governor, Barack Obama was well-known in Chicago as a community organizer. Unbelievably, the national media tried – with straight faces – to suggest Sarah Palin's seventeen years in public office, including six as mayor, did not give her the experience necessary to be a *vice presidential* candidate. Obama's total of *less* than two years of experience in politics as a new senator was not an issue. Obama was running for *president*, not vice president! Columnist Noel Sheppard did a piece for *Newsbusters* in 2008 and made an excellent argument:

> "After all, just days after winning his U.S. Senate seat in 2004, Barack Obama said he didn't have enough experience to sit in the White House. As he basically threw his hat in the presidential ring during an October 22, 2006, appearance on NBC's *Meet the Press*, it means that less than twenty-two months in the Senate is all he needed to be more qualified than he felt he was roughly two years prior."[7]

Plenty of Obama's time in the Senate was spent traveling and campaigning, which is one thing he does very well. What executive experience did he have? During his on the job training in the Illinois Senate, he voted "present" 129 times while representing his constituents. Voting "present" was one of three options in the Illinois Legislature, along with "yes" and "no." The primary job responsibility of a United States Senator is to review bills and vote on legislation passed by committee. At least he showed up physically.

In contrast, Sarah Palin had many years of executive experience in both the public and private sectors. As Governor of Alaska, she managed a $14 billion budget. As President of the United States, Obama failed to pass a budget in his first three years, so it is doubtful he knows how to manage one. As a young lawyer, Obama represented ACORN and was a successful community organizer and activist in Chicago. As Alaska's Governor, Palin fought government waste and won. Her financial administration was over a state whose revenue fluctuates widely, entirely dependent on the price of a barrel of oil.

Obama worked with liberal non-profit groups and big labor unions, wrote a book, made friends with Oprah and Bruce Springsteen, and lobbied for Hollywood support. Barely half of Illinois residents (51.8%) approved of the job Obama was doing in office as a senator.

Palin challenged both political parties in Alaska while cleaning up years of corruption. Her average job approval rating was in the 80's, and she had the highest voter-approval ratings of any governor in the United States (93% in May 2007). I'm sure the media simply overlooked these facts or didn't know where to find them.

It's not surprising the media acts and believes the way they do, and yet, they present themselves as unbiased reporters. This time they showed their true colors. *Front Page Magazine*'s John Perazzo has monitored years of media bias and said he had never seen it more pronounced than in the 2008 election cycle, Perazzo concluded:

> "The professionals who constitute America's mainstream news media – the reporters, editors, anchors, publishers, correspondents, bureau chiefs, and executives at the nation's major newspapers, magazines, radio networks, and television networks – are leftists and Democrats in far greater numbers than they are conservatives or Republicans... they have been transformed – by virtue of the one-sided, passionately partisan worldview shared by editors and reporters alike – into mouthpieces of the political Left."[8]

Do you understand why experience wasn't a factor? The media didn't *want* it to be a factor. By September 2008, both parties had either elected or selected their presidential and vice presidential candidates to represent them on the greatest stage in national politics. The nation was buzzing about the history-making 2008 Presidential Election, and the media were slobbering all over themselves. I'll let them tell the next part of the story...

THE QUOTES: ABOUT BARACK OBAMA

> "Barack Obama has prospered in this presidential campaign because of the steadiness of his temperament and the judicious quality of his decision-making. They are his best-known qualities. The most important decision he has made – the selection of a running mate – was done carefully, with an exhaustive attention to detail and contemplation of all the possible angles.

Two months later, John McCain's peremptory selection of Governor Sarah Palin has come to seem a liability…" –Joe Klein, *Time* magazine

"I see he is getting a standing ovation from all of the journalists who have come there [to hear the speech]…." – Wolf Blitzer, CNN

"Take pride that this nation can produce men and speakers such as that." – Keith Olberman, MSNBC, following an Obama speech

"It's part of reporting this…election, the feeling most people get when they hear Barack Obama's speech. My – I felt this thrill going up my leg. I mean, I don't have that too often." – MSNBC host Chris Matthews

"It's like running against God; you know the media has anointed him." – Female CNN host

"People have called you the savior, the messiah, the messenger of change…." – Matt Lauer, interviewing Senator Obama

"…we're [media] all just – on board – we're not embarrassed when we get together. We just talk about how much we love Obama." – Joel Stein, Los Angeles Times

"I've been criticized for saying that he inspires me and the hell with my critics … his speech was worthy of Abraham Lincoln." – Chris Matthews, MSNBC

"I keep hearing that we have our JFK…Lee [Cowan] says to me, 'it's hard to stay objective covering this guy.'" – Brian Williams, NBC

"and rally after rally, people literally faint" – ABC news reporter

"Maybe we should ask Barrack if he's comfortable and needs another pillow." – Hillary Clinton

"I haven't been actively engaged before because there hasn't been anything to be actively engaged in. But I am engaged now to make Barack Obama the next President of the United States." – Oprah Winfrey

"And let me tell you something – for the first time in my adult lifetime, I am really proud of my country. And not just because Barack has done well, but because I think people are hungry for change. And I have been desperate to see our country moving in that direction and just not feeling so alone in my frustration and disappointment." – Michelle Obama, 2008 campaign speech

This list could go on for pages so let's advance the story that made history. Upon winning the nomination for the 2008 Democratic Primary, Barack Obama stated:

"America, this is our moment. This is our time. Our time to turn the page on the policies of the past. Our time to bring new energy and new ideas to the challenges we face. Our time to offer a new direction for the country we love.… I am absolutely certain that generations from now, we will be able to look back and tell our children that this was the moment when we began to provide care for the sick and good jobs to the jobless; this was the moment when the rise of the oceans began to slow and our planet began to heal; this was the moment when we ended a war and secured our nation and restored our image as the last, best hope on earth. This was the moment – this was the time – when we came together to remake this great nation…."[9] –Barack Obama, June 2008

Now let's hear more from the experts and celebrities, remembering to look closer at statements by those who pretend to be unbiased, objective news people.

THE QUOTES: ABOUT SARAH PALIN (LANGUAGE WARNING)

"After McCain announced his VP candidate, and she gave her [record TV audience] lightning bolt convention speech, and when the polls reflected her high likability…the media was petrified of Sarah Palin." – Radio talk show host and documentary film director John Zeigler

"This woman is trouble." – Karen Dunn, strategic campaign assistant to David Axelrod

"You can put lipstick on a pig, but it's still a pig." – Barrack Obama

"We still don't have the date of first issuance of her passport." – Washington Post journalist Carl Bernstein

"Is she indeed incompetent as even some conservatives would say?" – CNN male host

"There's also this issue that on April 18th, she gave birth to a baby with Down's Syndrome.... Children with Down's syndrome require an awful lot of attention." – CNN anchor John Roberts

"The fact of the matter is the comparison between her [Sarah Palin] and Hillary Clinton is the comparison between an igloo and the Empire State Building!" – MSNBC host Chris Matthews

"The broader question is if Sarah Palin becomes Vice President, will she be shortchanging her kids or will she be shortchanging the country?" – NBC reporter Amy Robach

"Palin would be a backward step for women." – Joe Biden

"And I can see Russia from my house." –Tina Fey, Saturday Night Live (86.9 % of those who voted for Obama thought this was a direct Palin quote even though it was Fey who said it.)

"You're up there in Alaska sneaking around doing anything you want and nobody cares." – David Letterman

"Bad Mother Palin is blabbing about how her pregnant teenage daughter has made the right CHOICE!!! Well, first of all, Ms. Palin, I mean MRS. Palin, your slutty daughter wouldn't have a CHOICE to make at all, if you had your way! ...I can see that she gets off talking badly to Barack, and I am sure the "N" word is rollin' around that empty head of hers somewhere." –Rosanne Barr

"Palin will be gang-raped by my big black brothers if she enters Manhattan…. It's about the extreme views of Gov. Sarah Palin – a woman who doesn't believe that other women should have the right to choose…. I certainly wish Gov. Palin no harm – I'd just like her to explain to me how she can hold such *outrageous* views … and then go back to Alaska." – Sandra Bernhard

"She said that small towns, that's the part of the country she really likes going to because that's the pro-America part of the country. You know, I just want to say to her, just very quickly: F_ck you." –Comedy Central's Jon Stewart

This list of quotes is by NO means close to exhaustive.

HATE: A SYMPTOM OF THE DISEASE

It's clear most elites, progressives, liberals, and socialists have contempt for Sarah Palin because of her faith in God. They are their own gods, and Christianity is a threat to them. As a result, they treat Palin with hostility, vitriol, disdain, nastiness, sarcasm, maliciousness, and hate. These are symptoms of the overall war against Jesus Christ in America. The root cause is always spiritual, and it begins in the human heart. Many have given their take on this phenomenon. In his outstanding book, *How Evil Works*, author David Kupelian brilliantly explained:

"Haven't you ever wondered why, when someone on the public stage radiates noble character, common sense and natural grace – like Ronald Reagan did, or more recently Sarah Palin – he or she is regarded by the 'big media' with an inexplicable revulsion? Hatred is almost too soft a word. It's because Reagan and Palin manifest the very qualities of character that the jaded media elite lost long ago, and since being thus reminded of their lost innocence is painful and unwelcome, they feel compelled to attack the 'reminder.'"

John Zeigler is the author of the eye-opening documentary *Media Malpractice: How Obama Got Elected and Palin was Targeted*. Like many analysts, Zeigler believes it is unfortunate Sarah Palin is not as popular with liberal women, because she unintentionally makes them feel badly about themselves. He was asked "why was the feminist Left so silent in witnessing the media treating a woman so badly?" Zeigler believed that Palin threatened many women because she's a beautiful woman who "clearly loves her husband" and "kills her own food."

A psychotherapist in California who goes by the pseudonym, "Robin of Berkeley" talked about why Leftists loathe Sarah Palin, explaining, "She has retained something that was stripped from them years ago: a wholesomeness, a purity of heart." Many others have noted Christians in the public eye cause people to feel shame, and yet they deny their need for God. Some are masking past pain while others are just jumping on the bandwagon of mob mentality.

THE JOKES

Because some people form political opinions based on comedy, we should look at some late night humor that influenced people's opinions. Below is a small sampling – there are literally hundreds available – from TV's entertainers. A study by the Center for Media and Public Affairs actually counted the number of jokes which Jay Leno and David Letterman told about the four major candidates.

Immediately following McCain's announcement that Palin would be his VP running mate, there were 180 jokes about Palin and 106 about McCain, compared to sixteen jokes about Biden and twenty-six about Obama in a five week period.[10] **That totaled 286 jokes about Republicans and 42 jokes about Democrats.**

> "Sarah Palin and McCain are a good pair. She's pro-life, and he's clinging to life…Actually, it was kind of a smart choice. McCain went with a woman because he didn't want to have to be in a position to have to get CPR from Mitt Romney." – Tonight Show's Jay Leno

> One of the "Highlights of Sarah Palin's trip to New York" was that she "Bought makeup from Bloomingdale's to update her 'slutty flight attendant' look." – David Letterman

Sarah Palin is so dumb; she thinks the capital of China is Chinatown... Palin thinks there are twenty-two letters in the alphabet." – The Daily Show

"The Republican Convention is under way. The theme for tonight's Republican Convention is, 'Who is John McCain?' Tomorrow night's theme is, 'Who forgot to check if the Vice President's daughter is pregnant?'" – Conan O'Brien

"What about the husband? You know he's *doing* those daughters. I mean, come on. It's Alaska," (*NY Times* assignment editor, portrayed by actor James Franco, responded): "He very well could be. Admittedly, there is no evidence of that, but on the other hand, there is no convincing evidence to the contrary. And these are just some of the lingering questions about Governor Palin." – SNL skit about Todd Palin and incest

"It could be her baby, but it is a little suspicious if what I read in *US* magazine has any weight." – Bill Maher, on Palin's son Trig (*US* magazine cover featured Sarah Palin and the title, "Babies, Lies & Scandal")

"She looks like one of those women in the Van Halen videos who takes off her glasses, shakes out her hair, and then all of a sudden, she's in high heels and a bikini. All of a sudden, I am FOR drilling in Alaska." – Jimmy Kimmel

"One awkward moment for Sarah Palin at the Yankee game, during the seventh inning, her daughter [14-year-old Willow] was knocked up by Alex Rodriguez." – David Letterman, monologue – joking about the rape of a minor

The scales were tilted seven to one with jokes about Republican candidates. Christians shouldn't expect different behavior from unbelievers. Hollywood and the media teamed up and the 2008 popular vote favored Obama/Biden approximately 69 million to 60 million for McCain/Palin. Remove Los Angeles, New York City, and Chicago and Obama would have lost the people's vote.

Americans knew (and still know) less about Barack Obama than any other presidential candidate in United States history and voted him into the most important office in the land. Many people – not just Christians – saw the nonstop hatred toward Sarah Palin and kept quiet. People knew there was bias and tragically accepted it as normal. Post-election, people were surveyed, and the media was questioned. Here are a few headlines and poll results:

Rasmussen: By 10-to-1 Public Says Reporters 'Tried to Hurt Palin'

By Nearly 8-to-1, Voters Say Journalists Wanted Obama to Win

By 5-to-1 Public Thinks Most Journalists Tried to Elect Obama

Pew Poll Finds Media Credibility Plummets to All-Time Lows

Rasmussen: '55% Say Media Bias Bigger Problem than Campaign Cash'

Fox News Poll: Two-Thirds Think Most Journalists Wanted Obama to Win

Pew: Many Recognize Media's Pro-Obama Bias, Democrats Prefer CNN

Rasmussen: 63% of ABC, CBS, CNN, NBC and MSNBC Viewers Back Obama

From a list of election issues, people were asked what they thought was the most and least important. At the *bottom* of the list for voters under thirty was the candidate's character and experience. *New York* magazine reporter John Heilmann added:

"No person with eyes in his head in 2008 could have failed to see the way that soft coverage helped to propel Obama first to the Democratic nomination and then into the White House...."

An *Investor's Business Daily* study exposed the lopsided ratio of campaign donations as journalists contributed to Democrats 11.5-to-1. Get this, in terms of dollars given, the ratio was 15-to-1.[11] If you look at those outside the news room, the industry standard is almost purely Democratic. Big media company employees were analyzed revealing shocking results: **the ratio in campaign donations is 100-to-1 in favor of the Democrats**.

Ratings are crashing, and the public has turned against the media, but they're too into denial to notice. Almost 70 percent of Americans thought there was a clear media bias favoring Obama, and a majority wanted to hear more reports on the issues instead of the candidates. Despite reader complaints, the elite media put out more favorable stories (73%) about Obama. Journalism is the only profession I know that ignores the wishes of its customers.

Another question that hasn't been answered is how could the AP, CNN, and other national outlets send over 100 reporters to Alaska to investigate Sarah Palin while sending no one to Chicago – the home of political corruption – to look into Barrack Obama's background? CNN's John King admitted that the media assumed Hillary Clinton was going to win the nomination because in Democratic politics "the Clinton name is the gold standard." King admitted the media didn't vet Obama, and they "need to learn that lesson." The criticism of the media is legitimate.[12]

The next year, within a matter of weeks, the mainstream media ran thirty-seven negative reports on Sarah Palin and only two positive stories. Tina Fey even got an Emmy nomination for mocking Sarah Palin on SNL and believe it or not, Katie Couric received a journalism award for her infamous interviews with VP candidate Palin. Couric's CBS crew edited hours of interview footage and aired only selected segments. Do you think they told the public the whole story?

ABORTION BIAS

The media labeled Sarah Palin a pro-life extremist, but why didn't they report on Barack Obama's pro-abortion position? Abortion was another unreported issue in the 2008 election cycle. In a 2012 Republican debate, the media tried to frame Republicans as anti-women because of Rick Santorum's conservative views on abortion and birth control. Newt Gingrich responded to a question on birth control from John King at the CNN debate by saying:

> "I just want to point out – in the 2008 campaign, not once did anybody in the elite media ask why Barrack Obama voted in

favor of legalizing infanticide. So let's be clear here. If we're going to have a debate about who is the extremist is on these issues, it is President Obama, who as a State Senator voted to protect doctors who killed babies that survived an abortion. It is not the Republicans."

President George W. Bush signed the federal version of the Born Alive Infant Protection Act. The bill allowed nurses to give aid to babies who survive abortions instead of having to leave them to die before of disposing them. Gingrich was referring to Obama's votes as a state senator opposing the Illinois Born Alive Infant Protection Act in 2001, 2002, and 2003.[13]

Jill Stanek, a nurse at Christ Hospital in Oak Lawn, Illinois, helped expose abortionists' practice of abandoning babies (born alive) after failed abortions, leaving them to die in a hospital utility room.[14] Ultimately, Obama gave ten different reasons for voting against the infant protection bill – from protests that it would undercut *Roe v. Wade* to allegations that Stanek and others lied under oath.[15]

Regarding Obama's radical views, Rush Limbaugh said the president's vote against the Illinois version of the Born Alive Infant Protection Act amounted to "the most shocking and underreported significant story I can ever remember."

CONCLUSION

America is a free country, and we have a free press, but the media fails to live up to their responsibility to bring factual information to the people. This is beyond conclusive when it comes to Sarah Palin, and it is a serious issue. We may not be able to change what they believe or how they present the news, but we can pray for their salvation and for more citizens to wake up and see the corruption. A remnant of truth seekers and defenders is stepping up. Will you join the ranks?

In this age of the 24/7 news cycle, the blogosphere, and very little media accountability, we know the attacks, distortions, and misinformation will continue to be aimed at Christians and conservatives. Let's not stoop to their level. Call attention to their hypocrisy, but don't lose focus. Having the freedom to speak about the Bible and share the Gospel is our priority before party, policy or politics.

The media is part of the culture to blot out God in America. Christians in the public eye, especially those as popular as Sarah Palin, are a threat to the progressive, socialist agenda to normalize and rationalize sinful behavior and destroy the moral fabric in America. If they had their way, we'd be prevented from talking about our faith. We'd stay home, we'd stop quoting the Bible or talking about Jesus Christ on the Internet. If they had their wish and we kept quiet, the hopeless, lost, and the hurting would not be reached with the good news.

According to our culture today, anything goes. Moral relativism is normal. On primetime TV, profanity is normal. In churches, it's normal to not make judgments, and Christians should conform to the world and live like everyone else. To those who are sleeping together, premarital sex is fine and dandy. Inconvenient pregnancy? Abortion is normal. To the world, homosexuality is normal. I believe it's time to know God better and get back to our Christian roots in America. It is time to revisit the old normal.

You will be hated by all because of My name, but it is the one who has endured to the end who will be saved (**Matthew 10:22**).

ENDNOTES

1   http://www.mediabistro.com/tvnewser/
    sarah-palins-alaska-premiere-draws-5-million-breaks-tlc-ratings-record_b39794
2   http://www.lifesitenews.com/news/
    liberal-blog-mocks-retarded-3-year-old-trig-palin-suggests-product-of-inces
3   http://frontpagemag.com/2011/01/18/why-the-left-hates-sarah-palin/
4   http://www.wnd.com/2011/10/352225/
5   http://www.youtube.com/watch?v=3s4YfBKs39Y
6   http://townhall.com/columnists/michellemalkin/2008/11/07/
    the_cowardly_character_assassination_of_sarah_palin/page/full/
7   http://newsbusters.org/blogs/noel-sheppard/2008/09/13/2004-flashback-obama-felt-he-
    lacked-experience-be-president#ixzz1mrrQ9F
8   John Perazzo, Front Page Magazine, 10/31/2008. In the Tank: A Statistical Analysis of
    Media Bias, http://archive.frontpagemag.com/readArticle.aspx?ARTID=32928
9   http://www.breitbart.com/article.php?id=D912VD200
10 Jennifer Lawinski, "Late-Night Comics Skewer Republicans 7-to-1, Study Finds," Fox
    News (October 16, 2008)
11 William Tate's July 2008 report in Investor's Business Daily. http://newsbusters.org/blogs/
    rich-noyes/2008/07/24/medias-campaign-donations-tilt-100-1-favor-democrats
12 http://www.scetv.org/index.php/press/release/
    john_king_critiques_media_election_coverage/
13 http://therightswriter.com/2011/01/
    obama-opposed-bill-to-ban-grisly-philadelphia-style-abortions/
14 http://www.lifesitenews.com/news/archive/ldn/2008/aug/08081209
15 http://illinoisreview.typepad.com/illinoisreview/2008/01/top-10-reasons.html

CHAPTER 8

NORMALIZING HOMOSEXUALITY

HOW HOLLYWOOD, GOVERNMENT, PUBLIC SCHOOLS, AND THE LIBERAL MEDIA ARE PUSHING A HOMOSEXUAL AGENDA

Or do you not know that the unrighteous will not inherit the kingdom of God? Do not be deceived; neither fornicators, nor idolaters, nor adulterers, nor effeminate, nor homosexuals, nor thieves, nor the covetous, nor drunkards, nor revilers, nor swindlers, will inherit the kingdom of God (**1 Corinthians 6:9-10**).

THE PROBLEM

Every one of us has the ability to fall into a life of sin. If it were not for God's grace, we'd be lost and without hope. But while we were still sinners, Christ died for us (Rom. 5:8), and the Father's love for us is so great that we are called His children (1 John 3:1). However, if any one of us is unrepentant and continues in a sinful lifestyle, whatever that sin may be, we will not inherit the kingdom of God and cannot be his child. Sadly, because of those who have promoted homosexuality as normal in our society, many have been confused or deceived. We need to pray they won't be lost forever!

It is undeniable that homosexuality has gained acceptance, approval, and momentum in America. Thanks to the marketers of sin, morality has been redefined in our culture. In the span of just over five decades, America has displayed a radical reversal in standards and attitudes toward sin in general, but specifically toward homosexuality. Either God, His Son Jesus Christ, and His Word are right – or Hollywood, the Human Rights Campaign, and the U.S. Department of Education are right.

Gay rights activists and media elites deny they have an agenda, but their actions tell a different story. Homosexuals not only want to legalize gay marriage nation-wide, they also seek to redefine marriage. They lobby our government, implement pro-gay curriculums in public schools and misuse bullying awareness to gain fake sympathy. When the media refers to gay rights, a "right" implies that someone is not being treated fairly and needs special protections. They also report approvingly of "same-sex unions." People can get a certificate or change the laws, but their relationship is not a marriage in God's eyes. Hate crimes legislation is being established and century-old laws are being challenged. The homosexual movement generally has the protection of the elite media, the NEA, the Obama administration, and the Democratic Party.

Some Christians feel it is wrong to point out any sin because we've bought the lie that we shouldn't make a judgment on behavior. We're all imperfect sinners, right? They refer to John chapter 8 where the Pharisees brought a prostitute to Jesus and demanded he obey the law and stone the woman. Jesus said to them, *He who is without sin among you, let him be the first to throw a stone at her* (John 8:7b). Those who defend sinners love to use that verse while ignoring the fact that Jesus did acknowledge she sinned. He also warned her to leave her lifestyle of sin and told her, *Go. From now on sin no more.*

Radio host, Peter Heck, stated emphatically that both Bible-believing Christians and progress-seeking homosexuals cannot live in the same culture where there is such a sharp public disagreement about sin. Heck quoted a national leader in the gay and lesbian movement that stressed the goal of "pushing the parameters of sex" while "transforming the very fabric of society." Heck clarified:

> "They know the success of their cause depends upon the total abolishment of the Judeo-Christian ethic and the Moral Authority it teaches. That is why any belief that the homosexual lobby is merely a passive group of individuals wanting to peacefully coexist with others who have different beliefs and values is naively absurd."[1]

Since there is now more approval of homosexuality in our culture, there must, proportionally, be more disapproval of God. Americans have allowed this gradual, progressive shift in values that would absolutely shock our great grandparents. The things that cause us to roll our eyes and change channels on television these days would make them roll over in their graves. What was once abnormal, indecent, offensive or even repulsive fifty years ago is now becoming normal.

Remember how gay activists and the media excoriated Kirk Cameron recently for saying homosexuality is "unnatural," referring to Romans chapter 1? Free speech is not what it used to be. We must understand homosexuality, the very sin most Americans used to believe went against God's Word, is freely being advanced, celebrated, and promoted.

Homosexuality is a sin and is not ordained by God. The apostle Paul writes that they "exchanged the truth of God for a lie" and worshiped themselves (Romans 1:25).

> *For this reason God gave them over to degrading passions; for their women exchanged the natural function for that which is unnatural, and in the same way also the men abandoned the natural function of the woman and burned in their desire toward one another, men with men committing indecent acts and receiving in their own persons the due penalty of their error* (**Romans 1:26-27**).

God allows people to rebel and choose sin over him. It is repeated in these verses that a relationship between a man and a woman is natural and necessary. Indecent sexual behavior leads to severe consequences. In the Old Testament, homosexuality is called an abomination. It's clear where the God of the Bible stands. Though it is not an unforgiveable sin, the Bible sternly warns about sexual sin, because it is a sin against your own body, against another person, and against the Holy Spirit.

Tragically, there are also homosexual pedophiles who make concerted efforts to recruit young people to their lifestyle of perversion, which can cause children to stumble. The North American Man Boy Love Association (NAMBLA) has been around for decades and is protected and represented by the ACLU. One of NAMBLA's goals is to end the "oppression of men and boys in mutually consensual relationships." They believe there should be no restrictions on age of sexual partners. Some associated with NAMBLA even conspire to sexually abuse children.

As disgusting and reprehensible as this may be, we are to love them. I admit it's easier to love the person who is genuinely struggling with his or her identity and sexuality or seeking help. I confess I have a harder time loving and praying for the loud and proud, bold and vocal gay activist who parades down a rainbow-lined street half naked. I also don't appreciate the push for wide-spread social acceptance of same-sex marriage, homosexual adoption, and gay foster parents. Then I remind myself I was also lost and hostile toward God at one time. It must grieve the Lord's heart to see such little resistance to blatant public sin. What country is this, and how did we get here?

Author and apologist, Pastor Joe Schimmel of Good Fight Ministries referred to the fact that we can't deny homosexuality is being marketed through America. He drew the parallel of the rapid spread of homosexuality with the expulsion of the Bible and prayer from public schools. What followed in the 1960's were the early stages of teaching Darwinism and moral relativism. Pastor Joe Schimmel explains:

> "Add to this the so-called 'free love' movement espoused by godless atheists and occultists in the hippie revolution of the 1960s, and you have a volatile recipe for apostasy. It was at this time, like never before, that the moral compass of America began to be buried under an avalanche of liberal propaganda.

> "In the 70's the American Psychiatric Association removed homosexuality from its list of mental illnesses, and it gained more and more approval in the academic world. Its spread slowed down precipitously with the advent of AIDS in the 80's, but this trend was soon reversed after homosexuality began to be intensely advertised and glorified in mainstream media."[2]

When activists pressured the American Psychiatric Association to remove homosexuality as a category of mental illness causing them to cave, Time magazine even described the change as "an awkward compromise by a confused and defensive profession." It has been proven that gay sex partners are not as physically or psychologically healthy as the rest of society.

Did you also know that "AIDS" (acquired immune deficiency syndrome) was not the original acronym? AIDS came about as the result of homosexual activism against the medical profession. The original name for AIDS was "GRID" (gay-related immunodeficiency disease). The reason they fought to rename and reframe the idea of contracting such a deadly disease is obvious. It was to convince the general public AIDS was something anyone could acquire, placing less emphasis on how it is spread. People will give more sympathy to a person thought to be a helpless victim. On the flipside, the definition of GRID implied it can either originate from or be spread by homosexuals.

Though homosexual sex left masses of deceased victims in its wake in the 1980's and early 1990's, it must also be noted drug users had a smaller role in the spread of AIDS. According the Center for Disease Control (CDC), almost 25% of those who were exposed to AIDS caught the disease from "injection drug use." Gay activists and lobbyists used this fact to downplay their role in the spread of the disease.

Regardless, there is overwhelming evidence of health risks that can result from homosexual lifestyles. These truths won't slow down the movement because this is the era of "gay pride." It saturates primetime television and is promoted in public schools. At the college level, there are lesbian and gay studies. Disneyland and Disney World hosts its annual "Gay Day." Walt would not have approved. Home Depot, McDonald's, Ford, Abercrombie & Fitch, Progressive, Bank of America, PepsiCo, and many others have funded the gay agenda, activities or advertising.

HARMFUL TO YOUR HEALTH

The spread of HIV, AIDS, or Anal Cancer are some of the health problems that have resulted from homosexual activity. Where there is rampant expansion of immorality in the form of promiscuity, sex experimentation promoted in public schools, pre-marital sex and adultery; disease is soon to follow. These diseases can spread and affect the lives of countless people, not just the individuals who had the direct sexual contact. As for heterosexuals, pre-marital sex leading to pregnancy which leads to an abortion is also a horrendous result of promiscuity, and tragically, Christians are not excluded from this category.

That said, according to *Life Site News,* a study which analyzed tens of thousands of gay obituaries and compared them with AIDS deaths data from the CDC, has shown the life expectancy for homosexuals is about twenty years shorter than that of the general public. The study, entitled "Gay obituaries closely track officially reported deaths from AIDS," has been published in *Psychological Reports.*[3]

Study after indisputable study has indicated that the average male homosexual has hundreds of sex partners in his lifetime. This further proves that behavior is the underlying issue. One classic study of homosexuality and lesbianism was done by A.P. Bell and M.S. Weinberg. They found that 43% of white male homosexuals had sex with 500 or more partners, with 28% having 1,000 or more sex partners.[4]

I honestly cannot imagine the emptiness of a homosexual lifestyle where sexual activity is the primary thing that provides fulfillment. I have read the average male homosexual live-in relationship only lasts between two and three years. In another documented study published in *Journal of Research,* Paul Van de Ven studied the sexual profiles of 2,583 older homosexuals. The study found only 2.7% "claimed to have sex with one partner only."

A 1997 CDC report revealed 45% of homosexuals who had unprotected anal intercourse during the previous six months did not know the HIV status of all their sex partners. Even more alarming, among those who reported having had unprotected anal intercourse *and multiple partners,* 68% did not know the HIV status of their partners.[5]

The media doesn't report on the societal dangers or health risks of homosexuality, and how often have you heard a gay or lesbian character on primetime TV talk about any of these concerns? Marketers of evil fail to mention the downside of expanding "gay rights" while they oppose the Defense of Marriage Act. Do the promoters of sexual experimentation in public schools warn young kids as they pass out condoms and Planned Parenthood pamphlets?

Let's address a few of the medical issues that should alarm us. Some of the facts provided here about the negative health effects of homosexuality are courtesy of the Family Research Council.

Human Papillomavirus (HPV): HPV is a collection of more than seventy types of viruses that can cause warts, or papillomas, on various parts of the body. More than twenty types of HPV are incurable STDs that can infect the genital tract of both men and women. *HPV infects over 90% of HIV-positive gay men* and 65% of HIV-negative gay men, according to a number of recent studies.[6]

Hepatitis A: The *Mortality and Morbidity Weekly Report* published by the CDC reports: "Outbreaks of hepatitis A among men who have sex with men are a recurring problem in many large cities in the industrialized world."[7]

Gonorrhea: An inflammatory disease of the genital tract, Gonorrhea traditionally occurs on the genitals, but has recently appeared in the rectal region and in the throat. Untreated gonorrhea can have serious and permanent health consequences, including infertility and damage to the prostate or urethra.

Syphilis: A venereal disease that, if left untreated, can spread throughout the body over time causing serious heart abnormalities, mental disorders, blindness, and death. According to the National Institutes of Health, the disease may be mistaken for other common illnesses. There is a two- to five-fold increased risk of acquiring HIV infection when syphilis is present.[8]

HIV/AIDS: The human immunodeficiency virus (HIV) is responsible for causing AIDS in America, for which there exists no cure. Homosexual men are the largest risk category. The CDC reports homosexuals comprise the single largest exposure category.[9]

According to the CDC, in 1999, a whopping 50% of all new AIDS cases were reported among young homosexuals. Stats are available on the CDC website under "Young People at Risk: HIV/AIDS among America's Youth."[10]

There have also been studies that include lesbians noting a high amount of depression and a greater suicide risk. Mental health issues were common among both homosexuals and lesbians. A national survey of lesbians published in the *Journal of Consulting and Clinical Psychology* found that 75% had pursued psychological counseling of some kind, many for treatment of long-term depression.

The promotion of promiscuity is practically everywhere in our secular-progressive culture so who and what contributed to altering traditional beliefs in America? We exposed Margaret Sanger and Planned Parenthood already. Who else helped progress the perversion?

ALFRED KINSEY AND SEXUAL ANARCHY

Some refer to Alfred C. Kinsey as the Father of the "Sexual Revolution" in America, while others refer to him as the most influential bisexual pedophile and child molester in this nation's history. In 1997, biographer James Jones called Kinsey a sadomasochistic homosexual.

One goal of Kinsey's research was to prove that humans are sexual beings, and the earlier in life we start to experience sexual pleasure, the better. Kinsey fed his perverted sex drive by selling his theory that there was "widespread ignorance of sexual structure and physiology." He believed waiting to have sex, especially until getting married, was psychologically harmful. This subject matter could be (and has been) expanded into an entire chapter or book of its own, but let's look at Kinsey's impact through the lens of gay activism in America.

Alfred Kinsey's research was funded by the Rockefeller Foundation in the late 1930's[11]. The Rockefellers also funded Margaret Sanger's first birth control clinic in 1923 and continue to fund abortion and population control research today.[12] Another of Kinsey's influences was Dr. Herrmann Muller, one of his colleagues at Indiana University. Muller was a member of the American Eugenics Society and had studied under Ernst Rudin. (Rudin became the head of the Nazi Racial Hygiene Society and contributed to Margaret Sanger's *Birth Control Review*.)

Kinsey had a lack of respect for human life, morality, and religion. The Human Life Foundation published Rebecca Messall's research "The Evolution of Genocide," also confirming that "Kinsey was a self-avowed eugenicist."[13] Alfred Kinsey founded the Institute for Sex Research at Indiana University in 1947, now known as the Kinsey Institute for Research in Sex, Gender, and Reproduction.

Early on, Kinsey conducted most of his research in the attic of his Bloomington, Indiana home. If you consider this horror, he truly inspired the future trend of pornography. Most notably, Kinsey influenced Hugh Hefner to launch *Playboy Magazine*, the "soft" approach to porn, which in time would escalate the widespread use of pornography through magazines, cable TV, and the Internet. America would be changed forever by the pornography pandemic.

Dr. Judith A. Reisman is an author, researcher, historian, and teacher who declared "Kinsey's fraudulent sex science research" led to the addicting of men, women, and children to pornography.[14] According to Dr. Reisman, Kinsey said his mission was to remove the Christian influence in America and eliminate the sexually "repressive" legacy of Judeo Christianity. In her exhaustive study of Alfred Kinsey, Dr. Reisman went on to conclude:

> "In large measure, Dr. Kinsey's mission has been accomplished, mostly posthumously, by his legion of true believers – elitists who have systematically brainwashed their fellow intellectual elites to adopt Kinsey's pan-sexual secular worldview and jettison the Judeo Christian worldview upon which this country was founded and flourished."[15]

Dr. Reisman also noted one of Alfred Kinsey's most ardent supporters is Dr. Carol Vance, a lesbian activist and Columbia University anthropologist. Vance spoke at a Kinsey symposium in 1998 to fellow sexologists at San Francisco State University:

> "Biography is the battleground." Should Kinsey be discredited, she warned, "200 years of sexual progress can be undone."[16]

From the time Kinsey's first report was released, his godless work drove the depravity and decay of American culture to the point that even churches would become infected. Many historians have noted that shortly after his work was issued, the problems of abuse in Catholic churches began. Years later, many scandals would be exposed.

When Hollywood released *Kinsey*, starring Liam Neisen, writer and columnist Selwyn Duke published "The re-whitewashing of pedophile Alfred Kinsey." Duke stated the movie portrayed Kinsey, not as the criminal he was but merely as a "conscientious but persecuted scientist whose only ambition was to push back the frontiers of ignorance." The film completely glossed over Kinsey's perversion and damage he caused to America. In real life, he padded and skewed many of his sex survey results. Selwyn Duke accused those who conceal the truth about Kinsey as being complicit in "crimes against humanity" concluding:

> "It is absolutely unconscionable that useful idiots, perverts and social-engineers would perpetuate one of the most pernicious lies ever foisted on the American public. To create any kind of work about the life of Alfred Kinsey and not place his deviance, criminality and wickedness front and center is akin to making a movie about Hitler and omitting mention of the Holocaust."[17]

Kinsey's work soon catapulted the homosexual movement in America. His reputation continues to be protected today by academia, Hollywood, and the elite media even though many critics insist he should have been convicted of child molestation, incest, and pedophilia. No one seems to care his privately conducted studies were not monitored. Kinsey's work was also blindly accepted as fact through the engineering of a Model Penal Code that *reduced* penalties for sex offenses, thus putting women and children at increased risk of harm.

Kinsey's research caused a warped formation of society's beliefs about human sexuality. Possibly most disturbing is the fact that his seldom challenged data is somewhat of a guide used at almost every level of education causing the expansion of the "sex education" industry. Kinsey's live sex surveys involved illegal experimentation on hundreds of children. In part of the description to her 1990 book, *Kinsey Sex and Fraud: the Indoctrination of a People*, Dr. Judith Reisman explained his surveys were done on (a non-representative group) hundreds of sex offenders, prostitutes, prison inmates, and exhibitionists.

> "Because of this fraudulent research, Kinsey's brand of social 'science' has led to one of the greatest hypocrisies of all time: the pretense of providing safe-sex instructions to children while in reality advancing Kinsey's agenda, including indulgence in high-risk lifestyles and behaviors."[18]

A pioneer of perversion, the man who regarded humans as animals is well respected today in colleges and universities. If you hear his name in the future, you'll now understand that tragically, there may be no bigger and more damaging influence on sexuality in America than Alfred Kinsey.

GET 'EM WHILE THEY'RE YOUNG

Friday, April 20, 2012 was the annual Day of Silence (DOS) in American public schools. Under the guise of "Anti-bullying," thousands of public schools allow students to participate by remaining silent throughout an entire day even during instructional time. The DOS is sponsored by GLSEN (Gay, Lesbian, Straight Education Network), and is a political action in public schools that promotes the homosexual movement. GLSEN's goal for DOS is to encourage sympathy and support for not only homosexual and lesbian students but also those involved in cross-dressing behaviors. Behind the veil, DOS is not led by students at all.

Linda Harvey of *Mission America* writes:

"GLSEN describes itself as 'championing LGBT issues in K-12 education since 1990.' Did you catch that – 'K through 12'? Younger and younger students are the target of this group. The younger, the better because they are easier to manipulate."

Of course, any activity considered sinful by biblical standards should not be promoted in public schools in any way. The DOS seems to justify immoral behavior under the blanket of tolerance yet prevents Christian students from sharing their faith with peers caught up in gender confusion. Amazingly, the DOS requires that teachers create activities around the students who are silent. Sadly, those students who choose not to go with the homosexual flow are a captive audience while an agenda they may disagree with is implemented in their classroom.

Attorney Robert Tyler, founder of Advocates for Faith and Freedom warns that the new tolerant terminology coming to public schools is "gender liberation." Evidently, this will be used to 'liberate children' from stereotypes and to eliminate our God-given distinctions between male and female. One of their solutions is gender neutral restrooms. Conservative and Pro-family groups have been warning that this assault on Christian values has been increasing. They even support gender change for elementary age children while suppressing objections by Christian parents. Calling it "blatant indoctrination," Linda Harvey also wrote "The Sleazy History of GLSEN," questioning how they achieve the "sexual enticement" of children.

"Behind GLSEN's window-dressing rhetoric about safe schools, bigotry, 'homophobia', oppression, and concerns about harassment, lies the reality: advocacy of actual homosexual sex, sometimes very explicit even for young kids. And sometimes it's with adults.... How can they get away with ... even soliciting the opinions of minors for sketchy, internally-constructed and analyzed school climate surveys, where no parental permission is needed to interview a sixth-grader about homosexual identity via the Internet?"

With access to kids, GLSEN will use children to normalize homosexuality as long as parents and public schools continue letting them do it. Harvey said "The gatekeepers are not watching."

The founder of GLSEN, Kevin Jennings, (appointed by President Obama in 2009) was forced to resign from his position in the Obama administration. The president appointed this radical activist to a post in the Department of Education, and this is no joke, as the Director of "Safe Schools." It should not surprise us that President Obama would appoint homosexuals to his administration as there are a record number more than any other president in our history. But how in the world did such a dangerous man like Jennings remain in the Obama administration for *two years*?

GOVERNMENT

Kevin Jennings has said that "twenty percent of people are hard-core, fair-minded, pro-homosexual people." However, he ridiculed Christians and discussed what he called "his strategy" at a speaking engagement a few years back and stated that:

"Twenty percent are hard-core [anti-homosexual] bigots. We need to ignore the hard-core bigots, get more of the hard-core fair-minded people to speak up, and we'll pull that 60 percent [of people in the middle] ... over to our side.

"We have to quit being afraid of the religious right. ...I'm trying to find a way to say this. I'm trying not to say, 'F*ck 'em!'

which is what I want to say, because I don't care what they think! [audience laughter] Drop dead!"[19]

I can see why Obama liked him. Kevin Jennings wrote the foreword of the book pushing indoctrination, *Queering Elementary Education*. One of six books Kevin Jennings wrote to promote homosexuality was *Becoming Visible: A Reader in Gay and Lesbian History for High School and College Students*. Jennings also founded the nation's first "gay/straight alliance" in Massachusetts. Harry Hay "inspired" Kevin Jennings to become a homosexual activist.

We all have our mentors, but since Jennings had access and influence on public school kids across America for two years, and Hay was such an infamous radical, we should probably take a closer look. Harry Hay, a known Marxist, was a founder of the homosexual movement, an open supporter of NAMBLA, and a prominent member of the Communist Party USA. Cliff Kincaid is the Director of the Center for Investigative Journalism at Accuracy in Media. In his article "NAMBLA-gate: the Strange Case of Kevin Jennings," Kincaid stated:

> "This is the real scandal – the degree to which the homosexual movement tolerates pedophiles in its midst and regards a champion of pedophilia as a hero."

In 2011, President Obama awarded Kevin Jennings $410 million to promote homosexuality in the public schools. National recession? No problem, this was important! Jennings received an increase of $45 million for his work to push through his agenda on school children regardless of the fact that America has massive federal budget deficits.[20]

As it happens with a Democratic administration, people are appointed to positions before the media reports on their backgrounds, if they ever do report on them. (I highly recommend Michelle Malkin's *Culture of Corruption*.) Shortly after Jennings was appointed, *The Washington Times* attempted to get more facts by questioning the Obama administration, including Education Secretary Arne Duncan. They made "serious inquiries about the filth propagated by a senior presidential appointee," but were being stonewalled.

It was alarming that someone like Kevin Jennings was put in a position responsible for implementing federal education policy. There was clear evidence from various sources that Jennings helped promote a "reading list for children thirteen years old" that made explicit adult-child sex appear normal and acceptable. This was under the guise of promoting so-called alternative lifestyles. The *Washington Times* reported:

> "Democrats clearly are terrified of ruffling the feathers of their activist homosexual supporters, who are an influential part of the Democratic Party's base. This scandal, however, is not merely about homosexual behavior; it is about promoting sex between children and adults."[21]

Perhaps even more disturbing is the fact some homosexual activists aren't just happy with being accepted, welcomed and even given special rights in our society; they are now working to squelch the free speech of Christians. The Obama administration and the NEA continue using taxpayer money to push their outrageous agenda.

WAKE UP AMERICA – IT STARTS AT THE TOP

The homosexual movement receives support from corporations, unions, the media, and Hollywood, but bills are passed and laws are enacted through government. The Obama administration wasted no time whatsoever implementing pro-gay policies. The day President Obama was inaugurated, his "civil rights" goals were immediately posted on the official White House website. Among his goals were to: allow homosexuals to serve openly in the military – repeal "Don't ask don't tell," use the federal government to expand adoptions of children by homosexuals, and encourage the federal government to promote sex-education and contraception in schools. Check, check, check!

More goals were publicly listed by the Obama Democrats: Protect cross-dressing and transgenderism in the workplace (including schools) through federal law, pass "Employment non-discrimination Act" [EDNA] to prohibit "discrimination based on sexual orientation or gender identity or expression," and expand hate crime statutes which includes giving the federal government the power to prosecute those crimes..., repeal the Defense of Marriage Act [DOMA], and push for full civil unions and federal recognition of homosexual couples, plus benefits equal to actual marriage.[22]

MISSION BEING ACCOMPLISHED FOR LGBT COMMUNITY

Portions of the following timeline were taken directly from the Obama/Biden website, BarackObama.com, which included these actions that have advanced the homosexual agenda:

2009

Ordered the federal government to extend key benefits to same-sex partners of federal employees (6/17), hosted the first-ever White House LGBT Pride reception (6/29), awarded the highest civilian honor, the Medal of Freedom, to Billie Jean King and Harvey Milk (8/12), signed the Matthew Shepard and James Byrd Jr. Hate Crimes Prevention Act into law (10/28).

2010

Banned discrimination in federal workplaces based on gender identity (1/01), lifted the ban that prohibited people with HIV/AIDS from entering the United States (1/04), clarified the Family and Medical Leave Act to ensure family leave for LGBT employees (6/22); Awarded a grant to the Los Angeles Gay and Lesbian Community Services Center to work with LGBT foster youth (10/1), led a United Nations measure to restore "sexual orientation" to the definition of human rights (12/21), signed the repeal of "Don't Ask, Don't Tell" (12/22).

2011

Declared the Defense of Marriage Act unconstitutional and announced the administration will no longer defend it in court (2/23), hosted first-ever White House Conference on Bullying Prevention in America's schools (3/10), clarified the meaning of "family" to include LGBT relationships, helping to protect bi-national families threatened by deportation (8/18), Alison Nathan becomes second openly gay appointee to be confirmed to the federal bench under President Obama's nomination (10/13); In his presidential proclamation of National Adoption Month, President Obama called for equal treatment for same-sex adoptive parents (11/1), Created first-ever U.S. government strategy dedicated to combating human rights abuses against LGBT persons abroad (12/6).

2012

Promoted equal access to quality health care by enabling searches for health plans with same-sex partner benefits on Healthcare.gov (2/7), Michael Fitzgerald, fourth openly gay nominee under President Obama, is confirmed to the federal bench in California (3/15), Came out against North Carolina's Amendment 1, which would prohibit same-sex marriage in the state (3/16).[23]

This is all part of the Democratic Party platform and has caused some conservative Democrats to convert to Independent or Republican. Before he was elected, people knew President Obama openly supported homosexuality, yet many didn't care! His administration is weakening the foundation of America, and more people now believe it to be intentional. Marriage, as defined by Jesus Christ, is one of the foundations under attack by President Obama.

> *He answered, 'Have you not read that he who created them from the beginning made them male and female,' and said, 'Therefore a man shall leave his father and his mother and hold fast to his wife, and the two shall become one flesh'? So they are no longer two but one flesh. What therefore God has joined together, let not man separate* (**Matthew 19:4-6** ESV).

God created the natural family unit beginning with the union between one man and one woman in marriage. To those fighting for state-sanctioned gay marriage, licensing the unnatural will not make it natural. So many blessings, including procreation, God's peace, and His protection cannot be fully enjoyed in a homosexual relationship. Marriage is a bedrock to American culture and a healthy society. Satan would prefer to have that foundation destroyed which is the main reason the battle to redefine marriage is so intense.

TAKING CUES FROM HOLLYWOOD

Do you think it is a coincidence or intentional that you can hardly find a scripted show on primetime television that does not feature a friendly, likeable, well-adjusted homosexual character? Hollywood is one of God's biggest offenders. We don't have the time to list all the organizations that promote the cause of the LGBT community, but people on both sides are keeping score.

Each year, the Gay and Lesbian Alliance Against Defamation (GLAAD) releases its listing of TV networks rated according to their friendliness or promotion of pro-homosexual propaganda shown during primetime programming. The CW network came in first place, and Fox came in second for gay-friendly programming in 2011.

As we would expect, the marketing of homosexuality increases massively on the cable networks. HBO and Showtime provide viewers with their usual filth, and then they added gay-friendly content to receive a "good" rating from the LGBT community. According to *Life Site News*:

> "Of its 103 hours of original primetime programming, 55% included LGBT-inclusive images which also reflected the ethnic and racial diversity of the LGBT community. It is notable that both *ABC Family* and MTV, which in 2010 received the first-ever 'Excellent' rating from GLAAD, are both youth-oriented networks."[24]

The only two cable networks that "Failed" to promote gay causes were A&E and TBS. In 2012, GLADD held their annual Media Awards for television and TV shows *Modern Family* and *Hot in Cleveland* won along with transsexual Chaz Bono taking home an individual award. Past Media Award recipients [promoting homosexuality] include: *Glee,* Oprah, Ellen, Keith Olberman, Joy Behar, Clay Aiken, Drew Barrymore, Wanda Sykes, and Tyra Banks.

When it comes to supporting corporate advertisers, does it matter to you what sponsors are behind the worst, most offensive shows on television? It should, because it matters to activists. When openly gay *Grey's Anatomy* actor T.R. Knight presented a significant LGBT award to Suze Orman, she emphasized the importance of advertisers:

> "I want every single one of you in this room to take note of what corporations put their time and money behind gays, behind lesbians – behind you…. Do you want to continue to give your money to people in corporations that oppress us; that keep us down? Or do you want to give your money to the corporations

who can help us rise and change what needs to be changed in the United States of America today.

"I ask you to honor those corporations not only with your support but with your money as well. We can do this – and here's how you're going to do it. You are going to think about every single penny you spend from this day forward. And the only thing I ask of you is to spend it and invest it in those companies that invest in you."[25]

Because this has not been important to Christians in the past, we (believers, conservatives, families, parents, traditional Americans) have lost some ground when it comes to what kind of programming invades our living rooms via the TV. We must take our business elsewhere if companies sponsor shows and movies supporting anti-biblical and homosexual propaganda.

Hollywood continues to nominate and award Oscars to gay-friendly movies almost every year, even if some films are practically unknown to the public. If you haven't figured it out yet, the Academy Awards are not geared toward conservative or traditional Americans. Let's take a quick look at a very brief and highlighted Oscar timeline:

1993 - Tom Hanks won Best Actor Academy Award for his portrayal of a friendly and loveable homosexual in *Philadelphia. (5 nominations)* This was a ground-breaking film for the homosexual community.

1997 – Greg Kinnear won Best Supporting Actor for being the gay victim across the hall in *As Good As It Gets. (7 nominations)* The movie earned Oscars for Best Picture, Actor and Actress, (Jack Nicholson and Helen Hunt)

1999 – Hillary Swank won Best Actress for her portrayal of transgender Brandon Teena in the movie *Boys Don't Cry. (2 nominations)* It was the first transgender film character to be nominated for an Oscar.

1999 – *American Beauty (8 nominations)* won: Best Picture, Best Directing, Best Writing, and Kevin Spacey won Best Actor for his portrayal of a depressed suburban father in a mid-life crisis who was infatuated with his daughter's attractive friend. (A gay couple was portrayed as the only normal people on the block)

2002 – Nicole Kidman won Best Actress for her role in *The Hours*. *(9 nominations)* Themes addressed included lesbianism, suicide, AIDS, and unhappy marriage.

2003 – *Monster:* A disturbing film based on a true story, Charlize Theron won Best Actress for portraying man-hating lesbian, Aileen Wuornos; based on the life of a Daytona Beach prostitute who became a serial killer.

2004 – *Kinsey:* The film about bisexual human sex research "pioneer" cost approximately $11 million to make. Directed by homosexual activist, Bill Condon, *Kinsey* flopped grossing $10 million domestically. Reviews were positive, and Hollywood loved it. Overall, Kinsey was portrayed in a positive light, almost heroically.

2005 – Phillip Seymour Hoffman took home Best Actor honors in *Capote (5 nominations)* based on the life of famous openly homosexual author Truman Capote.

2005 – America didn't love *Brokeback Mountain (8 nominations)* at the box office, but Hollywood went crazy for this gay cowboy romance film that they nominated for eight Academy Awards! It was the Best Picture frontrunner in 2005 but ultimately lost. Ang Lee won Best Director.

2008 – Sean Penn won Best Actor in *Milk (8 nominations)* for his portrayal of homosexual activist Harvey Milk. California's first openly gay elected official, Harvey Milk fought for gay rights and served on the San Francisco Board of Supervisors.

Before you looked at the above (partial) list, maybe you only remembered a few of these major productions. Each of these films elicited sympathy for gay characters or perverted lifestyles. Now imagine how many chapters we could fill if we talked about the hundreds of movies that have portrayed heterosexual marriage in a negative way or movies that portray fathers as dumb, ignorant, and even unnecessary. This is just the tip of the iceberg when it comes to the anti-God, anti-family, anti-marriage agenda that has existed in Hollywood for decades.

As Hollywood celebrities rub elbows with media elites and attack the biblical views of Christians and conservatives, the media like to tell their dwindling audiences that we are backwards, ignorant, or obsessed when it comes to the Bible and social issues. Their talking points have become tedious, and the people of America are catching on.

When discussing marriage, elite liberals do the bullying and then try to marginalize people who believe in the Bible by suggesting Christians are hateful. On CNN's *Piers Morgan Tonight*, for example, Morgan asked Michelle Bachmann to give her opinion of Kirk Cameron's view on homosexuality! Congresswoman and former Republican presidential candidate Bachmann politely responded:

> "I'm here as a member of Congress, and I'm not here as anybody's judge. That's what I have to say."

Morgan attacked her for this response and said she had "been pretty judgmental in the past" and insisted she give her views once again. This time, Bachmann answered back:

> "Well, that's absolutely rude. I'm not a judgmental person.... I believe in traditional values. I believe in marriage between a man and a woman. But I don't think that's bigoted."

Morgan pressed the issue:

> "What I don't like, is the rhetoric that is used against the gay community by those who don't agree with them."

Michelle Bachmann responded:

> "Actually, I would tell you, Piers, the rhetoric is far worse against people who stand for traditional marriage. If anyone gets attacked in this country, it's people who stand for traditional marriage.... There are people who claim Islam is their religion. They do not believe in the issue of marriage between anything other than a man or woman. They aren't bigoted. Or Hindus, they aren't bigoted because they take that religious view."[26]

Good point. Has the media ever asked a Muslim why they are against homosexuality? Michelle Bachmann has been happily married for over thirty years and has five children. The media don't like pro-life, Christian working moms who are happily married. The Bachmanns have also cared for twenty-three foster children, inspiring Michelle's tireless efforts in Congress on behalf of America's adopted and foster children.[27] Bachmann started a charter school for at-risk kids in Minnesota and has continuously worked to defend the right to life for *all* Americans, including the unborn. It doesn't matter what a person does; it's the Christian faith and views on protecting marriage that enrages parts of the homosexual community.

GROWING DISCRIMINATION AGAINST CHRISTIANS

Public school teacher Viki Knox, a New Jersey teacher, was suspended for her Christian beliefs. Because she disagreed with the promotion of homosexuality in her school, the media – led by the *New York Times* – had a field day. We also mentioned the vandalism at a Christian school in Chicago by gay activists that was caught on security cameras. One of the radicals even bragged about the crime on the Internet, but was not arrested. The media ignored the story.

How did America get to the point in our society where opposition to homosexuality became more "controversial" than homosexuality itself? We do a good job of talking about grace, but a lousy job talking about holiness. Let's take the investigation a step further and look at a few cases of blatant discrimination against Christians.

In December 2011, Macy's Department Store in San Antonio, Texas fired employee Natalie Johnson for refusing to let a man use the women's fitting room. The man was wearing make-up and girl's clothing and demanded to speak with a manager. The cross-dresser was accompanied by five other people. According to Liberty Counsel:

> "The group argued with expletives that Macy's is LGBT-friendly, to which Johnson replied that Macy's is also non-discriminatory toward religion, and that it would go against her religious beliefs to lie that he was a woman or compromise with homosexuality. The manager demanded that she comply with the LGBT policies or lose her job. Johnson refused to go against her sincerely held religious beliefs and was terminated."[28]

According to employment law, Natalie Johnson's rights were protected by the same policy that protects LGBT. Macy's claimed that transvestite rights superseded faith, and their decision opened up Macy's dressing rooms to any man who felt like using them.

Another woman who was harshly discriminated against is Oklahoma Congresswoman Sally Kern, a Christian pastor's wife. In 2008, a homosexual activist was funding political races to help elect candidates who supported the gay agenda, and Sally addressed the issue in a speech.

Kern spoke about the danger for a society in which homosexuality is fully embraced, and that she thought it was a greater threat than terrorism because it starts within the country, especially in public schools. (Kern was a former school teacher.) Someone recorded her speech, selectively edited it out of context, and posted it on YouTube. As you can imagine, the liberal media vilified this woman who had spent years working with AIDS patients. This resulted in hate mail from homosexual activists and in an attempt to embarrass her, Ellen DeGeneres called Sally at home during a live taping of the *Ellen* show.

Sally Kern was persecuted for her faith, yet did not back down from her statements and biblical convictions. Homosexual activists failed to prevent her from being re-elected, and she still talks about her passion to see people come to Christ. Her ordeal resulted in her writing a book, *The Stoning of Sally Kern: The liberal attack on Christian conservatism-and why we must take a stand.* The book is about her desire to see America return to the conservative, moral principles that guided America's founders. Kern warns conservatives about standing for their freedom now, before they no longer have the right to do so!

One last, but very tragic example of the danger of homosexuality took place in Prairie Grove, Arkansas, where thirteen-year-old Jesse (Yates) Dirkhising was killed by two homosexual men. Jesse was bound and drugged, tortured, raped, and he died due to a combination of the drugs and the position in which he was tied down. The *Washington Times* was the only national media outlet to report the story at first.

The reason I mention this case is because just one year earlier, the Matthew Shepard case received massive, ongoing national media attention because Shepard, the victim, was a homosexual. While both victims died as the result of assaults by two men, Dirkhising was a minor while Shepard was an adult. No protections have been issued or written on behalf of minors, but severe hate crimes legislations have been passed and implemented to protect homosexuals. Gays (it's an unwritten rule) cannot be portrayed as villains by the media even if they were convicted of rape, torture, and murder.

The *Washington Times* story was headlined, "Media tune out torture death of Arkansas boy." Tim Graham, director of media studies at the Media Research Center said that no one in the media wants to be on the wrong side of the issue by saying anything negative about homosexuals. The LexisNexis Group provides computer-assisted research services and revealed a drastic contrast in the two cases in a media search. One month after each murder, there were 3,007 stories about Matthew Shepard's death compared with only forty-six stories about Jesse Dirkhising's death.[29]

Finally, one of the most disappointing moves by the Obama administration in 2011 was the repeal of the "Don't Ask, Don't Tell" policy in our military. Allowing open homosexual behavior in our military is not only dangerous, it is homosexual activism by our own government. Will this policy weaken or undermine the effectiveness of our armed forces? An article in the Christian Science Monitor mentioned that some US troops voiced their concerns about the decision to allow openly gay troops to serve, worrying it would put them on the defensive. While touring Afghanistan in June of 2011, Defense Secretary Robert Gates was questioned by a marine who said:

> "Sir, we joined the Marine Corps because the Marine Corps has a set of standards and values that is better than that of the civilian sector," the Marine said. "And we have gone and changed those values and repealed the 'don't ask, don't tell' policy."[30]

SODOM AND GOMORRAH OR 2 CHRONICLES 7:14?

*In a similar way, Sodom and Gomorrah and the surrounding towns gave themselves up to sexual immorality and perversion. They serve as an example of those who suffer the punishment of eternal fire (**Jude 7**).*

One of the saddest things to see in America today is the infiltration of gay ministers and pastors in churches, along with the growing openness to homosexuality in Christian churches. I did not say 'openness to homosexuals'; we should be loving and compassionate toward any and every sinner. I said openness to homosexuality, meaning it has become rationalized not only in culture, but also in some churches.

It is the rise of apostasy: gay churches and leadership that preach accommodation and community instead of the conviction of sin. These deceived people are glossing over homosexuality and are not helping those in bondage. Regardless, we are not without hope for the Christian Church in America.

> *If My people who are called by My name humble themselves and pray and seek My face and turn from their wicked ways, then I will hear from heaven, will forgive their sin and will heal their land* (**2 Chronicles 7:14**).

Though many homosexuals publicly promote their lifestyle of sin like no other, we are all in need of a Savior. In a 2011 interview, Pastor Joe Schimmel reminded believers that God is not partial (Romans 2:9-11); we are all in the same boat, and homosexuals are on the same vice list with those who engage in other sins: drunkards, adulterers, revilers, extortionist, slanderers, swindlers, idolaters, and fornicators (1 Cor. 6:9-10). Pastor Joe shared some thought-provoking truths:

> "We need to distance ourselves from two extremes regarding homosexuality. One extreme is the 'God hates fags' crowd, who treat homosexual behavior as the unforgivable sin. The other extreme to taking a cavalier attitude toward homosexuality, and fail to recognize that the Scriptures teach that sexual sin is destructive in a way that other sins are not (**1 Cor. 6:18**)."[31]

We know God destroyed the cities of Sodom and Gomorrah due to their wickedness, but his wrath was not poured out without first rescuing righteous Lot and his family. The Bible recounts the story in Genesis 18 and 19, and archeological evidence also proves Sodom and Gomorrah were destroyed by fire. Violence accompanies rampant sexual sin, and one of those violent effects we have in America is the destruction of life through abortion.

Only Christians can stop the literal bleeding of our culture before it is too late. From the way some Christians talk about or vote for gay marriage, I am convinced there is far too much ignorance about what the Bible teaches. Furthermore, I don't understand why so many Christian leaders have remained silent or neutral, allowing evil to be pushed on young children.

Linda Harvey gave a plea to pastors and Christian leaders in which she shared concerns that homosexuality could destroy American culture and infect the Church. She, like many of us, believes the Church will have a lot of explaining to do on Judgment Day. In her article, "What's at Stake for Christians in the War over Homosexuality," Linda Harvey pleaded:

> "Why did you spend little or no time in the pulpit dealing with this and all the related sexuality issues - promiscuity, pornography, adultery, fornication - sins that are tearing apart the families and personal lives of even Bible-confessing Christians? Why did you constantly decry 'political involvement' when this is a deeply moral issue, one for which there are ready arguments to be made in the public square had more Christian leaders been willing to make them?"[32]

God has no pleasure in the death of the wicked (Ezekiel 33:11) so He is patiently waiting for Christians to speak up about sexual immorality instead of ignoring it – or worse – accepting it. We cannot blame nor can we depend on our pastors. We each must take responsibility.

God's Word is our standard and the foundation upon which America shaped its original laws and values. Don't allow the revisers of history to tell you otherwise and don't fall for their talking points. Someone's natural identity (who a person is) is not the same as their chosen sexual behavior (what a person does). The Bible teaches that we are born in God's image, and this includes the person struggling with homosexual behavior. The bottom line is the wonderful truth about the grace of God. It is for you, it is for me, it is for every other sinner under Heaven – and it is amazing.

It is important to remember that none of us is without sin, and Christians are called to love the homosexual. The Bible does not teach gay people are inferior any more than it teaches abortionists, alcoholics, child molesters, idol worshipers, wife abusers or pornographers are inferior people. Sin is any behavior contrary to God's law, and it is the very reason Jesus Christ suffered and died. He is the way out for us all, but the choice is up to each person who hears the gospel how they will respond; we are to ensure they hear it and compassion is the key.

We were all once enemies of God, but he has rescued and forgiven us. The enemy will still try to lure us back into sin, so we must be careful what we allow in our lives. This effort begins with the things we open our hearts and minds to; will we conform to culture and do as the world does or will we strive for a more holy standard? It begins at home. We'll tackle soul pollution next.

> *It is a trustworthy statement, deserving full acceptance, that Christ Jesus came into the world to save sinners, among whom I am foremost of all. Yet for this reason I found mercy, so that in me as the foremost, Jesus Christ might demonstrate His perfect patience as an example for those who would believe in Him for eternal life* (**1 Timothy 1:15-16**).

ENDNOTES

1　Peter Heck, 78 How Christians Can Save America, 2011 Attaboy Productions

2　http://www.gcmwatch.com/7414/pastor-joe-schimmel

3　http://www.lifesitenews.com/news/archive/ldn/2005/jun/05060606

4　A. P. Bell and M. S. Weinberg, Homosexualities: A Study of Diversity Among Men and Women (New York: Simon and Schuster, 1978), pp. 308, 9; see also Bell, Weinberg and Hammersmith, Sexual Preference (Bloomington: Indiana University Press, 1981).

5　Jon Garbo, "Gay and Bi Men Less Likely to Disclose They Have HIV," Gay-Health News (July 18, 2000). Available at: www.gayhealth.com/templates/0/news?record=136.

6　Richard A. Zmuda, "Rising Rates of Anal Cancer for Gay Men," Cancer News (August 17, 2000). Available at: cancerlinksusa.com/cancernews_sm/Aug2000/081700analcancer.

7　Mortality and Morbidity Weekly Report (Centers for Disease Control and Prevention) September 4, 1998, p. 708.

8　Family Research Council, Issue Analysis on homosexuality, http://www.frc.org/get.cfm?i=IS01B1

9　"Table 9. Male Adult/Adolescent AIDS Cases by Exposure Category and Race/Ethnicity, Reported through December 1999, United States," Centers for Disease Control and Prevention: Division of HIV/AIDS Prevention: available at: www/cdc.gov/hiv/stats/hasr1102/table9.

10 "Young People at Risk: HIV/AIDS among America's Youth," Divisions of HIV/AIDS Prevention (Centers for Disease Control) November 14, 2000. Available at: www.cdc.gov/hiv/pubs/facts/youth.htm.

11 http://en.wikipedia.org/wiki/Alfred_Kinsey

12 http://liveaction.org/blog/rockefeller-foundations-push-to-legalize-abortion-in-uruguay-is-no-surprise/

13 http://www.humanlifereview.com/index.php/component/content/article/11-1999-winter/7-the-evolution-of-genocide

14 http://www.drjudithreisman.com/about_dr_reisman.html

15 http://www.lifesitenews.com/news/sexual-anarchy-the-kinsey-legacy/

16 http://www.lifesitenews.com/news/sexual-anarchy-the-kinsey-legacy/

17 http://www.renewamerica.com/columns/duke/041202

18 http://www.drjudithreisman.com/archives/2005/08/kinsey_sex_and.html

19 http://www.worldviewweekend.com/worldview-times/print.php?&ArticleID=5352

20 http://www.massresistance.org/docs/issues/kevin_jennings/410_million/index.html

21 http://www.washingtontimes.com/news/2009/dec/09/obamas-risky-sex-czar/

22 http://www.massresistance.org/docs/issues/obama/first_day.html

23 https://s3.amazonaws.com/obama.3cdn.net/8b81d637f95493e38a_wlm6b5ril.pdf

24 http://www.lifesitenews.com/news/2011-list-of-tv-networks-which-most-promote-homosexuality

25 http://www.glaad.org/2009/04/01/20th-annual-glaad-media-awards-in-nyc-wrap-up

26 http://transcripts.cnn.com/TRANSCRIPTS/1203/05/pmt.01.html

27 http://bachmann.house.gov/Biography/

28 http://www.lc.org/index.cfm?PID=14100&PRID=1133

29 http://en.wikipedia.org/wiki/Murder_of_Jesse_Dirkhising

30 http://www.csmonitor.com/USA/Military/2011/0607/As-don-t-ask-don-t-tell-repeal-nears-concerns-crop-up-on-both-sides

31 http://www.gcmwatch.com/7414/pastor-joe-schimmel

32 http://www.missionamerica.com/church.php

CHAPTER 9

SOUL POLLUTION: THIS CHAPTER RATED "M" FOR MATURE

TELEVISION, MUSIC & MOVIES

For the one who sows to his own flesh will from the flesh reap corruption, but the one who sows to the Spirit will from the Spirit reap eternal life. Let us not lose heart in doing good, for in due time we will reap if we do not grow weary (**Galatians 6:8-9**).

What would our great grandparents say if they walked into a grocery store and saw the covers of today's magazines? They'd consider it to be pornographic material, and they'd probably shield the eyes of the nearest children in disgust. Now imagine our great grandparents bringing home their first television, but somehow when they turn it on, the programming mysteriously jumps to the year 2012. After picking themselves up off of the floor, they'd probably throw the TV set out the nearest door or window.

What changed? Has God and the Bible changed or has American culture changed? Today, Hollywood continually pushes filthy garbage right through our TV screens directly into our living rooms, and we say nothing because "that's entertainment." We are desensitized.

Case in point: *Don't Trust the B---- in Apartment 23.* The producer of this ABC show previously called *Don't Trust the Bi*ch in Apt 23*, boasted about pushing the boundaries of decency too far instead of being boring. The Parents Television Council (PTC) warned about the show:

"The program is a sexist mixed-bag of hedonism, drug-use, alcohol abuse (including the main character plying a 13-year-old boy with alcohol to get him drunk) and explicit levels of promiscuity that are shocking even by today's broadcast TV standards."[1]

Chloe, the actual character in Apt. 23, is described by a *Plugged-In* review as the prototypically cynical, slimy and slightly "psychotic New Yorker with a lack of ethics or morals or human decency." The star of the show drinks and sleeps around, lies, sells illicit Chinese sexual energy pills, and even steals money and flowers meant for cancer survivors. The show features "television's most shallow, carnal, self-absorbed and plain ol' wicked characters."

> "If Chloe's not walking around the apartment completely naked, then we've got to deal with Eli, who masturbates as he watches the girls from a nearby window. If Eli's not in the picture, chances are Luther – the homosexual fashion guru of Chloe's 'straight gay BFF' James Van Der Beek – is reciting some ooky double entendre."[2]

We're talking about primetime programming kids watch. There has been a gradual, disrespectful, progressive scheme by networks and advertisers to test any remaining moral barriers in America. The more they push, the more the public accepts. Thinking that we can't do anything about this home invasion, even Christian families do or say nothing at all.

TELEVISION, THE FCC, AND OUR HOMES

It's frustrating when we turn on the TV in our own 'safe' living room, and we're bombarded by what the Bible would consider appalling, indecent, offensive, unacceptable, and unholy. I confess that when my wife and I see a movie, a program or even commercials on TV that are offensive, we either flip over to another channel or turn the TV off. This is most likely what you and other families do as well. Some parents have cancelled their cable or digital service because of the awful programming. I don't blame anyone for protecting their family by doing so.

However, these simple actions, though they help us avoid soul pollution temporarily, do not change the cause or source of the problem. We have only treated an ongoing symptom. Our choices don't help other families that have been seduced by the monster. Should this be a concern? Some Christians don't have the discipline and self-control to turn the channel, shut off the TV, monitor their children's programs, or look into parental control services. Many other families, though maybe not Christian, still find today's programming just as offensive or disturbing, yet they just keep on helplessly watching and taking in the trash.

Talk to other Christians, friends, families and concerned parents and see if they have similar concerns. They probably will, unless they have been desensitized to the point they don't notice or don't want to notice. Another action step is to contact the local station that airs offending programs or commercials. If enough people do this, it may help with local or regional programming. The next option is to contact either the national network, such as ABC or TNT. We can also contact the advertisers who are supporting the shows in question. I realize this sounds like work, but the way the Federal Communications Commission (FCC) is set up, it is a bit neutral because of First Amendment issues.

Believe it or not, the FCC does not censor programming as we'd like to think. It is more of a business than a regulatory agency in the way it operates. Its purpose is to regulate interstate and international communications by radio, television, wire, satellite, and cable. On the "Complaint" section of its website, it reads:

> "The Federal Communications Commission regularly receives complaints from consumers on a wide variety of issues. Consumers are encouraged to always try to resolve the problem first with the company whose products, services or billing are at issue. However, if that does not succeed, they may file a complaint...."[3]

In 1938 when barely two percent of Americans owned a TV, American writer E.B. White made a statement that was more insightful than he could have known at the time:

> "I believe television is going to be the test of the modern world, and that in this new opportunity to see beyond the range of our vision we shall discover either a new and unbearable dis-

turbance of the general peace or a saving radiance in the sky. We shall stand or fall by television, of that I am sure."[4]

The average American family watches between four and six hours of television every day which means that they watch thirty-five hours a week or 155 hours a month. If you do the math this equates to over 1,200 hours of television every year. How many of us wish we'd have spent our time more wisely? It's not too late, but it will take effort.

CASE STUDY 1: "GOOD CHRISTIAN BI*CHES" (G.C.B.)

How many primetime television programs have you seen that have portrayed Christians in a positive light? You don't need to answer that. When the ABC television show *Good Christian Bi*ches* was first proposed in May of 2011, the show seemed to basically be a Christian-bashing version of *Desperate Housewives*. The premise was not a horrible one: people who love Jesus are not perfect, and there is too much gossip in the church. The book that the show is based on was not supposed to be used as just another way for Hollywood to make Christians look bad. Author Kim Gatlin from Dallas intended to "put a voice to the downside of gossip."

The show name was changed to *G.C.B.*, and the basic plot was to show that Christians are hypocrites, religion is a joke, and Christian women are especially wicked. The show depicts "Christians" drinking, back-stabbing, and being sexually aggressive (surprise!). According to the PTC, all the show's women were supposedly devout Christians yet villainous and "vengeance-crazed." The formula for the show was to take a bunch of "shallow, materialistic, sex-obsessed women" and give them reasons to go after each other. Then throw in some clueless, token husbands, and you had a new nighttime soap.

In May of 2012, ABC pulled the plug on G.C.B. Some of the advertisers that made G.C.B. possible were McDonald's, Progressive Insurance, Google, Mercedes Benz, Olive Garden, Clinique, Target, Honda, and JC Penney. Know the advertisers behind offensive shows; reward the good ones with your business, and boycott the bad ones, if you care to do so. How will they know unless we speak up?

Research shows the majority of American families do not approve of the level of indecency on television today; it's just that most families don't say anything about their preferences. It's important to note that one reason reality TV has done well in general is that people freely reference faith, God, and prayer on many reality shows. In fact, surveys show that "most Americans treat religious beliefs with respect." In a November 2006 Zogby poll, a large majority (84%) of adults stated they are not offended by references to God or the Bible on network television.

This reveals an agenda by Hollywood producers who continually show contempt for Christianity, as the PTC explained, by:

> "Deliberately portraying God as subject of ridicule, and followers of organized religion as oppressive, fanatical, hypocritical and hopelessly corrupt.... Mockery of God is a constant on comedies like *American Dad, The Family Guy* and *The Simpsons*...."[5]

Media Research Center's Matt Philbin wrote about Hollywood's hostility toward Christianity and used the show G.C.B. as an example. He cited that in just the first three episodes, there were "more than 100 instances of mocking or attacking Christians and their faith."[6] He added that the characters were portrayed as drunken adulterers, dishonest, materialistic or secretly gay. What Hollywood is doing is nothing new; it's just that the content is getting more vulgar.

WELL, AT LEAST IT'S AN ANIMATED SHOW

Cartoons are not what they used to be. I hope by now that most parents understand that animation is not always safe for kids. The networks have implemented a brilliantly deceptive plan to basically bypass the censors and push their perversion on children and young adults. Simply because they are animated shows, they don't get anywhere near the scrutiny non-animated shows receive. (I use the word "scrutiny" in the loosest possible way here.) The truth is that most of these "cartoons" contain things that make many adults blush, and they have no business being allowed in prime-time. TV producers constantly test the virtually non-existent limits for animation on television.

In 2011, the PTC released some disturbing and riveting results from their study in a documentary called "Cartoons Are No Laughing Matter." It revealed "shocking levels of adult content" on networks kids watched the most during primetime hours, especially teenagers, according to Nielsen data from March 21 – April 14, 2011. That study included: Adult Swim, Cartoon Network, Disney Channel and Nick at Nite. PTC President Tim Winter warned parents that describing a cartoon with the term 'adult' goes beyond the content or the show. It is a hint that advertisers are going to market more 'adult' products in the commercials as well.

Naturally, the networks want to target kids directly with adult entertainment such as TV-MA shows, mature games and DVDs, and R-rated movies. Winter added that during PG-rated cartoons, "harsh profanity and graphic sexual depictions aired." According to the study, Cartoon Network "failed to use the ratings system to warn parents about sexual content, suggestive dialogue and explicit language 100 percent of the time."[7] Violence is the most loosely regulated and is almost a given in most primetime shows. Other major findings are as follows:

- Sex (680 instances) surpassed every form of violence (674 instances) in animated primetime cable programming. Sexual depictions included simulations or obscured scenes of sexual intercourse, pornography, masturbation, pedophilia and prostitution.

- Drugs: There were a total of 208 incidents relating to drugs including cocaine, marijuana, crystal meth, psychedelics and alcohol. Eighty percent of the drug-related incidents were depictions rather than references.

- Profanity: The study identified 565 incidents of explicit language on shows rated TV-14 and TV-PG. 27% of the uses of "f**k" and "sh*t" occurred on TV-PG programs.

- Content Ratings: 85% of the TV-PG shows and 64% of the TV-14 shows containing sexual content did not have an "S" descriptor warning parents (sexual content).

This was all in a *three-week survey period!* Concerned citizens must be aware of how blatantly explicit these cartoons are so that they can make better viewing decisions for their families.

CASE STUDY 2: AMERICAN DAD

(Offensive and Graphic Content Warning for Younger Readers)

Let's look at one of the top offenders, *American Dad* on Fox. After reading details about many of the episodes of this vulgar show, it is hard to believe it is on television at all. It's repulsive. Every week, the PTC rates the 'Best and Worst Shows on TV' and have awarded *America Dad* the **Worst TV Show of the Week** many times. They explain *American Dad* is similar to *Family Guy*, replete with all the sex, violence, language and crude humor. According to a PTC episode summary:

> "In the 4th season premiere, Stan and Francine find it impossible to cope with the fact that Steve has begun puberty. The budding teen proudly shows off his solitary first pubic hair. In previous episodes, daughter Hayley and her boyfriend wear bondage gear, and Steve masturbates to a nude picture of his sister Hayley...."[8]

> "In another episode, (July 31, 2011), "Stan is invited to a houseboat during Spring Break, where he and his friends plan to wear "Sluts Gone Nuts" T-shirts and entice young co-eds to flash their breasts." He ends up taking his son along, and the next morning he throws up under the breakfast table. Stan also confides in his teenage son (Steve) that he thinks Francine (Steve's Mom) "fakes her orgasms."

Another PTC Worst TV Show of the Week award went to the November 11, 2010 episode of *American Dad*. To set-up this particular episode, the PTC wrote: "Anti-Semitism. Mocking the disabled. Sleazy sexual innuendo ... Graphic, gory violence. And all in cartoons aimed at children." Twisted show creator Seth MacFarlane had fun with this Halloween episode that included neighbor "Buckle" whose mailbox had a demon that popped out and screamed, "I'll fu**ing kill you! I'll skin you alive, you little whore!" (the f-word was bleeped over)

"The kids, Steve and Snot, visited their Japanese friends, and Steve made a reference to sexual arousal upon seeing their friend's little sister, Akiko. The PTC review continued by describing the parents getting ready for Halloween in an episode full of sleazy sexual references. Stan was dressed in tight leather bustier and panties with fishnet stockings while at one point, Roger strips off Francine's [nun] habit, revealing her in panties and a bra and presses her face against a plexiglass window."[9]

After all, these are only harmless cartoons.

CASE STUDY 3: REALITY TV

In the 2012 season of *Dancing with the Stars*, my wife and I tuned in to see Donald Driver of the Green Bay Packers. DWTS is probably one of the more family-friendly reality shows on television, which I truly appreciate. One of my definitions of good TV is when a seven-year old, their parent, and their grandparents can all watch and enjoy the same program. Now, the downside is that some of the dancer's costumes can be risqué and certain dance routines are too sensual for 7 p.m. Co-host, Brook Burke, also wears an occasional inappropriate dress.

Next, *American Idol* has become a huge, influential show. (Idolatry alert) There are some rare profanities during the audition process, and if language gets bad, it is bleeped out. It does seem the most controversial Idol episodes are always near the end of each season when they bring in the mega-stars to perform. Some of these stars have been less family-friendly than others, but overall, viewers have fun getting sucked into picking a favorite contestant and sticking with him or her. About former judge, Aerosmith's Steven Tyler's f-bomb habit, the *Los Angeles Times* once said that during the taping of *American Idol's* tenth season, Tyler "dropped enough of them to blow up a small European country."

CAMERAS FOLLOW PEOPLE ON DATES? REALLY?

One of the new entertainment fads seems to be television dating. Any so-called dating show on television may not only be awful entertainment, (unless we really enjoy watching others get humiliated), but could be potentially mind-numbing and insulting to your intelligence. Both *The Bachelor* and *The Bachelorette* were given the 'red stop sign' rating from the PTC, which means the shows are not recommended for viewers under eighteen. I can't understand what's fair about the bachelor dude having a choice of only twenty-five young, love-hungry women vying for his attention when the bachelorette gal has her pick from the litter of thirty testosterone-filled, about-to-be-embarrassed, studly young specimens.

Let's get this straight: the shows pay each star to go on dates with twenty-five or thirty people, rotating them over and over as contestants work feverishly to win the prize of fake love and avoiding humiliation. This is what people watch? Naturally, episodes are full of exactly what you'd expect from dating shows – lots of kissing, sexual innuendo, sexual references, and implied sexual activity. One *Bachelor* show featured plaster casts that were made of all the girls' busts that would later be auctioned off for charity. As far as language, it's pretty foul and quite typical. Both of the shows bleep the words f*ck, sh*t, pu**y, and sl*t – while letting other words fly unbleeped such as "a*s," "bi*ch," "cr*p," and "s*ck." (All airing at 7 p.m. Central!)

A true reality show would be filming a person's life *without* them knowing it, kind of what *Candid Camera* used to do. Once they give you permission and know you are filming them, sorry, it's no longer reality. It's bad entertainment. We've all seen people act more exaggerated or foolish when they knew a camera was filming them. Other than dancing, singing, or music competitions, why do so many people watch this so-called reality stuff? If the ratings were bad, advertisers wouldn't support the programs and networks wouldn't keep the shows on the air.

It's also hard to believe that millions of people sit in front of their television sets to watch the latest episode of *Big Brother*, *Jersey Shore*, or *Real Housewives*. Unfortunately, we sometimes make poor choices about how to escape our own reality. Many of us use technology to accomplish the same thing; to take a break from everyday life routines. Though this is common, the problem occurs when we shut out other people. Shutting ourselves down emotionally is one negative effect of using *any* form of entertainment to get away from the stresses of life. Diversions are fine, but we need to maintain a healthy balance and avoid soul pollution.

CASE STUDY 4: "GLEE"

Due to the popularity of *Glee*, this will be more extensive. The PTC cautions, **"WARNING: Graphic Content!"** For containing explicit sexual content in a show aimed at kids, *Glee* has been named "***Worst TV Show of the Week***" several times.[10] I understand that these reviews and my writing about the show are going to ruffle some feathers, but I don't know of a clearer example of conforming to culture than a Christian family gathering around the television to watch *Glee*. The PTC calls it an edgy adult series that is "sexually charged."

The roll out of *Glee* was done quite deceptively as the pilot episode premiered immediately after an *American Idol* finale, one of the most coveted slots on Fox. But a show following Idol aimed at teenagers gave the *impression* that it was a safe, family-friendly program. What could be bad about high school kids dancing and singing? *Glee* is definitely not *High School Musical*: the T.V. Series. According to the PTC:

> "What did those pre-adolescents tune into when the show finally premiered in its regular timeslot on September 9th? A veiled reference to fellatio, a speech denouncing abstinence, simulated sex during a musical dance number, and premature ejaculation."

In the pilot episode, teachers giggle about using and selling illegal drugs, homosexuality, and pedophilia. One of the main characters, Rachel, talks about how cool it is to have two gay dads.

Not surprisingly, *Glee* was created by Ryan Murphy, the same man credited with the unbelievably explicit FX drama *Nip/Tuck*, which has featured orgies, incest and necrophilia among other things, and both shows share a similar cynical view of America. *Newsweek*'s Ramin Setodeh has called *Glee* "TV's gayest product since Richard Simmons." According to a PluggedIn review, "The series wallows in sexuality and sacrilege, and it stumbles – often – with crass gags and sleazy stereotypes." Lots of Christians (at least on Facebook) are big fans of *Glee*, so we're taking a closer look at a few episodes to see what today's Christian family approves of as acceptable entertainment.

In the November 8, 2011 episode called **"The First Time,"** two couples – one homosexual couple and one heterosexual couple – talk about losing their virginity. One of the characters named Tina encouraged them all: "Losing my virginity was a great experience for me. Because I lost it with someone I love." What message does this send to your kids? The subject of waiting until getting married never came up, and both couples chose to have sex.

> "Both couples kiss passionately and talk about sex. Kurt and Blaine make out in a car. Masturbation is mentioned, as are condoms. When another boy makes passes at Blaine, the three sneak into a gay bar (with fake IDs) on Drag Queen Wednesday."[11]

In the October 5, 2010 *Glee* episode **"Grilled Cheesus,"** the character Finn has a cheese sandwich with an image of Christ burned onto it, and he prays to his "cheesy lord." He prayed for many things such as getting to second base with his girlfriend, and his prayers were answered. Another character, Sue, protests kids singing Christian songs on school property (to encourage Kurt whose father was in the hospital).

Sue says, "Asking someone to believe in a fantasy (praying to Jesus), however comforting, isn't a moral thing to do. It's cruel." Emma thinks Sue is being arrogant, to which Sue retorts:

> "It's as arrogant as telling someone how to believe in God, and if they don't accept it, no matter how openhearted or honest their dissent, they're going to hell. Well, that doesn't sound very Christian, does it?"

Kurt says God is "like Santa Claus for adults" and calls him an "evil dwarf" and a "great spaghetti monster in the sky." He has a few choice words for Christians, too. The episode wraps with Kurt telling his unconscious dad that he doesn't believe in God...."

In the April 20, 2010 episode **"The Power of Madonna,"** the aging, controversial pop star is idolized throughout the episode, which encourages teenagers to take "control" of your own body. Three of the school's virgin characters decide to "do the dirty deed," and a montage of their caressing preparations plays out to "Like a Virgin."

Glee's **"Hell-o"** episode on April 13, 2010 featured the character Sue blackmailing the school's principal. She drugged his wine during dinner, got him in bed and slept with him, and then she threatened to tell his church and his wife. Finn went on a date with two cheerleaders, who offered to "make out with each other for the pleasure of their shared date" while viewers hear veiled sexual references to whipped cream and going braless. Profanities are both spoken and sung, including misuses of God's name. Sue slams Sarah Palin for being dumb, girls lie, back-stabbing is common, and home schooled kids are insulted. Had enough?

CASE STUDY 5: TV AWARDS SHOWS

The *2011 MTV Video Music Awards* in Los Angeles were "maybe the most bleeped award show in history and certainly among the lewd-est" according to the *New York Times*. Apparently, Lady Gaga opened the show "spewing an aimless monologue while smoking a cigarette and cursing like a fourth grader" all while dressed in drag. Of course, Cloris Leachman got into the act by exchanging profanities with the "Jersey Shore" cast.

Next, the *2009 American Music Awards* featured *American Idol* runner-up Adam Lambert's controversial performance that included simulated oral sex with a male backup dancer and a passionate kiss with a male keyboardist. Backstage at the Nokia Theatre after the show, Lambert told *Rolling Stone* that for years, female performers have been pushing the envelope on sexuality. Lambert stated:

> "We're in 2009; it's time to take risks, be a little more brave, time to open people's eyes, and if it offends them, then maybe I'm not for them. My goal was not to piss people off, it was to promote freedom of expression...."[12]

I agree with Lambert's point that female performers have been pushing the sexuality envelope for years. America has accepted the promotion of female sexuality in most every form, and this is wrong. Countless performers think the same way Lambert does, having the attitude that if people don't like it, they don't have to watch or listen. This is incorrect at its premise because when families are watching an awards show, or *any* primetime program, they don't have time to scramble for the remote and turn the channel the moment something offensive comes on.

You may remember the famous kisses between Madonna and Brit-ney Spears & Madonna and Christina Aguilera at the *2003 MTV Video*

Music Awards that triggered a controversy. Of course, who can forget the censorship failure of the apparent Janet Jackson wardrobe malfunction, during the Super Bowl halftime show in 2004 when Justin Timberlake ripped off the piece of leather covering Jackson's right breast. (She had conveniently covered her nipple with a gold star before the performance.) This act of lewdness flashed across TV screens all around the world with entire families including young children watching the game. An appeals court tossed out the proposed fine to CBS for airing the unplanned "malfunction."[13]

One of the most foul-mouthed and rebellious entertainers was praised in 2007 when controversial comedienne Kathy Griffin was given an award for her Outstanding Reality Program, *My Life on the D-List* on Bravo. Fortunately, her Emmy acceptance speech was cut from the broadcast when she said, "I guess hell froze over," Griffin announced. "A lot of people come up here and thank Jesus for this award. I want you to know that no one had less to do with this award than Jesus.... Suck it, Jesus! This award is my god now."[14]

The next example is from the *2003 Golden Globe Awards* which was televised on NBC and featured U2 singer Bono dropping a non-censored f-bomb when he remarked that "This is really, really, f**king brilliant." You may not believe this, but even though over 18,000 complaints were filed with the FCC, they refused to take action. The FCC's Enforcement Bureau (I didn't realize there was such a thing) claimed that in Bono's case "the 'f-word' was used as an adjective instead of as a verb; NBC did not violate the federal code." Un-be-lieveable!

Fox network aired the *Billboard Music Awards* during primetime in December 2003 and the dialogue between Nicole Riche and Paris Hilton caused over 46,000 complaints according to the PTC. While announcing an award, Riche told Hilton: "Have you ever tried to get cow sh*t out of a Prada purse? It's not so f**king simple." There was no significant response from the FCC. Needless to say, millions of us have stopped watching meaningless awards shows.

I'm not expecting worldly celebrities in Hollywood and liberal entertainers to stop cussing or to live according to God's Word because Christian values are either foreign or offensive to them. They need the love and salvation of Jesus Christ! Since they have no standards other than the culture and environment in which they live, we can't expect them to clean up their acts for the typical TV viewing family.

We can't blame a non-Christian for sinning or for hating Christians. The biggest problem is not with the foul-mouthed, shock value-producing "stars," but with a permissive culture, a quiet church, and a federal commission that gets more than $278 million a year from Congress. It is baffling that the FCC does not seem to care about the very American families their bureau is supposedly looking out for by monitoring what comes across our TV screens. This is failed bureaucracy.

Have nothing to do with the fruitless deeds of darkness, but rather expose them (**Ephesians 5:11**).

CASE STUDY 6: MTV

A chapter on soul pollution wouldn't be complete without MTV. Some of us were actually around before Music Television blasted into our living rooms in the early 1980's. It began as cool entertainment, merged into cautionary content, and became perverted programming. The problem got worse when a music network tried producing quality TV.

MTV's 2011 teen filth show *Skins* was cancelled after one season, but still had millions of kids tune in. The fact that so many young Americans were attracted to such moral garbage shows how far we have fallen as a nation. The show promoted adult content including drugs, alcohol, simulated masturbation, implied sexual assault, and teenagers disrobing and jumping into bed together. Yes – teenagers.

Next up is the new 2012 MTV show featuring "advice" about sex from activist and homosexual host Dan Savage. The show is aimed at teens and, according to Brent Bozell of the Media Research Center, "documents Savage touring college campuses to offer snarky/smutty advice to college students." Co-host Lauren Hutchinson told the *Los Angeles Times* that they plan to talk to kids whether parents want them to or not! Some of the advice Savage gives is to "be good, giving, and game" where sex is concerned. Anything goes, basically. MTV producers call the show "a crash course in sex ed." However, it turns out that the show is more about provocative entertainment than any form of education. Brent Bozell wrote:

> "At one point in the MTV show, Savage lectures a couple having 'unprotected' sex that 'pregnancy is the ultimate sexually transmitted infection.' A child is a disease? How sick is that? He tells the female: 'You can get birth control that'll knock your eggs out for a year. You should. You must! Oh my God!'"[15]

While touring Maryland College, Savage interviewed a young girl at a bar in town who described the "sex culture" on campus as "very active." Another girl described the sex scene on campus by saying, "It's like a good yogurt." Another group of four friends had a sexual conquest competition. According to MTV, this all falls under sex education. Remember Kevin Jennings?

SHOCKING STATS, STUDIES & POLLS!

A Fox News-Opinion Dynamics poll asked people if they think Hollywood shares their values or not. You may be surprised that only 13 percent said yes, while 70 percent said no. In the same poll, people were asked if they thought Hollywood was in touch with average Americans or out of touch – just 19 percent said Hollywood is "in touch."

In a 2005 Kaiser Family Foundation study on sexual content on television:

Among the top twenty most watched shows by teens, 70 percent include sexual content, and nearly half (45%) include sexual behavior.

During prime time hours, sex is even more common with nearly 8 in 10 (77%) shows including sexual content, averaging 5.9 sexual scenes per hour.

Two-thirds (68%) of all shows include talk about sex, and 35% of all shows include sexual behaviors.

The percentage of shows with sexual content by genre includes movies 92%, sitcoms 87%, drama series 87%, and soap operas 85%.[16]

According to a 2005 poll conducted by Harris Interactive for Morality in Media, more than half of U.S. adults (53%) believe the FCC is doing a poor job of maintaining community standards of decency on broadcast TV.[17] Thirty-three percent believe the FCC is doing a *"very* poor" job compared to only 15% of adults who say the FCC is doing a *"very* good job" of protecting families from indecency on TV.

This time, kids were surveyed in a 2004 study by Huston and Wright, University of Kansas called "Television and Socialization of Young Children." Surprisingly, 77% of kids said there is too much sex before marriage on television.[18]

In another 2005 poll, this one by *Time* Magazine, 53% of respondents said they think the FCC should place stricter controls on broadcast-channel shows depicting sex and violence.[19] Other findings from the poll:

66% said there is too much violence on TV

58% said too much cursing

50% said there is too much sexual content

49% say FCC regulation should be extended to cover basic cable.

Forty-six percent of high school students in the United States have had sexual intercourse. Although sex is common, most sexually active teens wish they had waited longer to have sex, which suggests sex is occurring before youths are prepared for its consequences. For every four sexually active teens, one case of a STD is diagnosed.

According to the Kaiser Family Foundation, about four in ten (39%) say most TV shows are not rated accurately. In a national opinion poll conducted for Common Sense Media ("New Attempt to Monitor Media Content," *NY Times*, 5/21/03), only one in five parents 'fully trusted' the industry-controlled rating systems.

Finally, and perhaps one of the more surprising results in considering decisions about contraceptives, STDs and sexual health choices, sixty percent of teens are almost as likely to get their information from TV as from a health care provider.[20]

ONLY YOU CAN PREVENT SOUL POLLUTION

With the backwards bureaucratic FCC, the responsibility of providing evidence of a bad, offensive product is on the consumer. I have never watched any of these shows, but I have come across them in primetime when turning channels and typically turn to my wife in disbelief, saying something like, "Can you believe this?" If you happen to catch a segment that is overtly indecent or obscene, you can contact the station, the advertisers, or the FCC. If you prefer to call, have all the details written down so you can be as specific as possible. The hours and numbers for the FCC are:

Monday - Friday, 8:00 a.m. to 5:30 p.m. Eastern. Call toll-free, 1-888-CALL-FCC (1-888-225-5322) or 1-888-TELL-FCC (1-888-835-5322). They can help you file a complaint or answer any questions. You can also file online and look for "Form 475B – Obscene, Profane, and/ or Indecent Broadcast Complaints." (www.fcc.gov/complaints)

Remember to provide as many details of the incident/show as possible. You will need to give them the date and time of the broadcast, the call sign of the TV station, excerpts from the program and at least a partial transcript (dialogue). Believe it or not, the FCC does not "actively monitor television broadcasts for indecency violations – nor does it keep a record of television broadcasts." The more information you can provide the better.

WHAT'S WRONG WITH THE FCC?

First, the "burden of proof" is on us, the viewers, to file complaints because the FCC relies on our documented information. I know – it is bewildering. The FCC was created, in part, to serve the interests of local communities, but sadly, the definition of "indecency" seems to be changing with the culture. In addition, the FCC must respect the protection of artistic expression and free speech as stated in the First Amendment. This is a quagmire of sorts because the limitations on the FCC taking action are already somewhat fluid.

The FCC cannot take action unless a program contains – the FCC's definition of broadcast indecency:

"Language or material that, in context, depicts or describes, *in terms patently offensive as measured by contemporary community standards* for the broadcast medium, sexual or excretory organs or activities."[21]

According to a PTC report, only after the FCC decides the material in question meets this definition can it regulate that expression in the future. Many programs on TV today clearly fall under this definition, but nothing changes without public concerns being voiced. First

Amendment considerations prohibit them from preventing what goes out over the airwaves in advance. They are, however, *authorized* by Congress to levy fines or pull broadcast licenses from stations *after* they air indecent or profane content.

There is a very detailed, thorough report on the PTC website called "Dereliction of Duty: How the Federal Communications Commission Has Failed the Public." Evidently, only two TV stations have ever been fined for airing indecent material in the history of the FCC. This is shocking when, as the PTC points out, every night in America homes are bombarded with "flagrant and repeated instances of partial nudity, explicit sexual content, raw language and graphic violence" directly from the networks and programmers. In the extensive report, they ask some pressing questions, including:

> "Why does the FCC ignore its Congressionally mandated role to enforce broadcast decency standards over the publicly owned airways? Why does the FCC refuse to enforce statutes the courts have repeatedly upheld as a reasonable balance between the First Amendment's right to free speech and the compelling public interest to protect the well-being of its youth?"[22]

Government trumps God once again. The solutions are obvious, but the red tape is thick. This is bureaucracy at its finest. In a 2003 hearing on Broadcast Ownership Rules in Richmond, Virginia, FCC Commissioner Kathleen Abernathy suggested that **it is the responsibility of parents and television viewers to avoid programming they do not agree with or approve of**. She said people can just change the channel, and that watching bad TV shows was a conscious choice. You and I both know it is nearly impossible and improbable for a parent to monitor the viewing habits of their children at all times.

I believe another solution is that fines and penalties for violations should increase dramatically. I agree with the PTC that with the millions of dollars these programs make from advertisers, the maximum $27,000 fine for TV stations is a joke, and that the FCC should fine each violation within a particular broadcast.

Thank God for organizations who make a difference in the lives of Christians and families in America by standing in the gap when it comes to these important cultural battles. Here are just a few of them: Parents Television Council, American Family Association, Morality in Media, Family Research Council, Focus on the Family, Movie Guide, and Plugged-In on line.

BAD ROLE MODELS AND DANGEROUS TV

FLASHBACK: What could go wrong with a show about six friends, a popular coffee shop, and a few apartments? *Friends* was one of the biggest shows ever on television. Throughout the series' ten-season run that includes 236 episodes, the six primary characters on *Friends* had a total of eighty-five sexual partners. According to a *Fox News* article reporting the results of research by splitsider.com, Joe Tribbiani (Matt LeBlanc) was the most promiscuous, sleeping with seventeen different partners. Phoebe Buffay (Lisa Kudrow) and Ross Gellar (David Schwimmer) weren't far behind, each racking up sixteen sexual conquests. Rachel Green (Jennifer Aniston) had fourteen partners – also producing a baby with daddy Ross, and Monica Gellar (Courtney Cox) had thirteen partners. Awkward and comedic character Chandler Bing (Matthew Perry) was the most reserved of the bunch: He only had sex with nine women.[23]

Who is TV's Worst Role Model for Kids today? Topping one list was, drum roll please...*Jersey Shore's* Snooki.[24] An article from Common Sense Media on parenting explained that one of the problems with kids emulating Snooki is obviously drinking too much and too frequently, which in her case often leads to questionable sexual behavior, getting arrested, or both. The sad thing is people on reality shows get paid to attract negative attention to themselves, and the message it sends kids is that society rewards lewd, obnoxious behavior! The article also noted Kim Kardashian was in the top five, and that she "and her sisters are the ultimate celebrity role models with nothing worth copying."

In a recent article called "What are the Most Dangerous Shows Your Kids are Watching Without You?", parenting experts and TV watchdog groups were asked to name the most dangerous shows aimed at young people. Let's look at just a few. The list included *Gossip Girl, American*

Dad, The Secret Life of the American Teenager, 2 Broke Girls, American Horror Story, Teen Mom, and *16 and Pregnant*.[25]

The marketing for the CBS comedy *2 Broke Girls* prior to the television season promoted the fact that the show was from the creator of the adult comedy *Sex and the City* on HBO. Why do you suppose they wanted to make this connection? They wanted to let people know there would be plenty of sexual content and from reviews by the PTC, not only is the language deplorable and reprehensible, but also, "Sexual jokes and references are abundant, including breast and vagina references, two audio depictions of couples having sex, an orgasm joke, and references to prostitution and masturbation."[26]

Gossip Girl on the CW Network is even worse. It's just another show conveying that sex can be used to get what you want. Like many shows geared toward impressionable youth, there are no consequences to having multiple and shared sex partners. Naturally, the show features countless make-out sessions, "erotic situations, and skimpy clothing." Ironically, the characters are all under the legal drinking age but there is plenty of drug and alcohol use among them.[27] As for bad language, the PTC noted quite frequent use of words such as "whore," "a*s," "b*tch," "sl*t," "screw," "damn," and "hell." (8 p.m. Central!)

KIDS WILL IMITATE THEIR 'ROLE MODELS'

I can understand why many young people look up to or even idolize actors, music artists, and movie stars. I just don't understand the fascination with reality TV personalities. (I cannot bring myself to call them "stars") These people are famous for being vain (or desperate) enough to allow camera crews to follow them around in their daily lives. They act outrageously, help a network attract an audience and, presto – they become famous! Unfortunately for your children, many of these people also become role models. Dictionary.com defines '**role model**' as a person regarded by others, especially younger people, as a good example to follow: a person whose behavior, example, or success serves as a model for another person to emulate.

According to The Hollywood Gossip site in 2011, for the second year in a row, Miley Cyrus was named the Worst Celebrity Influence in a poll of 99,000 people.[28] Ironically, the site's main audience is ages nine to fifteen, which is her core fan base. Cyrus even beat out Lindsay Lohan, who has earned her share of negative awards. There are some who are concerned Cyrus is in danger of becoming the next Hollywood train wreck. We need to pray for her and others like her. You may wonder what happened to good old pure, family-friendly Miley. She went from Disney's *Hannah Montana* to teen idol in a hurry, and in 2009, through her best-selling single "Party in the USA," she seemed to cultivate her adult image and sex appeal when she was only seventeen years old.

Cyrus's performance of *Party in the U.S.A.* at the *2009 Teen Choice Awards* incited a media uproar, with some viewers criticizing Cyrus's provocative outfit and inclusion of a brief pole dance as inappropriate for her age (16), and for her young fans.[29]

In 2010, Miley Cyrus released *Can't Be Tamed*, which was basically a sexed-up version of her changing image. *Christianity Today* questioned: "And how will a faith-based audience that has appreciated Cyrus's outspokenness about her Christianity and love for Jesus – themes which are nowhere to be found on this album – react to the Miley?"[30] Her video for the single featured "half-naked dancers and risqué bumping and grinding." Naturally, her song lyrics have taken a turn for the worse. In the lyrics for Miley Cyrus' *Can't Be Tamed*, she talks about getting crazy and getting her way and describes herself by saying, "I'm hot," and "I'm built like that." The song also talks about her getting lots of attention from guys and that "I go through guys like money flyin' out the hands." Fortunately, she says in the song she's not here to "tell you to go to hell."

At her nineteenth birthday party in Hollywood, her friends brought out a Bob Marley birthday cake, and Cyrus said, "You know you're a stoner when your friends make you a Bob Marley cake. You know you smoke way too much fu**in' weed." Finally, in the 2012 remake of a film called *LOL: Laughing Out Loud*, in a role Cyrus said she fell in love with, her character loses her virginity, smokes cannabis, gets wasted, and kisses two girlfriends on the lips.

I can imagine the stress and temptations that come from being in the public eye from childhood and having famous parents must be tough, but she attended church regularly while growing up and even wore a purity ring. Miley was raised Christian and was baptized in a Southern Baptist church prior to moving to Hollywood in 2005. Today however, it appears she needs help as she may be headed down a similar path as Britney Spears and Lindsay Lohan.

SECULAR MUSIC: JUST ENTERTAINMENT?

"Raise your kids better or I'll be raising them for you."
– Admitted Satanist, **Marilyn Manson**

Music has been a powerfully influential force for centuries. It is no coincidence that with the addition of television in the 1950's, the way music was marketed and produced has changed to accommodate the visual element. We all know in today's pop culture, marketing is often more important than the actual quality of the product or talent being marketed. I remember when a song sold on its own merit, not on creative advertising. The artist or band didn't need to shock the audience in order to get attention.

In the 1960s and 70s, more popular music artists and rock stars began to set bad examples and establish a rebellious tone for teenagers and young kids, and then we all know what happened when MTV arrived on the scene. In addition, much of what would have been censored just a few decades ago is now protected as artistic expression and free speech no matter how offensive it might be to some of us. Much has been written about how far music industry standards have fallen. Nevertheless, these artists are sending a message to today's youth, and record companies continue to enjoy the proceeds of their provocative products.

Britney Spears released her 2009 single, *If U Seek Amy*, in which she cleverly and overtly used a cheap play on words. She sang that part of the chorus so that when she sang "If U Seek Amy" she sounded as if she was purposely spelling out the "F" word. Other artists have pulled stunts like this, but few have done it so openly and deliberately, knowing that very young girls would be listening to her CD's and singing along. Pastor Joe Schimmel of Good Fight Ministries in California has done many exposes on the occult, pop music, and culture, and is also known for his video series, "They Sold Their Souls for Rock and Roll." He said parents aren't parenting anymore, and they fail to examine what their kids are listening to. Schimmel warned parents, saying the blame does not fully belong to the music industry:

> "They [parents] fail to give moral guidelines and then follow up by doing the best to lovingly enforce them. *Rolling Stone Magazine*, which has done plenty in corrupting children, quoted shocked parents saying things like: 'I was astonished and totally taken back when I heard my 5 and 7 year old kids walking around the house singing 'F-U-C-K'... When I asked them what it was, they told me it was Britney Spears. I was horrified.'"[31]

In the big hair decade, the 1980s, the invention of music videos and the launch of MTV transformed the music industry into a dangerously addicting and influential product for kids and adults alike. It was a mix of non-stop visual music messages that promoted partying, night life, bizarre clothing trends, rebelling against authority, and bad behavior in general. It was "sex, drugs, and rock and roll" free of charge and in your living room. Kids will emulate the lifestyle or fashion of their favorite rock stars. It has been documented and established that in many cases, pop culture has been responsible for increased drug abuse, teen pregnancy, murders, suicides, rapes, abortion, and domestic violence.

In today's pop music, we are bombarded by profanity and sexual references. Just take a look at 'modern day Madonna' shock artist, Lady Gaga: her antics, beliefs, costumes, and lyrics. Your kids most likely have some of her songs memorized. Like many other pop artists, she sings about sex, adultery, homosexual and lesbian relationships, and other mind-filling garbage. Did you know that in August, 2011, China banned her music for being too vulgar? China! The last time I checked, China was an anti-Christian, communist nation. America, however, is apparently fine with ten-year-olds singing along.

In 2011's release *Born This Way,* Lady Gaga's second single "Judas" talks about being a "Holy Fool" and about bringing Jesus down; also, "Judas is the demon I cling to." The chorus and the bridge of the song talk about Gaga being beyond repentance as she sings "I'm still in love with Judas, baby." This is mild compared to some of her video antics and imagery.

We must guard what we allow into our hearts and minds. Chances are your kids like many artists similar to Gaga. We could fill up an entire book with questionable and offensive pop music artists and lyrics. We could also fill up a book with obscene and indecent television content. But I'd like to finish up this chapter by touching on the movie industry.

HOLLYWOOD & MOVIES

From the days of going to the movie theater to see the latest new release we can now watch movies right at home on Pay Per View, through Netflix, or Video on Demand, etc. This new market has put many movie rental stores out of business. Though we don't get the big theatre experience at home, it is easier to press a few buttons on the remote or have our latest movie selection delivered to our home. The movie business is always changing to keep up with culture trends. Why don't Hollywood movie producers change their products to accommodate American families hungry for cleaner entertainment?

I ask this because at the time of this writing, of the Top 40 highest-grossing (domestic) movies of *all time*, thirty-nine out of forty are rated G, PG, or PG-13.[32] In fact, five of the top 10 movies are rated "G." Number one is the 2011 blockbuster *Avatar* (which was criticized for demonizing big business and for celebrating the environmental movement) and number two is *Titanic*, while *The Dark Knight* holds the number three spot. Also included in the Top 10 are two of the *Star Wars* films, *Shrek 2*, *E.T.* from 1982, *Toy Story*, and *The Lion King*. For *Lord of the Ring*s enthusiasts, the three films rank number fifteen, twenty, and thirty of all time.

Perhaps even more fascinating is the one and only R-rated film in the Top 40 of all time. What blockbuster holds the number nineteen spot on the charts? Mel Gibson's 2004 *Passion of the Christ*. The movie was rated R for the obvious violence and torture of Jesus Christ, but Americans flocked to this epic movie. The *Passion of the Christ* holds records for being the #1 R-rated film of all time, #1 in films that opened in theatres in the winter, #2 highest opening weekend gross for an R-rated film, and the #3 highest-grossing movie of 2004 (#5 worldwide). The Passion of the Christ also holds the #62 highest-grossing movie of all time.[33]

We all know Hollywood does not reflect the values of most Americans, so we should proceed with caution when choosing our entertainment. (This warning includes video games!) Aside from technology, there is nothing in today's society that has never been seen before. The Ten Commandments were broken millions of times before America existed and before Hollywood ever came to be. So is it more profitable for movies to promote all the bad stuff?

A 2007 study done by Movieguide showed that G-rated movies powered the box office that year. Check this out: according to the study, G-rated family films performed 438% better than R-rated films at the box office! G-rated movies averaged nearly $92.2 million while R-rated movies made only $17.1 million.[34]

The most successful movies are always the more conservative ones. In 2010, *Fox News* reported that "with the exception of Christopher Nolan's psychological thriller *Inception*, the top-grossing films of 2010 were all aimed squarely at families." The highest-grossing movie in 2010 was *Toy Story 3* from Disney-Pixar, which hauled in $1.06 billion worldwide, according to Box Office Mojo. These facts tell us something about what Americans want and that family-friendly films are not only a safe bet, but almost always lucrative for movie studios.

For over a decade, the number one highest-grossing film for every year has been a family-friendly product. The exception was in 2008 when *The Dark Knight* starring Heath Ledger shot up to the number one spot as millions of movie-goers saw the film after his death to honor him. Since 2000, here are the number one movies from each year:[35]

2000 – *The Grinch*

2001 – *Harry Potter and the Sorcerer's Stone*

2002 – *Spider Man*

2003 – *Lord of the Rings: Return of the King*

2004 – *Shrek 2*

2005 – *Star Wars: Episode III – Revenge of the Sith*

2006 – *Pirates of the Caribbean: Dead Man's Chest*

2007 – *Spider Man 3*

2008 – *The Dark Knight*

2009 – *Avatar*

2010 – *Toy Story 3*

2011 – *Harry Potter and the Deathly Hollows*

The downside of the success of Harry Potter films is the emphasis on witchcraft and the occult, a satanic element Christians often excuse as harmless. Another observation is that the last several years have been the years of the movie sequel. Is Hollywood running out of ideas or creativity or are they just trying to go with what has already made money? In 2009, eight out of the top fifteen highest-grossing films were sequels or remakes. In 2010, *every one* of the top five highest-grossing films were all sequels, and another Shrek installment holds the #8 spot for that year. Then in 2011, once again the top five were all remakes or sequels. Amazingly, eleven of those top fifteen highest-grossing movies were sequels! That means Hollywood produced just four original movies out of the best fifteen from last year.

Movieguide's Dr. Ted Baehr is an American media critic, and Chairman of the Christian Film and Television Commission. Dr. Baehr may be one of those responsible for opening Hollywood producers up to more family-oriented movie content. In an article at WND, columnist and editor Drew Zahn discussed this subject in "GUESS AGAIN! SEX DOESN'T SELL" in 2010.

It was an exceptional year featuring a *decrease* in profanity, sex, and drug abuse in the movies. In North America, Movieguide reported that family-friendly films far exceeded their competition at the box office when you compare them under the MPAA rating system:

In 2010, only 4 major motion pictures were given a G rating, but those 4 films made an average of over $120 million at the box office;

The 47 PG-rated films averaged $69 million;

The 80 PG-13 films averaged $51 million;

The 121 R-rated films averaged only $18 million[36]

Furthermore, and Christians will be encouraged by this news, the report also showed that since the first Annual Movieguide Faith & Values Awards Gala, the number of movies with at least some "positive Christian, biblical, and/or moral content has increased overall from an average of 18.27% in 1991 to an average of 71.67% in 2010." If you've been out of math class for a while like me, that is more than a 260% increase in good movie content! It appears as though movies with positive, moral, biblical, redemptive content are still good for business.

GOOD FRUIT OR COMPROMISE?

It is a simple yet key biblical principle: we reap what we sow (Galatians 6:7). This also relates to the entertainment we've allowed to take root in our hearts and minds. Typically, the Holy Spirit will give us a nudge, if something is not edifying and it's up to us to obey his guidance. Pastor Joe Schimmel talks about how cleverly Satan goes under parental radar to get to children and that Christian parents must show "spiritual hyper-vigilance" when it comes to the programming they digest. Shimmel concluded an article on the dangers of today's entertainment by saying:

> "If we are to safeguard the moral and spiritual wellbeing of our children, we need to lovingly encourage them in the truth of God's Word and diligently pray for the sanctifying work of the Holy Spirit to be manifested in their lives."[37]

I didn't add it all up at the beginning of this chapter. The *average* American family watches TV non-stop for seventy-six days (1,825 hours) every year. That is a LOT of wasted time. Studies have shown that it takes an average of twenty-one days – just three weeks – to develop a new habit in our lives. If you have not been wise and discerning with your time and your entertainment habits, it is not too late to set new healthy standards in your home. Your family may not like it at first, but they will most likely respect your decision to seek first the kingdom of God (Matthew 6:33) instead of what Hollywood would rather program us with. Christians will stand before God one day and explain how we used our time, talents, and treasure.

Too many of us have wasted precious years of our lives and missed what has been going on in our country. In the next chapter, we'll look at some disturbing trends and very real threats. Remember, only YOU can prevent soul pollution!

Therefore if you have been raised up with Christ, keep seeking the things above, where Christ is, seated at the right hand of God. Set your mind on the things above, not on the things that are on earth (**Colossians 3:1-2**).

ENDNOTES

1 http://www.parentstv.org/ptc/publications/emailalerts/2012/0412.htm
2 http://www.pluggedin.com/tv/def/dont-trust-the-b-----in-apt-23.aspx
3 http://www.fcc.gov/topic/complaints
4 Time Magazine. Learning to live with TV. May 28, 1979. Available at: http://www.time.com/time/magazine/article/0,9171,947316,00.html Accessed January 4, 2008.
5 http://www.parentstv.org/PTC/publications/reports/religionstudy06/main.asp
6 http://www.mrc.org/eye-culture/crusade-against-faith
7 http://www.parentstv.org/PTC/news/release/2011/0816.asp
8 http://www.parentstv.org/ptc/shows/main.asp?shwid=1960
9 http://www.parentstv.org/PTC/publications/bw/2011/0722worst.asp
10 http://www.parentstv.org/ptc/publications/bw/2009/0911worst.asp
11 http://www.pluggedin.com/tv/ghi/glee.aspx
12 http://www.wnd.com/2009/11/116899/
13 http://www.reuters.com/article/2011/11/02/us-cbs-janetjackson-idUSTRE7A15AU20111102
14 http://www.wnd.com/2007/09/43470/
15 http://newsbusters.org/blogs/brent-bozell/2012/04/07/bozell-column-mtvs-savage-schoolyard
16 http://www.orthodoxytoday.org/articles5/KaiserFamily.php
17 http://www.moralityinmedia.org/full_article.php?article_no=106
18 http://www.parentstv.org/PTC/facts/mediafacts.asp
19 http://townhall.com/columnists/brentbozell/2005/03/25/time_for_a_clean-up/page/full/
20 http://www.parentstv.org/PTC/facts/mediafacts.asp
21 http://www.fcc.gov/guides/obscenity-indecency-and-profanity
22 http://www.parentstv.org/ptc/publications/reports/fccwhitepaper/main.asp
23 http://www.foxnews.com/entertainment/2011/07/28/friends-cast-had-85-sexual-partners-over-10-season-run/
24 http://shine.yahoo.com/parenting/tvs-5-worst-role-models-for-kids-2489712.html
25 http://www.foxnews.com/entertainment/2011/12/05/what-are-most-dangerous-shows-your-kids-are-watching-without/
26 http://www.parentstv.org/ptc/shows/main.asp?shwid=3383
27 http://www.parentstv.org/ptc/shows/main.asp?shwid=2633

28http://www.thehollywoodgossip.com/2011/01/
   miley-cyrus-voted-worst-celebrity-influence-again/
29http://en.wikipedia.org/wiki/Miley_Cyrus
30http://www.christianitytoday.com/ct/music/reviews/2010/canttamed.html
31 http://cupofjoe.goodfight.org/?p=41#more-41
32http://www.boxofficemojo.com/alltime/domestic.htm
33http://www.boxofficemojo.com/movies/?id=passionofthechrist.htm
34http://www.wnd.com/2008/03/58964/
35http://www.boxofficemojo.com/yearly/
36http://www.wnd.com/2011/02/266097/
37http://cupofjoe.goodfight.org/?p=1451

CHAPTER 10

IT COULD NEVER HAPPEN IN AMERICA

LIBERALS AND MARXISTS AND SOCIALISTS – OH MY!

"The Left wants you to think that the cultural changes that have taken place in America since the 1960's have done nothing but progress us forward to a brave new world ... they've done everything in their power to dumb down our children, undermine our families, rewrite our history, and promote obscenity and immorality everywhere they can ... the ideas that now dominate our educational system are focused on removing God and His influence from every part of our culture."[1] – **Curtis Bowers** (Agenda Documentary producer)

"We are five days away from fundamentally transforming the United States of America." – **Barack Obama** "To avoid being mistaken for a sellout, I chose my friends carefully. The more politically active black students. The foreign students. The Chicanos. The Marxist professors and structural feminists...." (From his 1995 book *Dreams From My Father*)

"I was a rowdy nationalist on April 28th, and then ... By August, I was a communist ... I met all these young radical people of color – I mean really radical: communists and anarchists. And it was, like, 'This is what I need to be a part of.' I spent the next 10 years of my life working with a lot of those people I met in jail, trying to be a revolutionary.... The white polluters and the white environmentalists are essen-

tially steering poison into the people of color communities
because they don't have a racial justice frame."[2]
– **Van Jones** (Obama administration 2009 "Green Czar")

WHILE WE WERE SLEEPING

The battle for the soul of America has long been waged. If only we
had seen it coming. If only we had been warned 100 years ago or fifty
… or twenty-five years ago, or maybe even in 2008. If only somebody
would have told us about the imminent danger and the threat to destroy
America. If only Christians could have seen the coming attack on Jesus
Christ and assault on morality. Maybe concerned citizens could have
resisted the transformation. If only one of the socialist leaders would
have openly broadcasted a call to arms for radicals to seize power so
we, our parents, or our grandparents could have known their intentions
and fought back. If only the anti-American movement would have made
their declaration of war public, then we would have stood against the
enemy and resisted, wouldn't we have?

But they were patient, and it happened gradually. It was a brilliant
plan. One strategy enemies of God have used to neutralize opponents
(we the people) is to convince us there was never an agenda against
this country; that there are only rumors and fabrications. They say the
deterioration of America has been natural and inevitable. To those of
us who are awake and who understand the Bible, they are absolutely
wrong; history reveals it, and evidence proves it true. If only we could
have saved the United States of America. Maybe it's not too late; perhaps there is still time….

Sadly, the rapid decline of our culture continues with little resistance;
it's happening right under our noses and right before our eyes. The
implementation of an anti-Christian socialist agenda has been thrust
on America over the last fifty-plus years and if not stopped, will lead
to communism. This is the goal of the Left, and too many ignorant,
uninformed citizens are jumping on their bandwagon without fully
knowing what they are supporting. Stalin called them "useful idiots."

We can either remain in denial, or we can join the awakened movement of conservatives, independents, people of faith, and average Americans who want their country back. Two key questions are "who is doing this" and "how are they doing it"? Most atheists, socialists and Marxists believe people would be much happier if Christianity was eradicated. Without strong people of faith standing for truth, their agenda would advance with little hindrance.

> "The first requisite for the happiness of the people is the abolition of religion." And, "Religion is the opium of the masses."
> – **Karl Marx**

RADICALS AMONG US

Socialism has taken over much of Europe, and the result has been chaos and unrest due to economic failures and increasing immorality. Though it is not always blatantly out in the open, socialism has been on our shores for over a century. There are those in America who are so focused on gaining power at *any* cost even some liberals question their tactics which is one reason we've seen divided factions in the Occupy Wall Street movement. They've always been here, but now more Americans are waking up.

Many of us were either oblivious that our country was in fact, drifting away from our roots, or we ignored it. Our culture has been compromised as they have purposefully achieved their objectives through many of America's most influential institutions. Radicals have been emboldened by allies in the White House who through their policies are helping to advance everything from environmental activism to social justice and wealth redistribution. They openly support anti-American countries and groups while disrespecting Israel and weakening our national defense.

As Christian conservatives, one of our main concerns must be the protection of free speech and religious liberty in America. They'd love to shut us up. Until we understand how deceptive and dishonest some of our opponents are, it will be hard to defend the constant attacks on our faith, family, and freedoms. We are seeing more and more class warfare, criticism of capitalism, and government intrusion on American citizen's basic rights including religious liberties.

Many liberals and progressives in the media, in OWS, and in public unions want to "reform" America's free enterprise system. They'd like to see complete government control of our economy and markets; the Obama administration has already started down this road as they attempt to overhaul our nation's health care laws and energy policies. Communist and socialist party organizers in America are now openly pushing their propaganda via the web and at public protests, including their failed efforts in Madison, Wisconsin.

But why socialism, and why did they choose this time in our history to try to make their move? Generations must have been dumbed down because anyone with a remote understanding of history knows millions lived under abject poverty and suffered worldwide under socialism. Never before have so many innocent people died while being subjected to narcissistic leaders and tyrants who fooled them by saying all the right things. But the media buries it, and our kids are not being taught the whole truth in government-run public education.

Whether it is communism, socialism, Marxism, or progressivism, they all lead to man's worship of the State as provider instead of the American system that allows for and encourages people to see God as provider. The fact more Americans are considering ideas and "isms" like what we see today – after all of the climactic failures of socialism around the world – is beyond comprehension. If people don't know biblical truth and American heritage, it's no wonder some are not capable of reasoning and resisting this anti-Christian agenda. You don't think our country could be destroyed from within?

President Obama's father, Barack Hussein Obama Sr., was an African socialist from Kenya. Obama's mother, Stanley Ann Dunham, was a 60's feminist and atheist. Barrack Sr. once wrote a research project called "Problems With Our Socialism" which advocated taxing the rich, community property, and the confiscation of privately owned land. He was married four times and his religion most likely changed from Islam to atheist, though he was born into a Muslim family. President Obama's early formative years feature a mixture of religious and political views, including those of his mentors, friends, and associations. Many of the relationships helped formulate his antipathy toward America, and his attraction to socialism is well ingrained into his ideology and worldview.

From questionable Chicago politics to unethical community activism, there is a clear pattern in Obama's past. A Republican with the same background would have been vetted extensively, covered 24/7 by the media, and would never be elected. To suggest the corrupt, radical, leftist, progressive individuals who make up President Obama's close friends, associations and his administration do not reflect his faith and his worldview is both naive and insulting to our intelligence.

LOOK OUT FOR THE UNION LABEL

Some of the president's biggest allies are union bosses. Big labor unions used to protect the little guy and look out for their interests, but they generally do not have the ideals they started out with many decades ago. Take for example AFL-CIO's president Richard Trumka; through his efforts, a longtime ban on communists in union leadership positions was repealed. The Communist Party USA in 1996 stated the move was both historic and positive. Trumka also created a program called "Union Summer" whose activists recite a pledge that union workers produced the world's wealth.

Writing in *Front Page Magazine*, Matthew Vadum noted how Trumka brags about his cozy relationship with President Obama, who named Trumka to his Economic Advisory Board shortly after his inauguration. The big union boss believes breaking the law is acceptable, if it advances their cause. Vadum writes:

> Trumka: "I'm at the White House a couple times a week – two, three times a week ... I have conversations every day with someone in the White House or in the administration. Every day."

> "Trumka doesn't even make an effort to conceal his radicalism. 'Being called a socialist is a step up for me,' he told Bloomberg News in June. In 1994, Trumka proudly accepted the Eugene Debs Award named after the five-time presidential candi-

date and labor organizer who founded the Socialist Party of America."[3]

In September 2011 Teamsters President Jimmy Hoffa Jr. made a speech to union workers in Detroit just before President Obama addressed the crowd. Hoffa called Motown "union town" saying the message he wanted to send to the rest of the country was that the workers were under attack and at war. He blamed the Tea Party, unemployment, and Wisconsin Governor Scott Walker. Hoffa stated taking back Wisconsin was priority number one, Ohio is number two, and Michigan is third. Hoffa also went on to say, "right to work ... ain't going to happen in Michigan. No way." He told the crowd that union people love a good fight, and "there is only going to be one winner."

"They've got a war with us and ... we are going to win that war....
We are going to hear from President Obama in a few minutes ... **President Obama, this is your army!** We are ready to march ... **let's take these sons-of-bi*ches out and give America back** to America where we belong."[4]

Are all unions bad? No. Are they evil? No. Corrupt leaders don't necessarily make all union employees bad either. Some employees disagree with the actions of union leadership, but just like in the NEA, they're at the mercy of their boss's agenda and are afraid for their jobs should they speak up.

The main goal of the progressive movement is power, and they have built a base among the underclass and urban poor. Their work to mobilize the "oppressed" and to bring down the entire American system is clearly evident by the increased level of activism in the country.

In March 2012, the *Daily Caller* began an investigation of the "politically aggressive Service Employees International Union" (SEIU) who has created a national network of radical community-organizing groups with connections to OWS. Some of these local non-profit groups that are incorporated by the SEIU are "waging concerted local political campaigns to publicly attack conservative political figures, banks, energy companies and other corporations." SEIU spent an estimated $80 million in 2008 to elect Democratic candidates – over $27 million of which went to Obama. SEIU is supporting and helping fund OWS protests.[5]

AN ACORN DOESN'T FALL FAR FROM THE TREE

SEIU was the same union involved with ACORN and voter-intimidation activity during the 2008 Presidential election. They worked together using questionable methods to get their candidates elected. ACORN has a long history of voter fraud. Newsbusters reported:

"Seventy ACORN staffers in 12 states have been convicted of voter registration fraud by adding such notables as Mickey Mouse and Donald Duck to the voter rolls ... ACORN is in fact the political dirty tricks muscle of liberal Democrats."[6]

In 2011, "Las Vegas Judge Donald Mosley fumed at his inability to impose a harsher punishment on the radical advocacy group...." Despite their bankruptcy filing, ACORN continues to operate. They just use different names. Project Vote and ACORN Housing, renamed Affordable Housing Centers of America, are still in business.[7]

ACORN officials openly acknowledge the network is currently restructuring and will help re-elect President Obama, so they can have the money and power to allocate more funds to Left-wing causes. Benjamin Franklin once said,

"When the people find that they can vote themselves money, that will herald the end of the republic."

ACORN had succeeded in duping Americans for years, and too many citizens still remain in the dark regarding Obama's work with Saul Alinsky-influenced ACORN.

Former 1960's Left-wing radical David Horowitz converted to conservatism in the late 1970s and knows the inside of the socialist movement extremely well. Raised by parents who were both members of the Communist Party USA, Horowitz created Students for Academic Freedom, whose self-stated goal is combatting leftist indoctrination in academia.

In a booklet called *Barrack Obama's Rules for Revolution*, Horowitz wrote about the Alinsky strategy which includes the military tactic of deception in what radicals see as a *real* war to eliminate the enemy. In contrast, conservatives think of war as a metaphor which puts them at a disadvantage against those who are out to destroy America. One method of attack is the name calling and labeling of conservatives as "racists," "homophobes," "Islamophobes," and sometimes "sexists."

Deception is the radical's primary weapon. This Alinsky principle is about disarming the opponent by lying and pretending to be moderate. Horowitz explains:

> "Racial arsonists such as Al Sharpton and Jeremiah Wright pose as civil rights activists; anti-American radicals such as Bill Ayers pose as patriotic progressives....

> "Barack Obama is an enigma. He won the 2008 presidential election claiming to be a moderate and wanting to bring Americans together and govern from the center. But since he took office, his actions have been far from moderate.... He has used the economic crisis to take over whole industries and has attempted to nationalize the health care system. ...these actions had already made his presidency one of the most polarizing in history."[8]

There were die-hard socialists in America in the early 1900s who didn't hide their ideas. They wanted to abolish the U.S. military, state police forces, the Senate, and the presidency for starters. They have since become more subtle because they realized they wouldn't get very far if they continued to be that open about their agenda. Their strategy may have changed, but their agenda has not.

When Barack Obama boldly stated they were five days away from "fundamentally transforming the United States," most of us know he wasn't exaggerating. Some thought he sounded grandiose, and others assumed it was just campaign rhetoric, but an underground army of radicals was preparing to mobilize in Washington, D.C. and beyond. Obama's election appeared to be the perfect storm for those who believe Christianity is oppressive, and America is unjust. Saul Alinksy spent most of his life organizing a revolution to destroy America, and for several years, Obama himself taught workshops on the Alinsky method.

THE ALINSKY CONNECTION

Chicago-born Saul David Alinsky (1909-1972) was an American community organizer who dropped out of graduate school at the University of Chicago to work as a criminologist. He was drawn to the world of gangsters and was a confidant of the Al Capone mob. Alinsky became a "student" of enforcer Frank Nitti, who took over the mob when Capone was sent to prison. An Alinsky radical has one main goal – power. His motto was "The most effective means are whatever will achieve the desired results." Though he died in 1972, his vision gained traction.

According to David Horowitz, it was Alinsky who:

> "...helped to form the coalition of communists, anarchists, liberals, Democrats, black racialists, and social justice activists who spear-headed the anti-globalization movement just before 9/11, and then created the anti-Iraq War movement."

Communists played a formative role in the creation of the progressive CIO – the coalition of industrial unions – founded by John L. Lewis. Saul Alinsky was drawn to Lewis, the great labor leader, and he wondered if the same hardheaded tactics used by unions could be applied to the relationship between citizens and public officials. This may have been the first sign that radicals and union thuggery would be forever connected.

Alinsky influenced Wade Rathke, another radical who founded both ACORN and SEIU. Rathke was ACORN's chief agitator from its formation in 1970 until 2008 when he resigned due to his brother Dale embezzling nearly $1 million dollars from the organization. Alinsky was convinced large-scale socialist transformation would require an alliance between the struggling middle class and the poor. Does this idea sound familiar? Alinsky thought the key to radical social change was to turn the anger of America's middle class against large corporations.

Alinsky's ideas were later adapted by some U.S. college students and other young organizers in the late 1960s. They used his ideas to form their strategies for organizing on campuses. One particular college senior personally interviewed Alinsky and wrote a 92-page thesis on his theories entitled "There Is Only the Fight: An Analysis of the Alinsky Model." In her conclusion, she even compared Alinsky to Martin Luther King. The undergrad who wrote the thesis was Hillary Rodham (Clinton).

Three of Obama's mentors in Chicago were trained in the Alinsky method. One mentor, Gregory Galluzo had his own training manual that instructed organizers to "Get rid of do-gooders in your church and your organization." Jesse Jackson was another leader who was influenced by Saul Alinsky. Jackson dropped out of the Chicago Theological Seminary in 1966 to focus full time on the civil rights movement.

Since Alinsky mentored and motivated so many progressives, who or what else influenced *him*? On the opening dedication page of his book *Rules for Radicals*, Saul Alinksy writes:

> "Lest we forget, an over-the-shoulder acknowledgment to the very first radical…from all our legends, mythology, and history…the first radical known to man who rebelled against the establishment and did it so effectively that he at least won his own kingdom – Lucifer."

He was inspired by Satan. Christian friends, it's not a game to these people. Radicals often camouflage their agendas by calling them something else or associating themselves with various causes (such as social justice), but the most consistent is "progressive." The battle can be summed up in three words: God or man. We have leaders at every level in America who were influenced by either "Rules for Radicals" or the Marxist-socialist worldview, so we better understand their goals and where they acquired *their* ideas and values.

VLADMIR LENIN

One of Saul Alinsky's inspirations was Vladimir Lenin (1870-1924), a Russian Marxist revolutionary and communist politician. As leader of the Bolsheviks, he headed the Soviet state in its initial years. The Bolsheviks were a faction of the Marxist Russian Social Democratic Labor Party, and they envisioned a classless society. The state confiscated private property including the seizure of land and industry. Banks, railroads, farms, and factories were nationalized. Lenin destroyed 100,000 churches in the Soviet Union to purge Russia of reactionary (faith in God) ideas. The Bolsheviks assumed total control of the country.

During this period of revolution, war and famine, Lenin demonstrated a chilling disregard for the sufferings of his fellow countrymen and mercilessly crushed any opposition. Do you think Hitler was evil? **Lenin was responsible for the murder of 40 million people.** He used a massive propaganda campaign to tout the "benefits" of socialism. This is a classic history lesson as Russia traded one ruling class of elites – the aristocracy – for another: the Communist Party. Some Americans would like us to be the United Socialist States of America one day.

> "America is like a healthy body and its resistance is threefold: its patriotism, its morality and its spiritual life. If we can undermine these three areas, America will collapse from within."
> – **Joseph Stalin**

JOSEPH STALIN

Saul Alinsky also admired Joseph Stalin (1879-1953), another disciple of Karl Marx. One of the most powerful and murderous dictators in history, Stalin was the supreme ruler of the Soviet Union for a quarter of a century after taking over for Lenin. His regime of terror caused the death and suffering of tens of millions. Stalin once said, "A single death is a tragedy; a million deaths is a statistic." His path to power began when **he began to read Marxist literature.** He devoted his time to the revolutionary movement against the Russian monarchy. He spent the next fifteen years as an activist and on a number of occasions was arrested and exiled to Siberia.

In 1922, he was made general secretary of the Communist Party, a post not considered particularly significant at the time but which *gave him control over appointments and, thus, allowed him to build up a base of support.* Beginning in early 1930, the Stalin regime also initiated a campaign to rid the country of "all entrepreneurs" – self-employed shopkeepers and craftsmen of only moderate means who operated small, one-person businesses. Joseph Stalin intentionally engineered famine in Ukraine during 1932-33, resulting in the deaths of an estimated 10 million people.

Marxist revolutions are driven mainly by hatred of the perceived class enemy. Chief among those identified as "enemies of the people" by Stalin were landowning peasants, clergy, shopkeepers, and private business owners. Hunger and poverty became huge issues in Russia causing Stalin to begin his "Five-Year Plans." Part one was to nationalize Russian commerce and industrialize the economy. Unfortunately, part of the plan was also having the state take over all private land, even confiscating farms and forcing the peasants to produce quotas for the government without pay.

There were nearly 25 million working farmers who were allowed to keep only what they needed from the harvest to survive. What drove this program? It was the influence of Karl Marx and his dream of social equality and social justice. These terms are being used in America today, and we better hope there are still people who remember past history so we do not repeat it.

Part of an extremely in-depth Stalin biography from Discover the Networks explains:

> "Stalin's vision entailed the systematic replacement of small, unmechanized farms with large, mechanized alternatives that would theoretically produce food much more efficiently. In practice this meant that a nation which had once been Europe's breadbasket would experience famine and chronic agricultural scarcity for the next sixty years, until the system collapsed."[9]

For the record, *Time* Magazine named Stalin its "Man of the Year" for 1939.

MARX MADNESS

Karl Marx (1818-1883) has been described as one of the most influential figures in human history. Revolutionary socialist governments espousing Marxian concepts took power in a variety of countries in the 20th century, leading to the formation of such socialist states as the brutal regime of the Soviet Union – the USSR (United Soviet Socialist Republic) in 1922 and the People's Republic of China in 1949.

Many labor unions and worker's parties worldwide were also developed or influenced by Marxian ideas: Leninism, Socialism, Maoism, and Trotskyism. Be reminded these "Isms" gained power and fame by brutal, criminal, and immoral means.

Marxists have killed over 100 million of their own citizens – not during wars but at peacetime! Their ethics and politics justified the end by almost any means. Karl Marx's legacy lives on in the states through the manipulation of untold millions of American citizens. His poison has infested many of our schools at every level of education. **One of Marx's goals was a state-controlled godless "paradise."**

Marx claimed mankind's foundation was the history of the "class struggle," or war between the Haves and the Have Nots. Ironically, Marx came from a relatively wealthy family. He was a writer who made his living off of other people's money. In fact, he married Jenny von Westphalen, a "beautiful baroness of the Prussian ruling class." It was described as a marriage between individuals who belonged to the middle and upper class aristocracy.

The majority of the leaders in communist and socialist movements were intellectuals and not exactly from the "working class." The same thing holds true in America today. We hear talk about people needing to "pay their fair share." What you do not hear is what may be "fair" for them is not necessarily fair to you and me. There is more of a push for a post-modern society and a one world government.

German immigrants came to America in the mid 1800's, and some of them were socialists who brought with them *The Communist Manifesto*, written by Karl Marx. Many unions were formed as well as the Socialist Party of America (SPA). The Socialist Party was formed in 1901 by a merger between the Social Democratic Party of America and certain elements of the Socialist Labor Party.

THE FABIAN SOCIETY

Enter the British socialist movement called the Fabian Society which was founded in London in 1884. Instead of forcing change via revolution, the Fabians believed in more of a gradual, dissemination into society. In the early 1900's, Fabian Society members advocated the ideal of a scientifically planned society and supported eugenics by way of sterilization. This was implemented in Australia where children were systematically and forcibly removed from their parents. The sterilization movement was already progressing in America as the Socialist Democratic Party promoted these kinds of extreme ideas such as reducing or eliminating "inferior" races while breeding a superior race.

The famous writer, atheist **George Bernard Shaw**, said the Fabians made it possible for "an ordinary respectable religious citizen to profess and belong to a Socialist Society without any suspicion of lawlessness" because Fabians supposedly had better reputations. One tenet of their agenda was, after patiently waiting and plotting, to "strike hard" when the time was right. They focused on infiltrating American society through the upper and middle classes. Shaw wrote about his Fabian membership saying that to conservative parents and relatives fifty years ago it seemed shocking and unheard of that they'd become Socialists. Shaw proudly stated:

> "Under Socialism, you would not be allowed to be poor. You would be forcibly fed, clothed, lodged, taught, and employed whether you like it or not. If it were discovered that you had not character and industry enough to be worth all this trouble, you might possibly be executed in a kindly manner; but whilst you were permitted to live, you would have to live well."[10]

Shaw created the well-known Fabian Socialist Window which pictures men with large hammers striking the world to chisel it the way they saw fit. The Window has these words at the top: REMOULD IT NEARER TO THE HEART'S DESIRE. Not God's desire, man's desire. Also pictured is a wolf in sheep's clothing and a shield that reads "Pray Devoutly, Hammer Stoutly."

The Fabian Society was created in 1883, the same year Karl Marx died. Because early Fabians denied the God of the Bible, they used liberal clergy to infect the church. They succeeded in penetrating the major institutions of society and taught that man was not inherently evil or fallen. Fabians have attempted to dilute and ridicule Christianity, and they've had an obvious influence on colleges and Universities in America and in the erosion of our culture. It was perhaps one of the most cunning, creative plans to subvert the United States from within, knowing full well we were too strong a nation to use force to achieve their ends overtly.

STUDENTS FOR A DEMOCRATIC SOCIETY & BILL AYERS

"Guilty as hell, free as a bird – America is a great country."
– **Bill Ayers**

In the United States, Students for a Democratic Society (SDS) was a direct offshoot of the Fabians and a branch of the Intercollegiate Socialist Society. SDS was a student activist movement – the youth arm of the League for Industrial Democracy the American counterpart to the British Fabian Society founded to promote socialism throughout the West. A faction of SDS formed the Weather Underground, identified by the FBI as a "domestic terrorist group."

Bill Ayers, Barack Obama's close friend from Chicago, was the leader of the Weather Underground. Ayers participated in the bombings of New York City Police Headquarters in 1970, the Capitol building in 1971, and the Pentagon in 1972. Ayers once said, "Kill all the rich people. Break up their cars and apartments. Bring the revolution home. Kill your parents."[11] He worked as a professor of education at the University of Illinois.

In a 2004 interview Bill Ayers told the *New York Times* he didn't regret setting bombs and that he didn't do enough. In his 2001 memoir *Fugitive Days*, Ayers recounts his life as a 60's radical and talked about the day he bombed the Pentagon:

> "Everything was absolutely ideal.... The sky was blue. The birds were singing. And the bastards were finally going to get what was coming to them." He further recalls his fascination with the fact that "a good bomb" could render even "big buildings and wide streets ... fragile and destructible," leaving behind a "majestic scene" of utter destruction.[12]

This is the guy who co-authored a book in 1974 titled *Prairie Fire: The Politics of Revolutionary Anti-Imperialism,* and made the following statements:

> "We are a guerrilla organization. We are communist women and men...."

> "The only path to the final defeat of imperialism and the building of socialism is revolutionary war."

> "Without armed struggle there can be no victory."

"We need a revolutionary communist party in order to lead the struggle, give coherence and direction to the fight, seize power and build the new society."

"Socialism is the total opposite of capitalism/imperialism. It is the rejection of empire and white supremacy. Socialism is the violent overthrow of the bourgeoisie...."[13]

In 1995, Bill Ayers and his wife, Bernadine Dohrn (Dohrn was on the FBI's Ten Most Wanted list) hosted meetings at their Chicago home to introduce Barrack Obama to their neighbors and political allies as Obama prepared to make his first run for the Illinois State Senate. Astonishingly, Americans didn't care when conservatives shared this information in 2008.

REVEREND JIM WALLIS

Jim Wallis is another member of SDS and is currently President Obama's spiritual adviser. Wallis became the leader of SDS while at Michigan State University.[14] Over the years, Wallis has been pro-Vietcong and actually celebrated America's defeat in Vietnam. Wallis stated:

"I don't know how else to express the quiet emotion that rushed through me when the news reports showed that the United States had finally been defeated in Vietnam"[15]

Jim Wallis has had relationships with the communist Committee in Solidarity with the People of El Salvador (CISPES). Writing in the November 1983 issue of *Sojourners*, Jacob Laksin notes that "Jim Wallis and Jim Rice drafted what would become the charter of leftist activists committed to the proliferation of communist revolutions in Central America."[16]

In a 1982 Democratic Socialists of America (DSA) newsletter, Wallis was listed as one of three "Religion and Socialism Commission co-chairs." Wallis's *Sojourners* enterprise has been a socialistic undertaking from the start, claiming to help the poor with government aid. Wallis and the Christian Left promote equally distributed wealth, but this type of socialism has never been able to create the abundance needed to lift the poor out of poverty. Like Bill Ayres, Jim Wallis remains fiercely opposed to the free market system, and in many interviews he has stressed his belief that capitalism has proven to have failed the poor and the earth.

Jumping ahead to 2005, Wallis was hired by Senate Democrats to fool Americans into believing secular liberals had found "religion" in part by sprinkling references to God and faith into their speeches. In addition, fifteen Democrat House members made Wallis their guest of honor at a breakfast, and his topic was how to turn "religious voters" into Democrats. He is a self-described "activist preacher" known for his opposition to the religious right's policies. Appointed by President Obama in 2009, Wallis has a key political role in Washington, D.C. as he works his social justice, anti-American angles.

ANTONIO GRAMSCI

Antonio Gramsci (1891-1937) was another disciple of Marx. Gramsci was an Italian writer, politician, atheist, founder and one time leader of the Communist Party of Italy. Also influenced by Vladimir Lenin, Gramsci is seen by some to be one of the most important Marxist thinkers in the twentieth century. He also believed in overthrowing the capitalist system and that **the goals of Karl Marx would never be reached as long as Christianity was strong**. Gramsci was renowned for his concept of cultural hegemony.[17] This implemented strategy to grind down the morality of a culture has been one of the most damaging to America.

Antonio Gramsci believed a culturally diverse society could be ruled by one social class by manipulating the societal culture – beliefs, perceptions, values, etc. This would be done by converting intellectuals and working through academia, the media, entertainment, and government. He thought of it as a long, evolutionary, march through the major institutions in order to break down the wall of Christianity over a few generations.

Gramsci was another brilliantly evil mind. His effectiveness was accelerated due to the fact he was in prison for the last eleven years of his life, becoming a type of martyr for Marxism. He wrote his "Prison Notebooks," more than thirty notebooks and 3000 pages of history and analysis during his imprisonment. Gramsci's methods and teachings have diminished the Word of God in churches across America. The plan was to destroy Christianity and western civilization. Italy's Antonio Gramsci was one of the key influences of Chicago's Saul Alinsky.

Frankfort School: One more offshoot of Karl Marx was the Frankfurt School, a Marxist think-tank founded in 1923 in Weimar, Germany. Briefly known as the Institute for Marxism (aka Institute for Social Research), the primary goal of the Frankfurt School was to translate Marxism from economic terms into cultural terms. It would provide the ideas on which to base a new political theory of Cultural Revolution.

Among its founders was another fellow traveler and Marxist, Georg Lukacs. Many members of the Frankfurt School were Jewish atheists, and in 1933 when the Nazis came to power and National Socialism (Nazism) grew in Germany, they shut down the Frankfort School. Its members fled to New York City, and the Institute was reestablished there in 1933 with help from Columbia University. Even though they despised our Christian culture, they gladly accepted teaching jobs at major universities across the country. European atheists and Marxists got a foothold in higher education, and some eventually ventured into government.

VETTING THE PRESIDENT

By the time Barack Obama made it to college at Occidental, Columbia and Harvard, you can be sure he had formed enough anti-American views to build on what he had already gleaned from his childhood mentor, communist Frank Marshall Davis. Davis was a labor activist, writer, and community organizer as well as a Communist Party USA member.

In 2010, Dr. John Drew, one of Barack Obama's college friends, came forward and confirmed what many informed people already knew that Obama "was basically a Marxist-Leninist." Drew talked about his past arguments with Obama about the many brands of Marxism. In radio and phone interviews, Drew stated:

> "I see evidence of a continuing commitment to Marxist ideology…. In the Marxist model, the economy is the driving force behind change in the other spheres of society."

The media made sure the American public knew everything there was to know about former President George W. Bush. They vetted every detail of his past including: his college records, medical records, his grades, friendships, Air Force years, who he dated, his "wild years," music and sports interests, high school activities, mentors; the kind of deodorant he used, and what kind of underwear he preferred. And why do you suppose the American people know very little about a far left liberal Senator in Chicago who had ties to hard-core, radical, socialist, big-government ideologues?

Dr. John Drew did his senior honors thesis on Marxist economics at Occidental College, and he also founded the Democratic Student Socialist Alliance. He was a contemporary of Obama at Occidental and a Marxist himself. In fact, Drew was a well-known campus communist and was attracted to the college because Occidental was known for its Left-leaning politics and Marxist professors. Some even said it was considered "the Moscow of southern California."

Occidental College attracted America's future president. Drew believed Obama was looking for a social revolution during his college days, and he expected a movement where "the working class would overthrow the ruling class" leading to a socialist utopia in America. Drew admitted how extreme he thought Obama's views were at the time.

In 2010, John Drew was interviewed by Dr. Paul Kengor, an author, Reagan biographer, columnist, radio host, and *Executive Director of The Center for Vision & Values*. Drew admitted that at Occidental he was a comrade who leaned more toward the Frankfurt School of Marxism. Here is a partial transcript of Dr. Kengor's radio interview with John Drew:

> **Drew:** "I felt like I was doing Obama a favor by pointing out that the Marxist revolution that he and [our friends] were hoping for was really kind of a pipe dream, and that there was nothing in European history or the history of developed nations that would make that sort of fantasy – you know, Frank Marshall Davis fantasy of revolution – come true."

Kengor: "So you had a realistic sense that even though you liked these ideas, it really couldn't happen or really wouldn't even work."

Drew: "Right. I was … still a card-carrying Marxist, but I was kind of a more advanced, East Coast, Cornell University Marxist.…"

Kengor: "I know people are listening right now who want me to address this – and especially people who are Obama supporters. To be fair, I mean, look at where you were then and now where you are today."

Drew: "Well, yeah, now I'm a Ronald Reagan, churchgoing, Baptist conservative."

Kengor: "But now, okay, so what about Obama? Where do you think *he* is today? And to the people who are listening and are angry that we're even having this conversation, [I want to tell them this]: Look, you don't want us to talk about this because you don't like what it says about Obama's past, but *we have to know this stuff about our presidents*!

"You can't leave this out of biographies.… And that's what people need to understand.… That's why the background is so crucial – Frank Marshall Davis, what happened at Occidental, goes straight to Columbia from Occidental, the Bill Ayers affiliation, no real-world experience – this matters.…"

Drew: "Yeah, I think whenever he talks about people clinging to their guns and their religion due to economic stress, that's just the standard Marxist argument. In fact, that's the argument of alienation and class-consciousness … the superficial religious and cultural ideals of the capitalist culture … and I really think he's surrounded by people that share that mental architecture."[18]

Need a background check on a conservative Republican? You'll have the results in less than twenty-four hours. Liberal Democrat? This could take a while. We now know that after college, for three of his Chicago years Barack Obama did plenty of community organizing and was associated with a religious group called the Gamaliel Foundation. One reporter, David Freddoso, researched Obama's involvement in 2008 and concluded, "the proposed solution to *every* problem on the South Side was a distribution of government funds...."

Thanks to Breitbart TV, a 2009 video surfaced of the Gamaliel Foundation leading community organizers in prayer, not to God, but to President Obama. In the video they are seen lobbying for health care and social justice while repeating "Hear our cry, Obama" and "Deliver us, Obama."[19] Why did they worship him before he was president? As a trainer for Gamaliel and ACORN, Obama used his influence to secure a *major increase in funding* for both groups. They in turn supported him politically. Do you think the money has helped Chicago?

Because an enemy exists that must be eliminated, they have long ago declared war. Many radicals want not only to reform the system; they hope to destroy it completely.

Know this: there are enemies within. Anita Dunn, President Obama's *former* communications director, went on record and said that Mao Tse-tung – who murdered 60 to 70 million people – was one of her two favorite philosophers. Second, John Holdren, the Obama administration Science and Technology Czar is a huge promoter of population control. He believes that for us to enjoy a higher quality of life there must be fewer people. He has written about and considered forced abortions and sterilization as population control options.[20]

CLOWARD-PIVEN STRATEGY

In March 2012, Frances Fox Piven gave a lecture to a group of students at the University of Connecticut touting OWS and cheering socialism. Piven stated the Occupy movement may be in its second phase where it "makes trouble" and "threatens to shut down institutions." Fox Piven was thrilled OWS had moved into city neighborhoods and schools and added:

> "This spring, we'll see action against the banks, against the corporations.... I know one poll that shows something like

half of the youngest age group polled, probably 15 to 25, saw no problems with socialism...."[21]

In the 1960s, Piven gave traction to the radical strategy of forcing political change through orchestrated crisis. The "Cloward-Piven Strategy" aims to bring about the fall of capitalism by overloading the government bureaucracy with a flood of impossible demands. It is a political strategy outlined in 1966 by American sociologists and political activists Richard Cloward (1926-2001) and Frances Fox Piven (b. 1932) which called for overloading the U.S. public welfare system in order to precipitate a crisis that would lead to a replacement of the welfare system with a national system of "a guaranteed annual income." Cloward and Piven were a married couple who were both professors at the Columbia University School of Social Work.[22]

Not surprisingly, the two were both lifelong members of Democratic Socialists of America. The couple implemented their strategy by birthing several radical organizations one after the other, including ACORN, with the help of Wade Rathke. Journalist, columnist, and *former White House staff economist* James Simpson has been studying the Left and their radical movements for decades and noted the couple's most significant achievement was the "Motor Voter" act which was signed into law by Bill Clinton in 1993 as they stood right behind him. Simpson writes:

> "As we now know, ACORN was one of the chief drivers of high-risk mortgage lending that eventually led to the financial crisis. But the Motor Voter law was another component of the strategy. It created vast vulnerabilities in our electoral system, which ACORN then exploited.
>
> "ACORN's voter registration scandals throughout the U.S. are predictable fallout. The Motor Voter law has also been used to open another vulnerability in the system: the registration of vast numbers of illegal aliens, who then reliably vote Democrat. Herein lies the real reason Democrats are so anxious for open borders...."[23]

In June 2012 President Obama announced that the United States will stop deporting hundreds of thousands of young illegal immigrants and will give them work permits. The administration has side-stepped the country's legislative process and Obama's executive order will apply to illegal immigrants who came to the U.S. before they were sixteen and are younger than thirty.

"Racists, Sexists, Anti-Gay ... Right Wing bigots go away" – Occupy Activists chant 2-11-2012

"The only solution is World Revolution" – from the official Occupy website

CONNECTING OCCUPY WALL STREET DOTS

"Anonymous" is one of the anarchist groups behind OWS's most violent incidents and in February 2012 released a video declaration of war. On the video, they called for real change, democracy, and revolution and further stated "Anonymous has decided to openly declare war on the United States government. This is a call to arms." They called on U.S. citizens to support them in "overthrowing this corrupted body."[24]

These "Occupiers" rail against the wealthy in America, and based on its mob mentality there is more evidence the movement is open to using violent means to get what they want. A speaker at an Occupy Los Angeles rally shouted, "Revolution! Yes, revolution that is led by the working class. Long live revolution! Long live socialism!"

The origins of the OWS movement have been covered up. Certain news corporations are either ignorant or complicit in the evil they are promoting and protecting. You and I, Christianity and the majority of Americans stand in their way. I do not mind the protest of greed – there is far too much love of money in America – but it is a bit much to take down the American system.

Many of us may also agree with those who would call for reforming or even abolishing the Fed, Fannie Mae, and Freddie Mac because they do not promote free-enterprise capitalism; they promote crony capitalism. They are ugly arrangements of special treatment for political allies. These government agencies allow the funneling of taxpayer dollars from our pocket to politicians and bank executives. It's corrupt and immoral, so I don't mind talking about these issues, but the OWS movement trail of support leads from overseas and from key radical organizers including top socialists in America.

There are at least two things you and I did not want to believe: communist activism has been alive and well on American college campuses for decades, and our children are being softened toward socialist ideas in public schools and universities. Many of these influential OWS cogs are members and leaders of the Democratic Socialists of America, which is the U.S. branch of the infamous Socialist International. Their ultimate end would be a one world government.

Look up "climate change" and "Socialist International," and you'll see how much power they have attained in their quest. Sadly, this radical organization is virtually unknown to the majority of Americans because it rarely gets mentioned. There is mounting evidence the major U.S. media, billionaire progressives such as George Soros, the White House, and factions of the Occupy movement are working together.

Their revolution isn't just about reelecting a Democratic president; it's about completely transforming America. This is a huge endeavor so where does all the funding come from? Soon after the Occupy protests came to our shores, donations started to come in from all over the world to help destroy America. Since it was young in its development, Occupy leaders enlisted the services of a non-profit organization called the Alliance for Global Justice (AFGJ).

According to its own website, the AFGJ provides grassroots support for organizations that pursue a "socially, ecologically, and economically just world." Writing for the Heritage Foundation, journalist Lachlan Markay explained that Katherine Hoyt is their president and leads the Alliance's Nicaragua Network program. This supports their Marxist Sandinista political party and was founded to overthrow the Nicaraguan government. Hoyt supports and has worked for the Sandinista government. Markay explained:

> "The Sandinistas ruled from 1979 to 1990. Their leader, Daniel Ortega, was elected again in 2006.… Given the radical nature of many of its projects, it is perhaps unsurprising that the Alliance receives money from a host of progressive individuals

and organizations. Chief among them is George Soros's Open Society Institute."[25]

Hypocrisy alert: In a movement trying to convince Americans that capitalism, corruption, and greed are the biggest problems relating to the "working class" and the economy, a December 2011 report noted the top twenty-five Occupy backers are worth over $4 billion dollars! Making the list of those supportive of OWS are big names such as George Clooney, Jane Fonda, David Letterman, Brad Pitt, Roseanne Barr, Al Gore, Miley Cyrus, Matt Damon, Yoko Ono, Michael Moore, Katy Perry, Alec Baldwin, Stephen King, and Jay-Z.

Liberal celebrities and wealthy individuals are often a product of their own elite bubble, but their backing a protest of the "rich" is quite disingenuous. Note the irony of Yoko Ono's husband John Lennon writing "Imagine all the people living life in peace…. Imagine no possessions" from a Park Avenue penthouse in New York City while millions of dollars in Beatles income sat in his bank account.

Many of the unkempt Occupy activists need a bath and some breath mints, but they are *very* well organized, funded, and dangerous to America. I am not talking about those who are going along with the protests to make headlines, but those who understand *exactly* what the movement is about and what its goals are. Some have described OWS gatherings as counter-culture freak shows that feature bongo-banging tie-dyed Woodstock wannabes, but protests are full of banners and posters featuring images and quotes from, Marx, Lenin, Mao, and Che Guevara, a chief executioner and assassin for the Fidel Castro regime. Guevara was directly responsible for murdering thousands of people.

OWS has the media, unions, and the Left-wing of the Democratic Party behind them. Endorsements have come from all over the place, including the Marxist Student Union, American Nazi Party, Hugo Chavez, Black Panthers, the government of North Korea, Louis Farrakhan, and the Islamic terrorist group Hezbollah. OWS has enjoyed support from many labor unions and federations representing millions of public-sector workers, such as the AFL-CIO, the AFSCME, the SEIU, and the United Federation of Teachers.

Author, columnist, and speaker Robert Ringer wrote that OWS may not talk about communism, but that is exactly what they're shooting for. Ringer stated:

> "Whether it's the Occupy Wall Street protesters, rioters in Greece, public workers defacing the state capitol building in Madison, Wisconsin, or thugs tearing down the city of Oakland, brick by brick, they are all focused on the same objective: equal distribution of wealth and a classless society."[26]

According to *USA Today*, the Deputy Chief of Staff of the Iranian Armed Forces for Culture and Defense Publicity, General Seyed Massoud Jazzayeri, described OWS not only as "a revolution and a comprehensive movement against corruption in the U.S.," but as a force that "will no doubt end in the downfall of the Western capitalist system."

You won't be surprised that several individuals working for the *New York Times*, *National Public Radio* (NPR), and *NBC News* have portrayed the OWS movement as "a spontaneous uprising." Discover the Networks has a group of experts on the political left and have provided a comprehensive expose on OWS that includes these gems: Muslim New Yorkers are in solidarity with OWS, and *Rolling Stone's* Matt Taibbi expressed his love and support for the movement.

> "Another media figure, the infamous racist and MSNBC host Al Sharpton, made a very public appearance at an OWS rally, where he shouted: 'It's time for us to occupy Wall Street, occupy Washington, occupy Alabama. We've come to take our country back to the people.'"[27]

WE'RE ALL SOCIALISTS?

Shortly after President Obama was inaugurated in January 2009, *Newsweek* ran a cover story for its February 16 issue declaring: "We Are All Socialists Now: The Perils and Promise of the New Era of Big Government." The economic crisis was caused by too much government regulation, borrowing and spending, yet *Newsweek* claimed, "In the absence of a robust private sector, the government will fill in the gap." The publication inferred that with the election of Barack Obama,

America was becoming more like a European socialist country. Though I stopped reading *Newsweek* many years ago due to its liberal leanings, I recently learned the writer of that article was none other than Evan Thomas.

Thomas teaches journalism at Princeton University. He is also the grandson of previously mentioned Marxist radical, Norman Thomas. And you wonder why kids going into journalism end up with hostile views of Christians and friendly views toward liberalism? In addition, on June 5, 2009, while being interviewed by Mr. "Thrill up my leg" on *Hardball with Chris Matthews*, Evan Thomas provoked controversy by stating: "I mean, in a way, Obama's standing above the country, above – above the world, he's sort of god."[28]

Prior to *Newsweek*, Thomas also worked at *Time Magazine*. You can see his continued influence at *Time* as the 2011 Person of the Year cover story was – "The (Occupy) Protestor" with the socialist clenched fist representing the movement. Many conservative Americans stopped considering *Time* legitimate and unbiased years ago. These and many other publications have sanitized socialism. The lengthy, eight-page cover story praised the European revolutions, focused on OWS, and dedicated just two descriptive sentences to the Tea Party calling it a "radical populist movement."

Time did point out that, "In the U.S., the Obama campaign was in part a feel-good protest movement that galvanized young people." In 2008, Barack Obama was declared *Time's* Person of the Year.

Andrew Breitbart believed one purpose of OWS was to divert attention from the much larger, highly influential Tea Party movement. In October 2011, *New York* magazine published the results of a poll it had conducted with 100 committed OWS protesters in Manhattan, half of whom were in their twenties. Forty-five percent of respondents said capitalism "can't be saved" and is "inherently immoral."

In a different 2011 survey of OWS protesters by *The Wall Street Journal,* 65% said government has a moral responsibility to guarantee all citizens access to affordable health care, a college education, and a secure retirement – regardless of the cost. Pollster Doug Schoen concluded OWS is committed to radical policies and they hold "values that are dangerously out of touch" with most Americans. Other results of the survey of Occupy protesters were as revealing as they are disturbing:

> "77% supported tax hikes on the wealthiest Americans; 52% had participated in political movements before; 98% endorsed civil disobedience to achieve their goals; and 31% said they would support violence to promote their agendas."[29]

In a report by *The Daily Caller*, a series of leaked emails revealed specific OWS objectives. One particular email from *Adbusters* senior editor Micah White stated the movement wanted the "forgiveness of all student loan debt," a tax on the wealthiest one percent to fund public services, and another "Robin Hood" tax on financial transactions to be used to fund welfare programs and to combat climate change, and to devote large sums of money to creating union jobs.

Lisa Fithian, a top street-level organizer of the Occupy Wall Street movement and activist trainer for ACORN, once told the *Internationalist Socialist Review*:

> "I have no issue with property destruction. I think sometimes it's appropriate, sometimes it's not. ...Does it help us achieve our goal, or does it not? We're in a society where property is idolized, so a lot of people don't get it yet that it doesn't really matter...."

According to the American Nazi Party, which supports OWS, the movement strikes a welcome blow against an obscenely corrupt "Judeo-Capitalism." Los Angeles Unified School District employee Patricia McAllister told a television reporter: "I think that the Zionist Jews who are running these big banks and our Federal Reserve ... need to be run out of this country." There have been caricatures of Jewish bankers, and in Chicago there were flyers with the headline: "Refuse to Pay Taxes. Destroy Israel." These are intense times. How often have you heard people claim "It could never happen in America," but are now saying, "I can't believe this is happening in America?"

SPREADING THE WEALTH IN CHICAGO

Former ACORN chief executive Bertha Lewis has a new organization, The Black Institute (TBI), one of many ACORN reincarnations, dubs its protests "Occupy Black America" and "Occupy The Hood." During a March 2010 speech to the Young Democratic Socialists, Lewis told the audience, "First of all let me just say any group that says, 'I'm young, I'm democratic, and I'm a socialist,' is alright with me." In that speech, Bertha Lewis talked about immigration being America's "next big battle" and said the following:

> "And the reason this is so important is, you know, here's the secret [whispers]: We're getting ready to be a majority, minority country. Shhhh. [applause] We'll be like South Africa. More black people than white people. [laughter] Don't tell anybody...."

Just two years prior to making this speech, Lewis had focused her attention on organizing ACORN's national get-out-the-vote campaign for Barrack Obama. By October 2008, Lewis was facing widespread charges of voter fraud. ACORN has been called "the largest radical organization in America."

In a May 2008 article in *National Review*, Stanley Kurtz, a senior fellow at the Ethics and Public Policy Center, asked the question, "What if Barack Obama's most important radical connection has been hiding in plain sight all along?" Madeleine Talbot was the woman at ACORN who invited Obama to train organizers. Acorn was devious in its use of banking regulations to pressure financial institutions into massive "donations" that ACORN used to finance supposedly non-partisan voter turn-out drives. Kurtz reports:

> "Talbot turns out to have been a key leader of that attempt by Acorn to storm the Chicago City Council (during a living-wage debate).... On July 31, 1997, six people were arrested as 200 Acorn protesters tried to storm the Chicago City Council session. According to the *Chicago Daily Herald*, Acorn demonstrators pushed over the metal detector and table used to screen visitors, backed police against the doors to the council chamber, and blocked late-arriving aldermen and city staff from entering the session."[30]

Let's dig deeper: Barack Obama served on the boards of two chari-table foundations, including the Woods Fund of Chicago from 1993 to 2002. The Woods Fund supported the concept of an expanding welfare state allocating ever-increasing amounts of money to the public school system and the redistribution of wealth via taxes. During that time, the tax exempt foundation made some interesting grants, including one to Obama's church, Trinity United Church of Christ, headed by Rev. Jeremiah Wright.

Annual grants of around $70,000 were also made to ACORN from 2001-2005 for a total of $355,000 – courtesy of the Woods Fund. There were a few honest journalists who reported on the money trail, but the media gatekeepers prevented the stories from making prime time news. In addition to the reservoir of political support that came to Obama through his close ties with Jeremiah Wright, Father Michael Pfleger, and other Chicago churches, ACORN appears to have played a major role in Obama's political advance. But wait, there's more!

At one time, the board of directors included Obama, Bill Ayers, and Chairman Howard J. Stanback. Stanback headed New Kenwood LLC, a limited liability company founded by Obama's close friend and convicted felon, Tony Rezko. The fund provided a combined total of over $1 million to the Chicago Annenberg Challenge. Obama was its chief executive officer, and Ayers authored the $50 million grant that gave life to the Chicago Annenberg Challenge.

The Woods Fund also used Northern Trust for financial services, which is the same company that provided Obama his 2005 mortgage. The Obamas financed their upscale Hyde Park home in 2005 through Northern Trust and obtained an outstanding mortgage rate. Obama's memberships on foundation boards "allowed him to help direct tens of millions of dollars in grants" to various liberal organizations, includ-ing Chicago Acorn, "whose endorsement Obama sought and won in his State Senate race."[31]

Ten years prior, Obama joined the Board of Directors for the Chicago-based Joyce Foundation in 1994 and served on its board until 2002. The Joyce Foundation targets its grants toward organizations through agendas of social justice, prison reform, increased government spending for social services and radical environmentalism. Many of those recipient groups are hostile to the capitalist model. In 2003, Obama's close leftist friend and campaign adviser, Valerie Jarrett, also joined the Joyce Foundation board. In a *World Net Daily* exclusive, "The groups Obama kept off his resume," Brad O'Leary noted:

> "Between 1998 and 2001, the Obama and Ayers-led Woods Fund also gave nearly $300,000 to Northwestern University, where Bill Ayers and his wife, Castro-trained Bernadine Dohrn Ayers, had secured teaching jobs. Bill Ayers' father, Tom Ayers, also sat on the Board of Trustees for Northwestern.

> "If the funding and the relationships sound all too cozy, that's because they are. Joyce Foundation President Deborah Leff and Barack Obama served together on the Foundation's Board as late as 1999, and they also served together on the board of the Chicago Annenberg Challenge."[32]

WHAT HAS AMERICA LEARNED?

It is imperative you and I recognize the enemy has been working through people willing to forge his devious plan in America. We must alert others to the wickedness because the time to sound the alarm is almost past. Thomas Jefferson's timeless words should inspire us today:

> "Educate and inform the whole mass of the people. Enable them to see that it is their interest to preserve peace and order, and they will preserve them. And it requires no very high degree of education to convince them of this. They are the only sure reliance for the preservation of our liberty."[33]

What an honor and privilege it is that God has chosen you and me to be alive during this trying and exciting time in America. We are not here to be spectators. We were born during this generation to be a voice and an influence on others in order to draw people to Jesus Christ and to counteract what is happening in America. I don't believe our grandparents could deal with everything we have to deal with today. Conversely, we probably couldn't live through two World Wars and the

Great Depression like they did. God has a specific purpose for you and me today and His timing is perfect.

> *There is an appointed time for everything. And there is a time for every event under heaven. A time to be born and a time to die; a time to plant and a time to uproot, a time to kill and a time to heal, a time to break down and a time to build up, a time to weep and a time to laugh...a time to be silent and a time to speak, a time to love and a time to hate, a time for war and a time for peace...* (**Ecclesiastes 3:1-4, 8** ESV).

Do not allow today's news or the agenda of the Left to cause you to lose your focus or your effectiveness for the Lord. This is all temporary. He is eternal. We are here for such a time as this and God has chosen us. Don't give up and don't get tired of doing what is good because we will reap a harvest in due time (Galatians 6:9-10). Rally, stir up and strengthen fellow Christians. Regardless of the condition of culture and what is happening in America, we are responsible for using our time wisely while we're here. Enemy forces want to blot out God and our freedoms, but He has entrusted this generation with His commission and to infiltrate society for Christ.

> "Freedom is never more than one generation away from extinction. We didn't pass it to our children in the bloodstream. It must be fought for, protected and handed on for them to do the same." – **Ronald Reagan**

ENDNOTES

1 AGENDA, Grinding America Down, http://agendadocumentary.com/
2 http://www.wnd.com/2009/08/108083/
3 http://frontpagemag.com/2011/09/30/union-gangsters-richard-trumka/
4 Detroit Free Press, http://www.freep.com/article/20110906/NEWS15/110906056/Transcript-Teamsters-Jim-Hoffa-s-speech-Labor-Day
5 http://www.breitbart.com/Big-Government/2012/03/04/SEIU-lerner-Occupy
6 http://newsbusters.org/blogs/jack-coleman/2011/12/31/chris-hayes-equates-gingrich-worker-committing-voter-fraud-70-acorn-co#ixzz1oHC3u0X3
7 http://www.wnd.com/2011/08/332061/
8 David Horowitz, Barrack Obama's Rules for Revolution; Alinsky Model, 2009, David Horowitz Freedom Center
9 http://www.discoverthenetworks.org/individualProfile.asp?indid=2042

10 George Bernard Shaw: The Intelligent Woman's Guide to Socialism and Capitalism, 1928, pg. 470

11 http://www.chicagomag.com/Chicago-Magazine/August-2001/No-Regrets/

12 http://www.nationalreview.com/corner/167989/
bill-ayers-unrepentant-lying-terrorist-andrew-c-mccarthy

13 http://www.zombietime.com/prairie_fire/

14 http://romanticpoet.wordpress.com/2010/03/15/
obamas-faith-adviser-jim-wallis-mixes-with-socialists-radicals-and-truthers/

15 Ronald H. Nash, "Why The Left Is Not Right," p. 58

16 Laksin, "Sojourners: History, Activities and Agendas" in Discoverthenetworks.
org., 2005

17 http://en.wikipedia.org/wiki/Cultural_hegemony

18 Dr. Paul Kengor, 10/2010, http://www.americanthinker.com/2010/12/obamas_
missing_link_1.html

19 http://michellemalkin.com/2009/09/29/
creepy-o-cult-video-of-the-day-deliver-us-obama/

20 http://www.foxnews.com/politics/2009/07/21/obamas-science-czar-considered-
forced-abortions-sterilization-population-growth/

21 http://www.theblaze.com/stories/fri-a-m-this-spring-well-see-action-piven-
issues-dark-prediction-on-occupy-wall-street/

22 http://en.wikipedia.org/wiki/Cloward%E2%80%93Piven_strategy

23 http://www.americanthinker.com/2009/11/clowardpiven_government.html

24 http://www.breitbart.com/Breitbart-TV?id={6F1AA708-52F2-4F2D-9D4C-
D4E954861C72}&title=Anonymous%20Declares%20War%20On%20The%20
United%20States

25 http://blog.heritage.org/2011/11/07/
meet-the-radical-group-handling-occupy-wall-street-finances/

26 http://www.humanevents.com/article.php?id=47801

27 http://www.discoverthenetworks.org/groupProfile.asp?grpid=7694

28 http://www.americanthinker.com/blog/2009/06/evan_thomas_on_obama_hes_
sort.html

29 http://www.discoverthenetworks.org/viewSubCategory.asp?id=1533

30 http://www.nationalreview.com/articles/224610/inside-obamas-acorn/
stanley-kurtz

31 Richard Henry Lee, Obama and the Woods fund of Chicago, 7/7/2008, http://
www.americanthinker.com/2008/07/obama_and_the_woods_fund_of_ch.html

32 Brad O'Leary, World Net Daily, http://www.wnd.com/2008/10/78106/

33 http://foundersquotes.com/quotes/
educate-and-inform-the-whole-mass-of-the-people/

CHAPTER 11

SOCIAL JUSTICE AND THE BIBLE

HOW THE SOCIAL GOSPEL GOT A BAD NAME

I know that the LORD will maintain the cause of the
afflicted and justice for the poor...Who executes justice
for the oppressed; Who gives food to the hungry. The
LORD sets the prisoners free (**Psalm 140:12; 146:7**).

Social Justice means different things to different people. According to Dictionary.com, *social justice* is defined as "the distribution of advantages and disadvantages within a society."[1] The definition has been altered by big government proponents, and its modern manipulation gives a black eye to what is in theory a good cause. Most of us would absolutely agree that the church in America must do a better job of helping the poor and less fortunate, but progressives place more emphasis on man's ability to fix the problem than on God's power, provision, and sovereignty.

Some Social Justice Christians seem more concerned about economic issues and the environment than they are about injustices done to babies ripped out of a mother's womb. They need to drop the moral pretense, because they're looking for leftist solutions to cultural problems.

When we consider the various definitions of "advantages" (benefit, gain, profit, opportunity, advancement, superiority, etc.), social justice becomes a bit confusing. Moreover, what is considered an advantage to some is not an advantage to others. I happen to believe owning a Bible and being educated in its principles is one of the most important advantages you can have.

In America, social justice has taken on a disputable and variable meaning, depending on who is using the term. A good rule of thumb may be that whenever there is an adjective added to a value-based noun such as "justice," there is an agenda right behind it. People do the same thing with the word "rights."

Other meanings of social justice support the idea of creating a society or institution that is based on the principles of equality and solidarity, progressive taxation, income redistribution, and in some cases even property redistribution. It appears the beneficiaries on the receiving end are often determined by those who are promoting social justice. Social Justice proponents typically protest capitalism and engage in anti-war activism, which will start up again if Mitt Romney is elected president. (If Obama is re-elected, the anti-war mob gets another four years off.)

Social Justice is a code phrase of the left which believes in a class-less society and that all differences in wealth and property should be eliminated. It is a political movement that generally believes people are born into an inflexible social order.

Religious liberals have invaded evangelical Christian churches with their version of social justice. They claim to back up their fight for poverty and world hunger by the use of selected Scriptures about helping the poor. *Every* individual Christian is responsible to obey God's Word and do what we can to manage our resources to help those in need, and humanitarian efforts should coincide with the preaching of the gospel. Christians need to be the hands and feet of Jesus, but poverty and hunger will never completely be eradicated.

The poor you will always have with you, and you can help them any time you want. But you will not always have me (**Mark 14:7** NIV).

To liberals, social justice means a level of fairness as defined by them and enforced by the state. Their argument is that the church has not done a good job taking care of the poor so the government must step in. The solution should never be government intervention. When government gets involved, who decides how to allocate money? This promotes an unholy alliance between the church and state. The apostle Paul wrote in 1 Timothy 5 that it is our responsibility to take care of "widows and orphans" and those who are unable to care for themselves.

Most Christians try to heed Jesus' warning to care for "the least of these" in Matthew 25:35-46. The key is through charitable giving,

Christians are to *voluntarily* tithe to the church and share their finances (distribute wealth) with the needy, not be forced by the government through taxes to unwillingly (redistribute wealth) give to whoever the government decides needs it the most. Can government be trusted to use the people's money honestly?

If their definition of social justice is implemented and many poor people are fed, this meets their temporary physical need. With government involved, however, it would then be illegal for Christians to share the gospel with the poor to meet their spiritual need. Physical food and water will satisfy them short term, but spiritual food and drink are what can satisfy permanently. Only Jesus can give us the bread of (eternal) life and offer us living water:

> *Jesus answered and said to her, "Everyone who drinks of this water will thirst again; but whoever drinks of the water that I will give him shall never thirst; but the water that I will give him will become in him a well of water springing up to eternal life."* (**John 4:13-14**).

Immediately following that interaction with the Samaritan woman, the disciples returned and were urging him to eat something, and he told them he had food to eat that they didn't know about, saying *My food is to do the will of Him who sent me and to accomplish His work* (John 4:34). Jesus was pointing out the need to harvest souls that were ready.

Francis A. Schaefer cautioned about social justice in his book *The Great Evangelical Disaster*:

> "The socialist mentality as promoted by Evangelicals for Social Action and others, and endorsed by much of the evangelical world, is based upon a double error. First and foremost it is wrong theologically, fundamentally distorting the meaning of the gospel. But it is equally wrong in its naive assessment of the redistribution of wealth and its consequences. The answer is not some kind of socialistic or egalitarian redistribution."[2]

Under the Christian Left's idea of social justice, believers would be under federal control, and our basic freedoms such as sharing the gospel of Jesus Christ would be impossible without legal and financial repercussions.

> *For if you truly amend your ways and your deeds, if you truly*
> *practice justice between a man and his neighbor, if you do not*
> *oppress the alien, the orphan, or the widow; ...I will let you dwell*
> *in this place, in the land that I gave to your fathers forever and*
> *ever* (**Jeremiah 7:5-7**).

SOCIAL JUSTICE CHRISTIANS

Life is not fair, but God is good. He is sovereign, all powerful and He hates injustice. However, unfairness is inherent in the human condition. God is just; human beings typically are not. That's where the church comes in. Jesus did not commission the Roman Government to help the poor and He never advocated taxation on the wealthy to pay for the benefits of the less fortunate. The early church took care of the needs of the poor and also demonstrated how a system of heartfelt, *voluntary* distribution could work. The communal sharing of the early Christians in Acts chapter 2, for example, was virtually the opposite of the socio-economic Marxism some church leaders are calling for today.

We need to be careful about throwing the word "social" around. What is "socialized" is state-controlled. Here in the United States, we have tried throwing more money at the problem of poverty, and we have found it does not work (See Detroit). When corrupt men are in charge of distributing money, it most often does not get to the people who really need help. Communism has also failed worldwide, and Marxism should have taught the world a permanent lesson.

Over the years our churches and ministries in America have made the average citizen better, have fed countless millions around the world, and financed the spreading of the gospel. Without nations influenced by Jesus Christ and biblical Christianity, the world would be a much darker place, and there would be considerably more poverty both spiritually and economically. Would a system of socialism allow the church to do any of this?

Author and commentator, Erik Rush, the man credited with breaking the story about President Obama's former pastor, Reverend Jeremiah Wright and Black Liberation Theology, called social justice Christians another "well-organized group of traitors" to America. Rush said their religion has become superficial.

> "As with health-care reform … many are aware that social and environmental 'justice' issues are not about justice at all; they are calculated to deliver unprecedented levels of power to the federal government.

> "I declare that 'social justice Christianity' is apostasy; its adherents have abandoned their faith for a cause…. While some are misguided Christians, others (like Jim Wallis) are out-and-out Marxist posers. Proverbially, they now stand with the Sadducees and Rome, against Israel. While I pray that God will have mercy on their souls, *we* must show them no mercy politically."[3]

Jesus did not teach that the Spirit of the Lord anointed the federal government to preach. That's the job of the church so the power and will of God can be revealed. In **Isaiah 61:1-2**, a verse Jesus quoted in the Gospels as well, He gives six reasons for which God had anointed Him and not one of them mentions money:

> *The Spirit of the Sovereign Lord is on me, because the Lord has anointed me to preach good news to the poor. He has sent me to bind up the brokenhearted, to proclaim freedom for the captives and release from darkness for the prisoners, to proclaim the year of the Lord's favor and the day of vengeance of our God…*[NIV]

God calls us to give cheerfully from our hearts (2 Cor. 9:7), but God does not advocate additional tax burdens on the whole of society for any cause. When Jesus faced Roman prefect, Pontius Pilate, He didn't ask Pilate for financial aid for the poor. Jesus didn't complain about injustices in Galilee or Nazareth or Bethlehem. He didn't ask for the Roman government to step in and spread the wealth. In fact, Jesus stated, *My kingdom is not of this world* (John 18:36), and also proclaimed:

> *You say correctly that I am a king. For this I have been born, and for this I have come into the world, to testify to the truth….* **(John 18:37)**.

Eric Rush singled out Jim Wallis for a reason. Instead of promoting the true, unfiltered gospel of Christ, liberals such as Wallis are dangerous and divisive. In a 2006 radio broadcast, an interviewer asked: "Are you then calling for the redistribution of wealth in society?" Wallis replied, "Absolutely, without any hesitation. That's what the gospel is all about."[4]

Whose gospel is all about the redistribution of wealth? According to **1 Corinthians 15:1-4**, the gospel is all about faith in Jesus for eternal salvation:

> *Now I make known to you, brethren, the gospel which I preached to you, which also you received, in which also you stand, by which also you are saved, if you hold fast the word which I preached to you, unless you believed in vain. For I delivered to you as of first importance what I also received, that Christ died for our sins according to the Scriptures, and that He was buried, and that He was raised on the third day according to the Scriptures....*

WHERE'S WALLIS?

In 1979, *Time* magazine hailed Jim Wallis as one of the "50 Faces for America's Future." That same year, the journal *Mission Tracks* published an interview with Wallis, in which he expressed his hope that "more Christians will come to view the world through Marxist eyes."[5]

Reverend Jim Wallis serves on the White House Advisory Council on Faith-based and Neighborhood partnerships. Some say he is a progressive evangelical because his primary support is from leftists. In 2011, it was revealed by investigative journalists that Wallis's *Sojourners* magazine received hundreds of thousands of dollars from radical Left-wing Socialist George Soros through a huge grant in 2004.[6]

Sojourners is basically an interfaith movement that hides behind their version of the gospel, which promotes environmentalism and humanism. As its Chief Editor, Jim Wallis has a team of progressives as editors and regular contributors including Tony Campolo, Brian McLaren and Lynne Hybels, wife of Pastor Bill Hybels of Willow Creek mega church in Chicago. We'll talk more about these individuals in the next chapter, but according to author and Christian radio host, Mike LeMay:

> "They are anti-Israel and are promoters of the Palestinian cause – these same Palestinians who partner with Syria and

Iran to launch thousands of rockets into Israel every year, killing innocent children. Wallis applauded the Arab Spring as a great day for democracy, but has remained silent as Christians in Egypt are murdered, churches are burned, and the Muslim Brotherhood controlling Egypt has announced they will disregard Egypt's peace treaty with Israel."

Anti-Christian socialist George Soros has given several large grants to *Sojourners* since 2004 and has financed groups promoting abortion, atheism, homosexual activism, and government expansion. Both Soros and Wallis support the OWS movement. Jim Wallis first denied receiving any money from Soros, saying in an interview, "No, we don't receive money from George Soros. Our books are totally open, always have been. Our money comes from Christians who support us and who read *Sojourners*."[7]

George Soros is working to destroy America's system of capitalism and remove its influence of Christianity through his many radical organizations and control of various media outlets. This tie between Wallis and Soros should not be ignored. These guys are both anti-conservative and have very different desires for the United States than our founders had. Author and President of *Leading the Way* ministries, Dr. Michael Youssef wrote:

> "Called 'the leader of the Religious Left' by *The New York Times*, Rev. Jim Wallis has a long history of denouncing his own country. In *Agenda for Biblical People* (1976), Jim Wallis refers to America as a 'fallen nation'. In an article in *Mission Trends*, Wallis approvingly predicted that 'so-called young evangelicals' ... [will] see the impossibility of making capitalism work for justice and peace."[8]

Like Al Sharpton and Jesse Jackson, Wallis masquerades behind the label of "Reverend" to deceive evangelicals and others who are uninformed when in reality these men are diehard leftists, social activists, and agitators. Why would a radical financier like George Soros want to give so much money to a "Christian" organization such as *Sojourners*? Soros is a billionaire from Hungary with corrupt connections, and he wants to destroy America along with the ideals and freedoms that made us a great nation.[9]

On their website, *Sojourners* quotes people like Gandhi, the Dalai Lama, and new age leader Marianne Williamson. *Sojourners* emphasizes environmental activism, social justice, diversity, and immigration. I didn't see much on its website about holiness, sin, heaven, hell, abortion, family, or homosexuality. I did see an article about a two-day workshop with emergent Universalist Rob Bell, harsh criticism of Arizona for its immigration law, and an emphasis on "environmental stewardship," and racial justice.

Early in his career, Jim Wallis founded an anti-capitalist magazine called the *Post-American* which identified wealth redistribution and government-managed economies as the *keys* to achieving social justice. He changed the name to *Sojourners* in the early 1970s. During his college years, Wallis also joined the Students for a Democratic Society (SDS), a radical organization that aspired to overthrow America's institutions and remake its government in a Marxist image.

In 2009, when it was announced a Reverend named Jim Wallis was appointed to the Obama administration, people in many conservative Christian churches didn't know much about him. Seeing that he would be a close adviser to the leader of the United States of America, I was compelled to do some research on him and look into some history. What I learned just about floored me, so I contacted several pastors I knew from different states and asked them about Jim Wallis. Other than a few who had never heard about him, each pastor voiced concerns.

Wallis's popularity is not surprising considering the advance of liberal theology via emergent church movements and the current state of apostasy the church finds itself in today. His progressive gospel may offer government handouts, but it does little for a personal relationship with the living God. Some churches and denominations have embraced this social justice message, and it has become evident Wallis has found a prominent place of influence.

One pastor friend of mine from California called it "disturbing" that Jim Wallis has this position and noted Wallis seems to look at the

Bible in light of the world around him rather than looking at the world in light of God's Word.

Too many Christians are easily swayed into believing anything that sounds good when presented with big words, authority and passion. In this way, Wallis seems like an opportunist. From a White House platform, he attacks Christian conservatives while calling himself a "nonpartisan evangelical minister." The question we should ask is why is a reverend so popular among secularist liberals who routinely vilify Christians for their involvement in political issues?

As the church of God, we must stand against these winds of doctrine and not allow deceivers like Jim Wallis to be given a platform to propagate his message.

> *But there were also false prophets among the people, just as there will be false teachers among you. They will secretly introduce destructive heresies, even denying the sovereign Lord who bought them – bringing swift destruction on themselves. Many will follow their shameful ways...* (**2 Peter 2:1-2** NIV).

Jesus Christ loved and cared about the poor: He did not abandon them, nor did He feed them immediately with the resources at his disposal. The first thing Christ himself did for the poor was to teach them; Wallis seems to favor bureaucracy. Most independent thinkers admit government programs can't separate the truly needy from those who would cheat and take advantage of the system.

Conversely, private Christian charities and organizations are so much more effective at meeting needs and changing lives instead of basically throwing taxpayer money at the problem. Most charities run a tight ship by necessity and are just the opposite of government when it comes to eliminating fraud and waste while offering compassion to those in need.

America's free enterprise system is not keeping people poor; it is their best chance for economic advancement. Social justice advocates would have you believe it is the system that is the problem. *Renew America* columnist Robert Meyer points out how interesting it is that,

"Secularists who otherwise wish to absolutely separate church and state, anxiously merge them back together, if such a union can be used as a pretext for promoting a leftist political agenda."

Where Jim Wallis's theology is concerned, it does not stop with social justice. Sadly, there is a far left wing of "progressive Christianity" that includes collective salvation, Red Letter Christians, and universalism. Other heretics include Brian McLaren (Board Member for Wallis's *Sojourners*), Tony Campolo, Rob Bell, and Dan Kimball. I don't know the hearts of these men; however, I strongly question their agenda, authenticity and worldview. Some informed believers have shown concern about Wallis for years because he is a far left Liberation Theologian. According to Jim Wallis:

"As more Christians become influenced by liberation theology, finding themselves increasingly rejecting the values of institutions of capitalism, they will also be drawn to the Marxist analysis and praxis that is so central to the social justice movement."[10]

This type of social justice casts aside the Great Commission of Christ – to make disciples of all nations. Jesus came to save the lost, to destroy the work of the devil, and to give His life as a ransom for many so the world would know that He is God. He came to reveal the Father to us and destroy the penalty of sin through His sacrifice on the cross. We don't hear Jesus talking about various kinds of justice.

Author, editor-in-chief of *World Magazine*, and Provost of The King's College, Marvin Olasky has debated Jim Wallis and has written extensively about social justice:

"We can study the 150 or so times that *mishpat* in Hebrew and *kreesis* in Greek – words commonly translated as 'justice' – appear in the Bible. Biblically, justice – tied to righteousness – is what promotes faith in God, not faith in government.... Accept the left's focus on systemic problems, but not its faulty analysis. Learn about the biggest institutional hindrance to economic advancement for the poor: the government's monopoly control of taxpayer funds committed to education and welfare."

Wallis founded "Call to Renewal" in 1995 for the purposes of advocating for leftist economic agendas such as tax hikes and wealth distribution. Wallis met Barack Obama a few years later. Then, ten years after "Call to Renewal" was founded, Senate Minority Leader Harry Reid admitted he and other Democratic Senators met with Wallis in a closed session in 2005. One purpose of the meeting was to devise clever ways to use religious language in political speeches in order to pull evangelical voters away from Republicans.

The very next year in 2006, Wallis stated: "Whichever Democrat wins, Barack or Hillary, I'm going to work very hard to make abortion reduction a central Democratic Party plank in this election. It never has been before." I agree with Wallis that abortion reduction "never has been" a major focus in the Democratic Party. But more importantly, here we are in 2012 – six years since the promise that Wallis was "going to work very hard" to reduce abortions in America – and over 1.2 million babies continue to be aborted every year. He either lied or failed.

In the same interview with *Christianity Today*, Wallis also stated:

> "I don't think that abortion is the moral equivalent issue to slavery that Wilberforce dealt with. I think that poverty is the new slavery. Poverty and *global inequality* are the fundamental moral issues of our time. That's my judgment. People can disagree with my stance, and say the constitutional amendment to ban abortion is the prophetic stance. I don't believe it is."[11]

CUTTING THROUGH THE CHEESE IN WISCONSIN

In 2010, Wallis criticized conservative Christians and jumped on the race-card express saying, "Would there even be a Tea Party if the president of the United States weren't the first black man to occupy that office?" In the spring of that same year, Wallis was invited to be a keynote speaker at a Christian music festival in Oshkosh, Wisconsin called Lifest. This was not the first controversial speaker Lifest has had. Life Promotions, the organization that puts on Lifest, previously booked Tony Campolo, author of *The Shack* – William P. Young, Shane Claiborne, and others.

Every year Christian events and festivals across the country book questionable speakers, but not many as extreme and radical as Jim Wallis. I have only skimmed the surface in an attempt to encapsulate Wallis' background and worldview. The evidence presented here should be enough for sincere Christians to care about his politics.

It was an interesting decision to bring such a polarizing political figure to a Christian music event. More people should have been concerned, but apathy got the best of them. Wallis has been referred to as the "leading voice of the political arm of the emergent New Spirituality movement." Hearing about the decision, President of the Institute on Religion and Democracy, (IRD) Mark Tooley, shared his concerns:

> "Lifest seems to have crossed the threshold into the Evangelical Left orbit with Wallis's entrance. Adding to the leftward slant was the less high profile but still significant appearance of anti-American pacifist preacher Shane Claiborne, a popular 'urban monastic' who sinisterly equates America with ancient Babylon, the Roman Empire, and the Third Reich....
>
> "Some youthful concert goers and naïve evangelical organizers may be seduced by Wallis's throw-away lines. But most mature Christians understand that the Gospel is about considerably more than Wallis's current brand of 'White House theology.'"[12]

Jim Wallis took the main stage at Lifest on a Friday night in July 2010 and gave a presentation entitled "The Call to Jesus and his Kingdom of Justice." The next day, an article in the Appleton, Wisconsin Post Crescent newspaper read:

> "Jim Wallis shared his Bible-based message of serving the poor Friday night to a large, welcoming crowd at Lifest despite a *small number* of boos at his introduction. Wallis was 'effusively' introduced by Life Promotions president Bob Lenz. 'I've read his books, I've studied with him, I've been on retreats with him,' Lenz said. 'This is my brother in Christ. I believe he has a message from God for the church today. Part of who I am is because of this man.'"[13]

A man named Robert from Menasha, WI, a reader of the *Post Cres-cent* article on the paper's website, directed a comment at those whose "noses are bent out of shape because the liberal theologian, Jim Wallis, spoke at Lifest," and added:

> "I would like to point out that I, an atheist, spoke at Lifest, two years in a row. I was debating a local clergyman.... I don't recall anyone raising hell because of my appearance...."

People such as Robert completely missed the point: an open, healthy debate is fine, but Wallis was the headlining speaker on the main stage. Wallis gave an unchallenged presentation. Robert is *not* an influential national public figure with a radical background representing only one political party. No opportunity was given that night for a second voice to be heard representing Christians who are conservative, Republican, Independent, or Libertarian. According to the *Post Crescent*, Wallis said:

> "What unites us? The gospel of Jesus Christ and his kingdom. Sometimes conflicts and the attacking of each other push us away from Jesus. ...This [controversy] is not about social action or politics."

He asked what united Christians, and before he signed off, he could not resist dividing the crowd by criticizing conservatives. In his closing remarks, Wallis stated:

> "In America, everyone listens to information outlets they agree with. Replace the gospel of Glenn (Beck), Rush (Limbaugh), Sean (Hannity) and Bill (O'Reilly) with Matthew, Mark, Luke and John."

I would have been insulted had I been in the audience. This proved Wallis was loyal to President Obama's war on free speech at the time. Notice that Wallis didn't suggest we replace the gospel of Matt Lauer, Chris Matthews, Jon Stewart, Katie Couric, Rachel Maddow, Kieth Olberman, Brian Williams, Diane Sawyer, Anderson Cooper, Joy Behar, Barbara Walters, David Letterman, or George Stephanopolis with Matthew, Mark, Luke, and John. Wallis put down conservatives minutes after asking "what unites us?"

If he were more discerning about the Lifest controversy in the first place, he could have chosen to talk about solutions for the church in America. In addition to helping the poor and taking care of the planet, he could have promoted right to life issues or marriage between a man and a woman, but that was impossible because the man he advises in the White House vehemently opposes both. There was not a peep from the reverend on these major issues. However, when asked by local Christian radio station General Manager, Mike LeMay, if Wallis believed abortion and homosexuality were sins, Wallis shouted at him, called him a "right-wing Kool-Aid drinking Glen Beck follower" and hung up on him. Is that promoting unity?

The bottom line is, if we don't preach the gospel and lead souls to Christ, it won't matter if they're well fed come Judgment Day. In Romans 13, the people's taxes paid for governing authorities put in place by God for their good, but the government never had anything to do with practicing compassion or mercy.

We are accountable for what we know. We should know what kind of Christian a person really is. We need to be Bereans and search the Scriptures daily because we've been warned in God's word about those who use flowery talk to persuade less mature believers. Wallis is one such mouthpiece, and he knows how to work a crowd.

> *For the time will come when men will not put up with sound doctrine. Instead, to suit their own desires, they will gather around them a great number of teachers to say what their itching ears want to hear* (**2 Timothy 4:3**).

Wallis returned to Washington and, on his *Sojourners* blog, vented about Christians who disagreed with him being at the festival. He said they "looked pretty foolish," and he called their concerns "wild and fabricated charges" against him. In his summary, he claimed those who did not support Lifest because of him being there were stubborn and proved wrong in the end. Wallis went on to say:

> "But if the *attackers* had succeeded with *intimidation* to cancel a speaker they didn't agree with, there is no doubt that the *tactics of distortion* and intimidation would have been repeated in other places." (emphasis mine)

This is quite ironic because Wallis was a student of the Saul Alinsky school of activism and had used the very protest tactics he was erroneously accusing others of using: lies, distorted facts, pressure and intimidation. In his political activist career, Wallis had been arrested twenty-two times for acts of civil disobedience.[14]

FINDING COMMON GROUND?

In April 2012, the White House hosted a national interfaith conference where Jim Wallis spoke to college students about finding "common ground." In his goal to promote even more tolerance and many faith paths, he told the students that illegal aliens are being denied education and that immigration is another cause of injustice. This is a clear distortion of the gospel message. Wallis basically defines sin in his terms and embraces a recalibration of biblical morality that is not only ungodly, but also dangerous.

When Wallis was asked about Republican Mitt Romney's Mormon faith, he blurted out, "We have had a lot of incompetent Christians in the White House. Religion has no monopoly on morality." Wallis also minimized the importance of salvation by noting young people today are not as concerned about religious dogma. He literally encouraged them to be activists for injustice by telling them "Get arrested together and discuss theology in jail."[15]

You may wonder why it is so important for a liberal social justice advocate to bring students from all kinds of religious backgrounds together. He pushes tolerance and uniformity in order to water down sin and the gospel. One of his motives may be to help usher in a one world government. Why else would he be so open to other religions and attempt to reach (convert) millennials? When Wallis uses the word "unity," it is probably more accurate to say he is pursuing uniformity. He and other social justice advocates have their own agenda that sounds like the truth because it is sprinkled with carefully selected terminology, but it is not *the* truth.

Jim Wallis seeks uniformity, not unity. To him, Christ is not the measure of all things; man is the measure of things (humanism). The following is a great explanation from Pastor Darrin Mariot of Sonrise Westside Community Church in Venice, California:

> "**Unity** is our willingness to set aside our differences for a common goal. For Christians, that common goal is Christ and Him crucified - the Gospel (cf. 1 Cor. 1-3, 15, et al.). In unity we may not look alike or sound alike, and we may even have different preferences and priorities; but we all agree that the most important thing is Jesus Christ – His sinless life, death, burial, and bodily resurrection from the dead to set us free from the bonds of sin and Satan! When we deviate from this as our priority, then we are no longer in unity.

> "**Uniformity**, on the other hand, is when all look alike or sound alike or fail to note any real substantive distinctions among us. This is a caricature of the church and is what many of those outside the church think unity should look like. Far from it. The church is actually the most diverse organism on earth, but we all come around a common goal – Christ. Period. All those who appeal to something else are not looking for unity, but uniformity. For them, the focus is not salvation by grace, but by works (if there is even any need for salvation at all)."

Other leaders of the social justice movement subtly alter the biblical understanding of sin and salvation as well. They often place emphasis on this present temporary world and minimize the importance of repentance from sin against a holy God. Humanism and socialism – the way of man – will always fail, but God's ways always succeed.

His ways are definitely higher than our ways (Isaiah 55:8), and I believe that one reason He allowed Jim Wallis to speak in Wisconsin was to wake up sleepy Christians. To those who have ears to hear, please carefully consider these things. Complacency and compromise must be defeated and overcome in the power of Christ. God never promised us an easy path.

America finds itself in a dangerous place: we have a media and an administration selling class warfare and massive spending. The government is supposed to protect its citizens, not provide for us. If the federal government were in charge, how do you think it would process those in our society who are not able to contribute financially: such as the disabled, the elderly or those with Down syndrome? See where this could lead? Some elitists already see these people – created in the image of God – as less valuable, and it is this mentality that helps them justify abortion, euthanasia, or end of life "counseling." What type of justice is that?

If there was ever a time to avoid being an idle Christian, it is today. Let's sharpen some iron and gather as many allies as we can. There will always be opposition, but we cannot be caught off guard any longer. God gave us the Holy Spirit as a guarantee of what is to come, that he will take us safely home in due time. The Lord is faithful, and I cannot prognosticate how this journey of faith is going to end.

In this political, spiritual, and cultural war against Christ and the church, the Lord will have the final say, and He will be glorified and triumphant in all things and through all things. He is working even when we cannot see what He is doing. He works everything out, and for those of us who love Him and are obedient to His calling in our lives, He promises to bring good (Romans 8:28). Stay true to His Word and to sound doctrine, and don't buy the lies of the Left.

In the next chapter, we will investigate the emergent church movement and some key false teachings. There are over a dozen major evangelical leaders who are promoters of confusion and ambiguity instead of truth, and they are blotting out the God of Scripture from within the walls of evangelical Christianity.

Then we will no longer be infants, tossed back and forth by the waves, and blown here and there by every wind of teaching (**Ephesians 4:14a**).

ENDNOTES

1 http://dictionary.reference.com/browse/social+justice?s=t
2 http://www.banneroftruth.org/pages/articles/article_detail.php?812 ; The Great Evangelical Disaster, Francis A. Schaefer, pg 113
3 http://www.wnd.com/2010/05/155917/
4 http://www.onenewsnow.com/Perspectives/Default.aspx?id=1374980
5 http://www.americanthinker.com/2010/08/ soros_has_a_pastor_close_to_ob.html

6 http://www.theblaze.com/stories/
  george-soros-sends-150000-to-jim-wallis-left-wing-christian-magazine/
7 http://blog.american.com/
  jim-wallis-wants-to-change-the-story-now-to-glenn-beck/
8 http://www.michaelyoussef.com/michaels-blogs/keep-jesus-out-of-your-social-
  ism.html
9 Discover the Networks, George Soros: http://www.discoverthenetworks.org/
  individualProfile.asp?indid=977
10 http://www.worldviewweekend.com/worldview-times/article.php?articleid=1597
11 ChristianityToday, 5/9/2008, http://www.christianitytoday.com/ct/2008/
  may/9.52.html?start=2
12 http://frontpagemag.com/2010/07/27/
  jim-wallis-crashes-evangelical-music-festival/
13 Jim Wallis, Bob Lenz, Lifest intro 7/15/2010 http://www.theird.org/Page.
  aspx?pid=1558
14 http://www.usnews.com/news/religion/articles/2009/03/31/
  evangelical-minister-jim-wallis-is-in-demand-in-obamas-washington
15 http://standupforthetruth.com/2012/05/jim-wallis-interfaith-message-to-young-
  people-we-are-here-to-find-common-ground/

CHAPTER 12

EMERGING INTO CONFUSION

FROM BIBLE CLASS TO BUSINESS CLASS AND BEYOND

For I did not shrink from declaring to you the whole purpose of God. Be on guard for yourselves and for all the flock, among which the Holy Spirit has made you overseers, to shepherd the church of God which He purchased with His own blood. I know that after my departure savage wolves will come in among you, not sparing the flock; and from among your own selves men will arise, speaking perverse things, to draw away the disciples after them (**Acts 20:27-30**).

All the way back in the first century, the apostle Paul pleaded and warned believers to be on guard against men within their own ranks who would try to "draw away disciples after them." They would distort the truth of God's Word, teach only selected parts of it, or take Scripture out of context to deceive the flock. These are also tactics of modern day evangelical leaders who some might describe as emergent, liberal, or postmodern.

Postmodernism can be traced to the early 1970s and generally questions whether truth can be known with certainty, if it even exists at all. The danger, of course, with accepting ambiguity over truth is it leaves the door wide open to debate right and wrong in terms of feelings and experiences. Postmodernism rejects there is scientific, philosophical, or religious truth which is the same for everybody.

Doubt and uncertainty are the devil's tools going all the way back to the Garden of Eden when the serpent tempted Adam and Eve by getting them to question God's literal words. We can practically take those deceptive words, "Did God really say…?" and finish the question with whatever ending you'd like to plant seeds of doubt in the minds of believers. A recent example might be the debate over whether heaven and hell are actually real places. Maybe you've heard someone say, "A loving God wouldn't really send people to hell." We'll get to this when we discuss Rob Bell and Universalism, which basically suggests there is a final salvation for all souls, whether they believe in Jesus Christ or not.

Attempting to provide an overview of the emergent church and sum up various teachings in the "new evangelical" church movement in only one chapter would be nearly impossible. Furthermore, since I am not an apologist, pastor, or theologian, the task before me to provide a succinct overview is even more daunting. The emphasis of this book is on Christ, culture, and individual Christian responsibility. We now need to take a critically important look at how big of a threat false teachings are to the stability of the church in America.

You'd think the church would be a safe place for believers, but these are dangerous times in which we live. In the same way socialism has infected America, false teachings have infected Christianity. Some well-known leaders have gone astray and have taken some of the flock with them. You may not appreciate the fact that a pastor or religious leader you follow is mentioned in this book. Please pray for discernment, test every spirit according to the Word of God, and check with other sources.

It is unwise to put our pastor or favorite national religious leader up on a pedestal. We are all fallen beings looking up to the perfection of Jesus Christ, who is seated at the right hand of the Father in heaven. The Bible warns teachers to watch their doctrine closely (1 Tim. 4:16). Many emergent leaders do not focus on the deity of Christ and the authority of the Bible as much as they call attention to themselves or a doctrine they are espousing.

Remember this: we are more likely to defend and stand up for what we love. It is imperative we get back to loving the truth – the living Word of our God. As Christians who profess to be saved and believe in the Bible, not enough of us have a deep love and passion for the Word of God. An excellent chapter from the Bible about the greatness of God's law and His Word is Psalm 119. Here are a few selections from the 176 verses in **Psalm 119:**

Your word I have treasured in my heart, That I may not sin against You. Blessed are You, O LORD; Teach me Your statutes (verses 11-12).

Open my eyes, that I may behold Wonderful things from Your law. Your testimonies also are my delight; They are my counselors (v. 18, 24).

I will also speak of Your testimonies before kings And shall not be ashamed. I shall delight in Your commandments, Which I love. And I shall lift up my hands to Your commandments, Which I love; And I will meditate on Your statutes (v. 46-48).

Your hands made me and fashioned me; Give me understanding, that I may learn Your commandments. Forever, O LORD, Your word is settled in heaven. O how I love Your law! It is my meditation all the day (v. 73, 89, 97).

From Your precepts I get understanding; Therefore I hate every false way. Your word is a lamp to my feet And a light to my path. I hate those who are double-minded, But I love Your law (v. 104-105; 113).

The unfolding of Your words gives light; It gives understanding to the simple. I opened my mouth wide and panted, For I longed for Your commandments (v. 130-131).

My zeal has consumed me, Because my adversaries have forgotten Your words. Your word is very pure, Therefore Your servant loves it. My eyes anticipate the night watches, That I may meditate on Your word (v. 139-140; 148).

Consider how I love Your precepts; Revive me, O LORD, according to Your lovingkindness. The sum of Your word is truth, And every one of Your righteous ordinances is everlasting (v. 159-160).

I hate and despise falsehood, But I love Your law. My soul keeps Your testimonies, And I love them exceedingly. I long for Your salvation, O LORD, And Your law is my delight (v. 163, 167, 174)

Reading these verses reminds me how far I have to go in my own heart to fall in love again and be established on the Word. When we love the truth, we will be offended when others trample all over it. The Bible must be top priority in our lives. Books about the Bible and spiritual things are fine, but we must be spending most of our reading and study time in the Good Book. The better we know truth, the quicker we will recognize a counterfeit and avoid false teachings. I realize some believers are uninterested in discernment issues and don't want to deal with the sad reality of yucky church stuff. It is much easier to look away. Let's address it.

EMERGING FROM WHAT? [E.C. 101]

The Emergent Church movement is not just a fad among evangelicals; it has been gaining converts over the last few decades and has caused plenty of confusion when it comes to what the Bible teaches. The movement crosses a number of theological boundaries and stems from basic dissatisfaction with conservative teaching methods and traditional church services. Respected pastors and mature Christians have said describing the emerging church can be difficult since it has no official organizational model or statement of faith and is constantly being redefined.

Emergent church participants have been described as: evangelical, new-evangelical, post-evangelical, liberal, reformed, or post-charismatic. Many participants seek to live their faith in what they believe to be a "Post-modern" society. The emergent church is a rapidly growing network of individual believers and churches that have lost interest in church as a whole to the sad point of criticizing Christianity as a whole. Instead of reading straight from Scripture they prefer to have a conversation about the Bible and spiritual things. You'll notice "conversation" is a key buzz word to them. They are big on community rather than organization; however, many mega-churches across America fit right into the emergent model.

Having a common disdain and disillusionment with the institutional church, the emergent church favors the use of simple story and narrative, even to the point of paraphrasing the Bible. Followers and members of the movement often place a high value on good works, "practicing the presence of God," and social activism. Environmentalism is very important to many emergers. Some leaders emphasize environmental issues while glossing over the salvation of souls, and many subscribe to the Jim Wallis idea of social justice.

One hallmark of the emergent church is the new age aspect including the practice of contemplative monastic meditation and prayers. While some emphasize eternal salvation, many in the emerging church emphasize the here and now. Much of its doctrine rejects systematic Christian theology, the integrity of Scripture, and gospel exclusivity. They generally favor global initiatives, amnesty, pacifism, and homosexuality. They call for diversity, tolerance, and camaraderie among all religions, and they modify their teachings. It's a war against biblical truth and since Jesus Christ is the Truth, emergent theology often goes against the person of Christ.

In a sermon at Metropolitan Tabernacle in London back in March 1886, the highly-influential author, pastor, and preacher Charles Spurgeon talked about his lack of sympathy for "preaching that degrades the Truth of God into a hobbyhorse for its own thought" and preaching that uses Scripture to back up its own opinions. He told people not to believe him if he were to "go an atom beyond what is plainly taught" in Scripture:

> "I am content to live and to die as the mere repeater of Scriptural teaching – as a person who has thought out nothing and invented nothing – ...but who concluded that he was to take the message from the lips of God to the best of his ability and simply to be a mouth for God to the people – mourning much that anything of his own should come between – but never thinking that he was somehow to refine the message or to adapt it to the brilliance of this wonderful century and then to hand it out as being so much his own that he might take some share of the glory of it."[1]

Charles Spurgeon loved the unfiltered truth of God's Word. Over 100 years have passed since he gave that sermon, and it is painfully clear some American church leaders have chosen not to follow Spurgeon's example. Too many Christian leaders today suggest church services or sermons must be entertaining, relevant, and inviting. Sadly, what often happens while attempting to achieve this goal is that in the process of changing the methods used to reach people, the message also gets changed.

Those who think they need to adapt the Bible to secular culture or bring its teachings up to date are mistaken. Some Christians have gone right along with the deception and have bought the lie that the teachings of the old rugged cross are – well, old fashioned. In the New Testament, many verses describe Jesus Christ as consistent forever; in the Old Testament the Bible teaches God does not change (Malachi 3:6). Jesus never adjusted His message to fit the times so why should we try to be creative with God's Word in order to make the gospel more attractive or palatable?

Pastor Ken Silva, editor of Apprising Ministries, has described emergent church guru Tony Jones as a "prominent spokesman for the new cult of liberal theology." At an emergent church workshop in San Diego several years ago, Tony Jones said:

> "This is about our belief that theology changes. The message of the gospel changes. It's not just the method that changes."[2]

Christians who are serious about their faith understand we do not need to revise, rethink, or rewrite what Scripture teaches. Who are we to make the judgment that God's Word is not adequate as it is? What we need to do is to recommit our lives to Christ and rediscover Him! It is absolutely miraculous how Jesus changed the entire world with His message of repentance from sin using a dozen imperfect, rough around the edges, ordinary men. This is where you and I come in. We live in a secular culture, and God commissions us to take His message to the people and to stand against immorality.

The early church got its start in the midst of a corrupt and power-hungry Roman government. They had what we have today: massive immorality including drunkenness, violence, prostitution, attacks on Christians, idolatry, money worship, and corruption among religious leaders. Yet in a matter of decades, the original 120 believers and thousands of converts to Christianity turned the world upside down by preaching the good news. They taught about sin and judgment, and they weren't concerned that their message might turn people off.

Author and Pastor John MacArthur said:

"The primary message of the church should not be, 'This is a nice place,' you'll like us.' Instead, the message should be, "This is a holy place where sin is despised."

As Christians, we must build our faith on Christ alone and meditate on His word so we will never fall for the distractions or lies of the enemy. We must keep our eyes focused on His will and His return. False teachers cast doubt on Scripture and seek to divide believers.

These are the ones who cause divisions, worldly-minded, devoid of the Spirit. But you, beloved, building yourselves up on your most holy faith, praying in the Holy Spirit (**Jude 1:19-20**).

The main goal of the enemy is to lead us away from God. He uses many counterfeits to spread lies or half-truths. Some teachings even look or sound good on the surface, but are dangerously deceptive. Please keep this in mind as you read: We are addressing and exposing an overall belief system, not just a handful of leaders. Let's take a closer look at the backdrop of the emergent church, its leaders, as well as other threats to absolute truth.

THE BUSINESS MODEL AND EARLY INFLUENCES

When I rededicated my life to Jesus Christ back in the late 1980s, I had been reading books on positive thinking, including psychology, and self-help. I understand how easy it is to stray from sound Bible teachings and really convinced myself I could do anything I set my mind to. As you know, this kind of thinking removes God from the picture. Several books I read were by the "Father of Positive Thinking," Norman Vincent Peale.

During the 80s, business executives were already mentoring church leaders on how to build their church and grow their ministry. Austrian-born Peter Drucker was one of those men who, along with New Age business gurus Bob Buford and Ken Blanchard, influenced this alliance between the secular business world and evangelical Christian churches.

It is important we look at Drucker because America's most influential pastor, Rick Warren, has called Drucker his mentor, yet in a 2001 interview, Drucker denied being a born-again Christian.[3]

This is not surprising when we note that Drucker was a disciple of philosopher and mystic, Soren Kierkegaard, and was also influenced by Zen Buddhism. At a 2005 Pew Forum on religion, Warren proudly stated, "I've spent twenty years under his tutelage learning about leadership from him...."[4] I'm not at all suggesting Warren is not a Christian or that he hasn't done good works. His influences, however, should be noted. Drucker believed that in the twentieth century, the rise of the corporation was the "most significant sociological phenomenon" of the first half and the development of the mega-church was most significant in the second half of the twentieth century.

Another major player in the mega-church movement was one of Norman Vincent Peale's biggest disciples – none other than Robert Schuller of Crystal Cathedral fame. Schuller could be described as a non-traditional, New Age liberal and often used his positive thinking and positive imaging (visualization) in his messages mixed in with occasional Bible verses.

Prior to building America's first mega-church, Schuller literally went door to door passing out cards in the late 1970s in Orange County, CA and told people to write down what they wanted in a church. The concept many people preferred was an all-inclusive, liberal, social gospel of sorts. At a convention many years ago, Robert Schuller said, "If you want to know how to build a church, ask the community, and give them what they want." Kay Warren (Rick Warren's wife) spoke at Schuller's 2008 "Rethink Conference" held at the Crystal Cathedral.

Can you imagine Jesus Christ or any of the disciples asking people what they *wanted*? Instead of giving people what they need, which can save them from damnation and destruction, some pastors give people what they want, which oftentimes does not meet or satisfy their spiritual hunger and thirst. We can learn from successful businesses, but to pattern too much of the church after corporate models takes the focus off of Jesus Christ. He taught about going after individual sheep that have gone astray (Luke 15:3).

Bob Buford's Leadership Network (1984) aimed to "accelerate the emergence of effective churches." The business emphasis on tasks instead of theology came from business executive Peter Drucker. Another contributor was Arun Gandhi, grandson of Mohandas Gandhi. Anybody can do good works, and yes, Christians should do good works, but business philosophies such as Rick Warren's "deeds not creeds" have crept into churches emphasizing doing over doctrine.

Buford also worked with Bill Hybels and Willow Creek Community Church, and he described both Hybels and Warren as change makers. According to Roger Oakland in his outstanding book *Faith Undone*, the initial group of emerging leaders in the early 1990s included Doug Pagitt and Leith Anderson from a Minneapolis mega church.[5]

Pagitt wrote in his 2005 book, *Church Re-Imagined*, that he didn't think he'd be able to stay Christian in any useful sense ..."if I continued with the expression of Christianity I was currently living...." The more developed some of the emergent church concepts and ideas become, the further they must move away from Scripture because they directly oppose what the Bible already teaches. In order to get others involved in the emergent experience, Pagitt said they try to "create a community that's more like a potluck." Two major players on today's global-thinking mega-church team are Rick Warren and Bill Hybels.

It is important to distinguish that the emergent church was created and manufactured by corporate executives with new age influences and big business visions for church growth. It was not started by young evangelical Christians who were simply looking for a way to update and refresh the traditional church. The overall effect of the emergent church may be quite imponderable, but its influence is probably much greater and more devastating than we know. One thing we can be assured of, however, is that all pathways do NOT lead to heaven.

The Spirit clearly says that in later times some will abandon the faith and follow deceiving spirits and things taught by demons (1Timothy 4:1).

NEW AGE MOVEMENT

Because the New Age movement has been around for so long, many of us have grown accustomed to its influences. New Age teachings have been proven to be evil and malignant, especially seductive to young people. This belief system emphasizes human control which leaves people with the erroneous idea we are all gods in some way, and there are no moral absolutes. Humanism then comes into play through various forms of meditation and self-help activities. New Age proponents teach about "finding our inner spirit" or channeling our energy to meet a desired end.

Seeking anything that doesn't lead to the person of Jesus Christ is dangerous. There have been many labels used to describe branches of the movement, and the word "New" typically precedes the noun such as "New Christianity" or New- Evangelical, Faith, Light, Reformation, Spirituality, Life, Orthodoxy, Emergence, etc. Wasn't it Solomon who said there is "nothing new under the sun??" (Eccl. 1:9) Straying from the known truth opens the door to the demonic.

In his book, *For Many Shall Come in My Name,* Ray Yungen describes the term "New Age" as based on astrology. Some believe there are cosmic cycles in which the Earth passes through a time period when it falls "under the influence of a certain sign of the zodiac." This is a belief system that everything exists and revolves around energy containing tiny particles: atoms, molecules, protons, etc.

> "All is energy. That energy, they believe, is God, and therefore, all is God. They believe that since we are all part of this 'God-energy', then we, too, are God. God is not seen as a Being that dwells in heaven, but as the universe itself."[6]

Many New Age proponents strive for a "Christ consciousness" or a "higher consciousness" in an effort to become more aware of these spiritual realms. Yungen explains the teaching that the most direct way to achieve this consciousness is through meditation:

> "Meditation is the basic activity that underlies all metaphysics and is the primary source of spiritual direction for the New Age person. We need only observe the emphasis which is placed on meditation to see the importance of it in New Age thought."

There are great resources available on occult practices and history. It is so important to immerse ourselves into the Word of God and study to show ourselves approved by Him. We must be discerning about things such as: contemplative prayer, "centering prayer" and mantras, the law of attraction, witchcraft & Harry Potter, the Kabbala, spiritual formation, Labyrinth walking, and Wicca. Teachings promoted by well-known celebrities are even more dangerous because people tend to believe and follow those they idolize.

"How can there be only one way to heaven or to God?"
– **Oprah Winfrey**

LEARNING FROM OPRAH

Oprah Winfrey is one of the world's most influential women. She has launched book sales and resuscitated careers for many authors and gurus while continuing to give a number of proponents of higher spirituality a platform. You may have heard about *A Course in Miracles* which was written by a well-known New Age representative, Helen Schucman, who claims the book came directly from her inner voice. In the course, the listener is taught there is no sin, they are told not to make the "mistake" of "clinging to the old rugged cross," and that the name of "Jesus Christ as such is but a symbol."

Oprah has done many good things to help people, but does that mean we should trust her theology and religious beliefs? I'm sure she's a wonderful person, and I'm not judging her heart because we are all wicked without the atonement of Jesus Christ. Many Christian pastors have warned about the teachings promoted by Oprah. *A Course in Miracles* teaches that God is in everyone and everything and that "The oneness of the Creator and the creation is your wholeness, your sanity and your limitless power." Wow.

Maybe you're an Oprah fan and have always defended her or maybe you had no idea what she believes. In an interview with Oprah, New Age author and mystic, Eckhart Tolle, criticized Christianity and also took live calls from viewers. Tolle stated:

"The moment you say 'only my belief' or 'our belief' is true, and you deny other people's beliefs, then you've adopted an ideology.… And then religion becomes a closed door."

Oprah told the caller to simply realize Christianity is but one of *many* ways to achieve the "higher consciousness," and the belief that one must follow a set of doctrines is a consequence of "ego consciousness." She holds that while Christianity is a valid way to achieve high states of spirituality, it must not be considered a unique way, or a "correct way." Oprah believes God is all love, and she does not subscribe to the teaching that He is also a holy, jealous, just and vengeful God. She has told her audience:

"The new spirituality is that you are your own best authority as you work to know and love yourself, you discover how to live a more spiritual life."[7]

Sadly, millions of spiritual seekers have been led astray, and due to Oprah's popularity, people have opened themselves up to all kinds of practices, religions, and teachings contrary to the gospel of Jesus Christ and biblical Christianity. We need to pray for her and those who may blindly hang on her every word, or the words of any secular celebrity.

RED LETTER CHRISTIANS

Every word in the Bible is written exactly as God wants it to be. Our faith in the integrity of Scripture begins with permanence:

The grass withers, the flower fades, But the word of our God stands forever (**Isaiah 40:8**).

Bible publishers probably had good intentions when they highlighted the teachings of Jesus by printing them in red letters, but this has helped some emergent church leaders find another way to cast doubt on the entire Bible. Jesus Christ is the Truth and He is the Word – the Alpha and Omega, the beginning and the end. Jesus came to fulfill the law, the Old Testament. Every letter the apostle Paul wrote points to the perfect person of Jesus Christ. The Old Testament, the Gospels, and the New Testament are all in complete agreement and harmony.

Red Letter Christians teach that the sayings of Jesus are somehow more holy, sacred, or inspired than the rest of Scripture, but we know the whole counsel of God is perfect.

All Scripture is inspired by God and profitable for teaching, for reproof, for correction, for training in righteousness (**2 Timothy 3:16**).

One obvious agenda for this false teaching is to justify homosexuality. Emergent promoter of gay Christian ideology, Brian McLaren, is one of the leaders of the Red Letter Christians along with Tony Campolo, Jim Wallis, and well-known Catholic writer Richard Rohr.

These popular evangelical authors pit God and the apostle Paul against Jesus by telling their followers Jesus didn't specifically address homosexuality. By this they imply Jesus must approve of that which He did not address directly. This is ludicrous and would also lead to the false conclusion that Jesus also approves of cannibalism, rape, or vampires since He didn't specifically mention them. This is their logic.

These leaders argue that since Jesus taught about loving "the least of these," how can we call someone that Christ commands us to love, sinful? Wallis notes that the early church shared everything when he said, "In those red letters, Jesus calls us away from the consumerist values that dominate contemporary American consciousness." Wallis and Campolo have gained cult-like followings by speaking against the Christian establishment and against Republicans as they make the rounds on the college circuit. They can disagree with parts of the Bible if they'd like, but what amazes me is that people fall for it.

For truly I say to you, until heaven and earth pass away, not the smallest letter or stroke shall pass from the Law until all is accomplished (**Matthew 5:18**).

Red Letter Christians advocate unrestricted big government, often equating the welfare state with the Kingdom of God. Jan Markel of Olive Tree Views believes they are practicing a form of Neo-Marxism. Markel points out these leaders promote tolerance and mercy while claiming conservative evangelicals spend too much time worrying about abortion and homosexuality.

"Red-letter Christians champion 'social justice', the cause of illegal immigrants, environmentalism, high taxes, discrimination issues, socialized medicine, and getting rid of the death penalty. ...This crowd loves to spend other people's money. They put down conservative Christianity when, in fact, it is conservative Christians who are first to step up to the plate whenever there is a disaster at home or abroad!"[8]

Red Letter Christians profess to hate religion and love Jesus. Though there is not a clear statement of faith on their website, they do list the Apostle's Creed and give a charge to follow the words of Jesus (not the entire Bible). Their list of contributors and recommended authors is a roll call of the progressive evangelical hall of shame. When someone's theology seems to be driven by a desire to justify and promote a political agenda or a sinful lifestyle rather than honestly interpret what Scripture teaches, that's called handling the Word of God deceitfully. We must confront that which comes against truth.

We are destroying speculations and every lofty thing raised up against the knowledge of God, and we are taking every thought captive to the obedience of Christ (**2 Corinthians 10:5** ESV).

ISLAM AND MULTICULTURALISM

There are over 2.6 million Muslims in America, and most are friendly, hard-working citizens. The problem is a minority of the overall Muslim population in the U.S. has blended into our society with the goal of implementing acts of takeover or terror. There are those who are faithfully and patiently working and waiting for the call to jihad. On September 11, 2001, nearly 3,000 citizens were killed when terrorists hijacked fully-fueled American jetliners and crashed them into buildings. The men had been quietly living in America, plotting, and going about their business.

Both Christianity and Islam promote a standard of morality and doing good works, but the god of Islam is not the same as the living God of the Holy Bible. The Muslim holy book is called the Quran, which is an Arabic word that literally means "the recitation." The Quran considers

Jesus a prophet, but not the Son of God or Savior. Muslims do not believe Jesus died on the cross, but that he was assumed to heaven by Allah.

"Jesus is like Adam in the sight of Allah. Allah created him of dust and then said to him: 'Be,' and he was" (Quran 3:55, 58).

In other words, Jesus was a created being like us with no divine attributes. The Bible teaches:

In the beginning ... The Word was with God ... He [Jesus] was with God in the beginning; all things were created by Him and for Him (**John 1:1; Colossians 1:16**).

In the Muslim teachings of the end times, Jesus appears before Allah and is asked if He ever claimed to be Allah's son; Jesus says no. Jesus then gets angry and helps the Muslim Messiah kill every remaining Jew and Christian. The Trinity is also not supported by Allah.

The Bible was written by at least forty different authors over a period of at least 1,500 years, and its unity and continuity are still apparent and cohesive. The Prophet Muhammad is said to have received divine revelation (recitations) from Allah over a period of twenty-three years. Since Muhammad could not read or write, he "recited" the contents of his revelation to fellow companions. They in turn memorized and recited it to the next generation. The companions eventually wrote down what was recited to them on animal skins and bones, large stones, and on big palm leaves.

There are contradictions in the Quran; at times Allah commands Muslims to love Jews and Christians and at other times calls for their death, if they do not convert to Islam. Because there are verses that teach peace, you may hear Islam referred to as a religion of peace. However, other instructions in the Quran order Muslims to kill all unbelievers, especially the more recent verses relating to Jews and Christians. What does a follower of Islam do when two instructions seem to contradict each other? This word is a pivotal key to unlocking the answer: abrogation.

Abrogation is a recurring theme whenever apparent conflicting verses of the Quran are discussed. It means to cancel, repeal, or officially revoke something. In this situation, the later or more recent verses calling for Holy War override earlier verses counseling tolerance or peace.

Committed followers of Islam will settle for nothing short of universal conversion and eventual death to all infidels.

> "I will cast terror into the hearts of those who disbelieved, so strike [them] upon the necks and strike from them every fingertip" (Quran 8:12). And, "Strike off the heads of the unbelievers, and after making a wide slaughter among them, carefully tie up the remaining captives" (Quran 47:4).

One may argue our God commands violence just like Allah does. We must distinguish between commands given to nations and instructions to individuals. In addition, killing while under command and submission to an army is very different than murdering someone as a private citizen. Though there were wars and plenty of violence in the Old Testament, God warned enemies of Israel about his holiness, his covenant, and he used people as his instrument of judgment in the world at the time. Jehovah God even put to death some of his own people who violated their covenant with him, but he never commands us to take our own revenge.

> *You shall not take vengeance, nor bear any grudge against the sons of your people, but you shall love your neighbor as yourself; I am the LORD* (**Leviticus 19:18**).

> *Bless those who curse you, pray for those who mistreat you...* *"If you love those who love you, what credit is that to you? Even 'sinners' love those who love them* (**Luke 6:28, 32**).

> "And fight them until there is no fitnah [tumult, disorder, trial, test, unbelief] and until the religion, all of it, is for Allah. And if they cease - then indeed, Allah is Seeing of what they do" (Quran 8:39).

Islam is completely incompatible with a society such as America that values religious freedom. Islam will accept no other religions, no competing economic or political views and no legal system except Shariah Law which would outlaw Christianity. Islam teaches that good Muslims should lie to their enemies to win their confidence. Allah himself lies, and the teachings of the prophet Muhammad accuse Jesus of lying.

This may explain how Muslims have broken every peace treaty they have ever signed with Israel and other nations.

God is not a man that he should lie (**Numbers 23:19**).

Since many liberals, media, and progressives are hostile toward Christianity, they have blind support for Islam. They are either deceived, or they are part of the agenda to blot out the Judeo-Christian God from America. Islamic Law calls for potential death sentences for adulterers and homosexuals. Where are the gay protests of Muslims? Christianity teaches us to forgive, to love all men, and preach the gospel. We are to confront sin, but not hate the sinner. Islam also allows the treatment of women as property while Christianity teaches respect. Where are the feminist protests of Muslim women being oppressed or stoned?

Because Islam denies the deity of Jesus Christ, according to 1 John 4:1-3, it is a religion of antichrist. So, if the founder of Islam, Muhammad, was actually a false prophet who did not hear from the one true living God, then those who follow him are deceived. Furthermore, in the Quran it states they [Jews and Christians] are deluded and "may Allah destroy them" in Surah 9:30. This proves that to compare Islam to Christianity is like comparing oil and water.

Jesus did not come to earth to bring world peace (Matt. 10:34), and yet there are religious leaders in America preaching common ground with Islam hoping to unify religions. Nowhere in the Bible does God encourage joining with other religions. On the contrary, He warns against it. It's not that we shouldn't evangelize people of other faiths, but typically the faith that bends and compromises is Christianity, leaving a diluted gospel. This doesn't stop some from attempting to mix Christianity and Islam.

CHRISLAM

"Chrislam" is the idea that Muslims and Christians worship the same God and that there are similarities to unite around. We've already established this is impossible and that Allah is not the same as Jehovah God, YHWH. Though both Christianity and Islam have Abrahamic roots, and both religions promote morality, the similarities pretty much stop there. Teachings that line up with Chrislam gain popularity because tolerance has trumped truth in our modern culture. This is a small movement, but don't be surprised if it gains popularity.

We are to separate ourselves from unbelievers and those who worship other gods:

> *Do not be bound together with unbelievers; for what partnership have righteousness and lawlessness, or what fellowship has light with darkness? ...or what has a believer in common with an unbeliever?* (**2 Corinthians 6:14-15**).

Islam allows for lying and deception in order to advance their quest for world domination, so how can we work side by side with those who subscribe to what is called "Kitman," the practice of deceiving infidels with half-truths? In countries not yet dominated by Islam, it only coexists with other religions because they have not been fully converted to Islam yet. We, however, believe salvation is by faith in Christ alone. Islam rejects this teaching.

I don't care what evangelical leader backs this common ground movement. Conservative Christians must be loyal and obedient to the truth and the gospel of Jesus Christ and not be concerned with the approval of man. This does not mean we can't love them and have a heart for the lost. It means we must be cautious about a religion that teaches Jesus was an apostle of Allah and not the only Son of God. John MacArthur explains:

> "Islam today is the most powerful system on earth for the destruction of biblical truth and Christianity – thousands of Christians are dying under Islamic persecution, especially in the Middle East, Africa, Indonesia, and other parts of Asia.

> "Clearly, Islam and Christianity are mutually exclusive. Both claim to be the only true way to God, but both cannot be right. There is no atonement in Islam, no forgiveness, no savior, and no assurance of eternal life."[9]

UNCOMMON GROUND

In October 2007, leaders of Islam came up with an open letter to leaders of the Christian faith in America called *A Common Word Between Us and You* calling for peace between Muslims and Christians and an understanding among both religions. They sought to emphasize *two* of the Ten Commandments; the love of god and the love of our neighbor. What's wrong with that? Islamic leaders stated, "The future of the world depends on peace between Muslims and Christians."

Not only is the world's future in God's hands, but the Bible teaches a very different future than other religions believe. Jesus warned about false prophets, wars, and nation rising against nation in the end times. It should also be noted that Islam means absolute "submission." The Islamic model of the relationship between Allah and his followers is that of a master and servant. Christianity teaches that we are children of God and are privileged to call him our Father.

What did our best and brightest leaders do? Scholars from Yale Divinity School decided to respond to the letter from Islamic leaders by publishing a full page advertisement in the *New York Times* titled, *"Loving God and Neighbor Together: A Christian Response to A Common Word Between Us and You."* They promised to "work diligently together to reshape relations between our communities and our nations."

The response includes Christian repentance over the mistreatment of Muslims and, yet, does not include any mention of differences between Allah and Yahweh! This leaves us with one of two conclusions: either these liberal evangelicals and scholars are confused and deceived about the teachings of Islam or they are complicit in the goal of a one-world government and the minimizing of Christianity. Muslims are taught that if they are a minority in any country or region, they may smile at the infidel, but never love him in their heart. Could the letter from Islamic leaders be just another way to try to win the trust of America?

The document's signatories include many well-known church leaders as Leith Anderson (President of the National Association of Evangelicals), Bill Hybels (Founder and Pastor of Willow Creek Community Church), Tony Jones (Emergent Village), Brian McLaren (Author,

Speaker and Activist), Robert Schuller (The Crystal Cathedral), Rick Warren (Saddleback Church), and Jim Wallis (Sojourners).[10]

Having open dialogue about peace and love is fine, but Muslims seem to be fighting with just about every nation they have not conquered or dominated. They are killing one another in the Middle East, and they attack and kill non-Muslims across the globe. Since Ishmael, Abraham's first son, was born outside of God's perfect will to Abraham's servant Hagar, the Lord said the birthright and inheritance would go to Isaac, the son of Abraham's wife, Sarah. Muslims believe Abraham's first son Ishmael deserved the inheritance which explains the constant fighting and strife in Islamic nations fulfilling God's prophecy over Ishmael:

> *He will be a wild donkey of a man; his hand will be against everyone and everyone's hand against him. And he will live in hostility toward all his brothers* (**Genesis 16:12**).

In the previous chapter in Genesis, God spoke to Abraham regarding his sons Ishmael and Isaac:

> *Then behold, the word of the* LORD *came to him, saying, "This man will not be your heir; but one who will come forth from your own body, he shall be your heir* (**Genesis 15:4**).

To respect each other is a good thing, but to focus on the few common teachings without looking seriously at major doctrines that are diametrically opposed to one another is misguided.

UNIVERSALISM

Universalism teaches that all people will ultimately be saved no matter what they believe here on earth. You can live the way you want: sin, curse God or deny Christ and still make it into heaven. Some Universalists say their salvation is through the atonement of Jesus Christ while others think everybody will go to heaven eventually regardless of whether or not they have put their faith in Christ. Confusing? Apparently this universal redemption will be realized either during a person's lifetime or after their death in some future state. Since there are many variations of Universalists, it's not possible to place them all in one doctrinal category. In fact, there are even Universalist groups with conflicting teachings. Some are Arian (God is one person, Jesus is a creation) while others believe in the Trinity.

Christian Universalism holds that all of mankind will ultimately be saved through Jesus, whether we place our faith in Him as the Son of God or not. This salvation is not from hell, but from sin, thus pretty much eliminating the truth about a future Judgment Day. As you can imagine, this is a very appealing teaching to young people and an entire generation of evangelicals has already been poisoned with this unbiblical doctrine. After all, who *wouldn't* want to accept a God of love without having to hear about judgment and justice?

In his book, *The Suicide of American Christianity*, author and host of "Stand Up for the Truth" radio program, Mike LeMay warns about this:

> "While you will not find many Emergent Christians that admit it, when you read the entirety of their writings and beliefs, many are Christian Universalists. That is one reason their teaching is so appealing to a biblically illiterate generation of Christians… God is a holy God, who cannot tolerate sin, and heaven will be a place that is void of the very presence of sin according to Scripture…When we eliminate the righteous judgment of God, we diminish His holy, perfect character."[11]

Some Universalists believe they will make it to heaven because a loving God would never create a place like hell. They think they will have to make up for their sins in some way – in heaven – and that they are disciplined and purified in *this* life for their sins. Most believe punishment for sin is moral, not physical since there is no eternal damnation. Still another belief is that a person makes it to heaven no matter what, but they lose certain rewards if they didn't trust Jesus Christ while on earth. Christian Universalism boils down to the claim that any doctrine about a literal hell is wrong.

Some say God has taken various forms throughout history and revealed Himself through other religions like Hinduism and Islam. Others split hairs over the essential doctrine of Christ's physical resurrection believing He was taken into heaven by God instead of actually rising from the dead and coming out of the tomb. Groups that deny the physical resurrection of Jesus are not Christian, nor are groups who deny the teaching of the Trinity. One of the more dangerous Universalist beliefs is a type of reincarnation in which those who have rejected Christ get a second chance and can still come to faith in the next life!

Matt Slick, President and Founder of the Christian Apologetics and Research Ministry (CARM), has written extensively on cults and false teachings and states:

> "Christian Universalism" really isn't Christian, and it is meshed with many other unorthodox and erroneous teachings. This belief system should be avoided.[12]

CONTEMPLETAVE PRAYER

> *But you, when you pray, go into your inner room, close your door and pray to your Father who is in secret, and your Father who sees what is done in secret will reward you* (**Matthew 6:6**).

Contemplative Spirituality has also become more popular recently. It is a belief system that uses ancient mystical practices such as silence and word repetition to induce altered states of consciousness. Often mixed with Christian terminology, the premise of contemplative spirituality is that God is in all things (panentheism). This is different from the belief that God *is* all, the divine being synonymous with the universe (pantheism). Its influences come from Roman Catholicism and Eastern religions including Buddhism and Hinduism.

Contemplative prayer is one of the most esteemed spiritual disciplines taught in spiritual formation and seeks to empty the mind and sit in silence. In contrast, biblical prayer seeks to focus on God's will and pray according to the Scriptures. Other interchangeable names for contemplative prayer are: centering prayer, breath prayer, meditation, or listening prayer.

Evangelical Christianity has been seduced into trying to see God through various spiritual eyes thanks to people like eastern mantra meditation proponent Quaker Richard Foster and Catholic theologian Henri Nouwen who stated:

> "Today I personally believe that while Jesus came to open the door to God's house, all human beings can walk through that

door, whether they know about Jesus or not. Today I see it as my call to help every person claim his or her own way to God."[13]

Really? We get to claim our own way to God? Author of more than seventy books on subjects ranging from pacifism, social justice, and spirituality, Catholic writer and monk Thomas Merton (1915-1968) was one of the most influential individuals on this movement. He was a mystic and studied comparative religion, graduating from Columbia University with an English degree. In 1949, Merton was ordained to the priesthood and was given the name Father Louis. He once said he did not see a contradiction between Buddhism and Christianity. Merton also believed there is "a point of nothingness" at the center of our beings "which is untouched by sin" and is pure truth. Merton stated:

> "And I believe that by openness to Buddhism, to Hinduism, and to these great Asian traditions, we stand a wonderful chance of learning more about the potentiality of our own traditions, because they have gone, from the natural point of view, so much deeper into this than we have...."[14]

Spiritual Formation is a movement promoting the process of practicing various behaviors or disciplines (works) in order to mature and become more like Christ. This activity apparently causes spiritual growth and development through practicing the presence of God. There is less emphasis on understanding and teaching the Bible. Proponents of these disciplines claim they are necessary for spiritual growth, but they are clearly not commanded in Scripture. To impose such practices undermines the authority of and denies the sufficiency of Scripture.

Are you so foolish? Having begun by the Spirit, are you now being perfected by the flesh? (**Galatians 3:3**).

Some disciplines are good, but Spiritual formation is rooted in mysticism and teaches that man possesses innate goodness. Contrast this with Jeremiah 17:9 (the heart of man is deceitful and sick) and with what Jesus said, that no one is good except God alone (Mark 10:18). Mystical practices can invoke the wrong kind of spiritual experiences. When these disciplines cause reading and studying the Word of God to take a back seat, there's a problem. Jesus and the apostles placed a huge priority on teaching and preaching Scripture, and we should do the same.

Next, "Centering prayer" has many origins including the fourth century writings of the monk St. John Cassian that pointed to the Desert Fathers. Emergent Gurus Brian McLaren and Tony Jones promote these teachings on prayer, but it was not a practice or teaching of Jesus Christ or the apostles. Since we can conclude the practice of Contemplative or Centering Prayer did not originate in Scripture, it should not be part of a Christian's relationship with God. This style of prayer starts with detachment, which is an emptying of the mind. In the process, a person seeks to hear from God and fill their mind - but with what?

Repeating a mantra or a short phrase is another technique that apparently allows the heart to detach and the mind to open to thoughts, voices or visions. This is often accompanied by a mystical state. In both practice and purpose, Centering prayer, Contemplative prayer, and Spiritual Formation are not aligned with what Scripture teaches.

> As I urged you when I went into Macedonia, stay there in Ephesus so that you may command certain men not to teach false doctrines any longer nor to devote themselves to myths and endless genealogies. These promote controversies rather than God's work – which is by faith (**1 Timothy 1:3-4**).

YOGA AND "MINDFULNESS"

There is absolutely nothing wrong with taking good care of our bodies, our physical temples, while we're here on earth. Eating right, exercise and stretching are good things. It's common for Christians to be taking yoga classes, sometimes even at church, but yoga is taught within all sects of Hinduism, and it is taught as a means to salvation. The various types of yoga practices include chanting, meditation, breathing exercises, performing acrobatic exercises or trying to put one's own body in difficult postures. Because meditation is central to all forms of yoga, it is not simply an innocent stretching or relaxation method. Yoga is a 5,000-year-old system of self-realization and spiritual unfoldment.

According to former professional astrologer Marcia Montenegro, Christian Yoga is an oxymoron just like Christian astrology or a Christian Ouija board. She explains:

> "All forms of Yoga are part of a serious systematic spiritual path in Hinduism designed to lead one to realization of the self as divine, and to bypass the mind in order to yoke with Brahman, the Absolute. The Yoga most practiced by Christians is Hatha Yoga. The poses themselves are often depictions of Hindu deities, and the hand positions mimic the hand positions seen on the statues of Hindu gods."[15]

The point of yoga is to unite with God through combining body, mind, and soul together and directing one's focus on inward thoughts. The Yoga Journal tells people not to label or judge inner thought patterns as right or wrong, but to connect "the mind, body, and breath." Christians are instructed to be filled with the Holy Spirit and to meditate only on God and His Word. We are never instructed to focus on ourselves or to free our minds. Since yoga is religious in nature, and some teach it as a way to salvation, Christians should find other alternatives to practicing yoga. Salvation is only through Jesus Christ and is not found in any other religious discipline, exercise, or practice.

SUMMARY

The watering down of sin and the Bible has now spread like poison in American churches. Truth has sadly become vague or irrelevant to many Christians, and grace and tolerance are over-emphasized today, thanks in part to the seeker-sensitive church mentality. Sinners are attracted to these emergent teachings, and some end up liking what they see and hear because it is patterned after the world. It makes them comfortable, but is this the church's job? Whatever happened to preaching the whole truth and leading people to repentance?

Many churches in America now have beautiful buildings, coffee shops, bookstores, great music and sound systems, state of the art lighting, edgy drama, video presentations, and some even offer yoga classes. Some churches seem to put more of an emphasis on entertaining the flock than on feeding them God's word. Well, at least it keeps the young people occupied, but what will they do when the go out into the real world? Are they prepared to face spiritual warfare and withstand attacks on their faith?

The apostle John wrote about Jesus calling out the hypocrisy of the religious leaders and saying they were of the devil (John 8:44). The very existence of the Bible is divisive because it forces people to make a decision about its message. It offers two options; accept it as God's Word or reject all of it. Picking and choosing verses like a spiritual buffet is not permissible. Cafeteria Christianity won't cut it.

Jesus never backed down when it came to facing prideful religious leaders. He challenged both their teachings and their actions. Everything we hear today must be held to the standard of Scripture because the enemy is active within the church working to blot out God. We must strive to continue in the Word of God and its authority. In the next chapter, we will analyze some well-known Christian authors and evangelical leaders and hold their teachings up to the Bible.

> *Then Jesus again spoke to them, saying, "I am the Light of the world; he who follows Me will not walk in the darkness, but will have the Light of life." …Jesus was saying to those Jews who had believed Him, "If you continue in My word, then you are truly disciples of Mine, and you will know the truth, and the truth will make you free* (**John 8:12, 31-32**).

ENDNOTES

1 http://www.spurgeongems.org/vols49-51/chs2916.pdf
2 http://www.alwaysbeready.com/index.php?option=com_content&task=view&id=142&Itemid=0
3 http://apprising.org/2012/06/11/was-peter-drucker-a-christian-the-spin-versus-the-truth/
4 http://www.pewforum.org/Christian/Evangelical-Protestant-Churches/Myths-of-the-Modern-Megachurch.aspx
5 Roger Oakland, Faith Undone, 2007 Lighthouse Trails Publishing; page 29
6 http://www.lighthousetrailsresearch.com/blog/?cat=95
7 http://www.lifesitenews.com/news/archive/ldn/2008/mar/08030701
8 http://www.worldviewweekend.com/worldview-times/article.php?articleid=5457
9 http://blog.beliefnet.com/news/2011/10/what-is-chrislam-and-does-anybody-really-preach-it.php

10 http://www.yale.edu/divinity/news/071118_news_nytimes.pdf
11 Mike LeMay, The Suicide of American Christianity, Westbow Press, page 106
12 http://carm.org/christian-universalism
13 http://www.lighthousetrailsresearch.com/celebrationofdisciplinearticleprinter.htm
14 http://www.lighthousetrailsresearch.com/blog/?p=9313
15 http://www.christiananswersforthenewage.org/Articles_ChristianYoga.html

COUNTERFEIT CHRISTIANITY

QUOTING THE CONVERSATIONALISTS

*Dear friends, although I was very eager to write to you about
the salvation we share, I felt I had to write and urge you to con-
tend for the faith that was once for all entrusted to the saints.
For certain men whose condemnation was written about long
ago have secretly slipped in among you. They are godless men,
who change the grace of our God into a license for immorality
and deny Jesus Christ our only Sovereign and Lord* (**Jude 3-4**).

*You were running a good race. Who cut in on you and kept
you from obeying the truth? That kind of persuasion does
not come from the one who calls you. A little yeast works
through the whole batch of dough* (**Galatians 5:7-9**).

The better we know the Word of God, the quicker we will recognize false teachings. With a solid foundation rooted in absolute truth
and a faith based on Christ the Lord, it will be harder for us to fall for
counterfeits. You might be surprised by some of the statements and
beliefs of some of today's influential Christian leaders. Some church
leaders have been deceived while others are deceivers themselves, but
each of them has potentially influenced tens of thousands of people.
Theologian Dr. R.C. Sproul recently stated:

"In every age the church is threatened by heresy, and heresy
is bound up in false doctrine. It is the desire of all heretics to
minimize the importance of doctrine. When doctrine is minimized, heresy can exercise itself without restraint."

310 COUNTERFEIT CHRISTIANITY

Minimizing the person and the gospel of Jesus Christ is a good way to describe what many evangelical leaders do regardless of whether it is on purpose or not. Teachers will be held to account one day for everything they teach. Having said that, these men are best-selling authors, speakers at Christian music festivals and conferences, and several are mega-church pastors. Notice they often have a difficult time relating to Scripture through the lens of the following words: authority, inerrant, infallible, revelation, absolute, and literal. It's time to go under the microscope and look at some influential Christian leaders' fruit.

ROB 'NO SINNER LEFT BEHIND' BELL

The founding pastor of Mars Hill Bible Church in Grand Rapids, MI and a popular icon in the emergent church movement, Bell openly questions the authority of God's Word. He often uses suggestive questions rather than declarations to challenge traditional Christian doctrine. The subtitle of his latest book, *Love Wins*, describes the work as *"a book about heaven, hell, and the fate of every person who ever lived." In typical emergent fashion, Bell creates more ambiguity instead of clarity when it comes to the concept of eternity.*

Pastor Joe Schimmel noted emergent leaders such as Bell are always moving and redefining themselves. This is partly due to the fact "there is no genuine commitment to propositional truth, so emergent leaders tend to be very evasive, and their lies are as slippery as an eel. You never seem to get straight answers."[1]

The idea that has caused the most recent backlash is Rob Bell's suggestion that eventually all human beings are reconciled to God after a brief separation. Even MSNBC anchor Martin Bashir saw through Bell's duplicity in a 2011 interview and called his teaching unbiblical and historically unreliable. In part of the segment, Bashir confronts Rob Bell's pop culture-friendly theology:

> "You're amending the gospel so that it's palatable to contemporary people who find, for example, the idea of Hell and Heaven very difficult to stomach. So here comes Rob Bell, he's made a Christian gospel for you and it's perfectly palatable, it's much easier to swallow."[2]

You know there's an integrity issue when a TV cable host on an extremely liberal network calls someone out on their teachings! With all the scriptural evidence on hell it seems strange emergent evangelicals like Bell would reinterpret its reality. He's giving our culture exactly what it wants: nothing too confrontational, convicting or absolute. The world prefers that church be light hearted, that sin be less offensive, and hell be something they don't need to fear.

Throughout the Gospels, Jesus warned about hell and never once cast any doubt on its existence. He described hell as a fiery furnace, outer darkness, a place of destruction, agony, torment, and weeping and gnashing of teeth – to name a few. Bell creates vagueness instead of providing answers and clarity. Let's look at some statements and quotes by Rob Bell:

> "This is part of the problem with continually insisting that one of the absolutes of the Christian faith must be a belief that 'Scripture alone' is our guide. It sounds good, but it's not true."[3]

> "For Jesus, heaven and hell were *present* realities. Ways of living we can enter into here and now. He talked very little of the life beyond this one...."[4]

> "What if tomorrow someone digs up definitive proof that Jesus had a real, earthly, biological father named Larry, and archeologists find Larry's tomb and do DNA samples and prove beyond a shadow of a doubt that the virgin birth was just a bit of mythologizing the gospel writers threw in...? Could you still be a Christian? Is the way of Jesus still the best possible way to live?"[5]

> "Believing in God is important, but what about God believing in us? ...maybe if we had more insight into the culture that Jesus grew up in and some of the radical things he did, we'd understand the faith that God has in all of us."[6]

> "No amount of clever marketing will attract people if we teach that 'God will punish people for all of eternity.'"[7]

"The love of God will melt *every* hard heart, and even the most 'depraved sinners' will eventually give up their resistance and turn to God."[8]

Bible Scholar D.A. Carson has preached extensively about Jesus' teaching about eternal punishment found in Matthew 25:46 and stated:

"...there is no shred of evidence in the N.T. that hell ever brings about genuine repentance. Sin continues as part of the punishment and the ground for it."[9]

The Word of God leaves no doubt about the existence of and severity of hell. With clarity and authority, God has told us everything we need to know about hell and how to avoid it through the merits of Christ. Rob Bell is a good example of the product of Protestant Liberalism that evolved back in the nineteenth century. Confusion about hell can be dangerously misleading to millions.

"What Jesus does is declare that he, and he alone, is saving *everybody*. And then he leaves the door way, way open."[10] – **Rob Bell**

Enter through the narrow gate. For wide is the gate and broad is the road that leads to destruction, and many enter through it. But small is the gate and narrow the road that leads to life, and only a few find it (**Matthew 7:13-14**).

BRIAN MCLAREN

Founding pastor of Cedar Ridge Community Church in Spencerville, MD, Brian McLaren serves as a board chair for the Christian Left's *Sojourners* magazine with Jim Wallis. He is an emergent church leader and a founding member of Red Letter Christians. According to *Time* magazine, McLaren is one of the twenty-five most influential people in the evangelical church. His teaching dilutes the sacrifice of Jesus Christ and the finished work on the cross and questions what the Bible says about heaven and eternal life. He doubts the reliability of the Bible and avoids clarity when interpreting Scripture. Here is Brian McLaren in his own words:

"Frankly, many of us don't know what we should think about homosexuality. We've heard all sides, but no position has yet won our confidence so that we can say 'it seems good to the Holy Spirit and us ... If we think that there may actually be a legitimate context for some homosexual relationships.... We aren't sure if or where lines are to be drawn, nor do we know how to enforce with fairness whatever lines are drawn.'"[11]

"Sit down here next to me in this little restaurant and ask me if Christianity (my version of it, yours, the Pope's, whoever's) is orthodox, meaning true, and here's my honest answer: a little, but not yet."[12]

"Yes, I find a character named God who sends a flood that destroys all humanity except Noah's family, but that's almost trivial compared to a deity who tortures the greater part of humanity forever in infinite eternal conscious torment, three words that need to be read slowly and thoughtfully to feel their full impact."[13]

"At the end God gets his way thru coercion and violence and intimidation and uh domination just like every other kingdom does. The Cross isn't the center then, the Cross is almost a distraction and false advertising for God."[14]

"In this light, a god who mandates an intentional supernatural disaster leading to unparalleled genocide is hardly worthy of belief, much less worship. How can you ask your children ... to honor a deity so uncreative, over reactive, and utterly capricious regarding life?"[15]

Do these few quotes point to Jesus and the Bible or do they cast doubt? Scripture warns against using idle words – do these statements by McLaren exalt and glorify Christ? Jesus told His disciples to beware of the leaven (Matthew 16:6), false teaching of the religious leaders. Most often, it doesn't take an entire book, sermon or paragraph for bad theology to be exposed. Someone might argue these statements were taken out of context, and to draw a fair conclusion we'd have to read

McLaren's teachings in their entirety. There are way too many heresies out there to have to digest all they teach. The Holy Spirit is our guide.

> *See to it that no one takes you captive through philosophy and empty deception, according to the tradition of men, according to the elementary principles of the world, rather than according to Christ. For in Him all the fullness of Deity dwells in bodily form...* (**Colossians 2:8-9**)

TONY CAMPOLO

Author, professor of Sociology at Eastern College, and a leader of Red Letter Christians, Tony Campolo has been a major player for progressive thought and reform in the evangelical church for decades. He is another one of American Christianity's most well-known evangelists. Campolo is a moral relativist and a political ideologue. According to Apprising Ministries, he is a "leading spokesman for this postmodern form of progressive Liberalism 2.0 de-formation of the Christian faith."

As a spiritual adviser to Bill Clinton, Campolo rationalized unbiblical behavior in the White House during the Clinton administration. Rather than my providing further commentary and explanation, I am allowing you to evaluate each statement and discern for yourself. Let's look at some quotes by Tony Campolo:

> "On the other hand, we are hard-pressed to find any biblical basis for condemning deep love commitments between homosexual Christians as long as those commitments are not expressed in sexual intercourse."[16]

> "To be a Christian in today's world is to be opposed to America. Why? .... America says, 'Blessed are the rich.' Jesus said, 'Woe unto you who are rich, blessed are the poor.'"[17]

> "Going to heaven is like going to Philadelphia.... There are many ways ... It doesn't make any difference how we go there. We all end up in the same place."[18]

> "Not only do I love the feminine in Jesus, but the more I know Jesus, the more I realize that Jesus loves the feminine in me.

Until I accept the feminine in my humanness, there will be a part of me that cannot receive the Lord's love.... There is that feminine side of me that must be recovered and strengthened if I am to be like Christ.... And until I feel the feminine in Jesus, there is a part of Him which I cannot identify."[19]

"I've got to push everything out of mind, save the name of Jesus. I say His name over and over again, for as long as fifteen minutes, until I find my soul suspended in what the ancient Celtic Christians called a 'thin place' – a state where the boundary between heaven and earth, divine and human, dissolves. You could say that I use the name of Jesus as my koan."[20]

Many of Campolo's teachings add to the Word of God, the very thing the Bible warns against. He harshly criticizes conservative Christians and what Campolo calls the religious right for being too rigid and traditional. He also emphasizes "converting the systems" in American society through government intervention and talks about economic injustice and the "polluting of the atmosphere." Campolo has also stated that he also learns from other religions as they speak to him about Christ. He also does not believe it is necessary for someone from another religion to leave their worship practices and religious context in order to convert to Christianity.

I am astonished that you are so quickly deserting him who called you in the grace of Christ and are turning to a different gospel – not that there is another one, but there are some who trouble you and want to distort the gospel of Christ. But even if we or an angel from heaven should preach to you a gospel contrary to the one we preached to you, let him be accursed (**Galatians 1:6-8** ESV).

LEONARD SWEET

Once an atheist intellectual, Leonard Sweet is an author, ordained Methodist minister, and Dean of the Theological School at Drew University in New Jersey. Sweet has been a leading figure in bringing change and so-called new spirituality into the evangelical church for well over a decade. Sweet has enthusiastically written about being part of a "New Light movement."

Back in 1995, Leonard Sweet and Rick Warren headed up a workshop they called *The Tides of Change* in which they taught about working toward a "New Reformation" in the church. This was just another product of the New Age movement. Author Warren Smith would know. Former New Ager and spiritual seeker, Smith writes about the movement in his eye-opening book, *A Wonderful Deception*:

> "What has become clear over the last decade is that the 'New Spirituality' – with its bottom line belief that God is 'in' everything – is, in reality, the foundational New Age 'hub' for the coming New World Religion. This panentheistic New Age/New Spirituality teaching that God is 'in' everything will be the 'common ground' melting pot belief that the coming New World Religion will ultimately rest upon."[21]

In recent decades, denominations such as Sweet's United Methodist Church (UMC) have steered away from the authority of Scripture and toward the goals of the World Council of Churches and the UN some time ago. The UMC is a signatory member of the UN "United Religions Initiative" where the UN is encouraging dialogue between religions in an attempt to forge a one-world religion. This is where it's heading, friends.

In his book *Quantum Spirituality*, Sweet claims New Lights must "catch the waves of a spiritual Gulf Stream" taking them into the unknown regions of…. "Spiritual Sciences." Understanding the direction of Christianity today you may not be surprised that many of the books by Rob Bell, McLaren, Campolo, and Sweet are required reading in missions and evangelism classes at Christian colleges. There is plenty of apostasy and heresy floating around, and too many gullible followers have been duped. Sweet's ideology seems to be a mixture of Christianity, paganism, and New Age. He has spoken at Nazarene churches and universities, and they love him. At a 2009 seminar at a Nazarene church, the promo included the following:

> *"Leonard Sweet is an historian of American culture; a futurist who 'sees things the rest of us do not see, and dreams possibilities*

*that are beyond most of our imagining.' He is a preacher and
writer who communicates the gospel powerfully to a postmodern
age by bridging the worlds of academics and popular culture."*[22]

Sweet is referred to as an historian, a futurist, and a dreamer and
he bridges academia and pop culture. I'm wondering where the Holy
Bible fits into his imaginative presentation. It is important to look at
some of Sweet's teachings because he has been considered by some an
influential pioneer in the emergent church. He often talks about following the "great Light." It's time to let some teachings by Leonard Sweet
speak for themselves:

> "Deeper feeling and higher relating go together. The church is
> fundamentally one being, one person, a comm-union whose
> cells are connected to one another within the information
> network called the **Christ consciousness.**"[23]

> "Quantum spirituality bonds us to all creation as well as to other
> members of the human family.... This entails a radical doctrine
> of embodiment of God in the very substance of creation....
> But a spirituality that is not in some way entheistic (whether
> pan- or trans-), that does not extend to the spirit-matter of the
> cosmos, is not Christian."[24]

> *"Keep breathing quietly while holding your Bible. You have within
> you not just the powers of goodness resident in the great spiritual
> leaders like Moses, Jesus, Muhammed, Lao Tzu. You also have
> within you the forces of evil and destruction. Resident in each
> breath you take is the body of angels like Joan of Arc and devils
> like Gilles de Rais, Genghis Khan, Judas Iscariot, Herod, Hitler,
> Stalin and all the other destructive spirits throughout history."*[25]

Leonard Sweet received further credibility by Rick Warren's endors-
ing Sweet's 1999 book *Soul Tsunami: Sink or Swim in New Millennium
Culture.* With the endorsement on both the front and back covers of
the book, concerns about Sweet's theology were not an issue for Warren. In 2006 and 2007, Sweet was voted by his peers "One of the 50
Most Influential Christians in America" by ChurchReport Magazine.

Then He will also say to those on His left, 'Depart from Me, accursed ones, into the eternal fire which has been prepared for the devil and his angels; ... And if anyone's name was not found written in the book of life, he was thrown into the lake of fire (**Matthew 25:41; Revelation 20:15**).

DOUG PAGITT

Doug Pagitt is an author, pastor, and radio host hired in the mid 1990s by Leadership Network and has worked with Brian McLaren, Tony Jones, and Dan Kimball. Pagitt is another controversial leader of the emerging church movement who questions aspects of traditional evangelical Christianity. Before founding Solomon's Porch, he was a youth pastor at a Minneapolis megachurch and had become disillusioned with his faith. In his book *Church Re-Imagined, Pagitt wrote that on more than one occasion:*

"God's going to judge the life and repair and restore and heal the life of everybody in the same way...there's going to be no difference between the way God is going to interact with you when you die and the way God's going to interact with a Muslim when a Muslim dies."[26]

According to his church website, they are considered a "Holistic Missional Christian Community." Like many emergent leaders, Pagitt seems to mold Christianity into his view of the world instead of following the eternal, indisputable teachings of the gospel of Jesus Christ. On his personal website, Pagitt refers to himself as "a social and theological entrepreneur." At Solomon's Porch, they do not have services; they call them "Sunday Gatherings." Pagitt doesn't consider his sermons lessons that define belief, but rather "stories that welcome our hopes and ideas and participation."

About twelve years ago, Pagitt sensed the need to move away from traditional conservative Christianity that he felt wasn't up to date and culturally relevant and "move into a Christianity that somehow fit better with the world I lived in, not an expression reconstituted from another time."[27] Here are some revealing statements by Doug Pagitt:

"We also understand ourselves as part of a global community. We are required to live our local expressions of Christianity in harmony with those around the world."[28]

"God is never finished with creation, and God is never finished with us. We are constantly being re-created, and we are invited to join God as co-re-creators of the world."[29]

"Encourage young people who are Gay and Christian that their faith is legitimate."[30]

Hopefully, you will see through this changing theology for what it really is: a departure from the truth of God's Word. In Doug Pagitt's case, he openly describes his sermons at Solomon's Porch as "putting words around people's experiences" and reiterates the fact that his style is *not* about "extracting truth from the Bible to apply to people's lives."[31]

This is not uncommon. I've heard concerned Christians say their once solid church has changed. In his book *Faith Undone*, Roger Oakland sadly admits the Bible seems to have become a forbidden book. Some pastors no longer teach the Bible. Instead, "the Sunday morning service is a skit or a series of stories."[32]

In our travels, my wife and I have visited some churches where the pastor doesn't encourage people to bring their Bibles with them. In fact, at one church we attended for a short time in California, the church had the few Scriptures from his sermon printed in the bulletin, and he told the church to "open up your bulletin if you'd like to read along." The general implication is that if you prefer digging into the Word, do it on your own time. Let's not complain about it; instead, let's ask our pastors to please tell folks to bring their Bibles to church.

> *But false prophets also arose among the people, just as there will also be false teachers among you, who will secretly introduce destructive heresies, even denying the Master who bought them, bringing swift destruction upon themselves* (**2 Peter 2:1**).

TONY JONES

Another author and prominent spokesman for the emergent church movement, Tony Jones is a blogger, theologian-in-residence at Solomon's

Porch in Minneapolis and an adjunct professor at Fuller Theological Seminary. (Fuller is not what it used to be.) Jones and Doug Pagitt own a consulting business and work together at Solomon's Porch. On Jones' website it states: *"Tony Jones* is an ecclesiologist – that's like a proctologist for the church." A progressive evangelical and admitted relativist, Jones, according to his publisher, Zondervan, is the National Coordinator of the Emergent Village. It was the late Dr. Walter Martin that rightly called the emergent movement a "cult of liberal theology."

Jones was one of the first emergent leaders to come out in full support of homosexual Christians. Someone might ask why that's a problem, because pastors often support Christians who are alcoholics, adulterers, divorced, those who have had abortions, etc. The key is whether a person has *repented*, instead of continuing to *practice* or engage in sin. In a 2006 interview with *Relevant Magazine* on the emergent church, Jones said that there is no need for churches to break fellowship with *unrepentant* sinners. In this particular case, they are talking about ordaining gay ministers:

> *Relevant Magazine*: "You mentioned earlier that you have lesbian pastors and conservative absolutists. It seems that it would create a tension point when it comes to endorsing that person's view or platform."

Tony Jones: "If you believe that Christianity is – at its very heart – a tension-filled, dialectical endeavor, you have less problems with these tension-filled relationships with believers....Why would you break fellowship with someone because you have a different understanding of the atonement than they do? Or a different understanding of human sexuality than they do?"[33]

As you compare the following quotes with biblical truths, remember Scripture is the same today as it was when it was first written, and God never changes. People, fads, and trends, however, come and go. Here's much more from Tony Jones:

> "In any case, I now believe that GLBTQ (Gay Lesbian Bisexual Transgender Queer) can live lives in accord with Biblical Christianity (at least as much as any of us can!) and that their

monogamy can and should be sanctioned and blessed by church and state."[34]

"Maybe some evangelicals should tear the book of Romans out of their Bibles and read a Romans-free Bible for a few years. Then they can paste it back in."[35]

"I think the Bible is a f***ing scary book, pardon my French, but that's the only way I know how to convey how strongly I feel about this."[36]

"Some people today may find it compelling that some Great Cosmic Transaction took place on that day 1,980 years ago, that God's wrath burned against His Son instead of me. I find that version of atonement theory neither intellectually compelling, spiritually compelling, nor in keeping with the biblical narrative."[37]

"The idea is to purposefully shed the common methods most of us use in our everyday reading…. As you attend to those deeper meanings, begin to *meditate on the feelings and emotions* conjured in your inner self."[38] (Emphasis mine)

Author of *The Cult of Liberalism,* Dr. Walter Martin is a theologian and the founder of Christian Research Institute. He warned about testing all things, and he adamantly stated:

"It is a cult because it follows every outlined structure of cultism; its own revelations; its own gurus, and its denial – systematically – of all sound systematic Christian theology. … And it ends in immorality; because the only way you could have gotten to this homosexual, morally relativistic, garbage – which is today in our denominational structures – is if the leadership of those denominations denied the authority of the Scriptures and Jesus Christ as Lord … in the light of historic theology, and the Holy Bible … it is obvious they don't have any theology that is going to save anybody."

SHANE CLAIBORNE

Shane Claiborne is one of the founding members of a New Monastic community named the Potter Street Community in Philadelphia, a Red Letter Christian, and teacher of Christian Mysticism. Claiborne is a part of The Alternative Seminary in Philadelphia, PA. He is featured in the documentary *The Ordinary Radicals* and wrote the foreword to Ben Lowe's *Green Revolution: Coming Together to Care for Creation.* Claiborne is also a social justice activist and pacifist promoting non-violence and the redistribution of resources to the poor.

Claiborne has also blogged for Jim Wallis's left-wing *Sojourner's Magazine.* It's important to remember that any statement, idea or doctrine that strays from the foundation of the gospel and points people to things other than the Word of God is problematic. The enemy is clever and most deceptive with the use of subtleties and compassion-sprinkled opinions. Claiborne and others like to refer to the Beatitude in Matthew 5:3 where Jesus said, "Blessed are the poor," but they often leave out the second, most important part which is, "Blessed are the poor *in spirit*, for theirs is the kingdom of heaven." Here is a small sampling by Shane Claiborne:

> "Church Father Ignatius said that if our church is not marked by caring for the poor, the oppressed, and the hungry, then we are guilty of heresy."[39]

> "So for those of us who have nearly given up the church, may we take comfort in the words of St. Augustine: 'The Church is a whore, but she's my mother.' She is a mess and has many illegitimate children. But she is also our momma...."[40]

> "When a *devout Muslim brother* asked Tony [Campolo] and I to have this cross-generational dialogue about interreligious cooperation for an interfaith publication, we jumped on it."[41] (Emphasis mine)

> "Rarely are people converted by force or words, but through intimate encounters. Perhaps one of the best things we can do is stop talking with our mouths and cross the chasm between

us with our lives. Maybe we will even find a mystical union of the Spirit as [Saint] Francis [of Assisi] did."[42]

"One of the barriers seems to be the assumption that we have the truth and folks who experience things differently will all go to Hell. How do we unashamedly maintain a healthy desire for others to experience the love of God as we have experienced it without condemning others who experience God differently?"[43]

Shane Claiborne is not an evil person. He helps the homeless and the poor and walks his talk in that respect, but do not buy into his theology. He wrote a painstakingly neutral blog about the emerging church on the *Sojourner's* site and basically said the same thing about them you could say about atheists, Catholics, Christians, communists, or anyone: there are always going to be extreme views that don't represent the overall movement. Claiborne once said both Muslim and Christian extremists kill in the name of their gods,[44] but he fails to explain the percentage of terrorism carried out by Muslims worldwide today while Christians are being martyred for their faith.

I want to emphasize two things: First, there is a remnant of conservative evangelicals who love Jesus, believe in evangelism, and want to change the world; second, the Jesus that emergent church gurus talk about is not the same Jesus you and I believe in.

> *Now I urge you, brethren, keep your eye on those who cause dissensions and hindrances contrary to the teaching which you learned, and turn away from them. For such men are slaves, not of our Lord Christ but of their own appetites; and by their smooth and flattering speech they deceive the hearts of the unsuspecting* (**Romans 16:17-18**).

JOEL OSTEEN

Author, televangelist, and senior pastor of Lakewood Church in Houston, Texas, Joel Osteen seems like a very likeable and well-meaning Christian man. His ministry reaches about seven million people every week in countries around the world through radio and television. Prior to October 3, 1999, Osteen produced the church's television program for seventeen years. With no biblical education or experience, Joel Osteen succeeded his father. Prior to his father's death, Joel had only preached once in his entire life and had no theological training.

Today, he is one of the most popular, well-known Christian leaders in America. Barbara Walters named Osteen one of the year's "Ten Most Fascinating People," and his popularity earned him some attention at ABC News, naming him one of the "10 Most Fascinating People of 2006." His church rakes in approximately $70 million every year. Television news anchor Chris Wallace interviewed Joel Osteen in December 2007 on Fox News Channel and began the segment by saying Osteen "offers a message about personal growth and positive thinking, which may explain why he's now pastor of America's largest congregation." Wallace asked him what Osteen thought it was about his message that people want to hear. Osteen replied:

> "I don't know if I know exactly, but I think the fact that it's positive, it's hopeful, and I talk about everyday life.... And, too, I think, Chris, there's a lot of negative things trying to pull people down, and I think people respond when you tell them that, hey, there are good things up ahead."

What Osteen just described sounds like a motivational pep talk. Apparently, others notice how seldom Osteen gives his views or discusses what the Bible teaches on issues such as abortion, homosexuality, pornography, marriage, and other religions. Chris Wallace also asked why Osteen doesn't get involved in politics or talk much about "abortion and gays and the social issues." Joel Osteen explained:

> "Well, it started back with my father. He never did. And I just don't feel comfortable as well. I don't feel like that's my main gifting. And I feel like when I stay focused on encouraging people, and giving them hope, and helping them live their everyday life, I think that's where I can have the most impact."

He's in good company. Non-views have become the evangelical norm, and Osteen takes the neutral route. Critics say Osteen preaches a word-faith prosperity gospel lite, which I like to call Cotton Candy Christianity. He can be overly positive and at times a bit out of touch with human suffering. One popular quote by Joel Osteen is, "When you focus on being a blessing, God makes sure that you are always blessed in abundance." So all we need to do is focus on being good and doing good? Tell someone who is confined to a bed with an incurable disease, or someone who lost their home, or lost a loved one that they'll *always* be blessed in abundance.

In a 2011 interview with the *Washington Times*, Osteen told editors that he saw faith in America at an all-time high. He said that yes, people are struggling, but "our message is so much about hope." He naturally evaded most political questions saying, "I don't really take sides," as it divides the people, adding that he prefers to "stay in my own lane."

His latest book is *Every Day a Friday: How to Be Happier 7 Days a Week*, the follow up to his previous best seller, *Your Best Life Now*. Many of us would like to hear Joel Osteen dig into the Bible and give a bold presentation of the gospel of Christ without apology. With Mitt Romney running for president of the United States, Osteen is getting more questions from people about Romney's religion. From the *Washington Times* interview:

> "I believe that [Mormons] are Christians," Mr. Osteen said. "I don't know if it's the purest form of Christianity, like I grew up with. But you know what, I know Mormons. I hear Mitt Romney – and I've never met him – but I hear him say, 'I believe Jesus is the son of God,' 'I believe he's my savior,' and that's one of the core issues.
>
> "I'm sure there are other issues that we don't agree on. But you know, I can say that the Baptists and the Methodists and the Catholics don't all agree on everything. So that would be my take on it."[45]

Even though denominations may not agree on a few nonessential doctrines, they all base their faith on the Bible, not the Book of Mormon. Osteen has stated on several other occasions that Mitt Romney, a Mormon, "believes in his savior just like I do." What does that even mean?

Joseph Smith founded Mormonism and Latter Day Saints (LDS) less than 200 years ago. Mormonism teaches God was once a man who progressed to Godhood, there is no Trinity, Jesus was not born of a virgin, and he is not eternal. We can safely say this is another gospel which is cautioned against in the New Testament. Smith also taught all other religions are of the devil and according to Mormon teachings, Joseph Smith "received visitations from Moroni, an angel of light."

Mormon leaders have also taught that Jesus' incarnation was the result of a physical relationship between God the Father and Mary. They believe Jesus is a god (small "g"), but humans can also become gods and salvation can be earned by a combination of faith and good works. Osteen must be careful because God will scrutinize his statements as leaders have the power and responsibility to influence many lives. In Joel's case, it's millions of lives.

> *Let not many of you become teachers, my brethren, knowing that as such we will incur a stricter judgment* (**James 3:1**).

Did you ever wonder why there is so much opposition or resistance to Christians? The God of all creation is our help and strength. We pray to a *living* God while the bones of the gods (or founders) of other religions can be found at their tomb or burial site. We have a Savior who overcame death and the grave leaving an empty tomb that shouts to the world that Jesus is alive.

During interviews on his book promotion tours, Joel Osteen often gives similar responses about being positive, changing your life, developing better habits, not being stuck in the past, doing the best you can, hope, and abundance. Osteen claims Jesus wanted us to live a "great life." What about orphans? What about the handicapped, shut-ins, disabled Veterans, or the persecuted church? How is a great life defined?

Jesus said that in this life we can expect trouble, but to take heart because He has overcome this temporary world. (John 16:33). Jesus also talked about His kingdom in heaven and never mentioned visualizing a nicer house, car, boat or financial blessing. Christ came to give us life, to destroy the devil's work, to preach the good news to the afflicted and brokenhearted (Is. 61:1). He set us free from the law of sin and death (Rom. 8:2).

Osteen says that talking about sin isn't his main calling and that he's "trying to make God more relevant" in our society. Let's look at how Joel Osteen responded to a few more direct questions from Chris Wallace about Mormonism, from the 2007 interview on *Fox News Sunday With Chris Wallace:*

WALLACE: "And what about Mitt Romney? ...Is a Mormon a true Christian?"

OSTEEN: "Well, in my mind they are. Mitt Romney has said that he believes in Christ as his Savior, and that's what I believe, so, you know, I'm not the one to judge the little details of it. So I believe they are. And so, you know, Mitt Romney seems like a man of character and integrity to me...."

WALLACE: "So, for instance, when people start talking about Joseph Smith, the founder of the church, and the golden tablets in upstate New York, and God assumes the shape of a man, do you not get hung up in those theological issues?"

OSTEEN: *"I probably don't get hung up in them because I haven't really studied them or thought about them.* And you know, I just try to let God be the judge of that. I mean, I don't know. I certainly can't say that I agree with everything that I've heard about it, but from what I've heard from Mitt, *when he says that Christ is his savior, to me that's a common bond."*[46] (Emphasis mine)

So let's clarify here that Pastor Joel Osteen feels it is not his calling to get deeply into the Bible or to talk about sin. He also prefers not to think too much about other religions, but he believes Mormons are Christians. He focuses on the positive and promotes a word-faith theology that the more you do or say something the more you will get as a result. I know this teaching well because I followed it for several years in my early Christian days. It is both addictive and deceptive. Who doesn't want to be happy and "up" all the time? Most of us realize that not only is this unbiblical, it is not realistic.

The tragic thing is that hoards of young people are being influenced by Osteen's limited theology, and they end up looking at God as some kind of genie as a result. On page 306 of *Your Best Life Now,* Joel claims, "It's our faith that activates the power of God." When the emphasis is on the power of our own words instead of the power of the resurrection, something's wrong. He goes so far as to say it's more important to speak to your problem than pray about it (pg. 124). The following quotes are from *Your Best Life Now* by Pastor **Joel Osteen**:

"The first step to living at your full potential is to *enlarge your vision*. To live your best life now, you must start looking at life through eyes of faith, seeing yourself rising to new levels. See your business taking off. See your marriage restored. See your family prospering. See your dreams coming to pass. You must conceive it and believe it is possible if you ever hope to experience it" (p. 4, emphasis his).

"You will produce what you're continually seeing in your mind.... *If you develop an image* of victory, success, health, abundance, joy, peace, and happiness, nothing on earth will be able to hold those things from you ... God wants to increase you financially, by giving you promotions, fresh ideas and creativity" (p. 5).

"God wants you to live an overcoming life of victory. He doesn't want you to barely get by. He's called *El Shaddai*, 'the God of more than enough'" (p. 33).

"You will often receive preferential treatment simply because your Father is the King of kings, and His glory and honor spill over onto you" (p. 40).

"Our words have tremendous power, and whether we want to or not, we will give life to what we're saying, either good or bad.... Words are similar to seeds, by speaking them aloud, they are planted in our subconscious minds, and they take on a life of their own.... Get up each morning and look in the mirror and say, 'I am valuable. I am loved. God has a great plan for my life. I have favor wherever I go. God's blessings are chasing me down and overtaking me. Everything I touch prospers and succeeds!' (p. 122-123).

"It's going to happen.... Suddenly, your situation will change for the better ... He will bring your dreams to pass" (pp. 196-198).

Osteen has also said that believers will "often receive preferential treatment" in this life and that our spoken words "take on a life of their own" and will produce results. He encourages people to "get up each morning and look in the mirror and say, 'I am valuable. God's blessings are chasing me down' and one of my favorites, 'Everything I touch prospers and succeeds.'" There's nothing wrong with trying to be positive, but where is this found in the Bible?

Maybe you're a fan of Joel Osteen. You may have read his books and have watched him on TV and are having a tough time accepting this. I strongly encourage you to pray about everything he or anyone teaches. If you sincerely seek God's truth, He will reveal it to you. Osteen presents a kind of self-help program under the guise of Bible instruction. There's nothing wrong with optimism, but pastors need to stick with the Word of God.

People who follow Osteen's formula and fail to get the positive results he promises end up disillusioned and worse, get mad at God and fall away from him. Don't you think Christians are responsible for telling people what they need to hear instead of what they want to hear? You won't get that from Mr. Happy. Smooth talk. Positive vibes. Prosperity and abundance. Flattering speech. Deceptive doctrine with a smile.... Cotton Candy Christianity.

> *Pay close attention to yourself and to your teaching; persevere in these things, for as you do this you will ensure salvation both for yourself and for those who hear you* (**1 Timothy 4:16** ESV).

"AMERICA'S PASTOR" RICK WARREN

Rick Warren has impacted millions of lives, and his books and teachings have blessed people. Please understand, no man is without sin, and no one's teachings should be held above the teachings of Jesus Christ and the Bible. I've seen people idolize popular church leaders, and it must grieve the Lord.

Author of *The Purpose Driven Church* and *The Purpose Driven Life*, Rick Warren is the senior pastor at Saddleback Church in California which averages 22,000 attendees per week. I respect the fact that Warren seems to, at least in the past, separate himself from most liberal progressive church leaders in his views on abortion, marriage between one man and one woman, and stem cell research. He has stood for life and has been effective in battling AIDS abroad. He has done some good philanthropy, and we should pray for God's wisdom for him.

As a general rule, when the progressive, mainstream, anti-Christian media speaks well of a pastor or other Christian leader, it's probably not a good sign. *Time* magazine named Rick Warren one of "15 World Leaders Who Mattered Most" in 2004; and in 2005, Warren was named one of "America's Top 25 Leaders" in an issue of *U.S. News and World Report*. An elected member of the Council on Foreign Relations, he was also one of the "100 Most Influential People in the World" in 2005 according to *Time*. Warren was also called one of "15 People Who Make America Great" by *Newsweek*.

In the last chapter, I mentioned the influence of one of Warren's mentors, Peter Drucker, on modern Christianity. Drucker believed that the church should adopt a business model and the structure of a corporation in order for the church to be successful. In organizational structure, Saddleback Church was based on this model and followed the example of Robert Schuller's Crystal Cathedral. Drucker convinced many of today's prominent Christian leaders that being consumer-driven is what matters, and many pastors didn't think twice about operating a church like a secular business. In business, the customer is always right, and if they want a different product, they get it or the business may lose them.

Dan Kimball is another emergent, post-modern leader, and Warren wrote the foreword in Kimball's book *The Emerging Church*. The book was endorsed by Brian McLaren and Tony Jones as well. Warren wrote:

> "This book is a wonderful, detailed example of what a purpose-driven church can look like in a postmodern world. My friend Dan Kimball writes passionately from his heart, with a deep desire to reach emerging generations and cultures.... You need to pay attention to him because times are changing."[47]

Kimball was one of the early promoters of the emergent church and talked about re-imagining the church and re-thinking how to reach people. Kimball stated:

"The old paradigm taught that if you had the right teaching, you will experience God. The new paradigm says that if you experience God, you will have the right teaching."

Kimball and Warren imply that the old view is legalistic and narrow, but the five fundamentals of faith are: the deity of Jesus Christ, the virgin birth, the blood atonement, Jesus' bodily resurrection, and the inerrancy of the Scriptures. Sadly, in a typical evangelical church today, the rule is to not say anything that might make waves.

Let's look at the marriage issue in CA in which a majority of citizens voted in 2008 to define marriage as between one man and one woman. Two weeks before that election, Rick Warren encouraged his congregation to pray about how to vote on Proposition 8, "which is the proposition that had to be instituted because the courts threw out the will of the people. And a court of four guys actually voted to change a definition of marriage that has been going for 5,000 years," he explained. I was both surprised and thrilled to hear an evangelical pastor say what Warren said:

"Now let me say this really clearly: we support Proposition 8 – and if you believe what the Bible says about marriage, you need to support Proposition 8. I never support a candidate, but on moral issues I come out very clear.... There are about two percent of Americans [who] are homosexual or gay/lesbian people. We should not let two percent of the population determine to change a definition of marriage that has been supported by every single culture.... This is not even just a Christian issue – it's a humanitarian and human issue that God created marriage for the purpose of family, love, and procreation."

To Warren's credit, I cannot imagine a Jim Wallis, Brian McLaren, Tony Campolo or Rob Bell saying anything remotely close to this. But then it happened: the dreaded flip/flop in April 2009 on *Larry King Live*. Rick Warren was interviewed by the old guy and actually apologized for his stand on heterosexual marriage. He also denied publicly supporting Prop 8. Confused? So were a lot of Christians. Kudos to him for clarifying in a 2012 interview with Jake Tapper at ABC. When asked, Rick Warren replied:

"Well, if the Bible is the word of God, then I don't have the right to change it. Policies come and go over the years. And so if I'm unpopular for certain beliefs, well, then I'm unpopular for certain beliefs. And to me, the Bible is very clear that sex is for a man and a woman in marriage only."[48]

I'm thankful for that response. It tells me there's still hope for megachurches. Fame, success and power can corrupt, and Christians are not exempt. Generally, the bigger a church or ministry gets, the more difficult it is to stay grounded, humble, and not conform to the world.

You may remember in January 2009 that Rick Warren conducted the prayer for President Obama's inauguration. When it was announced that a Christian pastor was going to give the inaugural prayer, I was encouraged. I'm sure it was a political move, but I thought Warren would use the opportunity to proclaim Jesus. What he did say, however, may have caused more religious confusion. Warren prayed in the name of both Jesus and "Isa" (the name for Jesus in the Quran). Islam doesn't recognize Isa as the Son of God, and Isa did not die on the cross for our salvation according to the Muslim religion. Warren stated:

"I humbly ask this in the name of the one who changed my life, Yeshua, Isa, Jesús (pronounced 'Hey-sous', Spanish for Jesus), Jesus, who taught us to pray"[49]

Admittedly, Rick Warren was given a difficult task. Homosexuals, especially those in California who fought Warren on their Proposition 8 battle, were angry that he prayed in the name of Jesus and quoted the Lord's Prayer because it was a Christian tradition. Muslims, believing that Barack Obama was now their ally in the White House, wanted a little more than a brief mention of Isa and the "merciful and compassionate one," and Christian conservative evangelicals, questioning Warren's references to Islam, were hoping he would have quoted some Scripture in his prayer.

Him we proclaim, warning everyone and teaching everyone with all wisdom, that we may present everyone mature in Christ (**Colossians 1:28** ESV).

There have been many clues in Warren's ministry revealing what he has approved of and who he has partnered with. One item of importance was in 2009 when Warren spoke to eight thousand Muslim leaders at the forty-sixth annual conference of the Islamic Society of North America (ISNA) and did not share the gospel. ISNA is a known front for the *Muslim Brotherhood*. ISNA has also been charged with having links to other foreign terrorist organizations.

In *The Suicide of American Christianity*, Mike LeMay stated:

"We certainly should try to learn how to live with Muslims, not approaching Islam out of fear or ignorance. But to agree with them that Allah and YHWH are the same and promise to not share the gospel with them? This is nothing short of a betrayal of Christianity, and hatred, not love, for Muslims – people who need to know who Jesus really is and find salvation in Him. What about 'go and make disciples of all nations'?"[50]

Trying to find common ground is noble and yet naïve at the same time. Muslims believe the Christian and Jewish Bibles are false teachings. So it's fine to have dinner or talk about football, music, or politics, but when the Christian way to redemption and salvation is through the Lord Jesus Christ and the Muslim path to salvation is martyrdom, the contrasts are glaring.

"If you want to advertise your church to the unchurched, you must learn to think and speak like they do." – **Rick Warren**

THE DANIEL PLAN: In 2011, Warren and Saddleback hosted the kick-off for the 52-week health program called The Daniel Plan. The problem is not with doing these things, it is with *how* they are done as well as *who* implements them. The "experts" called in to head the program go way beyond promoting physical health and are absolute advocates and proponents of eastern-style meditation. Let's take a look:

Dr. Daniel Amen teaches techniques such as a twelve-minute form of meditation, Kriya Kirtan which includes chants and mantras for various purposes such as health and wealth. The promoted benefit of Kriya Kirtan is connecting with your inner divinity. This is a form of kundalini yoga (see Amen's book, *The Brain in Love*, p. 146). Those who have researched and understand New Age mysticism know that kundalini (or serpent power) is the spiritual "energy" behind meditation.

Another form of meditation that Dr. Amen advocates is called "Tantra" or tantric sex which is the use of Hinduistic-type mysticism during sexual intercourse. Tantra is the name of the ancient Hindu sacred texts that contain certain rituals and secrets. Some deal with taking the energies brought forth in meditation through the chakras and combining them with love-making to enhance sexual experiences. Rick Warren clearly stated Dr. Amen's resources would be available for those who attended the seminar and, of course, available on line. In almost all of Dr. Amen's resources, he advocates eastern meditation.

Dr. Mark Hyman is a nominee to President Obama's advisory group on prevention, health promotion, and public health. In his book *The Ultramind Solution*, Dr. Hyman emphasizes mystical meditation, saying it doesn't matter what religion one has in order to benefit from it (p. 322). Dr. Hyman suggests that "Mindful meditation is a powerful, well-researched tool, developed by Buddhists" (p. 384). On Dr. Hyman's website you can read the article, "How the Dalai Lama Can Help You Live to 120."[51] On the book's front cover sits an endorsement by Dr. Mehmet Oz, the third Daniel Plan doctor.

Dr. Mehmet Oz, a highly renowned cardiovascular surgeon was catapulted into American living rooms thanks to Oprah Winfrey who featured him on her show for five years, making him a household name. That eventually led to him getting his own television show, currently one of the more popular shows on TV. Like it or not, Oprah has influenced perhaps millions to at least check out the New Age movement and calls Oz her favorite doctor. Influenced by the mysticism of Sufi Muslims, Oz was raised as a Muslim and wrote an article called "Mehmet Oz Finds His Teacher" in which he shares his spiritual awakening.

According to one of Oz's mentors, mystic Emanuel Swedenborg, "heaven and hell are not merely places but spiritual states. We do not 'go there' when we die. We are already there." Dr. Oz is also a proponent of transcendental meditation and Reiki meditation, and his wife is a Reiki Master. Reiki is a type of "energy healing" based on the New

Age chakra system and puts those practicing it into contact with the realm of familiar spirits.

These three doctors worked with Warren to create a health plan that may already have been implemented by Purpose Driven Churches worldwide, and tragically, millions of people could possibly be introduced to their New Age influences. If he doesn't support their teachings, he sure gave them a big platform with which to promote them.

Next, in December 2011, Saddleback hosted a dinner attended by 300 Muslims and members of Saddleback's congregation. By partnering with Southern California mosques, Rick Warren hoped to focus on bringing Muslims and Christians together and heal past divisions. At the dinner, Saddleback pastor in charge of interfaith outreach, Abraham Meulenberg, and Jihad Turk, director of religious affairs at a mosque in Los Angeles, introduced King's Way as "a path to end the 1,400 years of misunderstanding between Muslims and Christians."[52]

Muslim leaders with whom Warren partners have stated that they embrace Warren because of his promise to not share the gospel with Muslims. Jihad Turk, director of religious affairs at a mosque in Los Angeles stated:

> "We agreed we wouldn't try to evangelize each other.... We'd witness to each other but it would be out of 'Love Thy Neighbor,' not focused on conversion."

Saddleback's "Interfaith Outreach Pastor," Abraham Meulenberg, teaches the concept of "Kingdom Circles" around the world. This theology teaches that all members of any religion can be saved *without* professing Jesus Christ as the Son of God. Warren's initial intentions may have been good, but the idea compromises the gospel and our ability to openly share it with unbelievers. Jan Markell of Olive Tree Views commented:

> "Do I think Rick loves God and is serving Him to the best of his ability? Yes. I just think 'Peace Plans' and global initiatives don't belong in the house of God. Cozying up to Mullahs and uttering words they want to hear produces nothing but a laughing Mullah."

Warren launched the original "PEACE Plan" at Saddleback in 2005 as part of an outreach to Muslims and a wide-ranging global effort to solve major world problems "by mobilizing governments, businesses and faith communities." He challenged his congregation to implement the tenants of his plan. The acronym stands for: Promote reconciliation (formerly, Plant churches), Equip servant leaders, Assist the poor, Care for the sick, and Educate the next generation. Sounds good, right?

The problem is when you get out of your own local church community and attempt something more far reaching, federal or global agencies and organizations get involved. Whenever the government gets their greedy paws on something a church is doing, red tape increases, effectiveness decreases, and the ability to evangelize becomes severely limited. Enter the United Nations, a secular organization that promotes humanism and universalism. Rick Warren's PEACE Plan goals are similar to the U.N.'s Millennium Goals. Both plans advocate social justice agendas.

The United Nations is an anti-Christian organization promoting environmentalism and earth worship through every program they offer. They have made it clear in many publications that they see religious fundamentalism as an obstacle to world peace. So why would they partner with Rick Warren to implement his PEACE Plan and spend millions of dollars on social justice programs? Perhaps because the U.N. knows that the Bible and the gospel won't be proclaimed.

Saddleback Church is located in multiethnic Orange County, California and home to 170,000 Muslims. Rick Warren's next door neighbor is Yasser Barakat, a Muslim from Syria who worships at a Mission Viejo mosque just four miles from Saddleback Church. Barakat invited Warren to learn more about Islam, and they travelled to Syria together in 2006. That is when Warren and his wife, Kay, began attending Iftar meals at the mosque. Iftar is the evening meal Muslims eat after a day of fasting during the holy month of Ramadan.

Through Warren's sincere attempts to live out his faith, this relationship has led to invitations to speak at Muslim conferences. In addition to some of the concerns previously mentioned, throughout the Old Testament God commanded the Israelites not to enter into agreements or covenants including marriage with people of other religions. The reasoning still applies to us today: it is easy to be led away from the one true God to worship other gods.

The danger of compromise is always on Christians who desire to partner with other organizations that have fundamentally contrasting beliefs and doctrines. One reason God takes partnership very seriously is that the concept of holiness has always revolved around the idea of separation. Joel Richardson, Bible Prophecy expert and author of *Why We Left Islam: Former Muslims Speak Out,* emphasizes his concerns about the direction Warren has taken:

> "...If Warren was pursuing friendships for the purpose of evangelism, I would openly stand with him in this goal. But I think it is clear that Warren is pursuing an agenda far more in line with the spirit of the age than with the goals of the early Christian Church."[53]

We are Christ's ambassadors and are called to be salt and light. We should be praying for Warren as well as the evangelical leaders mentioned earlier in this chapter. These men are highly influential on Christianity in America. I don't believe that Rick Warren is being purposely deceptive, but I could be wrong.

The apostle Paul wrote that we are not to pass judgment before the appointed time because the Lord will expose the "things hidden in the darkness and disclose the motives of men's hearts" (1 Corinthians 4:5). In these postmodern days, it appears too many leaders desire the approval of man more than the approval of God. To be honest, we're not all that different.

> *For the time will come when they will not endure sound doctrine; but wanting to have their ears tickled, they will accumulate for themselves teachers in accordance to their own desires, and will turn away their ears from the truth and will turn aside to myths. But you, be sober in all things, endure hardship, do the work of an evangelist, fulfill your ministry* (**2 Timothy 4:3-5** ESV).

CONCLUSION

These ideas and teachings were not accepted by Christians overnight. The progressive pathways of emergent leaders have gradually merged with the wide road that leads to destruction. I don't believe leaders set out at first with the agenda to poison Christianity, but their liberal theology has evolved to the point of contaminating the church. They intended to avoid harsh teachings regarding hell, judgment, and sin, but what has emerged is a wishy-washy, compromised and weakened message of a broad, tolerant gospel.

Conversely, Jesus was not very tolerant. He said even families would be divided over Him and that "For judgment I came into this world (John 9:39)."

> *And He was saying to them, "You are from below, I am from above; you are of this world, I am not of this world. Therefore I said to you that you will die in your sins; for unless you believe that I am He, you will die in your sins* (**John 8:23-24**).

Parents, please don't assume your kids aren't being swayed. Not everyone with a position or title at church can be trusted to correctly handle the word of truth (2 Tim. 2:15). Do you know what your Youth Pastor believes and teaches? It should be alarming that this next generation of leaders may be taking their cues from some of the progressive (evanjellyfish) Christian leaders we've touched on. Today's Christian youth may be headed down the tracks to destinations unknown, further from the truth and certainty of Scripture thanks to their emergent mentors.

"But wait," one might argue, "look at the size and growth of our church buildings and marketing campaigns and fundraisers! Look at how hip and relevant we are! We even serve cappuccino and lattes! Our sermons are catchy, our services are attractive, the kids are having fun, and we've blended in with culture!" This is my point exactly about the dangers of conforming to the world's ways.

When the Holy Spirit isn't invited by the preaching of solid Scripture to come in and work in our hearts, there can be no conviction. Without conviction and revelation of sin, there can be no repentance leading to forgiveness. The Lord Jesus said something very serious about those who cause people to sin. He said in Luke 17:2 that it would be better for them to have a millstone tied around their neck and be thrown into the sea! This is very serious to God.

Jesus warns us that He is returning quickly and said *Hold fast what you have, that no one may take your crown* (**Rev. 3:11**). It's up to individual Christians to live counter-culture for the Lord and resist those who oppose the light and truth of Christianity. Thankfully, there are some good churches and pastors out there who still teach the unfiltered truth. There is also a remnant that understands the times. These committed soldiers are seeking allies, kindred spirits to encourage and sharpen one another. Take up your position! There are watchmen exposing darkness and soldiers fighting the good fight of faith who are hoping to one day hear God say, "well done." Let's do our best to be counted among these.

> *Little children, you are from God and have overcome them, for he who is in you is greater than he who is in the world. They are from the world; therefore they speak from the world, and the world listens to them. We are from God. Whoever knows God listens to us; whoever is not from God does not listen to us. By this we know the Spirit of truth and the spirit of error* (**1 John 4:4-6**).

ENDNOTES

1 http://www.goodfight.org/a_t_rob_bell.html
2 http://www.youtube.com/watch?v=Vg-qgmJ7nzA
3 Rob Bell, Velvet Elvis: Repainting The Christian Faith (Zondervan, 2005), p. 067
4 Ibid p. 147
5 Ibid p. 26-27
6 Rob Bell, promotion for 2005 DUST video
7 Rob Bell, Love Wins (Harper Collins 2011) p. 175
8 Ibid p. 107
9 D.A. Carson, The Expositor's Bible Commentary (Matthew 13-28), Grand Rapids, Zondervan, 1995, p. 523
10 Ibid p. 155
11 http://blog.christianitytoday.com/outofur/archives/2006/01/brian_mclaren_o.html
12 Brian McLaren, A Generous Orthodoxy, Grand Rapids: Zondervan, 2004, p. 296
13 Brian McLaren; A New Kind of Christianity, 2010 Harper Collins, p. 98-99
14 http://www.deceptioninthechurch.com/wishfulthinking.html
15 Brian McLaren; A New Kind of Christianity, 2010 Harper Collins p. 109

16 20 Hot Potatoes Christians Are Afraid To Touch" page 117

17 http://www.michaelyoussef.com/michaels-blogs/keep-jesus-out-of-your-social-ism-part-3.html

18 Tony Campolo, *Carpe Diem: Seize the Day* (Word Publishing, 1994), 85-88.

19 Ibid p. 87-88

20 http://reformednazarene.wordpress.com/2010/10/21/
profiles-in-apostasy-tony-campolo/

21 http://cupofjoe.goodfight.org/?p=702

22 http://reformednazarene.wordpress.com/2009/11/05/
new_age_sympathizer_leonard_sweet_influencing_nazarenes/

23 Leonard Sweet, *Quantum Spirituality: A Postmodern Apologetic* (Dayton, OH: Whaleprints for SpiritVenture Ministries, Inc. 1991, 1994), p. 122

24 Ibid p. 125

25 Ibid p. 300-301

26 http://apprising.org/2010/01/20/
doug-pagitt-and-arrogance-of-liberalprogressive-christians/

27 Doug Pagitt, *Church Re-Imagined* (Grand Rapids, MI: Zondervan, 2005), p. 41

28 Ibid p. 27

29 Doug Pagitt and Kathryn Prill, *Body Prayer*, (Colorado Springs: WaterBrook Press, 2005) p. 27

30 http://apprising.org/2010/10/11/doug-pagitt-and-homosexual-sin/

31 Doug Pagitt, *Church ReImagined*, op. cit., p. 66

32 Roger Oakland, Faith Undone (Lighthouse Trails Publishing, 2007), p. 41

33 http://apprising.org/2006/12/22/
tony-jones-and-the-emergent-church-christian-gay-is-a-ok/

34 Tony Jones, Beliefnet.com 11/19/2008 blog

35 Tony Jones from his blog at tonyj.net, February 26, 2008 and Postmodern Youth Ministry

36 Tony Jones, "Why is the Emerging Church drawn to deconstructive theology?, *The church and postmodern culture: Conversation website*, 3-26-2007

37 http://blog.beliefnet.com/tonyjones/2009/04/why-jesus-died.html/

38 http://www.thebereancall.org/node/6365

39 http://www.thepathoftruth.com/falseteachers/shane-claiborne.htm

40 Ibid

41 http://www.thesimpleway.org/about/archive/
on-evangelicals-and-interfaith-cooperation/

42 Shane Claiborne, "On Evangelicals and Interfaith Cooperation," an Interview with Tony Campolo, *Cross Currents*, Spring 2005, No. 1.

43 http://apprising.org/2010/02/21/
mysticisms-gospel-of-goodness-and-shane-claiborne/

44 *Shane Claiborne, The Irresistible Revolution, living as an ordinary radical* (Grand Rapids, MI, Zondervan, 2006)

45 http://www.washingtontimes.com/news/2011/oct/24/
osteen-faith-at-all-time-high/

46 http://www.foxnews.com/story/0,2933,318054,00.html

47 Rick Warren foreword; Dan Kimball The Emergent Church Zondervan 2003

48 http://abcnews.go.com/blogs/politics/2012/04/rick-warren-on-same-sex-marriage-when-the-church-accommodates-culture-it-weakens-it/

49 http://blog.christianitytoday.com/ctpolitics/2009/01/rick_warrens_in.html

50 Mike LeMay, Suicide of American Christianity, Westbow Press 2012

51 http://drhyman.com/blog/2010/08/25/how-the-dalai-lama-can-help-you-live-to-120/

52 http://www.ocregister.com/articles/muslims-341669-warren-saddleback.html

53 http://www.wnd.com/2012/02/rick-warrens-tower-of-babel/

CHAPTER 14

THE LAST 50 YEARS IN AMERICA

A CONDENSED CHRONOLOGICAL
LOOK AT AMERICA'S MORAL DECLINE

1962 – 2012

By the end of this timeline you'll see massive evidence of the fading impact of Christianity on American culture. The church is on life support. We've been examining how false teachings have led to a weakened witness for Jesus Christ. Because of our ineffectiveness, morals and values have eroded in America over many decades. So much has happened in the last fifty years that has shaped the United States; some events impacted our nation for the better while some chipped away at us for the worse.

America was a much friendlier, safer, and simpler place to live in 1962. Unlike the fast-paced, impersonal, high-tech, Internet age today, there was a sense of community. Churches, libraries, and playgrounds were always packed, and families spent plenty of time together.

The average price of a brand new house was $12,500. *The Jetsons* premiered while *The Flintstones* cartoon was into its second full season on television. John F. Kennedy was still alive, and Johnny Carson took the seat for the first time as host of *The Tonight Show*. Elvis Presley's big hit was "Return to Sender," and if Americans weren't twisting to Chubby Checker, they were doing "The Loco-Motion." The first James Bond movie, *Dr. No,* was in theatres and a few of the top movies were *Laurence of Arabia, The Miracle Worker,* and *West Side Story.*

The Beach Boys also got their start in 1962 and surfed to success with their fun harmonies. The Isley Brothers recorded the original "Twist and Shout," and in a decision that would prove fortuitous, Ringo Starr replaced the Beatles original drummer Pete Best. Astronaut John Glenn became the first American to orbit the Earth. People were more kind, optimistic, and hard working. The unemployment rate was 5.2%, and the average family income was $5,800 a year.

Ninety percent of American households owned a television set, and Zenith marketed its first color TV with a 21-inch round screen! A gallon of gas was just 28 cents and a dozen eggs were 32 cents. The first K-Mart and the first Wal-Mart opened in 1962. An electric popcorn maker was $38.95, and a pair of roller skates cost $36. *Dick Van Dyke* and the *Beverly Hillbillies* were on television. Marilyn Monroe died, and Marvel Comics' Spider-Man first appeared.

Families were still thriving, and many people even knew their neighbors! I remember in the early 70s, men from the neighborhood helping my dad paint and put a new roof on our home while my mom brought out cold lemonade, beer, or soda. In turn, when they needed a hand, Dad would be on a ladder working over on their house. We can honestly say those were happier times.

Unknown to most people, there were some well-established underground movements working to blot out God in America. Some past historical events were morally and spiritually devastating. We have fallen for creative rhetoric that would have us believe in nothing, but tolerate everything. I wonder how different things might be today if Christians had taken a stand or had put up a fight through the years. People of faith need to wake up fast.

1960s

1962: Engle v. Vitale. This landmark ruling starts our selected timeline. Suddenly, after about 184 years of American history and progress, the court became concerned with reinterpreting the First Amendment. Why? Some parents of public school students complained that the voluntary prayer to "Almighty God" contradicted their religious beliefs. This was the school prayer:

"Almighty God, we acknowledge our dependence upon Thee, and we beg Thy blessings upon us, our parents, our teachers and our country. Amen."[1]

The court decided prayer in public schools breached the constitution's wall of separation between church and state. Looking back now, we see that under the extremely liberal-leaning Warren Court in the 1950s and 1960s, secular progressives gained new ground. It's crucial to remember presidents appoint justices and judges. The church did not resist, and the moral slide continued.

1962: The Beatles release their first single "Love Me Do" followed by "Please Please Me." They would go on to be one of the biggest influences in the world on culture, entertainment and on the entire music industry.

1962: The American Law Institute (ALI) advocates for a change in national abortion laws. A panel of lawyers, scholars and jurists develop the "Model Penal Code on Abortion," which recommends abortion be legal in cases of rape, incest, severe fetal defects, and when the women's life or health was at risk.

1963: The Bible is kicked out of public schools. In this case, (Abington v. Schempp) the court ruled that no state law or school board could require the reading of Bible passages at the beginning of each school day. Edward Schempp, a Unitarian Universalist from Abington Township, Pennsylvania, filed suit against the School District. The school district appealed to the Supreme Court, and the case was consolidated with a similar Maryland case launched by Madalyn Murray.

1963: Militant activist Madalyn Murray O'Hair creates the group American Atheists. O'Hair was the mother of plaintiff William J. Murray III, in *Murray v. Curlett*. O'Hare took the school board of Baltimore to court for allowing prayer in school. Attorneys representing the school districts stated **the purpose of Bible reading and prayer was to keep order in schools and provide a proper moral climate for students.** Christian organizations were silent so the case went virtually uncontested before the Court. The Supreme Court ruled 8 to 1 in favor of abolishing school prayer and Bible reading in the public schools.

1963: Betty Friedan publishes *The Feminine Mystique*, frequently seen as beginning of modern women's movement. In her book, Friedan examines and confronts the stay-at-home mom role for women. By doing so, Friedan awakens renewed discussion about roles for women in society, and this book becomes credited as one of the major influences of feminism.

1963: President John F. Kennedy is assassinated in Dallas, Texas on November 22. Lee Harvey Oswald is arrested and two days later is shot and killed by Jack Ruby. It shocked America. This was just two years shy of the 100 year anniversary of the assassination of Abraham Lincoln. Many didn't believe it could happen again … and a nation mourned.

1964: The Beatles make their first trip to America drawing tens of thousands of fans to airports just to get a glimpse of the Fab Four. They are the first band in history to play at a baseball stadium, Shea Stadium in New York. Wherever they went from this point on, there were fans screaming, some fainting, and crowds barely being contained by police and security.

1964: The Beatles had twelve songs on the Billboard Top 100 chart. In April of that year, they held all five of the top five spots on the chart including "Can't Buy Me Love" at number one –something that will most likely never happen again in music history.

1964-1968: President Lyndon Johnson launches his Great Society, establishing Medicare, Medicaid, The Housing Act, and dozens of other programs intended to lift Americans out of poverty. In his 1964 State of the Union speech, Johnson declared a War on Poverty. He and the Democrat-controlled congress funded programs that were supposed to provide a safety net for Americans and other programs such as the Food Stamp Program that were supposed to help hurting families in the nation. Congress also gave Johnson the green light to begin funding education and environmental programs. The era of big government spending was underway.

In a 1965 speech, President Johnson said his Great Society "is a society where no child will go unfed, and no youngster will go unschooled." The **"War on Poverty"** failed to help those who needed it the most and has piled massive debt on future generations. (In fiscal year 2011, the number of people receiving food stamps has soared to an average of 44.7 million, up 33% from fiscal year 2009 when President Obama's stimulus act made it easier for childless, jobless adults to qualify for the program and increased the monthly benefit by about 15 %.)[2]

1965: Homosexual activists picket the White House and Pentagon. San Francisco's first gay drag ball takes place; the first gay community center opens in San Francisco.

1965: Griswold v. Connecticut – the Executive Director of the Planned Parenthood League of Connecticut, Estelle Griswold, and her Medical Director are arrested and convicted for giving information, instruction, and other medical advice to married couples about birth control. After a series of appeals, the case lands before the U.S. Supreme Court. (Since 1879, Connecticut had a law against providing information on birth control and using drugs or instruments to prevent pregnancy.) The court nullified the Connecticut statute. *Griswold v. Connecticut* was a landmark case because it established that the U.S. Constitution guaranteed Americans the "right to privacy" even though this was not explicitly stated as such in the original document! The right to privacy set up a legal precedent that would be used in *Roe v. Wade.*[3]

1965 - 1969: VIETNAM – America officially enters the Vietnam War. Democratic President Lyndon Johnson sends over 200,000 troops to the conflict. His goal for U.S. involvement in Vietnam was not for the U.S. to win the war, but for U.S. troops to bolster South Vietnam's defenses until South Vietnam could take over. By entering the Vietnam War without a goal to win, Johnson set the stage for future public and troop disappointment when the U.S. found themselves in a stalemate with the North Vietnamese and the Viet Cong.

1965: Voting Rights Act is passed, authorizing direct federal intervention to enable blacks to vote. Muslim minister Malcolm X, also known as El-Hajj Malik El-Shabazz is assassinated by members of the Nation of Islam (Black Muslims) in New York City.[4]

1966: By August, *The Beatles* have sold 150 million records worldwide in the last few years. Within nine months, the Beatles' global gross would be $98 million in sales.

1966: *Time* **Magazine** celebrates Easter with cover story **"Is God Dead?"** William Hamilton, the leading radical theologian who helped influence the controversial Death of God movement during the 1960s was quoted by The Oregonian as saying, "We need to redefine Christianity as a possibility without the presence of God." Hamilton wasn't the only theologian with this view and others sought to construct "a post-theistic theology without the existence of an omnipotent God." Episcopalian priest and religion professor at Temple University, Paul Van Buren, rejected God yet presented Jesus as a model *human*.[5]

1967: The first gay campus group is formed at Columbia College in New York City.

1967: It's the Summer of Love in San Francisco as the hippie movement becomes increasingly prominent. One hundred thousand hippies celebrate the sexual revolution which is known for "free love" (sex with no thought of consequence). During the Vietnam War, "make love, not war" is the motto.

1967: The Beatles release an innovative new album, *Sgt. Pepper's Lonely Hearts Club Band.* One of the most influential lines from the title track is "I get high with a little help from my friends." With the Summer of Love in full swing, many assumed the song supported LSD, and drug use skyrocketed.[6]

1967: *Bonnie and Clyde* hits the theatres, shooting up the restrictive code that guarded movie violence for thirty-three years and launches a new era of American film.

1967: "The 'New' Social Studies" is published in the *NEA Journal,* describing the addition of sociology and social psychology curriculums in public schools.[7]

1968: Race riots erupt across the country. Black Panther Party members carry loaded weapons and numerous civil rights organizations take up the mantra "Black Power!" As a Baptist minister, Martin Luther King kept encouraging nonviolent protests in the Civil Rights Movement, but the movement was becoming divided.

Violence is what brought King back to Memphis on April 3, 1968. He was delayed due to a bomb threat for his flight in Atlanta before takeoff, but that night he gave his "I've Been to the Mountaintop" speech and again encouraged taking a nonviolent stand. King's thoughts were on history, on his mission, and on his mortality as he said there are difficult days ahead, and he didn't know what was going to happen. He concluded the speech saying:

> "I just want to do God's will. And He's allowed me to go up to the mountain. And I've looked over, and I've seen the Promised Land. I may not get there with you. But I want you to know tonight, that we, as a people will get to the Promised Land. And so I'm happy tonight; I'm not worried about anything; I'm not fearing any man. Mine eyes have seen the glory of the coming of the Lord."[8]

1968: Thirty-nine year old Martin Luther King is assassinated outside his second floor room at the Lorraine Motel in Memphis, Tennessee, April 4, at 6:01 PM, just after getting ready to go to dinner.

1968: The Beatles travel to Rishikesh, India, to study yoga and transcendental meditation (TM) with Hindu mystic Maharishi Mahesh Yogi. During their retreat, the Beatles, especially Lennon and Harrison, were looking for more 'cosmic awareness' and had been experimenting with LSD. Maharishi helped them process the death of their manager, Brian Epstein, who had died of a drug overdose. Joining the Beatles in India was Mick Jagger of the Rolling Stones, Frank Sinatra's wife Mia Farrow, her sister Prudence Farrow, Yoko Ono, as well as several other celebrities. Prudence Farrow, a UC Berkeley graduate, went on to teach TM for thirty-seven years.

The 1968 gathering in India, with all its high-powered celebrity, attracted a press following. *The Saturday Evening Post* ran a cover story on the trip in a May 1968 edition, having sent a reporter to go with the Beatles to Rishikesh. Because of this exposure, millions of people in America chose to follow their pop idols by experimenting with drugs, practicing TM or both. Epstein's death, the Beatle's world fame, lack of privacy, and that trip to India began a process of unraveling that would lead to the group's demise. They would not perform another concert together. Today, people throughout society including many church leaders and Christians in America have been influenced by Hindu mysticism.

1968: The Motion Picture Association of America (MPAA) film rating system was instituted. One reason for its creation at the time was to have an alternative to the government doing the regulating of movie content. For decades, many other countries already had movie rating systems, but due to the increase of violence, "realism" portrayed in films, and some sexual content in the 1960's, the United States had to implement a form of regulation. Further describing the changing times, *Entertainment Weekly's* Mark Harris pointed out that the movie ratings system wasn't designed for automated ticket purchasing. Harris explains:

> "The ratings system was created at a time when American movie houses were single-screen venues with on-site managers, adult ushers, and a ticket saleslady who looked like your homeroom teacher. The rule that kids must be accompanied to R-rated movies by a "parent or adult guardian" has always rested on the fiction that a fifteen-year-old can be "protected" from distressing content by the presence of an eighteen-year-old. In the age of pay cable, online porn, and one-touch downloads, that's preposterously quaint."[9]

1968: U.S. troop numbers in Vietnam reach 540,000 in December.

1969: Republican President Richard Nixon is sworn in as the thirty-seventh American President on January 20. Nixon takes over the office of the presidency and within five months, Nixon orders the first of many U.S. troop withdrawals from Vietnam.

1969: Apollo 11 Lunar Landing Mission. America boasts the first manned mission to land on the Moon. The first steps by human beings on another planet were taken by Neil Armstrong and Buzz Aldrin on July 20, 1969. Americans celebrated the achievement with amazement.

1969: Woodstock! It was billed as "An Aquarian Exhibition: 3 Days of Peace and Music" in White Lake, New York, on rented dairy farmland August 15-17. Promoters expected 150 – 200,000 people, but during the sometimes rainy weekend, thirty-two acts performed outdoors in front of nearly 500,000 concert-goers. Despite the thirty-minute lines for water, at least hour-long wait to use a toilet, and many lawsuits that would follow, the festival was a huge success overall.

There were drugs, sex, rock and roll, and a lot of mud from the periods of rain. It is widely regarded as a pivotal moment in pop music history. *Rolling Stone* called it one of the *50 Moments That Changed the History of Rock and Roll.* Woodstock 1969 marked the peak for hippie counter-culture. Their naive ideals of peace, love, tolerance, and unity resonated throughout the country at a time when Americans were divided over politics, race, religion, and war – not too different than today.

1969: In a Gallup poll, 68% of respondents said premarital sex was wrong and 21% said it was not. *(By 2009, forty years later, in response to the same question only 32% said premarital sex was wrong and 60% said it was not wrong.)*

1970s

1970: The EPA is created to enforce increasing number of environmental protection laws and regulatory agencies. The first Earth Day protests take place.

1972: Abortion is addressed for the first time on television in the primetime sitcom *Maude.* In a two part episode entitled "Maude's Dilemma" forty-five-year-old Maude Findlay (Beatrice Arthur) finds she is unexpectedly pregnant and chooses an abortion. Leading up to her decision, *her daughter reminds her abortion is now legal.* The episode draws millions of protest letters.

1973: In the *Saturday Review of Education*, radical feminist leader Gloria Steinem declares, "By the year 2000 we will, I hope, raise our children to **believe in human potential, not God**."

AMERICA, YOU MAY NOW KILL YOUR BABIES

1973: **Roe v. Wade – court makes final decision to legalize abortion in all states.** This single, detrimental decision by seven unelected justices defines life and death via federal abortion policy in America. Invalidating 200 years of state law, the ruling is made on the naive basis claiming that "no one knows when life begins." The judgments made in *Roe v. Wade* were argued based on a "right to privacy."

1973: President Richard Nixon orders all remaining U.S. troops to leave Vietnam.

1974: After the Watergate scandal, Richard Nixon is the first US president forced to resign.

1975: First Uncensored Comedy Special HBO features Robert Klein exclaiming, "It's subscription … we can say anything. Sh*t! How'd you like that? Sh*t!"

1976: State laws requiring parental or spousal consent for abortion are thrown out. Planned Parenthood challenges abortion regulations in Missouri. Abortion again makes its way to the Supreme Court in *Planned Parenthood v. Danforth*. Court decides that husbands have no say over their wives decision to abort, and parents have no say over their daughter's decision to abort. In his dissent from this landmark opinion, Justice William Rehnquist argued that the State should recognize the husband's interest in the life of his child and that this decision was "tantamount to the biological disenfranchisement of fathers."

1976: Jonestown, Guyana Massacre. On November 18, 1978, "Peoples Temple" cult leader Jim Jones instructs his followers to commit "revolutionary suicide" by drinking cyanide-laced fruit punch. Many drink willingly while some drink by force. At the Jonestown compound in Guyana, 912 Peoples Temple members (276 of whom were children) died. Jim Jones died the same day from a gunshot wound to the head. Earlier, California Rep. Leo Ryan took reporters and a camera crew to Guyana to investigate suspicions that some people were being held against their will. Their visit went fine until Ryan offered to take a few people back to America with his team. While leaving, they were shot and killed near the plane on the air strip.

Jim Jones envisioned a communist community and Jonestown was to be a utopia away from U.S. influence and under his control. He was simply a lying cult leader who manipulated sincere Americans who wanted a better life. He sought an isolated community where they could escape American capitalism and practice a more communal way of life.

According to CNN, Jones was a phony faith healer, and much of his money came in mail-order donations. Elderly members handed over their Social Security checks, working adults gave 25 percent of their wages to the church, and some signed over all their property. Government investigators would later find at least $10 million in Swiss banks, mainly in Panama. Another $1 million in cash was recovered in Jonestown. Jones, a leftist who had no formal theological training, based his ministry on a combination of religious and socialist philosophies.

1976: The Hyde Amendment is enacted. Congress adopts the first version of the legislation proposed by pro-life Congressman Henry Hyde (R-IL), barring the use of federal funds to pay for abortions.

1977: The ACLU opposes the Hyde Amendment claiming it unfairly targets low-income women and the amendment is revised. The original measure made no exceptions for cases of pregnancies that were the result of rape or incest or that threatened the lives of pregnant women. As a result, beginning in 1977 language was added to provide for such circumstances.

1978: *Federal Communications Commission v. Pacifica Foundation* – the **"Seven Dirty Words"** case. The Supreme Court holds that the government can constitutionally regulate indecent broadcasts. It came about when a father complained to the FCC about his son hearing George Carlin's "Filthy words" routine one afternoon on the radio. The station received a letter of reprimand from the FCC. The U.S. Supreme Court upheld the FCC action by a vote of 5 to 4, ruling the routine was **"indecent but not obscene."** The Court stated the FCC had the authority to prohibit such broadcasts during hours when children were likely to be among the audience

1979: The Iran Hostage Crisis - American Hostages are taken in Tehran. Islamic radicals take over the American embassy holding sixty-six Americans hostage for 444 days. The crisis was a diplomatic one between Iran and the United States over the support of the Iranian Revolution. President Carter called the hostages "victims of terrorism and anarchy." The crisis which followed this seizure created a near state of war, ruined Jimmy Carter's presidency, and began an environment of hostility between America and Iran which continues to this day. In 1981, the hostages were formally released into United States custody shortly after the new American president, Ronald Reagan, was sworn into office.

1980s

1980: Take the Ten Commandments down! In a five to four decision, the Supreme Court rules a Kentucky law, requiring the Ten Commandments to be posted, is unconstitutional. For years, the schools in

Kentucky had copies of the Ten Commandments posted in the hallway. In the case *Stone v. Graham*, it was ruled: "If the posted copies of the Ten Commandments are to have any effect at all, it will be to induce schoolchildren to read, meditate upon, perhaps to venerate and obey the Commandments … this … is not a permissible state objective."

1981: "Music Television" – MTV launches an entirely unique new product that would be one of the biggest influences on American youth for twenty-five years. Having a profound influence on the music industry, fashion and pop culture, MTV's moral influence on young people, including issues related to censorship and social activism, become subject of intense debate.

In 1992, MTV started a pro-democracy campaign called *Choose or Lose*, to encourage millions of people to register to vote, and the channel hosted a town hall forum for then-candidate, Bill Clinton.[10]

In 2001, MTV's hate crimes awareness campaign included airing a made-for-TV movie *Anatomy of a Hate Crime*, based on the 1998 murder of twenty-one-year old homosexual Matthew Shepard.

In 2005, the Parents Television Council released a study, *MTV Smut Peddlers*, which sought to expose MTV's excessive sexual, profane, and violent content.

In 2010, a study by the GLADD found that of the 207.5 hours of prime time programming, 42% included content reflecting the lives of gay, bisexual and transgendered people – the highest gay-friendly percentage ever.

1981: Gay-Related Immune Deficiency (GRID) identified by CDC (Later changed to "AIDS").

1981: An Arkansas state law passes, mandating the teaching of Creation Science in schools. Equal time was to be given also to evolution. A legal action was mounted (*McLean vs. Arkansas*) to overturn the law. Scientists and many main-line Christian churches were pitted against conservative Christian groups. The law was declared unconstitutional.

1984: Berkeley, California becomes first city with a domestic partner law.

1984: President Ronald Reagan announces the "Mexico City Policy." The Reagan Administration denies U.S. family planning funds to any overseas organizations that used their own private funds for abortion services, counseling, or referral.

1986: The first time the word "condom" is used in primetime on the show *Cagney & Lacey*.

1986: The first openly lesbian couple is granted legal joint adoption (California).

1986: No more abortion restrictions whatsoever! In a five to four court decision in *Thornburg v. American College of Obstetricians and Gynecologists*, all restrictions on abortion were struck down. No more requirements to inform women about alternatives to abortion. No more requirement to: educate women about prenatal development, to inform women about the potential risks of abortion, to keep medical records of abortions, and no requirement that third trimester abortions be performed in such a way as to spare the life of the viable child. All these were argued to be violations of a woman's right to privacy.[11]

1987: The Gay and Lesbian Caucus of the National Education Association is established.

1987: *The Last Temptation of Christ* hits theatres. Like the novel, the film depicts the life of Jesus Christ and His struggle with various forms of temptation including fear, doubt, depression, and lust. The movie depicts Christ being tempted by imagining Himself engaged in sexual activities. Naturally, secular reviewers including Roger Ebert gave the film four stars out of five. Though the movie tanked at the box office, Martin Scorsese received an Oscar nomination for Best Director. In one offensive scene, Jesus and Mary Magdalene consummate their marriage.

1989: *Seinfeld* airs for the first time on NBC. The sitcom runs until 1998 and becomes a classic. In 2002, *TV Guide* named *Seinfeld* the greatest television program of all time. E! named it the "number 1 reason the '90s ruled." The show had a dramatic impact on American culture. For example, in 2009, the episode on masturbation was ranked #1 on *TV Guide's* list of "TV's Top 100 Episodes of All Time." The prevalent theme on *Seinfeld* was that life is pretty much meaningless or irrational. This is consistent with the philosophy of absurdism. The characters had an indifference to morality and never seemed to learn their lessons.

1989: Denmark is the first country to legalize same-sex marriage.

1989: Communism fails and the Berlin Wall comes crashing down, signaling the end of the Cold War. In Poland, Hungary, and Czechoslovakia in 1988 and 1989, communism falter and new exodus points are opened to East Germans who want to flee to the West. People are in shock that the borders are really open. Jennifer Roesnberg writes in *The Rise and Fall of the Berlin Wall* that there was a spontaneous and "huge celebration along the Berlin Wall with people hugging, kissing, singing, cheering, and crying."[12]

1990s

1991: The first lesbian kiss on network television occurs on *L.A. Law* which featured a prolonged kiss between two female lawyers.

1992: In a five to four decision, the Supreme Court rules a graduation prayer violated the Establishment Clause. At the disputed graduation, a Rabbi thanked God for the legacy of America where diversity is celebrated:

> "O God, we are grateful for the learning which we have celebrated on this joyous commencement ... we give thanks to you, Lord, for keeping us alive, sustaining us and allowing us to reach this special, happy occasion."

The Bush administration agreed with the school board which argued the prayer did *not* demonstrate a religious endorsement. Regardless, the court ruled on benedictions and invocations: "Religious invocation ... conveyed the message that district had given its endorsement to prayer and religion, so that school district was properly [prohibited] from including invocation." Graham v. Central, 1985; Kay v. Douglas, 1986; Jager v. Douglas, 1989; Lee v. Weisman, 1992.

1993: With *NYPD Blue*, Steven Bochco launches network **TV's first R-rated primetime series.** A quarter of ABC's 225 affiliates preempt the first episode. *NYPD Blue* would also gain infamy as one of the first prime time network series to regularly show naked buttocks.

1993: In the movie *Philadelphia*, Tom Hanks wins an Oscar for Best Actor for his portrayal of a homosexual man who dies from AIDS.

The 90s were the "let the language fly" decade. According to the Parent's Television Council, between 1993 and 1999, the first recorded use of these words took place on primetime television: "a**hole," "screw," "p*ss," "d*ck," "t*ts," and bullsh*t. Also included in PTC's ETS database, the word "sh*t" heard first on CBS's *Chicago Hope*.[13]

1993: The first law established to protect lesbian/gay students in public schools. (MA)

1993: A group led by terrorist Ramzi Yousef tries to bring down the World Trade Center with a truck bomb. They kill six and wound a thousand. (Yousef's uncle is none other than Khalid Sheikh Mohammed, the mastermind of 9/11.)

1993: "Black Hawk down" – Somali tribesmen shoot down U.S. helicopters, killing eighteen and wounding seventy-three. It was discovered that those Somali tribesmen had received help from al Qaeda.

1994: The first school sanctioned gay-youth prom is held in Los Angeles.

1994: *Friends* Premiers on NBC and makes a ten-year run until 2004. According to *TV Guide* readers, *Friends* was the Best Comedy cast of all time, even beating *Seinfeld*. In the chapter on Hollywood, we already noted the high number of times in the series that the characters had sex. Another thing to note was the overused and disrespectful use of the expression "Oh – my – God," which is still popular today. *Friends* was a trend-setter among youth and culture.

1995: Police in Manila uncover a plot by Ramzi Yousef to blow up a dozen U.S. airliners while they were flying over the Pacific.

1997: Norm MacDonald lets the f-word slip during SNL's "Weekend Update." He is not fired.

1997: Ellen DeGeneres becomes the first lesbian character to star in a lead role in a prime time series. During the fourth season of *Ellen*, DeGeneres "comes out" publicly as a lesbian in an appearance on *The Oprah Winfrey Show*. Her bravery was celebrated, but the show was cancelled the next season.

1997: Bill Clinton becomes the first U.S. President to address a gay organization (Human Rights Campaign).

1997: New Hampshire and Maine pass gay rights laws.

1998: The FDA approves Pfizer's Viagra as the first prescription drug for the treatment of male impotence, now known as "erectile dysfunction." By 2003, Viagra would generate $1.9 billion in annual sales for Pfizer.

1998: *Will and Grace* Premiers on NBC from 1998 through 2006. It features a main character who is homosexual and contains frequent references to gay sex.

1998: Usama Bin Laden and four others issued a self-styled fatwa, publicly declaring it is God's decree that **every Muslim should try his utmost to kill any American**, military or civilian, anywhere in the world. It is a call for "Jihad Against Jews and Crusaders."[14]

1998: America's First Playboy President – Bill "I screwed up with that girl" Clinton and Monica Lewinsky dominate headlines. When the truth about the scandal comes out, the media basically rationalizes his behavior. Clinton also had issues with women back as Governor of Arkansas. In a PBS documentary, those closest to Clinton try warning him about his weakness toward young women.[15]

Marla Crider, a woman who worked with Mr. Clinton in Arkansas before he was president and had an affair with him, said that "he needed that kind of adoration" from women. When the Lewinski affair became public, Betsy Wright, Clinton's political aide, said his staff was deeply upset because he had lied to them and lied 'to a lot of people'.

When Gennifer Flowers came forward claiming to have had a twelve-year affair with Clinton, it was Hillary who revived his career by giving a TV interview in which she famously said she was going to "stand by my man." Paula Jones was another woman who went public, and Clinton settled with Jones for approximately $850,000. The Paula Jones case precipitated Clinton's impeachment. Americans were very forgiving as Clinton remained popular and left office with a 65% approval rating.

In his 2005 book, *The Marketing of Evil*, WND editor David Kupelian talked about the influence of Clinton's affairs and the epidemic of widespread, casual sex among young people known as "hooking up" – often with multiple partners.

> "Turbocharged by President Clinton and Monica Lewinsky's high-profile example – 'If it's okay for the president, it must be okay for me' – middle and high school children are experimenting with sex in the bathroom stalls at school, behind the gym,

and in the back of the school bus. Often the only way parents and school authorities find out is when confronted by an epidemic of sexually transmitted disease infecting large numbers of kids in the same social group."[16]

1999: Columbine High School Massacre. On April 20, 1999, in Littleton, Colorado, two high-school seniors, Dylan Klebold and Eric Harris, enact an all-out assault on Columbine High School during the middle of the day. Their plan was to kill hundreds of their peers by setting bombs in the school cafeteria, but when the bombs didn't go off, the two boys walked the hallways with pipe bombs, guns and knives and killed twelve students, one teacher, and themselves. They injured twenty-one more.

How was it possible that no one had a clue about the two killers? They fooled friends, parents, and teachers. When they got caught breaking into a van, they also fooled, psychologists, cops and judges. According to journals, notes, and videos, Klebold and Harris left to be discovered, Klebold had been thinking of committing suicide as early as 1997, and they both had begun thinking about a large massacre as early as April 1998. One psychologist would later say, "These are kids with serious psychological problems."[17]

Eric Harris wore a t-shirt with "Natural Selection" on the front. Natural selection is the process in nature by which, according to Darwin's theory of evolution, only the organisms best adapted to their environment tend to survive. Klebold's shirt said "Wrath." There has been plenty of speculation about what led to their rampage, such as lax parenting, lax gun laws, progressive schooling, antidepressant drugs, hard rock music, violent video games (Doom), violent movies (Natural Born Killers), or Goth. Few have suggested pure satanic evil.

Videotapes, journals, guns and bombs in their rooms would have been easily found if the parents had looked. Harris even made a website with hateful epithets that could have been followed up on. The Columbine Massacre changed the way society looked at children and at schools. Violence was no longer just an after-school, inner-city activity. It could happen anywhere, but it may not have happened at all **if God had not been blotted out** of public schools decades earlier.

2000s

2000: An al Qaeda team in Aden, Yemen, use a motorboat filled with explosives to blow a hole in the side of the *U.S.S. Cole*, almost sinking the vessel and killing seventeen American sailors.

2000: The State of Vermont passes HB847, legalizing Civil Unions for same-sex couples.

2000: George W. Bush is elected the forty-third President of the United States and takes office in January 2001.

SEPTEMBER 11 – THE DAY THAT CHANGED AMERICA

2001: Forever known as 9-11, TERRORISTS (already living in America) ATTACK AMERICA when nineteen Islamic fundamentalists, identified as al Qaeda terrorists, attack the United States killing 2,977 Americans by hijacking four fully fueled jetliners. Their plan was to crash them into the World Trade Center, the Pentagon, and the U.S. Capitol building. The fourth plane never made it to Washington as brave passengers overpowered the hijackers causing the plane to crash in a field in Pennsylvania. The well-planned terrorist attacks were part of a worldwide jihad against so-called "infidel" nations.

With the unanimous approval of Congress, the United States government responded to the attacks by launching the **"War on Terror."** America invaded Afghanistan to depose the Taliban regime that had provided a safe haven for al Qaeda, in an effort to prevent future attacks against American interests. A faction of liberals went along with the American Left, accusing the foreign policies of the United States for causing the 9-11 attacks. They believe Islamists hate America for its many sins, while many on the Right believe Islamists hate us for our many freedoms and success as capitalism. Others believe it is due to America's support for Israel, another "infidel" nation.

However, according to David Horowitz' September 11 report on his DiscovertheNetworks website, these views leave out a crucial reality. Yale University military historian, Mary Habeck, explains:

> "Radical Muslims today base their war against non-believers on the Islamic sacred writings – particularly the Sira, which tells the story of the Prophet Muhammad's life in chronological sequence.

"Jihadis pattern their thoughts and actions after those of Muhammad, who was not only the founder of Islam but also a brutal and most successful warrior.

"Islam's inherent desire for conquest, and not any particular provocation (real or imagined) by some outside power, is the key to understanding why jihadis, such as the 9/11 hijackers, do what they do."[18]

The impact of 9-11-2001 goes beyond the American economy, airport security, and anti-terror measures. There were some positive cultural indicators: immediate expressions of patriotism including more Americans flying the flag and an increase in patriotic songs. More people spent quality time with family, and there was a *temporary* increase in church attendance. America was hurt, but not humbled by the attacks, and sadly, our unity lasted about nine months.

2003: Parent Television Counsel Members file 18,000 complaints about "F-word" airing during Golden Globes Broadcast. (U2's Bono) FCC enforcement bureau finds the statement live on NBC "This is really, really f*ckin' brilliant," not indecent.

2003: In *Lawrence v. Texas*, the Supreme Court voids state sodomy laws, overturning an earlier Supreme Court ruling in *Bowers v. Hardwick* (1986). Lawrence's attorneys cite Alfred Kinsey's misleading statistics on homosexual sex! In the six to three ruling, the Court struck down the sodomy law in Texas and, by extension, invalidated sodomy laws in thirteen other states, making same-sex sexual activity legal in every U.S. state and territory.

2003: Renee Doyle, President of *EdWatch*, (Education for a Free Nation) reported in *'Social and Emotional Learning'* that The National Institute of Mental Health (NIMH) and the National Science Foundation (NSF) announced the results of their $1.2 million tax-payer funded study. Believe it or not, the study essentially stated that traditionalists are mentally disturbed! Scholars from the Universities of Maryland, California at Berkeley (naturally), and Stanford had determined that social conservatives ... suffer from 'mental rigidity,' 'dogmatism,' together with associated indicators for mental illness."[19]

Author and columnist Linda Kimball said that political correctness is a "diabolically crafted idea." Kimball wrote about Cultural Marxism, explaining:

"The strong suggestion here is that in order for one not to be thought of as racist or fascist, then one must not only be nonjudgmental but must also embrace the 'new' moral absolutes: *diversity, choice, sensitivity, sexual orientation, and tolerance.* Political correctness is a Machiavellian psychological *'command and control'* device. Its purpose is the imposition of uniformity in thought, speech, and behavior."[20]

2004: Janet Jackson exposes her breast with the help of Justin Timberlake during the Super Bowl half time show to a national audience of over 140 million including *more than 16 million children*. It was claimed to be a "wardrobe malfunction." More than 200,000 citizens file indecency complaints with the FCC about the Super Bowl half time show.

2004: *Degrassi: The Next Generation*: When Manny (Cassie Steele) becomes pregnant and is nervous about becoming a teen mom, she decides to have an abortion despite her boyfriend's desire to keep the baby. Her mother accompanies her to the clinic.

2004: *Kinsey,* starring Liam Neissen, is released and glosses over incriminating details of the radical sex experimentation techniques of anti-Christian, bisexual Alfred Kinsey.

2005: *Brokeback Mountain* fails miserably at the Box Office, but the gay cowboy film is nominated for eight Academy Awards.

2005: FCC denies thirty-six indecency complaints filed by the Parents Television Council.

2006: Atheist with a mission, Richard Dawkins, attacks Christianity in his book *The God Delusion*.

2006: President Bush signs the Broadcast Decency Enforcement Act into law on June 16.

2007: Al Gore produces *An Inconvenient Truth* documentary; a British court determines Gore's film contains *at least* eleven material falsehoods. The film is shown in public schools under the guise of scientific fact and truth instead of theory. It is a political work and promotes one side of the man-caused global warming argument.

2008: *Milk,* was released starring Sean Penn, who won Best Actor for his portrayal of gay-rights activist Harvey Milk. Hollywood loved the film, but the box office – not so much.

2008: Barack Hussein Obama is elected the first black President of the United States. *First president in our history to be elected without having to provide his college records, transcripts, financial, or medical records. Entire periods of his life are missing from his biography.*

2009: A Gallop poll reveals just 32% say premarital sex is wrong and 60 percent say it was not. (*In 1969, the same questions were asked and the poll had 68 percent of respondents saying premarital sex was wrong and 21 percent said it was not.)*

2009: *Newsweek* **proclaimed "The Decline and Fall of Christian America"** on its cover. In *Newsweek*'s April 14 cover story, "The End of Christian America," Editor Jon Meacham argues the falling numbers of self-identified Christians in America is a "good thing." Meacham takes a "small detail, a point of comparison" from a 24-page summary of the 2009 American Religious Identification Survey and builds a feature story that may reflect as much about the liberal media as it does about "Christian America."

2009: Rasmussen reports 88% of Americans believe the person known to history as Jesus Christ actually walked on the earth 2000 years ago – up five points from 2008. **Eighty-two percent believe Jesus Christ was the Son of God** who came to earth and died for our sins. Seventy-nine percent of Americans believe Jesus Christ rose from the dead![21]

2010: On NBC's *Friday Night Lights,* after a one-night stand with Luke, tenth-grader Becky becomes pregnant at fifteen. She's afraid to talk to her mother about it and goes to her guidance counselor, reads Planned Parenthood literature and has an abortion. There is little outrage over the episode and many critics applauded it.

2010: *Arizona v. U.S. Government* – The Obama administration files a lawsuit against the state of Arizona, forbidding them from implementing their own state law to protect its citizens from violence, primarily as a result of drug cartels at the U.S./Mexico border! According to the *Washington Times,* the Justice Department brought the lawsuit to stop the new immigration enforcement law in Arizona, saying, "It violated the Constitution by trying to supersede federal law and by impairing illegal immigrants' right to travel and conduct interstate commerce."

Sheriffs have asked the government for help because parts of Arizona are at the mercy of drug cartels. They have caused damage and destruction to the lives and property of farmers and ranchers, and have terrorized American citizens along the border. With the federal government having a sworn duty to protect its citizens, their solution was to put signs at the border warning travelers about the "Active drug and human smuggling area" characterized by "armed criminals" and speeding vehicles! You can't make this stuff up.

> "The federal government has posted signs along a major interstate highway in Arizona, more than 100 miles north of the U.S.-Mexico border, warning travelers the area is unsafe because of drug and alien smugglers, and a local sheriff says Mexican drug cartels now control some parts of the state."[22]

It is getting dangerous seventy-five miles from the Mexican border – thirty miles from Phoenix. Arizona has cried out to the Obama administration for 3,000 National Guard soldiers to patrol the border, but they gave them fifteen signs. Arizona Governor Jan Brewer condemned what she called the federal government's "continued failure to secure our international border." In a recent campaign video posted to YouTube, Mrs. Brewer – standing in front of one of the signs – attacked the administration, calling the signs "an outrage" and telling President Obama to "Do your job. Secure our borders."

2010: Over 46 million American people live below the poverty line in 2010. Remember Lyndon Johnson's Great Society and the billions of dollars that have since been spent to stop poverty?

2011: A record 44.7 million people – or one in seven Americans – are on food stamps. In fiscal year 2011, the federal government spent more than $75 billion on food stamps, which provided an average monthly benefit of $133.85 a month. That's up from $34.6 billion at the end of fiscal year 2008, when recipients collected an average benefit of $102.19.[23] The Heritage Foundation says that spending on income-based programs, such as food stamps, has increased by one-third to $900 billion under Obama. There are seventy such programs.

2011: Eighty percent of evangelical Christians from the age of twenty to twenty-nine have had premarital sex according to a study called National Campaign to Prevent Teen and Unplanned Pregnancy. In the same poll, about 88% of *all* single young people in that age range have had sex. The difference between Christians and non-Christians is about eight percent. Even more startling, the findings also revealed that just 76% of evangelicals believe premarital sex is immoral!

2012: On HBO's *Girls,* after the character Jessa reveals she's pregnant, her friends make a big deal about attending the abortion appointment. As hours pass and Jessa doesn't show up, her friends become angry and Hannah exclaims, "How could she ruin the beautiful abortion you threw?" Most notable about the episode is the sheer number of times it uses the word "abortion," says Hilary Busis at *Entertainment Weekly,* as if it's "trying to desensitize us to the word." *Girls* used it eleven times; *Sex and the City* used it three times.[24]

2012: Vice President Joe Biden endorses same-sex marriage in an interview on NBC's *Meet the Press* saying:

> "I am absolutely comfortable with the fact that men marrying men, women marrying women and heterosexual men and women marrying one another are entitled to the same exact rights, all the civil rights, all the civil liberties.... I think 'Will and Grace' probably did more to educate the American public than almost anybody's ever done so far. People fear that which is different. Now they're beginning to understand."[25]

Will and Grace educated America? This was obviously a political move in an election year to strengthen the liberal Democratic base and homosexual support.

2012: Barack Obama becomes the first president in United States history to openly support all forms of homosexuality, gay rights, gay adoptions, and civil unions.

2012: Democrats move to eradicate God from their Party platform and decide to remove all references of God during the 2012 Democratic National Convention. They take a vote to reconsider and the majority of Democrats boo![26]

2012: AMERICANS DECIDE THE FUTURE DIRECTION OF THE UNITED STATES BY VOTING IN THE 2012 PRESIDENTIAL ELECTION.

> *Since they hated knowledge and did not choose to fear the LORD, since they would not accept my advice and spurned my rebuke, they will eat the fruit of their ways and be filled with the fruit of their schemes. For the waywardness of the simple will kill them, and the complacency of fools will destroy them* (**Proverbs 1:29-32**).

Has America chosen to hate knowledge and to not fear the Lord? Is our complacency beyond cure? Are we at the point where God will not answer our cries? The Lord is a patient and compassionate God, but His anger won't be held back forever. We must choose this day whether we will serve our culture or Christ. America once had God's blessing and covering; His protection and His provision, but believers don't read, study, and live the Bible like we used to over fifty years ago. God is no longer top priority.

Though the forces of evil and the agenda to blot out God in America are advancing, He is sovereign and in control of all things at all times. The gospel and our commission to share His message have not changed so it's up to us from this point forward. It's not always easy, but taking a stand for Jesus Christ can be rewarding. If not in this life, we are sure to be richly rewarded in the next. Martin Luther once said "You are not only responsible for what you say, but also for what you do not say."

We are never fighting alone. When King Jehoshaphat and the people of Israel were outnumbered and facing impossible odds, they confessed their inability to the Lord and prayed to Him saying that their eyes were on Him. God responded by telling them the battle was His and to "go out and face them tomorrow and the Lord will be with you" (2 Chron. 20:12-17). God has our backs and He is trying to get through to us.

Author, evangelist and Reverend David Wilkerson (1931-2011) founded Teen Challenge ministries and World Challenge, Inc. He described how a loving parent gently shakes a sleeping child to wake him or her up. If the child doesn't wake up, the shaking must become more firm. God is shaking up America right now.

"At first, He shook us very tenderly but now His shaking has become violent, because He has not succeeded in awakening us. The writer of Hebrews says: 'Yet once more I shake not the earth only, but also heaven…. That [only] those things which cannot be shaken may remain' (Hebrews 12:26-27). God is going to shake everything in sight so that He is revealed as the only unshakable power!"[27]

The signs of the times indicate we should have an extreme sense of urgency. God has given us commands, instruction and all the tools we need to do the work required of us. Let's join the remnant of bold, committed Christians and not care about what people say, including those within the church who, because of their neutrality, may be convicted by our actions. This may require some extra effort and perhaps a lifestyle change, but it will be worth it in the end, because our labor in the Lord is never in vain (1 Cor. 15:58).

"If by excessive labor we die before reaching the average age of man, worn out in the Master's service, then glory be to God. We shall have so much less of earth and so much more of heaven. It is our duty and our privilege to exhaust our lives for Jesus. We are not to be living specimens of men in fine preservation, but living sacrifices [Rom. 12:1], whose lot is to be consumed."
– **Charles Spurgeon**

Christ is our future and our hope and He gives us purpose to live every day. We don't know when our journey will end, but until the Lord returns, there will always be an agenda to blot out the God of Christianity. Will the church continue conforming to culture? It will depend on the choices individual believers make. It is my hope that I have exhorted you to live a more undaunted life in passionate pursuit of Truth. It is my prayer that we work to impact America together. You and I are here for such a time as this.

You are the light of the world. A city on a hill cannot be hidden (**Matthew 5:14**).

ENDNOTES

1 http://en.wikipedia.org/wiki/Engel_v._Vitale
2 http://money.cnn.com/2012/01/17/news/economy/obama_food_stamps/index.htm
3 http://abortionusa.com/abortion.aspx#6
4 http://www.ushistory.org/more/timeline.htm
5 http://www.christianpost.com/news/
god-is-dead-theologian-william-hamilton-dies-at-87-70605/
6 http://www.pophistorydig.com/?tag=beatles-1967
7 http://www.cwfa.org/brochures/nea.pdf
8 http://history1900s.about.com/cs/martinlutherking/a/mlkassass.htm
9 http://www.pluggedin.com/cultureclips/2012/2012-04-16.aspx
10 http://en.wikipedia.org/wiki/MTV
11 http://www.abort73.com/abortion_facts/us_abortion_law/
12 http://history1900s.about.com/od/coldwa1/a/berlinwall.htm
13 http://www.parentstv.org/PTC/facts/tvtimeline.asp
14 http://www.freerepublic.com/focus/f-news/530420/posts
15 http://www.dailymail.co.uk/news/article-2100076/Bill-Clinton-documentary-reveals-
start-Monica-Lewinsky-affair.html
16 David Kupelian, The Marketing of Evil, 2005 WND Books/Cumberland Publishing, page
130
17 http://history1900s.about.com/od/famouscrimesscandals/a/columbine.htm
18 http://www.discoverthenetworks.org/guideDesc.asp?catid=146&type=issue
19 http://www.edwatch.org/
20 http://www.americanthinker.com/2007/02/cultural_marxism.html
21 http://www.rasmussenreports.com/public_content/lifestyle/holidays/
april_2009/79_believe_jesus_christ_rose_from_the_dead
22 http://www.washingtontimes.com/news/2010/aug/31/
signs-in-arizona-warn-of-smuggler-dangers/?page=all
23 http://money.cnn.com/2012/01/17/news/economy/obama_food_stamps/index.htm
24 http://theweek.com/article/index/227153/how-tv-shows-deal-with-abortion-a-timeline
25 http://www.cbn.com/cbnnews/politics/2012/May/
Biden-Im-Comfortable-with-Gay-Marriage/
26 http://www.wnd.com/2012/09/democrats-boo-idea-of-mentioning-god/
27 http://www.worldchallenge.org/en/node/17620?src=devo-email

ABOUT THE AUTHOR

David Fiorazo is an author, radio personality, speaker, and professional actor. He has worked in radio for 24 years and toured the United States as a drummer in Christian bands. While living in Los Angeles, he acted in television shows and commercials, and was very involved in the Christian community. David became concerned about fading family values in America and complacency among Christians. He also saw growing hostility toward Jesus Christ in every aspect of our culture. The catalyst that led him to start writing and eventually inspired this book was what David calls "the most corrupt, anti-Christian, one-sided media in American history, which refuses to report the truth." Seeing the increase of immorality and the attacks on conservatives, David prayed a dangerous prayer – that God would use his life and give him the strength to speak the truth regardless of the cost, the opposition or the resistance; and that he would find the balance of loving others while standing up for Jesus Christ without apology or compromise. He is undaunted in his belief that, though our time is short, America and the church are worth fighting for.

CONNECT WITH DAVID FIORAZO:

Book Site: www.BlottingoutGod.com

Facebook: www.facebook.com/
EradicateBlottingOutGodInAmerica

Blog: davefiorazo.blogspot.com

LinkedIn: www.linkedin.com/davefiorazo

Twitter: twitter.com/fiorazo

Personal Acting Site: www.davidfiorazo.com

CPSIA information can be obtained
at www.ICGtesting.com
Printed in the USA
LVHW111327090720
660236LV00002B/359